Zambia
Letters Home
1967-1969

Valerie Lapthorne

Copyright © 2016 Valerie Lapthorne

All rights reserved.

ISBN:-10:1530254469
ISBN:-13:1530254460

DEDICATION

To Mum and Dad and Richard,
and
To the Children and Grandchildren
who never knew us like this.

CONTENTS

1	The Journey	Pg 2
2	Introductions	Pg 10
3	My Birthday	Pg 17
4	Moving In	Pg 25
5	Sorting Things Out	Pg 30
6	Albert	Pg 34
7	Settling In	Pg 40
8	Small Creatures	Pg 50
9	Hockey Trial	Pg 55
10	Factory Visit	Pg 61
11	The Cars arrive	Pg 70
12	Obed Departs	Pg 81
13	Trade Fair	Pg 81
14	Pucci Arrives	Pg 106
15	Sculpture	Pg 120
16	Cooking	Pg 127
17	Dog Training	Pg 139
18	Office dresses	Pg 149
19	The Hoskyns-Abrahals	Pg 155
20	Christmas Shopping	Pg 168

21	Study Books	Pg 175
22	Independence Day	Pg 184
23	Molly	Pg 196
24	Thunderstorms	Pg 202
25	Puzzle of Shredded Clothes	Pg 209
26	Budgeting	Pg 216
27	Sewing and Post	Pg 226
28	Christmas 1967	Pg 236
29	Decimalisation	Pg 246
30	`No `Petrol	Pg 257
31	Chameleon	Pg 267
32	Rain and Mud	Pg 275
33	Marlene and Peter Leave	Pg 283
34	Missing Post	PG 292
35	Work and Study	Pg 299
36	Birthday	Pg 304
37	Rhodesia	Pg 311
38	Holiday Plans	Pg 320
39	Fraud	Pg 328
40	Budget Book	Pg 338
41	Travel Plans	Pg 348
42	Exam	Pg 355

43	Trade Fair	Pg 365
44	Overtime	Pg 375
45	Explosion	Pg 385
46	Sharing Gardens	Pg 395
47	Marlene and Margie to Rest	Pg 402
48	Nairobi	Pg 410
49	Heat	Pg 418
50	Inventory	Pg 428
51	Andre's Bike	Pg 438
52	Checking Hospital	Pg 448
53	Sewing	Pg 458
54	Layette	Pg 469
55	Replacements Arrive	Pg 478
56	Three of Us	Pg 487
57	Sleeplessness	Pg 499
58	Partying	Pg 508
59	Leaving	Pg 515
60	Fremantle to Melbourne	Pg 527
61	Raratonga	Pg 535

Misundu

ACKNOWLEDGMENTS

My Thanks to Linda Pitts

Zambia 1967 to 1969

Introduction

In January 1967, we married and were posted to Unilever's soap and oil factory in Zambia, less than three years after Independence in October 1964. We were twenty-two and twenty-three. Richard had his economics degree and his accountancy qualifications and I had never been away from home before, apart from a sedate holiday in Spain with the girls from the office, although this did include Dottie Rhone, Paul McCartney's recently ex-girlfriend who lent a little exoticism. I had complete confidence in Richard and had no idea what lay ahead and started writing these letters home to my Mum and Dad as soon as we made our first stop.

Gasp at my naivety. I do now. You see the experience all through my narrow and ignorant eyes. And for my parents and relatives, who shared these letters, it was also their first experience of Africa. When I gave in my notice to my boss and told him I was off to Ndola, he wished me all the best and said that it was his experience that Andover was quite a nice place.

Any italics are mine, written now, where more explanation is needed. The excerpts from The Times of Zambia are also recent additions, just to show what was going on in Zambia outside Unilever. I refer occasionally to Dougal, or more commonly Doodle. This is a stuffed toy dog, a character in The Magic Roundabout, which Mum gave me as a going away present, as we both watched the children's programme on TV when we got home from work and had a cup of tea together before starting on the evening meal. Was it really fifty years ago?

Valerie Lapthorne

Chapter One.   The journey

VC10. Somewhere south of England. 2.3.67

I'll start as far back as I can remember i.e. yesterday. We had a good journey down to London: it was sunny all the way and we saw England at its best. We had a meal on the train. It wasn't exciting but it was hot and filled in the majority of the journey. We checked in to the Grosvenor Hotel in Victoria, next door to the station. It was a huge monstrous hotel and the entrance hall was full of marble pillars, gold figuring on the walls and aspidistras and drooping ferns in pots like a tearoom. It only needed the Palm Court Orchestra. We wandered around London until time for an evening meal at The Paradiso Inferno in the Strand. We had an over rich lobster soup and a reliable steak done Italian style in a pepper sauce with anchovies. We then trudged around the theatres and got in to see The Taming of the Shrew, which was quite a romp, and it was late when we got back to the aspidistras.

This morning we checked in our baggage at the British United Airways terminus at Victoria Station. We kept all the heavy things in my blue train case and Richard's briefcase, about 36lbs in all. We knew that if this were weighed, it would take us tons over the limit. Anyway we took the other four cases for the weigh-in and were 7 kilos overweight. This is about 15 or 16 lbs. So it was vital not to have our "hand baggage" weighed. Then came the shock, this extra 7 kilos would lumber us with an excess baggage charge of £20.00 which is three times the value of the stuff in the cases. We therefore decided to send the little black case as unaccompanied freight, which costs 13/5d a kilo not 46/- a kilo.

We are therefore 2 kilos @ 46/- and 5 kilos @ 13/5 overweight. The black case only had a pair of shoes, a few files of Richard's and my bag of sewing cottons in it. Imagine paying so much excess. It would have been cheaper parcelling the stuff and posting it airmail, extraordinarily enough. As it is we won't see it for a week or so. It will arrive the same time as the things in the wooden trunk, which is also going by airfreight.

We went to see various people in Unilever House, and filled in loads of forms and tried to take in last minute instructions. We treated ourselves to a huge lunch, just in case we have to eat fish heads for the next few months.

I'm now 300 miles further south than when I started writing this letter. The Captain has now announced that we are crossing the French Riviera. I can see the coast for miles. It is all lit up. We are travelling at 600 miles per hour at 33,000 feet and now it's all disappeared and it's all black below. The hostesses are bringing dinner around. Its seven o'clock. I wonder if you have finished the dishes?

The take off was fantastic. We cruised along quite slowly, then, wham, we were lying almost backwards with our feet towards the sky. Excuse the blotchy ink, but you know how difficult it is flying at this height, what with the pressure and all that! The route is apparently from London to Paris, across the Med then over Khartoum and south to Entebbe.

False alarum. It's not dinner. It was only the children having their meal. There is a little girl of about six sitting next to Richard. It's quite like a kindergarten. There are lots of tiny children and there are four small babies, which at the moment are howling in hammocks slung from the luggage racks. The little girl is playing with two Tressy dolls complete with outfits. I'm longing to have a go. They've got hair combs. Her little brother opposite has made a garage on a tray. Richard doesn't know it but there's another little girl who has appeared over the back of his seat and she's aiming a full milk bottle at his head.

This looks like my dinner coming up. Excuse me.

I've just had smoked salmon for hors d'oeuvres and roast beef for main meal and that old standby caramel cream, and half a bottle of Bordeaux for 2/6 each. I'm now on fruit, and coffee is coming round. I've just started on a second bottle of Bordeaux. Well you did say you wanted all the details.

A small girl in red of about four is also eyeing up our neighbour's Tressy dolls but she has put the lid on the box and has made it clear that they are not to be shared.

By the way, Dougal says that it's not that he minds travelling, but he does object to lying on his back wrapped in a vest. It's most undignified.

12.30 a.m. The Captain has just announced that we are to start our descent into Entebbe, just as all the babies have got to sleep. There are now eight of them slung in hammocks. It's absolutely pitch black below. The only sign of life is a pair of white shorts attached to a short-sleeved white shirt and a pair of white pumps, waving the plane in with two paddles. We are to stop an hour and then there's a further two-hour run to Ndola.

4th March.   We've arrived and settled in. There are two airmail posts. One on Sunday and one on Friday and I must post this off even though there are reams to tell you.

Letter 2   Rhodes Hotel, Ndola.

I've just posted your first letter so I am starting on the next. We visited The Post Office today and bought a variety of stamps, and some airmail letters so that Richard will write home, which he is doing now. We are both sitting in bed having been out since ten this morning.

All I've seen so far would fill a letter the size of an encyclopaedia. We were two hours delayed at Entebbe Airport because of fog in Ndola. At least they thought there was fog, but couldn't be sure as there was no contact with Ndola Airport at that time of the morning. We arrived at Ndola at sixish but our watches had to be put on two hours. We were met at the airport by the personnel manager, the chief accountant and his wife and baby and the works accountant. They took us to an apartment attached to the Rhodes Hotel, which looked rather dingy and shabby, but when the curtains were opened, the sun streamed in and it looked a lot better. We are to stay here until we are found more permanent accommodation.

The drive from the airport was splendid. It is near the end of the rainy season and everywhere is lush green. There is a plant called mealie (or something), which is the main source of food for the Africans, who grow mealie on even six inches of ground. It's like sugar cane and grows to about eight feet in height. There is so much to photograph-everything is so strange and interesting and like the TV travelogues only in brilliant colour.

Along this road from the airport were the Africans coming to work or working. The women wear the most brilliantly coloured of outfits. They carry everything on their heads, even their lunches in stew pots with handles. Babies up to about two are carried on their backs and breast fed babies are carried around the stomach with one or both bosoms bared ready for lunch. Babies are fed anytime, anywhere, even on the steps of the Post Office, as I saw today. The houses on the outskirts are basic prefab type buildings, as you would find on a caravan site. Dozens of Africans travel together on bicycles, similar to Spain but with headgear as well. Getting out at the airport was wonderful. It was like a heat wave in the U.K. (No-one says England, always U.K). We both wanted to play tennis and swim before the sun disappeared, but it's nice to know that it will be there tomorrow. Everyone says it's cool now, because of the breeze, which is most pleasant and welcome, and they say. "You've not known heat yet, wait until it's October when it really gets hot."

We slept until midday. I had my first bath to remove travel dirt and the second to remove the sweat and wake me up. Two in as many hours!

We have been entertained for lunch today by Peter Rubner, the chief accountant, Richard's boss, at first glance, a taciturn bear of a fellow, and his jolly wife Marlene who smiles and chuckles as much as he glowers, and Sally Ann who is eleven months old and nicely sunburned and ever such a good, happy baby and rather shy.

Sunday 5th March

Just a minute to write, while we are waiting to be taken to the races at Kitwe by Tony, the works accountant. We have just had our breakfast. Steak and beans. Sausage and bacon are very expensive and not too nice, so steak and egg or beans is a popular breakfast.

You would be on the first plane back if you could see the crawlies we have. The first night was awful. We examined everything with an aerosol. There are flat spiders like starfish and cockroaches (not many) and red beetles and the most frightful buzzing and flying things and of course mosquitoes. When Richard opened the door on Friday morning, lizards ran all over the place. They had been sheltering under the door from the sun. They are about five inches long, rather like newts and harmless. They run like mad and when they are far enough away, peer at you with little beady, black eyes.

I have decided to number my letters to you so that you can tell if one is missing as things have a habit of disappearing en route according to reports, so don't worry if you don't hear because it only means someone is sitting on it or has lit a cigarette with it.

Sunday evening in bed. We went to Kitwe to the races with Tony and his nurse girlfriend who has been here for five weeks. It was like a miniature Ascot and I was recommended to wear my coat and hat, which I did. Incidentally my hat was shown in the Zambia Times. It was the same article, which I saw in the Daily Mail three weeks ago. In fact, all news except local stuff is apparently copied and printed here as up to date, about a month later. The main London news is News of the World type stuff. So people get together and take turns in reading the flimsy air mail Times and Observer at weekends, although we unfortunately can't get the colour supplements.

Back to the races. I took half my cine film. The course wasn't very crowded and you can go and inspect the horses at close range. I managed to take film of the horses parading, the jockeys mounting, the finish of a race and the winner being brought in. The sun was rather strong; I hope the film turns out. And wonderful, Richard and I have been parading in front of the mirror boasting who is reddest. I am, although he says he is. As well as a sunburnt nose, I have a streaming cold. Apparently this is not unusual and will go soon. It's the drastic change in temperature. Before the start of the race, the commentator shouts," Piccanins on the track." And sure enough there was a gang of little ragamuffins on the track, too far away to film. They were shooed away and ran past all eyes and grins. They hardly had any clothes on. I've never seen so many little black bottoms.

Although I've more to say, I'll close and start writing another, as four pages and an envelope weigh half an ounce and if there is insufficient postage it will be sent by sea automatically. Look after yourselves.

Letter 3   Monday, 6th March .67

Richard went to work today for the first time and got lost on the way. He starts at eight o'clock in the morning and finishes at five although it's now five forty and he's still not home. When he had gone I sorted out the laundry and filled in a little list detailing it. I then went to find the library, which I found a little way up the road. It costs 12/6 to join which is refundable on leaving Ndola, and I was surprised at the selection of books. The library is about as big as the Children's library in Borough Road but none of the books seem to be more than three or four years old. I was hoping to find out a lot about the locality, but it is full of the latest books. I did a little shopping for our lunch. Things are in reasonable supply but from half more to double the cost, but as Richard is on about £60.00 a week, (boast, boast) this should compensate. I ended up with tinned soup, rolls and butter, as everything was so dear. When Richard came home at lunchtime he explained that his salary was high to cover the increase in the cost of living, so tomorrow I must shop in a different light. There is a main shop that sells St. Michael things even to the packet biscuits, which bear the U.K. price. It feels extravagant to pay 1/9d and 4/10d for biscuits labelled 1/- and 2/3d. The bras I bought in cotton before coming away at 7/11 are 13/11 here. I think it would be easier if the money were cents and dollars and then I couldn't compare with U.K. prices. Dresses are similarly priced but are not too fashionable, although Tony's girlfriend has bought a very attractive navy and white dress and coat set which was 17 guineas and although slightly dearer compares favourably in style. It seems you have to shop around and pounce when you see something good.

The first time that I went to the Post Office to buy stamps, I joined a very long queue in front of a desk clerk, who had a notice over his head saying, amongst other things, Postage Stamps. It was hot and oppressive inside and overlaid with the smell of sweaty bodies and I was glad to reach the front of the queue. I requested my stamps, and the clerk made direct eye contact with me and said, "I don't have stamps. You are in the wrong queue. Go to the next queue." He pointed to the clerk on his left and then slowly and deliberately, still looking directly at me, slid the open ledger of sheets of stamps, from under his right hand across in front of him to the clerk on his left.

"But," I protested, "those are the stamps I want."

"Wrong queue", he repeated and looking beyond me, "Next".

Confused, but thinking there must be a reasonable explanation, I joined the end of the very long queue in front of his colleague. We shuffled slowly forward. The Post Office was full of people, but all standing in line like me. There was no jostling, so I didn't feel uncomfortable, just puzzled that I hadn't properly worked out the system.

I reached the front and put in my request for stamps. The clerk, with the same deliberate steadfast gaze as the previous clerk, said, "Wrong queue. Look at the sign. This desk doesn't say stamps" Which it didn't. "The next queue sells stamps", and he pushed the book of stamps back to his neighbouring colleague.

I left the Post Office feeling confused, not knowing how to get my stamps and ashamed to have to tell Richard that I hadn't even managed to successfully complete a simple task like buying some stamps. I did realise that newly empowered Zambians might delight in wielding this power, but wasn't sure how I was going to handle it, or indeed if I was going to have to accept that I was fair game.

At night the row is terrible outside. There are cricket type things about four inches long and praying mantis. They make the noise you hear in tropical films, that I never thought was genuine. We will try and tape it for you. There are snakes outside but only in the long grass, so you have to keep to the paths at night. We are at the back of the hotel- it's more like a motel- and have to walk through quite a few trees on rough paths in the dark for dinner. I go first and Richard follows- coward. Although I must admit he was brave the first night. I was examining the bed before getting in and sticking through the bottom sheet were pincers with a curly hairy body underneath. We had just run out of aerosol so Richard told me to lift the sheet in a swift movement and he would clobber the intruder with his shoe. I did this and Richard started knocking hell out of a feather. Relief!

10pm after dinner. Richard has been chasing a spider out of the dining room. It had a body as big as half a ping-pong ball and legs to match. Richard says that after this, Daddy will be shouting for me to remove spiders from the bathroom, not the other way around. Outside our window we have what I call a carnation tree. It is very bushy and covered with carnation type flowers <u>six inches</u> across in pink. There is also a tree across the road in bloom with flame coloured flowers as big as plates. Everything in the flower line is larger than life. There is also a yellow bell flower, which I picked up (in my handkerchief) and intended to press, but it dried up too quickly. It's called a franji panji. This is how it is pronounced although I don't know if you spell it that way. The flowers have been at their best, but are dying off now after the rainy season, for the winter.

I tried to photograph a lizard today and got to within a few feet of it, but it ran away when I stepped on a twig. The same happened when I tried to photograph a bird as common as a sparrow, a black and white bird rather like a wagtail, with a shrill but pretty song. I have also seen a snail with a shell as big as a teacup. They are common during the rainy season.

The water is O.K but the normal thing is to keep a plastic bottle of boiled water in your fridge. Drinking is common (alcoholic that is) but we are sticking to coke and beers and wine in the evening, as it is very easy to become drunk in this heat.

I must tell you about Peter and Marlene's "boy". The normal thing is to have a boy and a garden boy and a children's help if there are children. Marlene has a boy called Banda. Every other African is called Banda. He lives in a room, which is called a kahia and is usually attached to the garage at the bottom of the garden. This room has a toilet and shower combined, which is more than most Africans can boast, I'm afraid. Banda keeps his wife and baby here too and recently a four-year oldish girl has appeared. Marlene has no idea whom she belongs to. There is a high rush fence around Banda's house and he grows mealie here. When Richard and I went to the bottom of the garden to inspect Marlene and Peter's vegetables, Mrs Banda was making a pancake thing over a wood fire in a dish with the baby on her back. I was astonished at the backwardness of this, but was told that a house and garden tap was infinitely better than the bush or township where dozens had to share the same facilities. Banda is not bright and must be told every little thing to do. His duties are roughly as follows- makes tea at 6.30am (normal rising time) and then breakfast: dusts and tidies and maybe washes or irons; prepares lunch, which Marlene cooks as all the food is unfamiliar to Banda, who can only learn by watching. He then has the rest of the day off until the evening meal when he assists, serves and washes up. He has Saturday afternoon and Sunday off. He is paid once a month and 10/- a week ration money. This is because he (and every other African) spends his money the day after it is received, thus the necessity of providing 10/- ration money weekly. Otherwise Mrs Banda and babies would go hungry. Wives mean little to the African. Banda asked Marlene to send to England for a sweater for himself and a cheap one for his wife. He came back later to ask her to forget about his wife's sweater and get a pair of trousers for himself instead.

This letter is getting fat so I'll close. Looking forward to hearing from you.

Chapter Two   Introductions

Letter No 4   **10th March 1967**

We had a storm last night. The heat built up and the sky went purple and orange and then black. There were peals of thunder and then loads of sheet and multi-forked lightening without any thunder. It was very impressive. Then an hour or so later, down came the rain, or more appropriately, half the sky. This morning the ground is wet and steaming but the pavements are bone dry and the heat is just the same. It is half nine and I have been shopping for some biscuits and cheese. We are still eating in the hotel for breakfast and the evening meal, because Levers is paying and instructed us to have all our meals there, as it is difficult to cook with limited utensils. We have all our air stuff except the one case, but goodness knows when we will get our sea freight.

The firm has two houses empty and two couples, so at present they are deciding who is to have which. We have expressed a preference for the one near Marlene and Peter as we have become very friendly with them. Also the other house is on the farther side of town and although the houses are said to be more exclusive and are preferred by the majority, it is very close to a large African Compound and if any Iincidents occur they will be on that side of town.

I spend most of my afternoons with Marlene. She is very easy to get along with. I would say she is about ten years older than I am, but is so relaxed handling the baby and the servants. I wish I could become so capable. I feel she was a schoolteacher before she married, so perhaps that's where it comes from. I think she is quite glad to have some new company, although I know that, initially, looking after me for a while to settle me in, is probably part of her job

On Tuesday I met the younger girls, Bernice and Cecily who are 28ish. Bernice has three boys and Cecily has two. They are both from South Africa. In fact, the managing director, Peter and Marlene and us are the only English. The other Europeans are Rhodesians or South African or have been away from England so long they have become Rhodesian. On Tuesday evening, Marlene and Peter and us were taken to dinner in the Savoy, which is the best hotel in Ndola (out of three). We had a super meal, smoked salmon followed by steak and then strawberries and cream (fresh!) The bill was awful. The smoked salmon was 14/6 for a kick-off. The managing director paid, poor fellow|. *Did I really think he was paying out of his own pocket? It would appear so!*

I'm afraid I can't send anyone postcards, as I haven't seen any yet. I bought a birthday card for Joan and they were all Gordon Fraser cards, nothing at all with an African flavour. Africans probably don't even know their birthdays. There are no African things I can send home, not even an ivory elephant. Hardly anything is made locally. Even the copper, which is mined not far away, has to be sent to Rhodesia for processing so that copper things on sale are double English prices. Apparently at Christmas, things are chosen from a South African catalogue and you send a cheque to South Africa and your things are despatched home for you without you ever seeing them. That's not much fun. The nearest thing to an African elephant is a plaster dog or cat, Woollies quality. I was hoping to buy rugs and tapestries.

My suntan is peeling off my shoulders and Richard's nose is like Rudolph's. Doodle is sulking in our suitcase. I told him he had to have a rabies certificate and he was insulted. Also he has to be taken to the vets twice a week to be dipped in flea and insect repellent and his vanity was wounded. Marlene takes her dog, Pinky, a great big boxer, to be dipped in the insecticide and the dog then spends all day trying to run away from her own smell.

Wednesday afternoon was good. We, Marlene, Sally and I, went to the boating club. This is on the side of the Dambo, the local river. There are thatched shelters like at Formentor and a swimming and paddling pool. I had a swim in the pool, but not the river. That's just for boating. One drop of that water inside you and you'd drop dead. Within two hours my hair and costume were bone dry. The rainy season finishes in April; the showers become less frequent from the end of March. Apparently in October, the swimming pool is like stepping into a warm bath.

There are three to four children to every adult. Large families are popular as the climate is O.K. and there is plenty of assistance in the house. It's difficult with a tiny baby, as they are kept wrapped in mosquito netting as insects go for babies. A particular nasty is the putsie fly. This lays eggs on wet washing; therefore everything must be ironed thoroughly to destroy them (they are invisible). Sally had one. The eggs attach themselves under the skin and maggots grow and eat their way out. The result is like a large boil and shouldn't be burst until the maggot is ready to come out. Although it's not serious, it turns your stomach a bit. Richard examines the laundry calling " Here, Putsie, Putsie. Come out wherever you are" How safe and comfortable England seems.

On Wednesday evening we went to dinner with the marketing director and his wife. We had chicken with pirie pirie sauce. Wait till I try that one on you. It's very hot. Richard and my eyes were watering like mad. A friend was visiting them and was asked by the customs if he had anything to declare and he said "Yes, a teddy bear for a present." He was then asked to produce its rabies certificate and they weren't satisfied with his explanation until he produced the bear to confirm that it was inanimate.

You must buy a book, a paperback called "Tell Me Josephine" by Barbara Hall. It is a collection of letters from the problem page of the Zambia Mail and gives an insight into the life out here. It's very funny and true to life, I'm told. I've still not heard from you though. Letters arrive on the VC10 on Friday and Wednesday and are put into the P.O. Boxes on Friday and Monday, so I should hear on Monday. We got our X-ray certificates alright. We were given 20 days to produce them or we would be deported and as the X ray machines in Ndola aren't working at the moment, it was quicker to send home for them. Levers should have known we needed certificates.

I got your first and welcome letter on Friday afternoon. It is best to post your letter on a Wednesday as it gets the Thursday night VC10 and is delivered Friday or Monday. Even when we have a permanent address it is still better to send letters to Levers as all the P.O. Boxes are at The Post Office at the centre of town and we would have to go in and open it every day. Levers collect daily. There are no such things as postmen.

We went to the tennis club on Saturday afternoon. I didn't play as Richard thought the standard would be too high for me at weekends and, at weekends, you have to play with whoever you are given, to give everyone a game, but he now thinks I'll be good enough. This morning Richard got a lot of games and I chatted with the others waiting. It's a very sociable club. This afternoon I went in my kit. It looked good. Even my undies were new and I'm getting a nice healthy colour and I played with Richard for half an hour. This is as much as I could take. The sun and altitude affect everyone and people go to bed at nine thirtyish. It's difficult to stay up later on a working day. I start to wilt about eight.

I am writing this lying in bed with nothing on except a sheet. It is over eighty degrees and is 8.30 at night. We are in bed as it is too hot to sit around in clothes. The air is very close and heavy and my glasses are sliding down my nose. Even if you jump in the bath you soon heat up again. And this is the beginning of winter. It is also exhausting. We are still not used to this altitude.

This afternoon, Marlene and I went to the boat club, where the swimming pool is, to cool off, as it was so hot in the garden. I swam a breadth- Hurray! Then a cold wind started to blow from the river and we came back as Sally has had tonsillitis this last week and by the time we got back, we were just as hot, although if you draw the curtains it feels cooler.

Last night we took Marlene and Peter to dinner at our hotel and to the pictures. We saw "Ten Little Indians" It's about twelve months old and Richard had already seen it, but it didn't matter. It has just started to rain. It's belting down. I feel like running out in it just as I am. When it rains it really does rain. You just can't stand up in it. Here comes the thunder. On second thoughts I'm glad I'm in bed.

Sooty, *my yellow budgie at home*, would look pale after all the lovely birds I've seen. I've been trying to find out how to catch and preserve butterflies so I can bring some home, but can only find butterfly picture books in Ndola library. Can you help, Daddy? Have a look next time you are down at the library, as I would love to bring these home to show you. If not I will try to photograph some. Apparently there is a lot more to it than catching them and keeping them in a box.

Yesterday I made an appointment to see the personnel manager of the big mining company here. I went this morning, but he said that there were no vacancies at present and if there were, the policy at the moment is to offer jobs to locals however superior the qualifications are of any others. This apparently is the policy everywhere. Richard, as part of his job, is training someone with five O levels to take over his job. This is practically impossible. It took Richard five years of hard slog doing his degree and all his professional exams to get the job he's got.

Marlene and I stayed in this afternoon, as it was raining and much cooler. I am putting a blanket on the bed tonight. Richard and I ate at the Savoy this evening, as the food here at the Rhodes Hotel is pretty monotonous. I have found a curio shop, but the stuff seems to be imported from Nairobi and very expensive. The shop is attached to the Savoy and is possibly to attract the likes of our managing director, who stayed there before moving into his house.

Thursday. This morning, Richard's colleague at work, Tony, who took us to the races called at 8 o'clock and said he would take me to see a friend of his who might have a job. So I went along. Unfortunately, the job involved typing, so that was out, but I stayed and had coffee and everyone was very nice and chatty. Then one of the fellows there said that he knew another fellow who might need someone and he duly phoned up and the fellow said," Send her along" so along I went.

I am now the stock records clerk of Zambia Oxygen Ltd. It is not a tremendously good or exciting job, but will do for now. I'll be on £75.00 a month, which is £900 p.a. I was only on £638 at home, so that's not so bad. They said if I were O.K. after a probationary period of three months they would raise my salary-goody-I hope I'll like it

A Mr & Mrs Young have arrived for six months. He is on the technical side in the factory and is to train local men. They lived in Cobden Street off Union Street. *(A very shabby road of terrace houses.)* Fancy that. So I have told Mrs Young, who is motherly and a bit dull and mousey, to come and see you in September and tell you all about it and possibly take some photos.

I'll try and vary the stamps a bit for you, but we buy the 1/3 stamps from the factory for convenience.

At ten o'clock today, I dashed home from my job hunting and my lift to a tea party had arrived. Tea parties are held in the morning and are the equivalent of coffee mornings, I suppose. I met about six other wives of Lever men. One I met last week had been dashing around trying to find me a music teacher, which she has done, but I don't know how my job will affect this. I've got to find out.

Where was Daddy's line? Not even a "love from Daddy" on your last letter. I think he will have to write a whole letter every now and again if he can't fit on yours.

We went to North Rise this evening to give a lift to a boy from Richard's office. He came here from England two years ago and had to marry an African girl as she was expecting, and then he tried to start a farm in the bush and went bankrupt and then joined Levers. His wife was out when we called. Her great-great-grandfather was the first of three white settlers in Zambia and her family is reasonably wealthy but did not approve of their marriage and the two are outcasts from both sides as she is mainly African and therefore not accepted by African nor white and they live on the poor side of town. I'm longing to see their baby boy.

Richard is using a company car at the moment until our own arrive. We will then have to apply for our petrol ration coupons. I think we are allowed eight gallons per car per month. Our housing will be settled this weekend.

Letter 5

I burnt out a hotel kettle today. It was very old and had already been soldered and was on its last legs. Normally you boil drinking water and put it in a plastic water flask in the fridge. It's no trouble to do once you get used to it, but today I went for lunch and left the kettle on.

You always said I needed a ladies maid. Well I've got nearly the same thing. He's the hotel "boy". We had spaghetti Bolognese for lunch one day and then went out leaving a load of lousy dishes. When I came back, everything was washed and put away. Even the stove was polished. I don't even need to ask for more toilet paper. I just put the empty roll on top of the lav. And next time I go there's a new one. Ever had a feeling you were being watched? Some locals are excellent and friendly, others are sour and bitter and unpleasant, but perhaps we would be no different in the same position and I think of this when I encounter any rudeness or brusqueness e.g. when shopping. Richard bought two pairs of tennis socks for 10/9 each pair. The shop assistant said that the bill would be 15/6, then £1.13.6 and got in such a mess with his sums that he had to call the manager who showed him how to add it up. He was very willing however and made a lovely parcel of the socks.

Richard is defrosting the fridge. As it is on such a high setting the whole freezer is one big block of ice, and there's no room inside it. We've had more thunderstorms. The thunder rocked the car at one time and another time it shook my fork and my carrot fell off it. You'd really think the roof was coming in. If I'm ever on my own I'm getting under the bed. And I like thunder.

Tuesday. Hurray. Received your second letter.

Times of Zambia   **Sunday 12th March**

Petrol rationing is likely to be eased next month. After the start of the rains last year, contractors carrying badly needed petrol were hampered by quagmire conditions on parts of the Great North Road.

President Kaunda's personal turbo-prop jet, a Hawker Siddeley 748, being built in Britain at a cost of £600,000 should be ready for delivery in June.

March 14th

The father of a boy who was accused of blinding another with a pen refused to pay the £80.00 compensation, and demanded that the son pay with the sight of one eye, 'an eye for an eye". He would then be sure the act would not be repeated.

** Illegal schools problem. The Roberts Compound School is reported to be catering for more than five hundred children. The voluntary teachers, Mr Spadwell Lubaya and Mr Terrison Nkolola teach reading, writing, arithmetic, English, Nyanja and nature study all in the open.

** Dr Hubert Wilson, Livingstone's great grandson had removed thirty-nine objects from the Livingstone museum to display them in Scotland's Livingstone Museum. He felt that as the museum was near the border with Rhodesia, there would be fewer visitors.

Chapter Three My birthday.

Letter 6   Sunday 19/3/67

I have been playing tennis this morning. After breakfast at nine o'clock, Richard & I went to the club and were first there, so we had a knock up together. I was only going to play with Richard, but as other people began to arrive, I was asked to make up a four. I played three sets and in the last one, was playing against Richard. Thanks to a strong partner, we beat them! Everyone was very good and insisted that I played, saying it was the only way to improve. I was whacked. We came home just before one and jumped into the bath and then had our lunch at the hotel- four courses including some fish, which is scarce, and some turkey. We are now relaxing with last Sunday's newspapers. The Times is 3/- and the Observer 2/9 without colour supplements and is on flimsy airmail paper. Marlene buys one when they arrive and I buy the other and we swap on Friday. We are going back to the club at 3.30 when it cools down. The weekends are like a holiday, especially with no cooking to do.

Last night, Saturday, we had dinner at Marlene and Peter's and Bernice was there. Her husband is in Port Sunlight for six weeks, on a course. He is "doing" Wales this weekend. He is South African and has never been outside Africa before and he can't get over the fact that on the London to Liverpool run there wasn't a patch of ground that wasn't built on or cultivated. Here you can go for 400 miles along a straight road through exactly the same scenery of scrub. He thinks London is tremendous, thank goodness.

I wish Harold Wilson had let those shamrocks through for St Patrick's Day. There was a lot of fun made of that by The Rhodesians here.

On Saturday morning we went to look at furniture. We went to a small new shop called Bracaire. It is completely concrete on the outside with a small door. We went in, and what a sight! The place is lit from glass in the roof and the absence of glass windows made it cool. The roof light is filtered through slats. The inside was patterned concrete and Swedish furniture and coffee sets and rugs and candleholders and all sorts of beautiful knick-knacks were laid out. But! Snag! The prices were exorbitant. At home we had our eye on an egg shaped chair for £35.00. Here was the same chair for £95.00 and everything else was similarly graded. However, we may treat ourselves to a rug or vase or something. They had cast iron cooking things for roughly the same price. We also have our eye on a fondue set. Remember me telling you about the fat in a heater on a table at John and Sue's where we all cooked our own meat? As the entertaining standard is pretty high, Richard and I thought we would buy a set for our birthdays as we need something original and can do it to death.

We are going to a cocktail party at The Savoy tomorrow, for a fellow from London who is quite high up, and my cocktail things are still coming by sea, so I'll go in the blue dress that matches my coat (the coat incidentally, is a great success) and dress it up with a brooch. I'll have to stun them some other time.

I shall feel a little sad this afternoon as I did last Sunday, because the VCIO takes off over the tennis court and it seems funny that your letter is on board and that the plane is going all that way back and we are watching it go.

Monday The poor working girl has just arrived home and jumped in the bath. I am now just writing this before Richard comes home and before I get ready for the cocktail party. The job is very easy and consists roughly of keeping record of stock arriving and stock being used and keeping a running total. I should imagine that I shall be bored within a week but I would rather be bored in company than bored on my own, because mornings are long in a hotel with nothing to do.

Times of Zambia

March   A striking feature of literacy classes is that there were more women than men. Teacher Mr Chibola thought that this was

because men were more interested in drinking than furthering their education.

21st March The British pound is being maintained by Zambia, Foreign Minister, Simon Kapepwe said, "The £14 million aid was merely compensation for UDI. British goods were being imported; Zambian copper kept two million British in employment. We are keeping their economy alive."

22nd March Many urban Zambians are facing economic ruin because of their adherence to a centuries old system of supporting extended families.

Aerogramme No 7   Blue flimsy airmail letter.   23 March 1967

Just a quickie today because I have been working and we have been out in the evenings. Oh for an unhectic night.

I'm liking my job although it's not very interesting. The girls are alright and we have a laugh. When I arrived I saw two girls in the same dress but different colours, and I thought it was co-incidence, and then the others came. It is like a uniform dress in cotton and is very pretty. It has a Peter Pan colour and cap sleeves and is slightly fitted and is without a belt and had navy binding down the sleeves, collar and down the front and six buttons for show and are issued FREE in three colours, white, pink and blue. Goody, I wonder when I get measured. We enjoyed the cocktail party on Monday. We arrived at six and it finished at eight, so we and a few others stayed in the lounge until tennish and made an evening of it.

Last night Marlene, Bernice and I went to a fashion show at a club. It was very good and was put on by a shop in town. They had some nice dresses, pricey, but not too bad. I got a good idea of English prices when fishing around Chester, but the startling thing about the audience was that there were more fashions displayed there than on the dais. All the young ones were competing to see who could wear the most daring, way out outfits. There was even one with these short chiffon nightie type dresses with bloomers to the knee. I felt quite antwacky in my Rajah suit. It's at least four weeks old. We had fancy butties and things in the interval.

We are going to Marlene's tonight to dinner and the guest of honour is the fellow from London for whom the cocktail party was given. It's all going to be very formal   Longer next time.

Correction.

The reason that this letter was short is because I got appallingly drunk at the cocktail party.

All I ever drank was the occasional sherry or glass of Asti Spumanti. Dad served me orange juice, even at Christmas. When I was about forty, I mentioned that perhaps I could now start having a sherry like everyone else. He was a bit startled but gave me sherry for a couple of years, but then reverted out of habit and as I was only making a point and didn't really like sherry, I let it go. Once Daddy's girl, always Daddy's girl.

So I arrived at the cocktail party and was asked what I would like to drink. At parties, the cheapest thing you could take was six beers or a bottle of Martini. This Martini was little more than lemonade, so, because it wasn't very exciting and not drunk in large quantities, it wasn't really possible to get drunk on it.

I hesitated because I didn't know what to say, and martini was suggested and I gratefully concurred. Indeed it tasted very nice and wasn't a bit like the martini I was used to. It was, however a martini cocktail. The real McCoy. Gin based and Colonial gin ratios. As it was very nice, I drank a lot of it and we had a really good evening. I was very gregarious, nay, garrulous, but never thought I was going to be the worse for wear. Until I got outside in the fresh air, when I didn't appear to have any legs. I could see legs, but they didn't appear to belong to me. Richard hauled me along two blocks of unmade up road back to our bungalow at the back of the Rhodes hotel and boy, was I ill. Richard, possibly not too healthy himself, left me in the bathroom where, in the end I couldn't even lift my head up. I just lay there until the early hours in my own puke. I have never, ever, before or since, been so appallingly ill. At some point Richard stuck me in the bath and cleaned me up and did the best he could with everything else, even calling the poor servant to change the sheets.

I lay in bed all next day, unable to move or go to my second day of work. Richard called the doctor when he came home from work as I was so ill, and explained I'd had a stomach upset. The doctor agreed that it was something I had eaten and gave me some medicine and said to go easy on the food as my stomach was strained! I don't think, indeed I know, I didn't drink another drop of alcohol the whole three years we were there.

The office, happily, were very concerned about my food poisoning. Not surprising really, living in The Rhodes Hotel, they said. They were just glad I hadn't worked one day and decided I didn't like it enough to go back.

Letter 8   Good Friday

Its 10am and I'm sitting down at the tennis club under a little bower covered in flowers, which are trained around a trellis. I'm out of the sun and there is a pleasant breeze. Richard is playing tennis with Tony. The bowlers have just finished their match and they are coming in for their tea. They all wear white with white trilby hats, even the women. It's funny, but at home we would call a day like this a scorcher, but people are arriving and saying "Quite a breeze, much cooler than yesterday".

We went to Marlene and Peter's last might to dinner and it was excellent. We had curry with fourteen side dishes. The guest of honour, Hans Oei is Dutch Indonesian and has travelled all over the world. He was brought up in the Chinese manner, rice and sitting on the floor, and then went to Holland from Indonesia and has been in England for the past five years. He is a clever finance man apparently and speaks English better than I do, after only these five years. He said he couldn't count the languages and dialects he could speak. He was fascinating and an ideal dinner guest.

I have just received your photographs and your fat letter. Richard said yesterday at lunch. "I've a fat letter for you from your Mum, but I've left it in my coat in the office. I could have hit him.

We have Friday and Monday off for Easter so this will throw the letters out a bit. There are Easter eggs in the shops but they are very expensive, 25/- for a normal size and they are often white or melty inside. Did Daddy give you the box of chocs I left? They were very expensive {*expense again, probably comes from being permanently hard up and careful*) You must eat them all yourself, except for Daddy. I got them at Fullers in Chester.

21

A hen and cock with lots of little chickens have just walked past. They belong to the local who keeps the courts in good nick. One of the fellows has just tried to catch one for me and they all ran everywhere. The poor old mother hen is now dashing around clucking trying to round them all up.

Richard wrote home, against my wishes for his two hockey sticks. We worked it out to be £1-0-0 at the most by sea. He wrote and said if it were more, not to bother, but his mother sent them by airfreight and it cost £5, and his father wrote a stiff letter telling him off for asking for them, so I've told Richard to send a cheque by return. She was a bit thick though paying £5 for two old hockey sticks. I should have thought she'd have had more sense. He could have bought two new ones for that.

The same applies to you. If you send Christmas presents, send them by sea because It's only 3/6 a pound. There are only two Christmases so it shouldn't amount to too much. Keep your eyes open in C & A's for a tennis dress, because I think that's what I would like for Christmas. I'm mentioning it now because in October the shops won't have any, and you did say to let you know what I wanted, in good time, didn't you?

It's Sally Anne Rubner's first birthday a week on Wednesday and I'll miss her party because I'm working. Well, I can't have it all ways.

I had a nice surprise yesterday. I received a formal invitation through the post - Zambia Oxygen requests the pleasure of the company of Mr & Mrs R.D. Lapthorne etc. to celebrate someone's twenty-one years with the company. It's to be held on Friday at the home of the managing director, so I'm making a new circle of friends for us.

I've found a shop which had a box of postcards, but they had dozens of the same two views about 600 miles from here, which is like sending a postcard of Dover from Liverpool, I suppose, but as it's all I had, I might drop a few to people I want to remember but have no time to write full letters to. As well as letters from Mary and Joan, I had one from a woman in the office. Joan said that the oddest of people have copied down my address. But it's very nice to hear from everyone.

The best vegetables are bought from boys in the street. These are washed and in plastic bags and you can get potatoes, runner beans, carrots and tomatoes, the big Spanish ones, *(the cry was "Pot<u>aaa</u>toes, Ca<u>aaa</u>rrots, Tom<u>aaaa</u>toes, Grin bins." That's why R and I always call runner beans and French beans "grin bins ")* They are dearer than the shops but are fresher. Our office has slatted windows rather like Venetian blinds and these boys poke their hands through the windows with bags of potatoes and recite what they are selling all in one breath, so the girls who are all younger than me and married, do all their green grocery shopping through the window. After about ten o'clock it gets a bit much having a bag of beans thrust under your nose when you are trying to add up a long column of figures so we close the slats.

We've had to get tennis balls specially made for Zambia. They are Slazenger but are special high altitude ones. Fancy that.

Easter Monday. Saturday afternoon was a downpour and tennis was rained off. In the evening we went to Marlene and Peter's for dinner. Yesterday, Easter Sunday, we played tennis until 10 o'clock and then went to Muirhead's, the commercial director's for cocktails, which lasted from 11am to 2.30, and we missed our lunch at the hotel. The Youngs (who are here for six months, remember?) were there. Mr Young, who is only a supervisor, came here to train staff in the factory, has kicked up a big fuss and has a house and staff already and they have only been here for just over a week. We are moving into a maisonette at the weekend. It has a bathroom, two bedrooms, big downstairs room and a kitchen; half the size of ours in Chester and open plan stairs in the main room. It is all we need, but nowhere near as big as the Young's house, which has annoyed us a bit, but Mr Young was friendly with the current managing director in Ghana. Funny, isn't it. Mr Young lives in a terrace house in Cobden Street and runs a Wolseley and runs down England like mad. His wife has complained that there is no social life and no bingo, and they spend their evenings in the bar. They are no advertisement for England and we are afraid we will be judged as the same as them and are going the opposite way, not daring to admit that anything English is wrong.

We went to the pictures on Friday, the second time since we've been here. The films change three to four times a week. Our new home is on the edge of the golf course and overlooks the bush. It is about three minutes from the centre of town and we are pleased with its location. It is ten seconds from the tennis club.

Valerie Lapthorne

I received your lovely birthday card on Saturday with others from the family. I was so pleased to get them. There is no mantelpiece in our new house, but I'll put them on the sideboard until long after my birthday is over.

Chapter Four   Moving in.

Letter 9   29th March 67

On Easter Monday, it rained, not much better than an English Bank Holiday and as we had enough petrol, having travelled not more than necessary, we went to a place about 17 miles away called Luanshya.

We travelled on a road called the M6, which is tarmac but barely sufficient for two cars to pass, with a mud track either side. As Richard says- it even has a hard shoulder. This road goes through the bush in a dead straight line and is rather monotonous, except for the people we saw en route. Lining this route are charcoal burners, who erect little huts of thatch and tarpaulin and cardboard and corrugated iron, as big as a child would make on a bombed site. I don't know how they keep the rain out. These fellows prepare smouldering fires and when they have processed their charcoal, it is put into sacks propped on sticks at the side of the road. I wish I could have photographed them, but it's not the sort of place you can stop in, least of all to photograph. When it rains, the most extraordinary rainwear appears. One fellow had a large golfing umbrella with the spokes dangling on one side. Black sou'westers are popular, and can be hazardous when driving down an unlit road. I have seen younger more debonair young men in polka dot or floral plastic macs. On the Luanshya road there was a fellow, perhaps going home to see his mother and girlfriend and wanting to look his best with an umbrella and his polished winkle pickers on his head. A young girl at a bus stop in town was in a mini-skirted mod dress, with her handbag on her head.

Luanshya is a mining town. The entrance has a beautiful line of trees in drastic contrast to the bush, and formal flower beds and rambling houses, but the rest is like a mining town in a Western, even to the shops set slightly higher than the street. There were two banks, two churches, two schools, various shops, a "liquor store" and a beer hall and that was that. There is however a swimming pool and a police camp which we didn't see. On the way home a little boy waved to us as we passed. He had khaki shorts and a bicycle tyre and was highly delighted when we waved back. I'm sure he wouldn't have minded being photographed, but his Dad might have been around. The children fascinate me and if I see any on their own, watching me, I give a big cheesy smile, which makes them giggle.

March 30th. Happy Birthday to me. Happy Birthday to me. I have just come in after celebrating my birthday at the Savoy with Marlene and Peter. We had a lovely evening and I am scribbling this to catch the post. I missed you coming into my room singing Happy Birthday and Richard only remembered halfway through breakfast, but that would have been the same if we had been in Chester in our own house. Richard came in this evening with a teak ice bucket. It's Danish and is made from one piece of wood, and a fondue set with forks. The whole lot came to £25, but I got my wages cheque yesterday and it was £129 after deductions. I had only actually worked six days it being Easter. Not bad for six days, was it?

One of the girls in the office is coming to Liverpool for three months for a working holiday. Do you mind if I give her your address? She's a bit dizzy but rather nice. She gives me a lift sometimes at lunchtimes and she might be glad of someone to get in touch with.

I'm looking at my birthday cards. I have put them on my dressing table this evening-nine of them. I'm going to put them up in the house when I move in.

This is the first time I allowed myself to be miserable. I put my pathetic collection of birthday cards on the dressing table in that flyblown hotel's dingy, hot, dark, shuttered room and sat on the creaky metal bed with the lumpy mattress and wept.

Times of Zambia

30th March   Good News. Petrol ration goes up to 12 gallons a month.

31st March   New names for Zambian towns.

Broken Hill	Kabwe
Fort Jameson	Kapata
Fort Roseberry	Mansa
Bancroft	Kirilabombwe

Abercorn   Mbala

Letter 10   2nd April 1967

I've brought the camera to photograph the chicks but they have grown since last week and are looking very gawky and henny, not a bit like the balls of fluff they were three weeks ago.

We've had a lot of rain and couldn't play tennis yesterday but we have been to see the house and been arranging the furniture. We have a green lounge suite with a four-seater settee, a dark imitation Regency six-seater dining table and sideboard and a writing desk, which hasn't arrived yet. The kitchen is small but has enough cupboard space and the hall has built in wardrobe/cupboards. The bedrooms (two) are Marley tiled as downstairs and shine like mad. You can see your face in them.

Upstairs we have built-in wardrobes and cupboards in each room. We have twin beds (only until the double one arrives) a dressing table and stool with a chest of drawers to come, in the main bedroom. The second room is to be furnished with a single bed and a chest of drawers. I shall store the trunks here and cover the airfreight chest with material and disguise it and make a window seat, and put our valuables in there, well screwed down.

Valuables! We didn't have anything worth taking. The two chests of drawers never materialised

The main bedroom has full width metal windows and two chairs to sit on to survey the view. The windows are only 12 inches from the ground so you can lie on the bed and watch all the comings and goings.

A girl called Sue sitting next to me at the club has just realised she is moving next door but one to us. Her husband is in a bank for two years and they have moved from South Africa and she has been in leave houses (occupied while the owners are away on leave from a month to three months at a time) and is moving on the first of May. She was highly delighted to hear we would be neighbours and has invited me to play squash with her.

We had a good time at my office party. It was a huge rambling house and we had lots of food and dancing and champagne for toasts. Richard thought them all a friendly crowd

Sunday. We went to the house this afternoon at 4 o'clock and I set up the camera and did a few practice runs across the view, the idea being to start the camera when the "lift off" jets start, A tremendous roar and by the time I had panned to the middle, the jet would have left the runway and be rising above the trees. When 5 o'clock came we heard the engine start up and I had my finger on the button and zoom at the ready. Wonderful. But when I looked at the camera indicator to see how much I had left the film hadn't moved. I opened it up thinking it had come unthreaded at the beginning but I had put the spool on back to front and the take-up spool hadn't moved, but the spool with the film on had unwound and was raveled in the box and it all shot out.

Yesterday we went to the house just as a storm was starting. From the bedroom window we could see it moving and building up across the bush with the lightning coming down in forks. It was magnificent. We had a close shave last week. The lightening hit the bar in the tennis club and travelled down a wire grid and crackled and there was a big flash and everyone ducked.

Richard bought me two carved wooden antelopes from a roadside vendor. They have real horn horns, a mother and baby to go together on my sideboard,

I've just had a big moth on my finger. A boy caught it and said it was tame and would walk on my finger and it did. It had great bulging eyes

Monday. We have moved in very hectically, and the electricity has not been switched on, and I'm writing this by the light of a candle. As it goes dark at six, you can imagine the chaos. We've also no curtains up. The previous owners sold them to Levers and they are currently at the dry cleaners. We went out for a meal, as there is no electricity for the fridge or cooker. It would be funny, but we've loads of sorting and unpacking and odd jobs to do. We've some extra bits and pieces for the house, which Levers have bought. I'll tell you more next letter as I'm getting eyestrain by candlelight. That's a new excuse for ending a letter isn't it?

Times of Zambia

2nd April   Angola freedom fighters blew up the Lobito Congo rail line forcing all goods for Zambia to be held back.

**   A spokesman for Lever Bros said his company was only producing Surf in limited quantities. There was only one machine for producing for Persil and Surf and that had been out of order for some time. Last November an Italian engineer was flown in but had not been allowed to enter, as he had no visa.

7th April Shortage of Sugar hits shops. Custom officials are believed to be holding up several tons of sugar because the consignment includes bags bearing the names of Rhodesian firms.

**   There is no shortage of soap powder, says the Managing Director of Lever Bros, Ndola, Archie Mackie, and the detergent plant is running as anticipated.

Chapter Five Sorting things out

Letter 11 4th April 1967

Well, we're in. The electricity is on and everything is functioning quite normally at the moment. After a lazy month in the hotel, I've come down to earth, but it's lovely using our own towels and sheets instead of the grey, carbolicky hotel ones, and the change of diet is nice, two one course meals instead of two four course meals. We have been unable to get any meat yet. The butcher calls at the factory on Friday morning and collects orders and delivers Friday afternoon. This means we are meatless until Friday when we shall order for the following week. However we had our first chips this evening, with fried eggs and at lunchtime, luncheon meat and pickles.

We also get milk straight from a cow. We have two churns delivered in the morning at the office and everyone has bottles and we take turns to do the milk order. I took my first two pints home in Coca Cola bottles, but now use a two pint orange bottle. What a performance. However, you can drink the milk straight. Next month this finishes as the fellow who brings the milk from a farm is moving into town. We will then have to use the normal milk, which is apparently mainly powdered and treated, as demand exceeds supply. It tastes a bit like condensed milk and is a bit sickly, and you can't drink it on its own, although it is passable in tea and coffee.

Breakfast cereals are out at the moment. Things come and go like this and if you see something you may need in the far distant future, you buy it. Today I bought a tin of Heinz vegetable salad and a tin of anchovies, the last on the shelf, as when I would want to use these, there will probably be none. There was also a consignment of Surprise peas in, which we like and which will store indefinitely and which only come in once in a blue moon, so we bought a dozen packets. As you can imagine this requires a lot of storage space. We have a huge shoulder high fridge which I keep even vegetables in and we have bought a big hamper thing which is a vacuum and when the lid is on it keeps cold. It will be useful for picnics. It will save loads of string bags. It has a small plastic bag of something, which Daddy will probably know about, which you can freeze solid and put inside the hamper and it stays frozen and keeps the box cold for weeks.

We have lots of base units and a wall cupboard which, although clean were a bit dingy and only wood so we asked for some Contact which the company bought and Richard has covered the shelves and six drawers. The Contact is beige so we can see a crawly from six feet away.

We've some red ants, which are a nuisance. You can't keep spraying, as you will probably poison yourself, so the only thing is to discourage them. I've tried to keep all foods in the fridge except unopened tins. You can see how difficult it is- I left a tiny piece of meat on the draining board and when I came to wash up, the ants were marching off with it. In the evening yesterday, Richard had a glass of milk and duly washed both glass and bottle, but the bottle had left a milky ring on the cupboard top and we found the ants in a ring around it, lapping it up. Any dishes that I can't wash before a meal, because it will go cold, I immerse in hot water and make do with wiping the stove and draining board clean. This will teach me to be tidy the hard way. I've got to hang clothes up or the bugs will be walking round wearing them.

Thursday 6th April

Answers to Daddy's questions. The personnel manager is Bob Buchanan, a Scots nit of about 55 who is about 5'3 and wears a dickey bow. He is the one who is arranging the house or rather not arranging the house and sends us twin beds not a double, no light bulbs, no electric, a lav that doesn't work, a bathroom cabinet with the shelves missing, a dressing table with no wooden things to hold the mirrors up, and no chests of drawers. That's why we don't mention him. I wish I knew what had happened to him too.

Tony. Richard plays tennis a lot with him at the weekends. He is very happy go lucky and fancies himself as THE gay bachelor. He's about 26/28. His girlfriend's name is Eileen, but Tony, being true to his image, hasn't brought her with him the last week or so, which is unfortunate as she offered to help us move in as she was on nights. She is very pleasant and quite definitely on the husband hunt. She came here at twenty-five, as she said London had nothing to offer. She's a buxom blonde too.

The commercial director is Graham Muirhead and his wife's name is Chessie. (Mr Young keeps calling her Jessie) The Managing Director is Archie Mackie and his wife is Margaret. These two are the big nobs. But the wife is awful. She gave us a crummy coffee table that she ordered and didn't like, and she also gave us a white dressing table for the second room, which we were pleased with and then she changed her mind and took it back. The production line stopped one morning and when they went to see what had happened, they found that the men had been taken off to move a tree in her garden that she didn't like. Richard has difficulty in getting his car at lunchtime as she has it (chauffer driven) to take her shopping. She is also very hammy at cocktail parties shouting across the room "Ah, Mr. So and So, I haven't spoken to you all evening." I do better myself.

A colleague of Richard's brought a boy along for us to interview and we have taken him on. We pay him once a month, give him a rent allowance as we have no housing for him and 10/- a week ration money as the pay is spent all at once at the end of the month. And guess what, his name is not Mbongwi, its Albert. He starts tomorrow at seven. He understands and speaks a reasonable amount of English and is youngish-it's difficult to judge age. He was rather nervous and said "Yes please" to almost everything we asked him. For example, can you wash? Iron? Polish floors? Polishing floors is a big thing as it's Marley tiles up and down, and has a very high gloss, which takes some maintaining and would need an electric polisher if I had to do it and go out to work. John, who brought him, said that he knew he was nervous because he was chewing a bit of twig.

We believe there are toilets and showers in the central part of Dolphin Court. This is important, as you couldn't risk your own being used because of diseases. He is to work until I come home in the evening at 4.30 to 5, but is to stay later if we have visitors. We will provide two sets of uniform in khaki, although this is not essential, but he'll probably be more proud of a uniform and will keep it clean. He will also have a white uniform for serving at the table and such occasions.

As we are out all day, we will have to lock all lockable cupboards and wardrobes. This is a nuisance. Your life is not quite natural. During the day, I can't wander round in next to nothing or lounge about with my feet up, as Albert will probably be dusting or polishing. It was bad enough for Daddy when Nanny was around. *(My Gran, not a nanny)* Also, I'll have to be tidy and keep valuables out of temptation's way. We think it seems more trouble than it's worth, but couldn't cope with the tremendous amount of washing that there is, it being so hot, by hand, and in the bath, at that. Anyway how could I play tennis all weekend with ironing to do!

Last week I saw the sweetest little frog, only instead of long back legs it had short ones and ran rather than hopped. It puffed itself up like a little balloon and I thought it would burst and it stayed like that until we moved away. It was about the size of a ping-pong ball.

Well I'll let you know how Albert gets on. I hope I can be organised enough to find things for him to do. I haven't even got a broom or dusters yet. What a hectic responsible life.

Times of Zambia

8th April Zambia Bottlers may close down because of a lack of sugar. Broken Hill, Monza and Choma had already run out of Coca Cola.

9th April Shortage of sugar and flour eased yesterday on the Copperbelt and canned fruit, jams and vegetables, also in short supply, are expected to be back on the shelves next week.

**   There was no shortage of flour, said a spokesman of National Milling Company. What we were short of was packets."

Chapter Six   Albert

Letter 13

Can you find out about Quarantine regulations for a Maltese poodle from here? This arises because someone had the most beautiful Maltese poodle puppy for 7 guineas, and we nearly bought it, but hesitated, being unsure about quarantine, as if we bought it, we would want to bring it home. Had we been in a house with a large garden, we would have had a boxer, which we would have left as they are always in demand being good guard dogs but still good with children. This poodle is not a proper poodle, which I loathe, but was like a ball of wool. It would not grow very big and would have had long curly hair. He was beautiful. However, Sue who is going to be next door but one, put in for it, so I can still share the fun of it without the mess.

Albert has just finished his first day. I gave him clean sheets and a horrible amount of washing, mainly Richard's shirts and underclothes and tennis gear with towels and sheets for two beds. I left soap powder and a bar of Sunlight. When I came home at lunchtime, I expected to see him up to his eyes in suds, but everything was on the line and he was washing his own dusters. I bought a very big roll of dish cloth stuff and said he could use that for dusters and he had found the scissors and cut himself a few. When I came in, he switched the kettle on. I nearly choked when I saw the dining table. He had tried to lay it. He had put side plates on tablemats and a fish knife and a dessert fork on each plate, and cups and saucers on little mats with spoons in. I don't know what he thought we would eat. The bedroom had been cleaned and dusted, the bathroom and stairs likewise. I told him to take a half hour break, but he said, "Excuse me Madam. I stay. Too long go home." I think it takes him twenty minutes to get home. I meant him to go to the building they have for domestics with showers and toilets and a mess room for him to sit and have his lunch, but he didn't appear to have anything for his lunch As he had put the kettle on, I told him to have some tea. I hope he wasn't hungry. He is quite well turned out. He has a watch and wears shoes and has linen type trousers. Richard said he would get him a uniform and he proceeds to give Richard his precise measurements. A khaki shirt and trousers will cost about £2-15-0d. We intend to teach him to wait on table, which he says he can do, but judging from his table laying, I am not sure.

I came home from work at half four as I got a lift. I usually have to wait for Richard in the lounge of the Rhodes Hotel until six, which is a waste of time. Albert was in the middle of the ironing of this morning's washing. We have a huge airer and this was full. I told him to pack up and go home and he tidied up and emptied the rubbish and then he came in and made coughing noises and when I looked up, (I was writing at the desk, he said " I finish Madame" so Madame says " Thank you Albert. Goodnight, See you at seven tomorrow." Very necessary or he probably wouldn't arrive. And off he goes. Goodness knows what I can find for him to do Tuesday to Friday. However, polishing floors should take a day. He has had a nosey in all the cupboards, as he knows where everything is. My shoes are on a shelf in Richard's cupboard. Usually they take tea and sugar and you find your tea and sugar go down rapidly. I think he has taken some sugar, which is expensive. But even if I gave him a bag of tea and sugar a week, it would still go. I think it's the principle. As long as it's only sugar and tea. I do hope he's honest, as he's pleasant enough. When I said to Richard that he had a watch and trousers, he said he was just casing the joint for a week. Albert is two months younger than me, which makes it easier for me to tell him what to do than if he were an old man.

We had a lovely day on Sunday. We played tennis from 9 until 11.30. We then dashed home and got out the new cold hamper and put our swim things in the bottom and added lager and coca cola, tinned meat and a jelly I had made with fruit and went to the boat club where we were made official members at 12 0'clock. We came back home in time to film the VC10 and fell into bed at 9.30 having tidied around as Albert was coming.

We paid about £5.0.0 for assorted dusters and brushes. A wooden broom, which he broke the first time he used it, was 12/9, a floor polisher brush 10/6, a special one with a loop for his foot which he puts on and runs round like mad in the polish. We keep it all in a cupboard which we call Albert's cupboard. We have a special heavy iron without a thermostat, which he uses, although I am sure he could cope with a thermostat. He seems quite sharp. He filled a Coke bottle with water and put it in the fridge and he uses the light nylon brush for the upholstery. I gave him all the brushes and said that he was to tell me if he was short of anything. I suppose he's enthusiastic as he's on a month's trial.

Work is going down well. Its getting more interesting as I get into it and the girls are good company.

Richard has been tanned while playing tennis and the part covered by his shirt and shorts is white. He won't sit at the boat club in his trunks until he has evened his tan up in the garden. When he's undressed, he looks as though he has his shirt and shorts on. He looks a scream.

I sat in my bikini and have started a tan. I never wear anything on my arms now that they have their initial tan and won't burn. I don't wear make-up any more during the day as I have a good colour. Make-up now makes me look ill.

Letter 14   13.4.67

Jill from the office brought me home. Her Mum met her from work yesterday and took me back with them for tea and biscuits. They have a larger house on the other side of Dolphin Court. Jill is coming to Liverpool in May for twelve months She has already done a two-year secretarial course there. Do you have anything going in your place?   She seems good at work and is very smart. She has some super clothes. Her Mum is nice. I might pop in and see her when Jill goes.

Albert is slacking up a bit now-only four days after he started, but as Richard says it's cheaper than hiring a washing machine and a floor polisher, which are very, very expensive here. He pinches the sugar every day. We won't say anything unless it really increases. I also found half the toothpaste missing. He might have tried it out of curiosity and then couldn't get it back. He keeps the place dusted though and peels the vegetables that I leave out. After he had made a few useless efforts to lay the table, I showed him how. At lunchtime on Monday, he had the kettle on and I had to make a pot of tea. I gave him a cup. Aren't I good? He had probably already had three pots. On Tuesday, he had the teapot out, the cups and saucers in the kitchen, not on the dining table and the bag of tea and sugar out with spoons in them. We only keep a bowl of sugar out; the rest is in a Tupperware bowl in the locked sideboard. We can then control his sugar pinching. Today as I came in, he was making the tea himself. He had obviously picked it up from watching me. And what a strong pot.

I was pleased to see he was only using half the packet of Tide for the wash as they are reputed to love loads of soap for washing- until I came to use my Lux flakes which I had been saving as it was so expensive, for my woollies and my undies. It was half empty. I had tried to hide it on a back shelf, but he found it.

This morning he came and put a little bundle in the broom cupboard, which is his cupboard, and I thought it was his lunch. When I went into his cupboard this evening for a cloth, there was his shirt all washed and ironed. As I was in the kitchen when he went home he probably didn't take it home. I don't mind him doing his own shirts. I'd rather he was clean than smelly. (Although he doesn't exactly cover himself with Old Spice, so I shall say to him tomorrow "You forgot to take your shirt home. Don't forget tonight" or something like that to let him know I know, but don't mind. I would rather he wasn't sneaky about it. What a problem. However I hope we can teach him something useful so that he can better himself on leaving us.

Richard is doing the meal tonight so that I can write to you, because we play cards in the evening for an hour and if I write to you, we don't play and he gets grumpy, so I don't mind. We've got some meat today. Its not too fresh, but is a huge piece of fillet steak for 7/-, enough for only two meals with Richard's appetite. It's not the cost, but trying to get what you want which is the problem. We also bought four lamb chops. When we can't get meat, we have egg and chips or corned beef hash which is tasty enough, or omelette and tinned mushrooms. I dare say we can survive.

Richard says that the factory is rationing the soap powder because they can't meet demand because the raw materials aren't arriving because of UDI so we are going to buy half a dozen boxes of Tide (especially given the rate at which Albert uses it) I now lock the Lux away. Albert probably likes the scenty smell on his shirt. I am looking forward to walking into a shop and buying what I want. The flour here is not too good either. It must be sieved because of the maggots. Ugh! I was going to make pancakes but can't pluck up the courage to open the bag. I've found two worms in a bar of chocolate. There is special specie of worm that loves raisins and bores holes through the chocolate. And the way I've been gobbling Fruit and Nut. However we now buy ours from a delicatessen with a bigger turnover.

Later after meal. We didn't know how to grill the steak as it was such a funny shape until we realised we had to slice it down and turn the slices on their sides to grill. We cut eight steaks so you can tell how big it was. We ate two and will keep the rest.

Our accountant at work, with whom Richard and I were chatty at the party, invited us to a Treasure Hunt with their motor club, who have been saving up their petrol for it, but we will have to refuse as we are using a company car and petrol and don't want to abuse the privilege. I will tell him to ask us if they have one again and we have our own car. Also Richard wouldn't want anything to happen to the car on a dirt road out of town when he is only really to use it for necessary journeys. The car we are using is a Peugeot estate and bigger than our Hillman.

Shush! Richard is doing the dishes. He must really be keen on his cards. The game we play is one taught by Marlene and Peter and can only be played by two. They have kept a running score since Marlene arrived last May and she now has a score 2000 more than Peter.

I have been going to the library on Fridays and Richard is going to join this Friday, as I get annoyed when he wants a book on my ticket. As we are in our own house, we are not going out so much. We only finish our meal at eight and are in bed by 9.30 if we haven't fallen asleep beforehand.

Richard has pulled out the coffee table and is now dealing so I suppose I must close.

Times of Zambia   13th April

**   **Western Style Democracy not for us.**

A western type democracy would be a luxury Zambia could not afford, said Mr. Andrew Mutemba. If the opposition were to be effective, it would mean that instead of all the brains going to serve

the Government, they would be dissipated in the luxury of opposition. He said that chiefs, although without an opposition, were not absolute rulers. They had councillors, section chiefs and village headmen to advise them.

** The Rhodesia Railways manager in Lusaka has been declared a Prohibited Immigrant.

Chapter Seven   Settling In

Letter 15

Dear Mummy and Daddy

(Should be Mom & Dad if I really wanted to be colloquial.)

I was working this morning. I work one Saturday in nine, doing the switchboard which is very easy and which I learnt yesterday morning. All calls, which aren't Ndola, are long distance and I have rung Rhodesia. The only difficulty is that when you get strong accents, either Local or Afrikaans. I also do the milk. The milk churns come from the farm and during the morning all members of staff drop in with jugs and bottles and usually stop for a chat. The members of staff on Saturday wear shorts and casual shirts and I had no shoes or stockings on. It was quite pleasant and Richard did the shopping, which he is better at than I, as I am still saying, " I'm not paying 3/6. You can get it at home for 1/9" and end up getting very little. Also Richard grabs things that have not been around for a while. No cereals have come in yet and soap powder is in short supply. Eggs are also sold out after eight a.m. and we went to a bakery after I finished today and they only had half a dozen or so small cakes. Here again demand exceeds supply and stocks disappear by ten. This is the only bakery in town and is rather inaccessible but I wanted a cake as Marlene and Peter and Sally Ann are coming tomorrow for afternoon tea. I hope to have it on our terrace if it's not too insecty. I bought the little cakes and have made a jelly, which I shall have with tinned fruit and <u>fresh</u> cream. Marlene will envy me as I bought half a pint for 7/- a pint. Four pints of cream were bought in with the milk for first comers, so I was able to have some. It was a good job, as Richard couldn't get cream in a tin or ice cream. Richard also bought a white lamp with a marble base and white stand and a silk shade. The gilt was already tarnished a bit and it was £7-10-0 but he still bought it. We are allowed £15.00 by the company for a standard lamp, but we would rather have two table lamps, (wouldn't you in a large room which needs extra light?) but when we put this to them, they said that the people following us might not have the same taste. We need the extra light so will get the standard lamp, but I am sure we will be forever tripping over it.

The Youngs didn't get the house we particularly like. They just got a big detached house with a lovely big garden, which is silly when they are here for six months and we are here for two years. They have come under different arrangements and even pots and pans and bedding and ornaments and TV and a radio have been supplied. He gets his normal pay at home and, as he is not paid by this company, he is given living expenses of so much plus 25% extra as he has his wife with him. They pay no rent. We pay £6.00 a week They also have a birdbath and a rock pool, which attracts the birds and things. They also moaned because the kitchen was too big!! Anyway, we have a tap on our communal lawn, which drips, and when I went to switch it off (but it was too stiff), underneath was a little fat frog. I dashed for my camera but he had gone. Richard says I am like an angler. All my best ones get away. But I noticed the birds hung from the tap catching the drips, so I sat for a while and was rewarded as the birds came down. I was stiff from sitting but hope to have a few good shots to send you.

Played tennis until six and then Richard did bar duty. All members do a bit and it's quite fun. All I did was prop up the other side of the bar with an orange still in tennis kit. Me, not the orange.

I am now cooking a chicken, which we can also have with our picnic lunch tomorrow at the boat club. We must be very careful with ground vegetables like lettuce and cabbage, as there is a snail called a bilharzia snail which lives in rivers and gives off some sort of germ, hence no river bathing or fishing and when river water is used for irrigating crops, passes it on. Even a splash of river water can carry it. It is like TB, I think. A sort of weakening disease. Scrub and chilling then for lettuce. *What rubbish. It's a fascinating life cycle. Parasite eggs are released into fresh water and hatch. They then infect snails and migrate and develop within the snail and pass pass out as different parasites, which seek out mammals whose presence they can sense in the water. As they burrow through the flesh, they transform again and passing through the lungs end up in the liver and then migrate out of the body as eggs, but not before wrecking it. It can be treated if recognised. There is currently no vaccine.*

I've taught Albert how to set two places at a table with the forks and things the right way round. I told him it was very good and he was so pleased that he went mad and put two dinner plates on the table, two glasses and a jar of pickles. This was because we have been having tinned meat and pickles for lunch so he must think we always have them.

He asked for an advance on his ration money which is paid on Saturday, on Friday, so we gave him half, as it was his first week, but we mustn't do it again as borrowing is a habit. Even managers in Richard's factory earning £150 a month ask for advances, one fellow because his electricity bill had arrived. They don't appear to have any idea of budgeting.

One chubby little boy came to me in a very ragged shirt and clasped his hands and gazed at me with those big eyes and pleaded, " Sixpence please, Madame. I am so hungry" and I told him to clear off. His friends were around the corner, cashing up the takings. Begging is illegal as there are state benefits.

On Saturday nights we can hear the drums. It's a regular rhythm and quite groovy. It's eerie coming from the bush. And it goes on until the early hours. A local girl was telling me that when a village woman goes into labour, they have a noisy party to encourage her. I think it is to drown out the groans and yells, because nobody would be able to sleep anyway. When we first heard the drums in the early hours, Richard said he wished Sanders[1] would hurry up and get here so we could get some sleep. *Sanders from Sanders of the River Korda 1935*

Trucks take working people to the outlying townships and they sing going home. I love this sound. It really makes me feel I'm in Africa and its so nice to hear people singing going home from work. I think Birkenhead Corporation should try it. How about it Daddy? You could start a fashion. Sing with your cab window down. Mummy could start it on the Mersey Railway. I'll come and visit you when they carry you off to Deva. *The local lunatic asylum in Chester.*

Monday evening 4.45   I'm sitting on the terrace. The sun has gone down past the house and it's lovely and cool. Like the evening of a hot day at home. I'm going to have half an hour's sit before the mosquitoes start appearing. In the corner of the terrace is a hornet's nest. There appears to be only two coming and going. They have made a mud cone under a ledge near the floor and are working on the rim

At the tennis club, a little boy of about eight said he could find me lots of tree frogs and went shinning up the drainpipes. There was one sitting on the bowls club hat stand. He was blinking slowly and looked as though he were watching the bowls.

My slides are back. They are not as well exposed as I would have hoped. There is one of some black children in the shade and you can't see them! I'll send them soon, when I've written a commentary for Mummy to read out during slide shows.

We were talking about the post and someone said that things are O.K. once you get past the "What shall we pinch today brigade." So when you send something undervalue as much as realistic and make it sound as unattractive as possible. Clothing is very popular so write " haberdashery" or "no commercial value" wherever possible. I would love a second tennis dress, but watch the expense. The girls at the club love my dress, mainly because it is so obviously not homemade, but as we play Saturday and Sunday, I wear it most of the weekend. I don't wear any other dresses two days on the run. My shorts are still with the sea freight. I very much regret not being able to bring the tape recorder by airfreight as we have no radio or TV and I miss my music.

I asked Albert if we had his name right, as it had OBED on his identification card. His name is really Obed, but I keep calling him Albert. It now comes out like Albed. Touch Wood, he's still O.K. He has singed one of Richard's shirts, but otherwise they look like Daddy's evening shirts straight from the Chinky.

Times of Zambia

15th April   Pupils starving in Classrooms. A national nutrition programme is being formed to fight widespread malnutrition in

Zambia's schoolchildren.

21ˢᵗ April   Keep away from the Copperbelt

There was no need for people to flock to the Copperbelt in search for employment says Mr Hanky Kalanga, parliamentary secretary to the Mininstry of Health. Your government is prepared to give you fishing and carpentry loans to become better fishermen.

I wish I had taken more close-ups of flowers as they are beginning to die off. I've bought myself a 6/- book on trees and flowers. I've seen some of the flowers but the tree part only shows the tree leaves not the whole tree. Marlene's Banda must have thought I was mad because I went round on Friday afternoon and stood under the trees with my book open gazing upwards. He must have thought I was part of some funny English religious cult.

You ask if I provide Obed with meals. We should give him a meal break, but as he doesn't go home and has nothing much to do in the afternoon and sits round anyway; he doesn't actually go out for lunch. We don't give him any and he doesn't appear to bring any but he does smoke so he must prefer cigarettes to lunch. I give him apples and bananas if they are going soft and anything else left over like meat or chicken. I say "Throw that away for me" and I don't put it in the bin as I could, but leave it in the dish for him to leave or eat as he wishes. We had cold lamb chops left and I told him to throw them away, but noted he hadn't done so by the time we had gone back to work. His diet, remember, is different to ours and the national staple is mealie meal which is maize, I think. Even Richard's " new" managers can't eat in the staff canteen, but eat in the work's canteen because they can't get used to the different diet. He looks perfectly healthy and well nourished and I'm not providing food if he is smoking. He gets his wage and 10/- a week for food. There was a case in the paper where a woman's year's supply of mealie meal was eaten by cattle and she was offered £50.0.0 compensation.

Goodness knows when our sea things will arrive as apparently, because of the split up between Rhodesia and Zambia railways, things are held up. The Rhodesians want Zambia to share liabilities as well as assets when the railway split and as Zambia was keeping all the trains when they got over the border, trains are now swapped over the border on a truck for truck basis. There is therefore a hold up of trucks waiting to be swapped. Its like Toyland, isn't it?

A fellow came home with Richard last night as he told Richard he had some personal problems. As he was a member of his staff, he couldn't very well say no. I had just washed my hair, but luckily had the meal on the go and was able to slice another lump off the 3lb piece of steak, our week's meat supply. I also had tinned mushrooms and chips and was able to open some tins of tomato juice so it was a respectable meal. We must be doing alright and have a reasonable standard of living if we are able to ask someone to share our meal without embarrassment, so despite food difficulties, we have no reason to moan.

However all this person wanted was some advice on accountancy careers. He is 21 with three O levels. Richard was very diplomatic and gave him some addresses to write to for information and was, I thought very helpful considering that this bloke wasted our evening. I excused myself and started labelling my slides. The fellow did nothing but talk about himself and what he wanted to do and which exams he would pass easily. He seemed to me to be all talk and no do. I think he just wanted a free nosh.

Joan, the girl who is coming to Liverpool in June, is getting all excited and says she can't believe that she is actually going to the UK and can't imagine herself there. Just as I was last February. It seems very strange the other way around and I feel homesick when she is asking what to see and do, although it's nice to be able to tell her.

Letter 16   Sunday afternoon.

We had a storm yesterday evening and Friday evening and we were rained off tennis this weekend. Richard said we might as well be playing at Neston. The rains should have been over by now, and it has been the first for three weeks. However, we managed two games yesterday and three this morning, but it is too unsettled for our boat club picnic. Yesterday morning we were up at our usual time of 6.30am and were shopping at eight and had completed our shopping by 10.15. As so many people have to shop once a week, the earlier the better. This week, I managed some scones (a bit doughy) and a chocolate cake about 1½ inches deep, but well iced and quite light. Sue, next door but one, went to the bakers at eleven and couldn't get a thing except a loaf. We don't buy bread, as it is too doughy. If you press it in the middle it stays pressed in, and is even too stale for toast next day. Oh for a narna buttie. I bought half a dozen bananas for 1/-; we eat them in jellies and custards mainly. We buy melon, but these are surprisingly dear seeing that they grow locally, 3/- for a small one. I've seen flower seeds in the shops, but can't make out which are local and which are grown at home. I've bought some morning glory for the box outside the kitchen, but this is too weed-like to send home.

We've got loads of pamphlets on South Africa to plan our route home to see as much as possible and also to gen up on the game reserves. This is so we can plan our next year's leave and our terminal leave. We don't get any leave until July/August 1968. That's pretty poor isn't it? We will book our boat home next January as the boats fill up quickly. When you get this letter we will have done two months. A twelfth of the total time.

As it was dull this afternoon, Richard went to the factory to collect some work and I had a nosey in his office and a peep in the rooms in the directors' suite. All very posh. The gateman stands at attention and salutes. Richard says he salutes only managers and he was surprised how quickly he knew he was a manager. The road from the factory to home is past a township and is swarming with locals. I think we will go again and film the drive. The film might be bumpy, but it's the only way I am going to catch local colour. The township consists of houses like prefabs, but more barracky. Some have little gardens and fences and are cared for while others are very slummy. One of the first community buildings to go up is the council run beer hall, which is only the same as a pub goes up on a council estate at home, I suppose. But although the women are taught hygiene and baby care etc., we have been told that if we went into a township we wouldn't be seen again. There have been incidents before, stonings and car overturnings. The councils are trying their very best to rehouse vagrants and jobless and homeless and is creating employment. Recent figures show that only 10% of the population is in paid employment. The jobless sponge on working relatives without shame, because of the tribal customs of share and share alike. This pattern does not fit in to urban economics and hardworking locals are starting to resent the fact of having to support their relatives. This has been much discussed in the local paper.

I love our Sunday papers coming. I read every inch with relish, even the TV reviews.

I hope you got your card and present O.K. It wasn't anything like 7/11, but this was to discourage anyone who might fancy it from the description. We thought of putting "lump of rock on a pin" which would have been true wouldn't it? Richard said I must tell you in case you thought we were skimping on you.

A bumper mail today including Richard's pyjamas and the Liverpool Illustrated. Richard is very pleased with his pyjamas and as his birthday is tomorrow, you couldn't have timed it better, although I don't know about the birthday card. He got that in March. Did you post them at the same time? There was an article in the Illustrated, which said that attractive mews houses were being built within walking distance of Chester city centre. Our house! I hope it puts the value up a bit. "A mews house in a desirable area as featured in the Liverpool Illustrated!"

Did you see my floppy hat in last weeks Observer? I am ahead of fashion. (No pun intended). Last night we had one of our nicest meals- a shoulder of lamb done in all sorts of herbs. We have accumulated about 20 jars and packets of different spices, vinegars and herbs from South Africa to experiment with. Our meat bill this week was super. The shoulder of lamb is dearest at 12/-. A pound of liver is 3/-, 2lb of filet steak 7/- and four pork chops 5/-. The chops are very thick with kidney attached. We divided them into meal-sized portions and stacked in the freezer compartment of the fridge. When we last asked for four pork chops, the butcher brought out a whole pig and then an assistant sliced it with an electric thing like a chainsaw and in two seconds we had our chops. Couldn't be fresher as the pigs are bred locally. Nothing so antwacky as slinging the pig up in the shop doorway and slicing down the middle with a chopper like old Dillon does at home. This was done with a surgeon's precision.

A poor girl in the office had a burglary at the weekend, but the burglar couldn't get in as the house was too well locked. He broke a window, cut through the metal mosquito net, but couldn't get past the burglar bars. He then proceeded to strip the bedding off the beds using a pole with a hook on the end, the tablecloth from the table and the baby clothes that were airing on clothes drier. It's quite funny to think of him fishing through the bars, but I think I'm going to sew tapes to the corners of my bedding to tie them to the legs of the bed. Everyone takes burglaries very lightly as they are so frequent. I am glad we are amongst so many other houses, as a burglar would be more easily spotted than in a secluded house with a big garden,

Obed informs me that we have a lemon tree growing in our terrace box. I thought it was a tangly weed and would have pulled it out. We are going to transplant it into the middle when it is a bit stronger. It is about ten inches high now.

About a dog. Obed could easily look after a dog, but I would like to be home to train it. I've not decided how long I should work yet. I'll keep on as long as I enjoy it, because the money is useful and I like the company. The job is interesting as it is a new one and is being built up from nothing and I have new ledgers and cabinets and I am free to make suggestions. However when it is all in order I would imagine it would become tedious. Perhaps in the very hot weather next October/November I shall finish to build up a tan to come home.

Another Liverpool Illustrated arrived at lunchtime. It has been all round the office. I told one girl that Speke Hall was our house and she said, "Gosh, is it?" until she twigged. But you must understand that the girls in the office know as much about Chester and England as we did about Ndola and Zambia. I pointed out a picture of the Mersey ferry and this rang a bell all round, so the girls were singing Jerry and The Pacemakers' Ferry Across the Mersey, to make me feel at home. When I said I missed the radio and TV last night, Richard did an hour's imitation of Pete and Dud, Morecombe and Wise, Kenneth Horne, Family Favourites and The Archers and had me in pleats.

Have bought six tins of St Michael potatoes. Spuds here have gone soft and have doubled in price.

Times of Zambia

26th April   Petrol ration increased from 12 to 14 gallons a month

Chapter Eight   Small creatures

Letter 17

A blue writing pad this time. The boy from the office bought it for me and I omitted to say I wanted a white one; blue is 3d dearer than white. This tiny pad is 4/3d. Make the most of it because next time it's only going to be a 4/- one.

Please excuse the thumbprints, but I'm writing whilst cooking the dinner. We are having pork chops in wine. In my letter I said that the chops were 1 ½ inches thick but I have measured them and they are 2 ¼ inches thick. I just hope they cook through. You blanch the chops then drain and flour them and then fry in oil until brown and then cover in freshly ground black pepper, onions and white wine. The only thing I couldn't get was onions, but my spice collection had onion salt which I used instead of salt, and dried onion flakes, so I think that will do just as well. I'm sitting on Obed's kitchen stool, a high counter stool thrown out from the office, and supper smells delicious simmering there. I hope it tastes as good.

Spirits are very reasonable here and we are building up a collection, but they are only for visitors. We buy wine in gallon jars from South Africa - white and red. The red is a bit rough, but the white is medium dry and very good. It works out at 7/- a bottle. We alternate it with milk, as milk is precious. Oh for a slice of buttered bread. I dream of great plates of it. The bacon here is very salted, but someone said to boil it before frying and that should do the trick.

A woman called Nancy from the tennis club has just called to see if Richard would play in a tennis tournament on Monday, at a place called the Raylton Club. She says Monday, May 1st, is a holiday. The Russians have 1st May too, don't they?

It is Penguin week at the library next week and I have picked up the lists. I shall tick off the books I would like and will try to order them from the library. However there is a "Buildings of England" series I would like to collect and I will have to order them from the bookshop. I was talking to the girl in the bookshop, as she said four weeks ago that some butterfly books would be in. She said they hadn't had any deliveries for eight weeks. Apparently food and industrial supplies are taking priority.

Richard is avidly reading the library's Hi Fi books and browsing a Telefunken catalogue for the hi-fi he would like best. He says he will now know whether it has been put together properly when he gets it.

One of Richard's staff, John Hudson (who got us Obed) had some seeds in a box and at the weekend lifted one up to transplant and there was a black mamba underneath. These are the most deadly snakes in Africa and their poison is instantly fatal. Fortunately it was only 18inches long and just as surprised as he was. His wife's brother threw an axe at it and chopped it in half. Don't worry though. Hudson lives in a rather wild area north of town, with houses with uncut grass ideal for snakes. Also snakes hide under things and I wouldn't move stones and things as, if there wasn't a snake, there would be crawlies. Also Obed keeps our terrace brushed and boxes weeded and I only poke around in the flowers when I can see clearly.

Obed has just come to the door (seven o'clock) and asked for 10/-. He said his uncle had died and he wanted to send his brother to the funeral and he himself would go on Saturday. Obed is due to be paid three weeks wages on Friday. I thought this tale was a bit thin, but Richard said that if he wanted 10/- he could have asked me before he went home, if he were going drinking. In any case it is half an hour's walk to his home so he would hardly go home and come back. He also said that staff in the office often ask for money to go home for funerals, as they are big family occasions. Anyway, I hope he turns up tomorrow, as he appears reasonable.

You remember a fellow coming for a meal last Tuesday, who bored me silly? Well, he's gone round the bend. His brother is a priest in Italy and he went to join him in Italy to train in the priesthood, but cracked up and came home twelve months ago. This morning a supervisor came to Richard and said he was behaving oddly, saying he was seeing double and having dizzy spells. He had also written a letter to the Pope in Latin,

English and Italian, apparently last time he went funny he wrote cheques like mad, buying all sorts of soft things and as he is in charge of money in the office, Richard wasn't taking any chances. The fellow had been to a local doctor for an Insurance medical, so Richard rang his mother, his own doctor and the Insurance Doctor and sent the boy home (he is in digs here) under the impression that he is to have a further Insurance medical with his own doctor. His own doctor, who knows his history, can then see what is to happen. Poor fellow.

Jill called this evening after work. She has offered to take the slides to Liverpool and will call in at Custom House to give them to you. She is staying with relatives so will need no looking after, but perhaps you could invite her one weekend for tea, just for something different.

Obed turned up this morning quite sober. The Monday holiday is called Labour Day. It used to be Commonwealth Day, so that's a nice surprise. Mondays are the same as at home. Even with the sun waking you up, it is just as difficult to get out of bed and go to work. Obed must have thought we were unfriendly as we have temporary twin beds (metal framed like camp beds, but with ordinary mattresses. Wooden beds encourage termites.[2] We have them pushed together with separate sheets but one blanket. Obed has kept the bottom sheets separate but stretches the two top sheets on top of one another over the two beds. Last night Richard rolled over and the light beds parted and he fell down the gap in the middle. Chuckle, chuckle.

We now have four drinks tables to go at the side of the chairs and a standard lamp to match the table lamp, courtesy of the company. The tables are four legs screwed on to blocks, extremely crude and not well polished. I can now give tea parties. We keep the coffee table under the stairs and will put the tape deck on it when it arrives. It is laden at present with month old papers, that I don't want to part with. Obed is staying Friday evening but is having Saturday off, as we are having two technicians who are here for six months, for a meal. They are Norman Ravenscroft and Alan Williams who are married with grown up families, Norman has taken two boxes of slides and Tony has lent us his projector so we will have a photo show.

[2] *Who on earth fed me that rubbish?*

P.S by Richard in hardly legible spidery scrawl. Thank you very much for my pyjamas, a truly unexpected yet welcome gift. My present pairs resemble Aertex, and unfortunately the shops were out of stock of non-stripy poplin pyjamas when we were looking around. Incidentally whilst I am writing this, your daughter is sitting in the bathroom talking to Fred our resident gecko. Must be the heat I suppose.

P.S. Doodle is hiding on a shelf as he says he doesn't want to be hooked through the window on a pole.

Letter 19   1st May Happy Birthday to Mummy, Happy Birthday to you.

We have just had our breakfast on today's holiday for Labour Day.

On Friday, Norman Ravenscroft and Tony Wisdom came for a meal and Tony showed our slides on his projector. They seemed darker on the projector but it only had a 100watt bulb in it. I hope they show up better on your projector. Jill is taking them on tomorrow's VC10 so you should have them roughly the week after.

On Saturday, we bought, with the company's money, two armchairs for the bedroom to put in front of the view. (They are meant to supplement the chairs downstairs when we have visitors.) <u>and</u> two bedside lamps, which go out every now and then because of poor connections. We just thump them and they come on again.

As I am writing this on the terrace, a few geckoes have come belting out in front of me. They had been disturbed by a big fat lizard, with a big blue head. Correction. Two big lizards. They seemed out to catch the geckoes. I thought there was going to be a fight, but no, the little ones are too quick.

This morning Richard came downstairs and there was a green tree frog on the carpet. It wouldn't be chased out through the French window and I tickled it with the curtain to move it, but it jumped towards me. I ran because I was in my nightie and didn't fancy getting it on me, as they have sticky tummies, which helps them climb trees [3] He is now stuck to the back of the writing desk. At least we know where he is.

---

[3] *Rubbish, the frogs have sucker pads on their feet*

Yesterday at the tennis club, we saw a chameleon. It was fascinating and the boys put it onto a purple and green towel to make it change colour, but all it did was to run onto a green stripe- lazy thing. It was only a baby one, about six inches long with a six-inch tail. The boys broke off a branch and put it on it. It is quite happy as long as it is on a branch with leaves. As usual my camera was at home. You should have seen it catch flies. Both eyes move independently and once he fixes onto a fly, his tongue shoots out. His tongue is longer than himself and very fat and sticky. I don't know where he rolled his tongue. There seemed too much of it to keep in his mouth.

Yesterday afternoon after tennis, we packed our Sunday picnic and went to a place called the Bull and Bush. It is six miles down a dirt road into the bush and was supposed to be a pub on the side of a lake. It turned out to be rather like a caff with no food only ale, and the lake, although pleasant from a distance and reputedly good for fishing, was like a muddy bog and stank to high heaven and was thick with insects. The water level had dropped leaving a mud coating half way up the trees. I half expected to see crocodiles in the mud at the edge. Walking back up the track to the pub, we heard a rustling in the bushes and saw a fawn and brown back. Our first antelope? Giraffe? Lion? No. It was a flippin' cow. What a disappointment.

On our way back from the Bull and Bush there was a storm. The rain came in such sheets that we had to slow to almost a stop and the dirt road quickly became muddy and rutted. Richard said that we mustn't stop or we would get bogged down. I was glad when we reached the tarred road again. As the Bull and Bush wasn't up to much, we were taking our picnic to the boat club, but the rain stopped that, so Richard put the chairs out and we had our picnic in the lounge. When I went to get a piece of cake from the kitchen, Richard said I couldn't have any, as we had forgotten to bring the cake.

Times of Zambia   5th May   Russians rude at Lusaka luncheon.

Chapter Nine   Hockey trial

Letter 20.   **3/5/67**

I am writing this watching Richard at hockey practice. To be selected you have to attend practices once a week. The only team is Ndola, which is probably about County level. He is playing in his tennis kit and sticks out like a sore thumb. He can buy new kit if he's selected for the Ndola team. A lot practice in their bare feet.

On Monday we went to the Monkey Fountain Park. This is quite pleasant and has a lake with lilies on it and waterfalls and laid out gardens. Inside is a small zoo rather like the one at Folkestone. We didn't go inside as we were only there for an hour just to take a few snaps. I got cine of a little boy washing his face in the pond. When he spotted me he demanded sixpence. About the only English he knew was "Gimme sixpence". He was a nuisance and by hovering around prevented me from getting any close up stills of the lilies.

On Monday afternoon, there was a tennis tournament at the Raylton Club. This club has four courts (ours has two) a training wall and a ball machine for practicing with. However our club still said they preferred our club as it was friendlier and I agree. Anyway our tea and cakes in the mid morning or mid afternoon are only 6d and theirs are 1/6d. They are all keen and play to win, not for the fun of it. But this also meant that our club played good tennis with such competition and although we had no winners, one of our girls won the ladies' booby prize, a big box of chocs. I'm sorry I didn't enter, as she is much better than I am. Richard came in the middle somewhere of the men's group.

In the evening they had a braavleis. This is a barbeque and was jolly good. They had three charcoal fires going and you paid 5/- for two pieces of fillet steak and cooked them with a long fork on a grill over the charcoal. Also for your 5/- there were salads and sauces and batch type rolls. I really ate well but we had to eat with our fingers. This is quite amusing when you get to vegetable salad with mayonnaise and stuff. There is a knack in mopping up with your bread rolls. The atmosphere was good too, a few lights and the glow from the coals. Rather like bonfire night with no rain. These barbeques are very popular in the winter (the dry season).

The tree frog was still behind the writing desk last night but I couldn't find him this morning. He can't get out so I will probably find him on the table or on a chair, as I'm about to sit down. I'll walk around with my shoes on until he's found.

Obed came back on Friday to help with dinner. It was rather good. I bought an apple pie and had it in the oven and had him whipping cream (tinned) and passing things and as soon as I dirtied anything, he washed it. We let him gently into waiting at the table. We had tomato juice and he cleared the table while I dished out the grill in the kitchen. I had instructed him to take the pie out of the oven and put it on a plate and take the cream out of the fridge etc. I went over every detail as Marlene's Banda put out the ice cream in a serving dish without taking it out of the paper.

Richard and his crowd are now running around the field and every now and then on a given instruction do an exercise. Richard has to watch the others first. They all look a bit thick.

Someone gave me an avocado pear. You are supposed to eat it with pepper and salt. It is very soft inside rather like egg custard and I couldn't see Richard just eating it, so out came the Robert Carrier and I mashed it with celery salt and black pepper and put in part of our precious onion supply and slopped it on a plate and decorated it with tomatoes. Richard had bought a French type loaf (plaited with seeds on it) and I fried half a dozen slices in oil, onion, tomatoes and garlic. It looked nice on the plate. We both agreed the fried bread, onions and tomatoes were delicious. The avocado was just tasteless and we both left half of it. Well we've tried it. I suppose it is a delicacy because of its "subtle" flavour.

Richard didn't much like the hockey. He said that none of the team could receive and hit a ball and the practice was too concerned with keeping fit than hockey tactics and actual shooting and hitting. He reckons he is fit enough with tennis and squash.

Ah, squash. Last night John and Sue took us to the squash club where they are members. Its nearer than the bin as we empty our rubbish behind the squash club (in the bins I hasten to add) I didn't play as I had never seen it played, but Richard caught on quickly and was as usual all set for a game. He played three. All the fellows playing were whacked. It's very fast and exhausting. Richard was a bit chesty and wondered if it were with playing indoors. Anyway, he'll try again, as it's just the sport for the rainy season and we can sprint back to the house in between games and keep an eye on the cooking.

Thank you for the doggy quarantine details. Doodle says he wants to be smuggled back in, as he says he will pine away in quarantine.

On Friday, as I started to say, when Obed was waiting, he was instructed to bring the full tray to me and I would empty it and he could then take away the empty plates. He was slow when we pressed the buzzer and he then came in, in such a flap. He had forgotten who to give the tray to and stood rooted to the spot with a tray of hot plates and apple pie and jug of cream. With a little encouragement, he cleared the table, concentrating like mad and he was, so I noticed, chewing on a matchstick again. Buzzer again and he troops in with the tray of coffee cups and percolator. He had asked Richard, when being shown how to plug in the percolator (which he sensibly called the coffee kettle) whether he should stand and wait for it to boil, but he said he could just tidy up and go, which he did only popping in to say goodnight about 8.30. I gave him Friday afternoon off in lieu. The kitchen was lovely. It was spotless. That's the way to entertain. However there is a loss of privacy. He would know if your bedding was shabby. He puts out clean nightclothes when he changes the bed. However it encourages me to be tidy and all our things are new wedding presents. It certainly is no problem sewing the odd buttons on when things are washed and ironed. I have a linen cupboard in the bathroom and it always looks so organised. Richard's shirts and underclothes are washed every morning and back in the cupboard in the evening. Our shoes, too, have never been so clean. He sits on the step first thing and cleans them. This is quite a social occasion as all the other boys in the court are doing likewise, or cleaning the cars. The condensation builds up overnight and it is a common sight to see cars being pushed to start, because with the violent changes in temperature the water evaporates in the batteries.

Times of Zambia

6th May   An estimate of 100 have been killed on the TanZam Hell Run, route of Zambia's oil lifeline

Letter 21   7th May 1967

We played tennis this morning. I have reached a level where I can join in mixed doubles. Richard thinks his tennis isn't as good as it was, as the competition was much fiercer at Neston and he was forced to play better. Also the heat and altitude make one more lethargic. (Don't say that I don't need the heat to make me lethargic.)

This weekend, on Saturday morning, we spotted a blue-headed lizard, a blauskop, I think they're called. It was on the tree outside our kitchen window. They are about 14" long and very fat with a big head. All weekend we've spotted him dashing up and down the tree. Although they bite, they are very timid and he's up the tree in a flash. It was nice watching him as I was pottering about the kitchen. We were coming in from tennis this morning and as we turned into the court, there he was in our way. I got out and shooed him up the tree and told him to be more careful. The tree is in the middle of the court where all the cars are parked. We told John and Sue about him this evening and John said " Is it that dead one outside?" and sure enough poor old lizard had been hit by a car. So that was a short acquaintance.

After tennis, we packed a picnic in our hamper. I made a jelly with half peaches in the top and cream and chocolate bits on that and had bought a swiss roll and chocolate cake and shredded cabbage and vegetable salad and potato salad, the last two being in Heinz tins.

Sue roasted two chickens and roast potatoes and peas (cold but tasty) and we all went off to the boat club. We stayed until 6 when it went dark. It is cooler now in the evening and when we came in tonight our main room was chilly, but the kitchen was hot. The kitchen gets the sun all day but the main room gets none. It will get cooler in the evenings until June and then heat up again. We have been told we will need a fire in June, which is unfortunate as we haven't one and don't intend to get one as it will be no use at home in Chester. Perhaps the company will fork out. Our flat has no fireplace or heating. A girl at the tennis club said she was so cold last night that she put on bed socks. I was lovely and warm. Apparently, the first year you don't notice it getting colder. The second year it seems chilly and the third year you are searching for sweaters and having fires up the chimney. Give me this sort of winter any day. Richard is sitting here in shorts, shirt, sandals and I am in a cotton frock and sandals.

Our sea things are on their way by rail from Lobito Bay. But the railway they come on is very odd. No matter where the train is, at 6pm it stops and everyone gets out and sleeps until daylight. Goods trains only, not passenger trains.

I think Grace Keith's book is mistitled. It should be The Reversing Colour Bar not The Fading Colour Bar. When was it written, I should like to know? Things have altered for the worse even in the last twelve months so we are told, although we don't notice it as much as people who have known the place for years.

We collected our new curtains today. I wasn't enthusiastic about them and only bought them because we had none. The salesgirl thought we should have fish in the bathroom and a pan and wooden spoon design for the kitchen. I chose bulrushes.

Obed is pleased with them. Our orange squash bottle was nearly empty today. Must have a word with him tomorrow and squash is now on the lock up list with coffee and sugar. Sugar is in again. I bought two 5lb bags today, although caster and icing sugar and brown sugar are still out. We were down to about three spoons full and I hadn't done any baking except for a banana cake. This is normal sponge with mashed banana instead of liquid. It was a bit hard but Richard had a slice. I have nothing to measure with. My scales are on the high seas and you need less sugar here because of the altitude, so its very much trial and error.

Wonderful news. Joan Crowe has had an 8lb 2oz baby boy. She says it is a highly recommended experience, but I'm afraid we shall wait as the hospital here has the patients' families cooking and living outside and wailing in sympathy according to the state of the patient and I'm not sure I could produce in such an atmosphere although it might be nice to have a sympathetic audience. I went out to buy a baby coat pattern as I have time to knit here and could cope with an easy pattern, but the first shop I tried had none. A fellow shopper said that none of the other shops had any either and she had been trying to get one for two months. Richard said Simon had been spared, as it would be too grubby and small with sleeves of different sizes by the time I had finished.

I have received a letter with my Graduated Pension Statement. Apparently I will get 4/6 a week when I am 60!!

Times of Zambia   7th May   This land is mine, tribal chief tells court in Inyanga.

Chapter 10 Factory Visit

Letter 22   10/05/67

I still have my hair long. I can think of nothing else to do with it. It is cooler than short hair as I can tie it away from my neck and face. A lot of the girls wear their hair long and loose-the heat doesn't deter them. The teenagers are all highly fashionable; cotton trousers are very popular as are mini-mini skirts. In fact they go out of their way to be mod, despite the unsuitability of the clothes to the climate. I've even seen mini-skirts with knee length frilly bloomers. African girls can be smart too, but they seem to prefer extra tight skirts and skimpy sweaters and blouses, and elaborate figure accentuating dresses rather than shifts, like the old teddy-girl styles. The rural local people wear floor length, vivid print skirts and those who wear bras seem to have a liking for black and scarlet, judging by the drooping straps. Every woman of childbearing age usually has one baby, either on her back or on the way, or both, so another item of dress is the shawl to tie the baby on. Very mod. mums usually have this in the same material as the skirt. These are various ways of baby carrying.

As the wrap loosens, baby slips into the oddest positions, sometimes hanging sidewards, when the wrap is over the shoulder, with baby's head peering under Mum's arm. This is also useful for feeding as you just swivel baby around a bit. If baby cries, Mum just does a hippy dance on the spot, and baby bounces up and down on a usually ample backside. Tiny babies just look like rugby balls, as their heads are covered as well. I'm afraid of them slipping out.

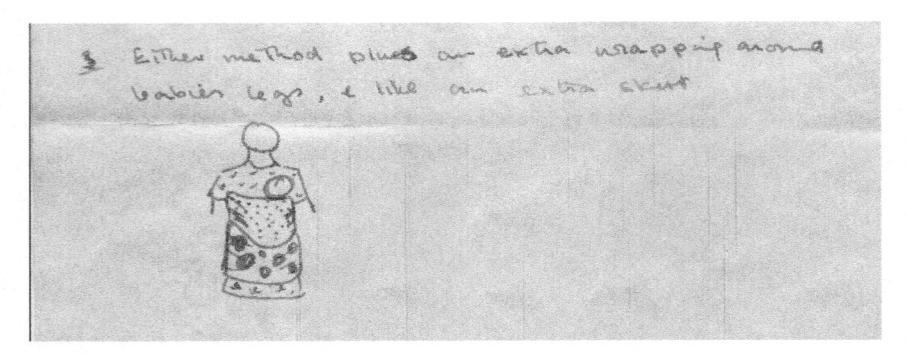

Either method plus an extra wrapping around babies legs, & like an extra skirt

Eileen, the nurse, told me this did babies' legs no good at all. This is a pity as I think this contact with the mother continually in its early years must be better than shoving it in a pram, although it restricts exercise. And both hands are free to knit as you go along.

A lot of the young girls here prop their babies up with bottles on cushions, and crèche from the age of two months is nothing new. Of the five I work with, Joan is single, Hilda is a granny, Cookie has four children, two at boarding school, one at local school and one at nursery and Margie and Vivienne have a girl of fifteen months and a boy of eight months respectively, the latter in crèche from two months. They are both younger than me. This is not unusual. One European baby of about eighteen months called Steven, sits with his nanny on the verge outside our office, while nanny chats up all the men from the factory. I see nanny and Steven walking into town each morning at 7.30am and she is still around town when I go home at 4.30. Steven probably doesn't know his mother very well.

John and Sue have been moving some things in and popping in and out, and stopped by finally at 9.30 for a drink. (but not supper, as tea and dinner are called supper). They are South African and had lots of stories to tell us as a new and appreciative audience. Being South African our politics are more compatible than the Rhodesians, but we only touch lightly on apartheid, without developing any arguments. Some Rhodesians are very anti- British and most are only first or second generation English-hardly very loyal. Their parents and ancestors were probably misfits anyway.

It's Whit this weekend. The tennis club is doing a braaivleis. (a barbeque, literally "cooked meat".) I am down for salad. They asked me to do cakes, but I opted for salad as none of my baking trays had yet arrived. I was hoping no-one would offer me any, as I have still not mastered high altitude cooking. People are apt to think I'm being modest when I say I can't do a thing, such as play in a tennis tournament, and insist I have a try. I say I would play, just to keep them quiet, but when I arrive in my frock, I'll hope that I don't get sent home again to change into my kit.

Richard is making exaggerated snores alongside me so I'll close.

Letter 23   14/05/67   Whit Sunday.

I didn't have to play tennis as they had enough players. It has been beautiful weather, but I stayed in the shade under a bower. Mother-in-law told my friend we were ebony, but she's making that up. Our arms and legs are brown but our bodies aren't, as they haven't had enough sun. We look healthy but not brown. I think it is sea air that gives a tan, and that is what we lack. Also, it's not like being on holiday. We can only sit out at the boat club and tennis club as, apart from the terrace, which loses the sun at 10am' there is only the communal lawn and I would feel a bit of a nit sitting there. If we were offered a house now, with an enclosed garden, I don't think I would take it, as we now have this house organised and looking nice and it only has a small number of beetles and things, compared with houses surrounded by garden, and it is not so unpleasant being near other people and I would miss my lovely view. It would have to be a superlative house before we took it, I think.

As I didn't play in the tournament, I kept score. Richard has been made tournament and match organiser on the committee. He has been organising people to play from when he started. Originally, people played with whoever they liked, but this meant that poorer players didn't get a chance, so he has set up a blackboard thing and your name goes into a different column depending on whether you won or lost and you put your name down when you arrive and when you come off court. This works well as the next four are ready to go on when a match finishes and no one hogs a court all afternoon. It was accepted well and the system hasn't failed yet. So he was roped in to act officially. He has shown me a list of the things he will arrange and they sound good. I did my salad and was relieved to see it was all eaten. Everyone paid three shillings for the days games and 2/6 for the drinks. Richard was pleased it was a cheap day, although my salad probably cost five shillings even though the lettuce were free from Marlene's garden.

Marlene and Peter came for supper on Saturday evening. It was funny as they are both so casual around their house. Peter wears sandals, shorts and shirt and Marlene, shift and sandals, and Marlene arrives in a chiffon dress with a lovely stole and Peter in collar, jacket and tie. I wish my meal had been up to it. I did prawn cocktail, which was my only success. I had topside of beef, sliced thinly and rolled them around a mixture of sage and onion stuffing and sausage meat and casseroled them in red wine. However the meat was tough and my cooking in no way improved it. I also decided to make a rum baba. Remember the one they demonstrated at the Gas Showroom? It was supposed to stand for an hour to let the yeast act and it was meant to double in size, but it didn't budge. I tried a second lot and the same happened. I put both lots together. Well, it was supposed to double in size! But it was a flop in the oven. Instead of rising, it just dried up. However, I'd made the rum syrup so served that with tinned apricots and cream, which was fine.

I am having tomorrow afternoon off as the ex-mayoress of Bebington, for some unknown reason, is visiting the factory. The technician, who is also from Bebington, is showing her around and I have been asked to accompany her. I only hope Mrs Young isn't going; she wouldn't give a very good impression. We are having tea with the directors and Richard has to go for tea too. I don't know why she gets all this fuss. On Wednesday evening there is a cocktail party at Mackie's for a financial fellow called Brock. Richard is the only one who knows him, as he met him in London before we came. No one knows why this Brock is coming.

I got a £5.00 rise at the end of April. I'm now on £80.00 a month. Goodness knows why. It might have been a birthday rise. I pay £6.00

odd tax, £2.00 pension (refundable), £2.00 government levy (purpose unknown) 5/- tea money (three cups a day) so my cheque was £67.00, which went straight into our English account. Good, hey?

Letter 24 16/05/67

This afternoon was great fun. Apparently the couple who had asked to see the factory were the ex Mayor and Mayoress of Bebington. These two, myself and the advertising manager, Dennis Bratton, who makes me laugh, went round the factory, with Dennis explaining all the processes.

The two were typical town councillors, with broad Lancashire accents, which made it worse, and social climbers. Good grief, I'd never seen anything more blatant. The conversation dotted with loads of name-dropping, "when I was talking to Lord Leverhulme", "Dear Lady Leverhulme, she was such a good friend before she passed away", "the Queen asked me if." and she was that patronising to the factory workers. "Oh, how clever", " I suppose you don't feel the heat", 'What lovely (or luvly) pieces of sorp (soap). Dennis and I were raising our eyes to heaven at every comment.

However, I was interested myself in the factory processes. A lot are very primitive; boxes filled by hand, labels stuck on by hand. But these were to supplement expensive machinery or were such small runs that an expensive packing machine wasn't warranted. Afterwards, some of the directors, Richard, the two Port Sunlight technicians and of course, the Youngs, had tea in the boardroom and we had loads of photographs taken in groups, standing around supping tea.

Me, Dennis Bratton and Richard at the tea party

They presented the woman with a wicker basket full of Lever's Zambia products all done up in cellophane. Dennis said he didn't know whether I was coming or not as I only asked for the afternoon off at the last moment and he would make me one too. I said it didn't matter as I wasn't a VIP, but doing my bit for the factory and anyway Mrs Young would only have wanted one. Anyway, I'll see if he does one for me. The basket would be useful. We don't use baskets for shopping as we have those stiff paper bags like Gay Gambol in the Express.

Letter 25   21/05/67

Started to write yesterday but something started burning in the kitchen. Sue has a lovely basic cookbook. Every recipe has its picture alongside, so it's a great help in presentation and in picking a recipe, and she lent it to me. I did roast fillet steak. Imagine-we folded the fillet in half and roasted it- not an ounce of fat. We'll have to get out of that habit. And roast potatoes, which turned out very well. I also made tiny little pancakes about four inches in diameter and alternated them with jam until there were about five in each pile and put them in the oven where they would keep hot until I needed them. I'm having a job cooking, as I have no dishes or measuring things. I tried to do a pie in the oven roasting pan, but the pastry wouldn't grip the rim and fell in. It was also a bit dry, as I couldn't measure for the pastry. Ah, well!

I won't give another dinner until my dishes arrive. I will also have to buy fruit dishes, which I haven't got, but the cheapest was five guineas for a bowl and six glass dishes and red glass at that. I do begrudge paying such a lot.

Its now lovely and warm during the day, but very chilly in the evening and has dropped as low as 45F. This may not sound much, but when the house has no heating and you only have one blanket, it's flipping cold. Its funny how it gets hot and cold so quickly. It's misty in the morning and smells cool and fresh, the sort of morning when at home you say it's going to be a lovely day. The weather during the day is hot but with a cool welcome breeze. It's most pleasant.

We are popping along to a woman tonight, Enid Case, who works with Richard at Levers and who plays tennis at the club, and she is going to lend us a blanket, the first thing we have had to borrow in three months, a thing of which I am rather proud.

We are finding the cost of living high. My wages go untouched back home together with £20.00 of Richard's per month to pay off our overdraft (the second car). I am so glad we are able to have the second car, as we will be able to sell it here with little loss when we leave and it will be invaluable to me, as I can't walk anywhere on my own and would be so reliant on Richard, who can be delayed and unable to get away promptly. I finish at 4.30 and wait in the library, sometimes until after six. Although I enjoy the read and the browse, I could be preparing the meal. As it is we are still eating at 7.30 and the evening is gone.

Yesterday we went along a dirt road past the boat club, as the VC10 was reputed to lift off just in front of the road. We heard its engines start up and waited. The road we were on was built on a raised up bank together with a railway line, across a swamp. On either side it looked like fields of wheat but every now and again you could catch a glimpse of water. We stopped the car and switched off our engine and could hear crickets and whooping birds and all sorts of strange sounds like you get in TV jungle plays, which I thought were exaggerated. It was eerie. The whistle of the VC10 was in the distance and we waited expectantly on hearing the roar, only to see it take off in the opposite direction, miles away. All the weeks we have watched it and it has only taken off the other way once.

We have collected the blanket and stayed for a sundowner (dig the lingo). Enid and her husband are English and have been here fifteen years. Their ten-year-old daughter is a broad Zambian European. I hope to get some accents on tape for you.

Poor Graeme Muir was "cleaned out" last night, an expression becoming too familiar. He arrived home at six to find half of his rockery through his French window and everything in the house except heavy furniture and unsaleable items like ornaments and pictures, missing. Wardrobes had been smashed and every item of clothing of his, his wife and baby and all bed linen and towels were taken. Can you imagine it? His wife and baby were visiting her mum in Salisbury. I can do no more here than lock away as much as possible and hope for the best. Perhaps being in a block of houses would deter a thief and we have a security patrol, but as Richard said, he wouldn't go out if he heard a noise next door, so we couldn't rely on neighbours.

I got my basket. It's a lovely wicker one and had in it a bottle of Covo, two packets of Surf (Omo at home), one of Persil (Surf), a big bar of Lux soap, small bars of Lifebuoy (carbolic) Reward (Lifebuoy), large long bar of Sunlight, Signal toothpaste and a bottle of shampoo (egg) and all done up in red cellophane with a big bow.

I left it in the kitchen, with the compliment slip in the bow. I wanted to photograph it on Saturday morning to show you, but when I got home on Friday, the compliment slip was on the sideboard and no basket. "Obed, where's my basket?" " In the cupboard, Madame" " Why did you take this piece of paper off?" "I tidied the basket away. Madame. And he shows me all my soap tidied away in his cleaning cupboard, the toilet soap in the bathroom and the cellophane in the bucket. I rescued the paper later and tried to reconstruct it, but the paper was torn. His curiosity had got the better of him, I'm afraid, but I would have liked to have unpacked it myself as you couldn't see everything from the top and it would have been like unpacking a Christmas Stocking, but I suppose employers of servants aren't supposed to get excited about unpacking soap.

Valerie Lapthorne

Chapter Eleven The Cars Arrive

Times of Zambia

11th May   Rebel sugar seized by Customs, believed to have come from Rhodesia for sale in Zambia.

Letter No. 26

The cars are due to arrive tomorrow at a place called Chirundu. This is about a day's journey from here. We are hoping to start in the early hours of tomorrow morning and collect the cars mid afternoon and stop at a motel overnight and drive back the following day. Tomorrow and Thursday are public holidays, Africa Freedom day (previously Rhodes and Founders day) and Commonwealth Day. Chirundu is about forty miles from Kariba Dam which we hoped we would see, but it is out of our way-it depends how time goes. It's on the Rhodesian border-in Rhodesia, but the cars will be pushed across the border by the shipping agents who brought them from Beira. We are picking them up, as it may be another three months before they can be driven through Zambia, and we do need that second car- can you imagine no transport! You would have to walk to work to Woodside and paddle a canoe across to Liverpool.

You will be pleased to know that I'm not driving back. Richard has enlisted the help of one of his nineteen-year-old clerks and he will drive back with us in the Imp and I will alternate between the two cars, to keep them company. This boy has already driven from Durban in his car (also an Imp). The journey is four hundred miles there and four hundred miles back (brilliant deduction) so it's going to be as far as Cornwall. I was going to drive the little car and Richard the big one, but people have said that it's a long, long, long straight road for about ten hours without seeing anything but road and scrubland and its very easy to doze off or be hypnotised by the sun and the road. I don't know whether Richard was thinking more of the car or of me. Anyway I'm happier about the present arrangement, having not driven since my test.

We are being taken down to the border by a fellow who is going to Salisbury and our only expense will be the motel for three, but Chrysler, who are in charge of the cars have to refund the charge of shipping up to Ndola (if shipping is the correct word) as we have already paid for that. We won't see any animals or villages or anything of note, unfortunately and will only see the oil lorries, (the route is known as The Hell Run) but we will be stopping at Lusaka, which is just the same as Ndola only bigger. The petrol coupons for the return journey will be provided by Chrysler.

Ndola has now been given the official title of city, which is much the same as calling Claughton Village a city or better, Heswall, a city.

I met Jill's Mum today and she said that Jill had seen you. I have started to knit a cardigan for Joan's baby but lost one of the needles. I went back to the shop and asked for some more, but they had none. As it is, I was using nines instead of tens. Anyway the girl found a little set of 4 sock needles, which are nines, but of course had points at each end. Who'd live in the middle of the jungle?

Thursday. Arrived back safely from Chirundu with the cars. They are covered in grease and dirt. Mine is black with dirt instead of white and all the way back people were staring at it. (*The cars were coated in thick grease as they travelled on deck all the way around Africa and it was to protect them from the sea spray. It was like thick axle grease-probably was thick axle grease.*) However it's super to have them and they are both running well. However the aerial had gone from the Minx and the two ashtrays had been ripped out but these are replaceable and were insured. What would anyone want with car ashtrays? The steering wheel glove had also gone, but I suppose we were daft to leave it on. I have driven mine from Broken Hill to Kapiri Mposhi about forty miles and it was a dead straight run all the way and got me used to the car again. I found I had remembered all my driving and was confident on my own. There were no real traffic hazards like monstrous hill starts. The only nuisances are other drivers and cyclists. The driving standard is awful.

Times of Zambia

12th May   **No room in Zambia for black capitalists says Kapepwe.**

*   **Business booms in Lusaka's out of town brothels**

*   **Beer and milk still short**

Letter 27   29th May 1967

Got your letter Sunday this week instead of Monday. This was because we emptied the P.O. Box ourselves as the fellow who usually does it was on leave and couldn't take it in to the office on Monday. We had a big briefcase packed. It was great fun looking for your letter. I had them all over the carpet. It was nice to see everyone getting mail. One for Marlene from her sister, some for the technicians-cards for the Muirheads', wedding anniversary? Cine films for three people, bills for others.

Our trip to Chirundu went very smoothly. We travelled down Wednesday morning and arrived at about lunchtime. The fellow that took the three of us down, left us on the Rhodesian border, on rebel territory! We were searched on both sides for newspapers, propaganda and petrol and had our daily paper impounded. The cars were to be delivered to the border to the agent at the border post. All there is at Chirundu is the bridge over the Zambezi, the two border posts and loads of insects and stinking hot sun. We arrived at mid-day too! There was a hill at the side of the border post with a tree on top so we climbed up there and sat on some rocks with our picnic hamper. The rock Richard sat on was alongside a lizard's home and we disturbed the lizards, which were about eighteen inches long. At first we thought they were snakes because all we could see were their heads and the bodies slithering through the grass. Whew! We were covered in bites, as the insects were thick, it being so hot and in a valley and the Zambezi Valley at that.

The whole hill was a home for blauskop lizards. The longer we stayed there the bolder they got and these big blue heads were popping out of their holes all around us. Fortunately, when we all got up, thinking to get the hell out of there, they all dived below ground, so as we sat and ate our picnic, if we decided they were getting too close for comfort we would stand up or clap and they would move away. This was also my first sighting of the baobab tree and I picked up the seedpod as a souvenir. The Africans say that the baobab tree became too vain because of its beautiful foliage, and God plucked it out and jammed it back in upside down. *(Still have the seedpod on top of the cupboard in the library)* We had our picnic and at about half past three, over the hill came the cars. Just think, it's the same car you had a ride in and its travelled all that way for three months, and we met again at the border post. Quite romantic really.

In fact it was a great relief that they arrived at all. There was no guarantee that they would arrive on the date stated in the letter, let alone the hour, and if anything had gone wrong they wouldn't have been able to let us know and we would have been stranded miles from anywhere with the remains of our picnic and a change of clothes.)

We got back to Lusaka and stayed in a hotel, which was clean and comfortable but nothing elaborate. Lusaka was the way I thought Ndola would be, well designed and laid out. There is the space for it. The main area had an avenue of trees down the middle and was quite pleasant. The shops were the same names as Ndola and I presume the same quality. Away from the town are the old government buildings and the governor's house, now Kaunda's. It's really colonial with huge grounds. There were slummy areas with Indian shops, but even these were tidy compared with ordinary city slums. We had a meal at THE good restaurant/nightclub, which was up to normal restaurant standards and they had a group of double bass, two guitars and drums, which was very slick. We went on to Eric and Peggy Hannaford-Hill's who runs the Lusaka depot. We had coffee and drinks with them and they kept us until the early hours despite the fact that we could hardly keep our eyes open. We had a good evening and were up at seven and home for lunch. Sue had us all in for lunch and Alan went home and we went with Sue and John up to the club and played tennis.

Joan Williamson had a farewell party before going to Liverpool and invited us. The street outside was full of cars on the verges (there are only pavements in town) and at the back of the house there were forty more. There were people sitting on roofs and bonnets of cars with eats and ale and all in very casual sports clothes. I was O.K in my tunic, but Richard had his "good suit" on and looked a right Pommie, much to his dismay. We couldn't get into the house for people. In the kitchen they were sitting on the draining board. We poked our noses around but I couldn't see anyone I knew, so we eventually gave it up and came away with our bottle *(Bit tight that?)* I was all dressed up and ready for a night out, so we went to the pictures, but it was half way through (starts 9.30 on Saturdays and this was 10 o'clock). Peter and Marlene would be in bed. Tony is on holiday. The Savoy was too expensive. John and Sue were at the pictures, or the bioscope as they call it. So we went home and to bed.

I've finished the cardigan for Joan's baby, but I had to pick up the stitches at the edge for the buttonholes and didn't know how to do it and it's a little bit pulled, although you would have to look closely. I'll press it and it may look better.

We went to a braai at Marlene and Peter's today at lunchtime. We cooked steak and chips on the barbeque thing and sat under the trees to eat it. It was very pleasant and good fun. We then all trooped to Bernice's to see excerpts from the Cup Final on their TV, but it was one of its off days and we got a wobbly picture but no clear sound. Anyway Richard and Peter saw the goals and things. I'm getting used to Peter. He's got a dry sense of humour, particularly after his first gin and tonic. Richard says he's a good boss, gives the right amount of guidance, but leaves him free to manage as he thinks best.

I'm going to wash my bits and pieces now and will finish this tomorrow. But before I do, I must tell you about Obed. We found he had taken a tin of oysters of all things. We knew he was taking sugar and flour and other small things, but ignored this, but the tin was too much. I was blazing mad. As it is we lock everything lockable. You can't have anyone untrustworthy in the house. Richard gave him his ration money and asked him what he thought he was up to and asked what else he had taken. We thought he would deny everything but he came out with a list. Coffee, tea, sugar, drinking chocolate, lemonade and beer, oysters and milk. Richard asked him why and he said he was hungry. He then asked what he had spent his ration money on and he said charcoal because he had been out of work for 18 months. I noticed also he had sold his shirt for 5/- to a fellow collecting second hand clothes. (*I don't know how I knew this. What was a second hand dealer doing coming round the court buying second hand clothes. I would have thought it would have been the employer's kit that was going on to the second-hand market. I wonder why I didn't check. Perhaps we had so few clothes that anything would have been missed. Our clothes were only stacked one or two deep on the shelves.*) Anyway we have said if he touches anything else, he's out. We let him off this time as he could have been hard up and he does do his work well. I shall buy him his own tea and sugar per month. I can't do much more and we mustn't be too soft. Also, if we sacked him, he could go to UNIP, the government party and we would get it in the neck. He has now had adequate warning and we won't hesitate to sack him next time. There is also the bother of training someone else, who might drink or be lazy. Who'd be an employer?

John, next door is a chartered accountant with Price Waterhouse. They leave Ndola in July and then go to South Africa to see their parents and then are travelling on the continent until September when John is due to start in London, where they will stay for 18 months and then return to SA just before we leave so we will probably visit them on our tour home.

A cockroach has just run out of the chair behind me. Richard found one yesterday. Obed brushes the chairs and takes the cushions off every day, so it looks as though they will need a periodic spray too.

Times of Zambia 16th May Children in Congo cash racket. Illegal currency racketeers at Makumba border post have thought of a new trick. They use children as fronts. The youngsters crowd the 100-yard stretch between Zambia and the Congo waving 1,000-franc notes at Zambians.

Letter 28 31st May 1967

Having a frustrating time with your tape. We received it Monday and I dashed to work to see if it would work on the Dictaphone. However, it was broken and being repaired. Margie said she had a portable and would bring it in, which she did this morning, but the batteries were flat.

The drums are going like mad tonight. Probably because its payday.

Obed went home tonight in his best trousers and a shirt with a tie. He keeps all his clothes in a parcel in our hall cupboard, which houses the stepladder and watering can and ironing board and ale. It's a bit spidery inside, so I won't use it for clothes only tinned food. Sue uses hers as a pantry, but I don't fancy that.

I'm glad we are not going out tonight, as it's the locals' drinking night. Most will have spent their wages by Friday. On Saturday, on the way to Joan's party, a fellow came round the roundabout on the wrong side and his bike hit the kerb in the middle of the road. He fell off his bike, got up and righted himself, by which time we had slowed up. Then he fell over along side us bringing his bike with him. Fortunately we didn't hit him, but he just stood in the middle of the road. He was paralytic and hadn't the vaguest notion of what he was doing. On our way home, another was swaying home, steadying himself with his hands on the pavement every now and then.

I can't go shopping tomorrow as the locals will be on a big spend and you can't get near anything.

The car is going well, although it conks out very easily. It won't tick over or idle at all. The girls at the office say that the "timing needs adjusting to cope with the altitude". Going back to SA, you need to have it adjusted for sea level. It's lovely having my car and coming home early. I did shopping on Monday, library on Tuesday and was home at 4.40 tonight.

The drums are loud and there is singing and shouting too. This will go on all night. I don't know where they find the stamina. It sounds rather like Red Indians with all that whooping.

Obed is buying a big loaf with icing on the top, each morning for his lunch and on Monday bought a pint of milk. He makes a point of sitting down with a cup of tea and his loaf cut into big thick butties. Richard and I were having corned beef butties and tomatoes as usual. I can't think of anything for lunch except ham and eggs and bacon and things like that. I would have loved a slice of bun. This is a thing plugged in the Government daily paper, because the African thinks that when he is full, that's all that matters, hence mealie porridge and bread, all bulk and no vitamins.

Am reading and enjoying Dr Zhivago. I've ordered two books from the library. Samuel Butlers, The Way of all Flesh and Shelagh Delaney's "A Taste of Honey" You write your title in a Book Suggestion Book, which is examined every now and then. The comment against the former was "Ordered". It was in a Penguin Book list under "Classics" I hope it's not a Lady Chatterley type classic. The second book I ordered after reading another Shelagh Delaney book. Other comments by the mysterious person who wrote "ordered" were "in paperback only" " Author quoted incorrectly" and most humiliating of all "already in the library". So it seems that within reason I could get any book at all. I shall work my way through the Penguin lists. I have also got out Tolstoy's "War and Peace" which is tough going.

Unfortunately, I find that music isn't sold anywhere and has to be ordered from England or SA. This is bad because you need to browse though music. Luckily the music I have brought is stuff I haven't tackled or difficult so I shall have to work hard on them. We are trying to find a piano, but they are in demand. A friend at the tennis club sold theirs for £50 and it was in bad repair and they were going to throw it out. They also need tuning once a month due to changes in the temperature.

Here is my first " Will you send me?" This will only cost a shilling though. Can you send a baby knitting pattern of jackets or cardigans for under six months for my friend Vivienne in the office's baby. It is Vivienne who lent me the one I am using at the moment. If there are booties on the pattern, so much the better as I thought I could tackle a pair for Sheila from the office in the UK who is having a baby in September. They will be cheap to post and show I have remembered her. The jersey I knitted for Joan's baby has washed huge and the neckband is a bit baggy, so I'm trying another and Vivienne is going to show me how to pick up stitches around the neck.

Times of Zambia

1st June   Mini skirt campaign hots up in Kitwe

5th June   Kapepwe calls British hyenas

Letter 29   5th June 1967

Saturday evening, we had Marlene and Peter and John and Sue for a fondue dinner and it was a success. I am glad it was, as Marlene has to pay for a babysitter every time they go out, so it's an expense even to go to the pictures. I said that I would be happy to babysit anytime, but she said she didn't like to ask. Anyway the only places they have been to recently is to us! I covered grapefruit, or rather oranges in rum essences and sugar and grilled them and put some cinnamon on top and a cherry. I wrote grapefruit as it was supposed to be grapefruit, but they were out and I could only get oranges. Sue said she got some nice ones last week. The rest was easy. We got 3lb of steak for 12/- and diced it and I did salady things like stuffed eggs. I halved the eggs and took out the yolks, hardboiled of course and mixed it with tomato juice and Worcester sauce and whipped it and put it back in the eggs. For pud, I made a jelly and beat in condensed milk as it was setting and put it on top of a jelly into which I had set swiss roll slices. I froze the lot and surrounded it with peaches. The jelly was peach too. I can get a wide variety of jelly flavours.

Richard just dashed in and said he was going to a committee meeting of the Bowls and Tennis club, so I hurried Obed off home and now I am here in the bar at the tennis club waiting for Richard. Back to food. I can now get some lovely cereals, cornflakes with strawberries, cornflakes and prune flakes, cornflakes and raisins. They are all South African and they are crisper than home and are super with cold milk, although, need I add, expensive.

We did nothing but laugh over the meal. The two bottles of wine helped no doubt. *(What! On two glasses each?)* Marlene and Peter left early as it's expensive after eleven and double rate after midnight, but John and Sue stayed until after midnight.

Yesterday afternoon, we took a young couple, Sally and Stuart Parker, to the Boat Club as they have only been here a month. They are about the same age as us and have been married nearly three years and have travelled around quite a bit. We then went to see the VC10 off. There were crowds there. We stood alongside the runway and had to cover our ears. The ground trembled. It left us all breathless. Apparently it's a Sunday drive. Quite the event of the week. If you ask someone what they did at the weekend, they say, "We went to see the VC10 off", as though they had said, "We went to the Zoo".

Sally and Stuart then came back for coffee, this being 5.15 ish. Richard and I (after putting our leg of pork in the oven, sat until about seven with them chatting. We then said, you must stay for dinner, but they refused saying they had letters to write etc. At seven thirty, we were hungry and persuaded them that they must eat and we did and I enjoyed this meal as much as yesterday, partly because there was no anxiety planning and we had tomato juice, pork, runner beans (*those grin bins again*) and peas and Sally made a nice gravy for me and just as we were about to sit down Sue knocked on the door with two slices of lemon meringue for Richard and I, that she had made. On seeing our visitors, she dashed back for two more pieces and we had this for afters.

Sally had asked about the boat club when we were at the tennis club, so it was then that we threw out the invitation, thinking it would be an opportunity to get to know them better (Sue and John are leaving in July) and we are glad we did as we had a good day.

More news. We are getting a dog. We have gone into it carefully and decided that as there are kennels close to Chester within frequent visiting distance during quarantine and he will be 21 months when we come home, it will work out O.K. He is at present two weeks old and is a pedigree Maltese terrier. We are going to visit him at the weekend in Luanshya where he was born. He is one of two dog puppies. The other is promised to the father's owner, and we have the remaining one. One of Richard's clerks heard Richard was looking for a Maltese terrier and her father's dog had just had these two. I am working on Saturday morning and have a day off in lieu therefore Marlene is taking me to a blind school where they make dog baskets. This week we bought a rubber ball and a bone. We have been reading oodles of books on dogs and have worked out a rough diet and where to keep him. I shall be home to give him breakfast lunch and two evening meals and the only meal Obed will have to give him is warm milk at three o'clock. He is a completely white dog with hair to the ground with a tail curling over his back, when he grows that is. I want to call him Pucci as in the designer, pronounced Poochy.

Clever pun! Richard thinks it's a terrible name, but can't suggest anything better. He wants to call it Mackie after the Managing Director, so that he can shout, " Get down, Mackie. Sit Mackie. I'll rub your nose in it Mackie", etc.

This evening, John called in with a SA newspaper cutting showing a piece of land for auction that he wanted, but he got the paper too late to put in a bid. It is in Port Elizabeth and above a river on the opposite side of which is a pine forest. They are both disappointed.

We have heard your tape on a borrowed tape recorder. It was great fun. I thought it would make me very homesick but it was so nice hearing you all and it was so natural it was like sitting in the same room with you. In fact, Richard had it on and I went into the kitchen and it did sound odd hearing you all in the lounge chatting away. *(I didn't always have pretensions about "sitting room")*

Times of Zambia

16th June   Copper exports in peril. Rail Bridge blasted on Lobito route.

Chapter Twelve   Obed departs

Letter 30   7-6-67

Sue has a cook-boy and he does all the cooking except on special occasions, and very well too. He just asks for the meat and gets on with it. I would rather cook for myself as they go through a huge amount of food. Yesterday, she bought six crayfish tails for about £2, for dinner guests tomorrow and she had worked out a good menu. At lunchtime, she came in to find a plate beautifully decorated with lettuce and tomatoes and in the middle-two crayfish tails. Luckily, four will still suffice for her dinner party, but this is the sort of thing that happens. She said that the lunch was jolly good, however.

You know the blue bikini you bought me? They've got them in our shop for 59/11d! And those bikini flowery pants that I bought for 3/11 are here for 9/11. You can understand freight charges being heavy on weighty items, but not on undies. They are making nearly 100% on the retail let alone the wholesale.

Our sea things are on their way from Lobito Bay to Ndola, by rail, as the firm has received the bill. I am longing to get them, as it is difficult entertaining with no extra bits and pieces, although we picked some nice things to bring by air. The "useless things" have been things like my table mats and my posh gilt tray, but they have been invaluable and make the house seem furnished. I have my ice bucket, tray and deer on the sideboard like this. Picture coming up.

We are having trouble buying a piano, as they are so expensive. The cheapest is £50 and they are all pretty awful. A woman in the office said, " I only got £5 for mine as it wasn't in very good shape. You can't get music, although there is a shop in Kitwe, 32 miles away and most people order from England or South Africa. I was thinking of sending home for some, but I don't know the names of the publishers, so will wait until my music arrives by sea, and will glean some information from them and write direct to the publishers. *(How wonderfully easy it is now to search and examine music on line and have it despatched or downloaded immediately.)*

There is a tremendous turnover in second hand stuff. Although it is dear, it's a lot cheaper than new. A girl in the office, Vivienne, her father sold the contents of his garage for £300!! This was old nuts and bolts, hosepipes, wire, sacking, old tools and all sorts of old rubbish. So leave Daddy's shed alone. It may all be valuable.

Daddy, are you taking any black and white photographs? I would like some photos during the year of the children, as they will alter so much in two years. (Actually, 21 months now). I also want to see snaps of the garden. I might get a black and white film for Richard's camera, so you can put faces to names and see our puppy growing up. We are going to see him this weekend.

I have seen a lovely photo album for £2/5/-. It has a heavy back, but only has 10 pages in it. Each page has a layer of polythene stuff attached to the edge and you put the photographs on the page with titles on slips of paper, and then smooth the polythene over the top. This holds the pictures in place. You can change the photos as you do not write upon, or damage the pages. I think they are South African.

Letter 31   10-6-67

Many thanks for the knitting patterns. I'm sorry they were expensive to post (I thought they would be quite light and not very expensive!) but believe me it was worth it. I've already got waiting lists to borrow them. Vivienne has borrowed the one with the hood of all things. It will keep the cold out of his ears when she takes him to crèche in the morning, so she says. The fact that she takes him in a car, and it is only round the corner from her own road doesn't enter into it. Any old excuse to knit a hood! The pattern is now on its way to Mufilira, as her mother-in-law is going to knit it. As soon as I said she could borrow it, she rang up mother-in-law with the news!

You and Mrs L. have the same idea about Obed – poor fellow, he must have been very hungry. This is what we thought at first too, and that is why we gave him a second chance and didn't knock any money off his pay. We said if it happened again he would be sacked. For about three days after payday, he brought lunch. This consisted of a pint of milk, an iced loaf with currants in, and his mealie porridge. Don't say that this isn't much. This is the staple diet for him and everyone else, no matter what the pay they earn, and is the staple diet like curry to the Indians and rice to the Chinese. We gave him tea and sugar and also the meat that was left at the end of the week, being about ½ lb of kidney and four sausages (I have told you before that I have seen the locals buying animal skins, which they must render into stew). This was considered fair by our friends, who thought "Pommies" are a bit soft that way, any way. They also tell a tale of Oxfam tractors, which are given to co-ops and farms and are left to rot because no one knows how to use them and they prefer ploughs anyway. However, this is by the way and may be 'wicked' South African propaganda!'

Anyway, the first Saturday in the month, we had John and Sue, and Marlene and Peter for dinner, and Obed turns up at 8 instead of 7 and is absolutely paralytic. All he could do was the dishes and he had both windows wide open, and he was so much in the way that I sent him home. However, I excused this, and just resolved not to have any dinners on the first Saturday after pay-day. Last week, when we were looking for a missing clothes brush, Richard spotted that a packet of candles (remember when we had no electricity?) was missing. He had taken not one or two used ones, but an unopened packet! This is not good and it was just less than a week after pay-day, and his warning. On Saturday, he asked for 10/-. Previously we have given advances, the last being to get his watch repaired, which he didn't, but turned up later wearing a ladies gold watch – far above 10/- worth. I wonder where he or his cronies got that! This meant he was broke, so today I checked on food and found my flour gone and my cereal gone. I always fold the bags a special way to stop insects getting in and he hadn't folded them back and had not wiped up the spilt flour. I couldn't check if anything else had gone. Back to the clothes brush we 'lost'! We looked everywhere for it; it is usually kept in the clothes bucket and Obed uses it every washday. However he couldn't recall the brush or its whereabouts, so I told him to have a jolly good look for it. Next day it was back in the normal place, and he said it had been there all the time! It was getting so that we were arranging things so we could tell if anything was missing. (He has also had airmail letters) This might make us tidy, but is no way to live. I was dreading coming home to see what the fool had taken, as I wanted not to know about it. Although 'hungry', he always has a full packet of cigarettes and matches.

So to keep on the right side of the government, we rang the equivalent of the labour exchange and gave them the facts, and they said to sack him. John and Sue's boy, who is very loyal and a good worker, has a friend whom they interviewed for us, and who, when we sack Obed sometime this week, will start for us. His name is Andres. Don't we get them!

I still feel sorry for Obed for being so stupid. As we threatened to sack him and he still steals, then we must sack him, or he will take us for real thick heads, and will try his hand at something bigger I'm sure. Do you see now? I'm sure Daddy is not so sentimental and will see our side. He has little or no rent to pay and no rates or electricity or things like that. This is paid for by the employer of the fellow, whose house he is living in.

On Saturday morning I was working and we played tennis in the afternoon and we stayed at the tennis club until 8.30 as about 12 of us younger ones got this fellow playing the piano and we had a good sing song. One fellow Costa, who is of Greek origin, sang Never on Sunday in Greek and did that Greek dancing for us. It was quite good fun.

But on Sunday morning I felt lousy – all fluey, but we were up at 7.00 because I couldn't sleep and had no voice, and by 8.30 we were on the way to Luanshya to see our puppy.

There has been a circus here over the weekend, but it was 25/- to 30/- a seat, and too much to pay, when neither of us were keen on circuses, but everyone said the animals were outside in cages, so on Friday evening we went to the field and couldn't get anywhere near for locals. We were busy all Saturday, and as we were told it would be there until Sunday night's performance, we went on Sunday morning at about 8.15. There wasn't a soul about. It had vanished. Nothing but wheel ruts at the entrance. There had been so much commotion on the Friday! Anyway, apparently there wasn't an elephant over 6' tall and all the lions had had their teeth out, and were a bit mangy. Guess whose circus it was. Wilkies. Aren't they the people who used to have the fair in New Ferry and a circus of some sort?

So we went on to Luanshya. Our puppy is about 8" long and is white all over with its hair just starting to curl. It wasn't walking properly, just wobbling and couldn't see properly. I didn't know which to choose, one was a bit bigger with more hair, the other smaller with curlier hair. I would be delighted with either. I took along a Spratts rubber ball – a tiny one, as I thought he could play with it until we brought him home in July and could bring it with him so that something would be familiar, but it was miles too big for him and he kept bumping into it. The owners were very nice and gave us coffee, and chatted. They had in the house, two puppies and the mother, a huge Alsatian, a West African Grey parrot, two canaries, a budgie and a visiting nephew and niece with squawking twins of about 3 / 4 months old! It was chaos. We stopped from 9.00 to 9.30a.m, and were at the tennis club just after 10.15! Good going hey! Luanshya is 17 miles away and we did about 70/80 all the way. Don't gasp, we weren't rushing. It was a dead straight completely empty road for the 16 ½ miles between.

Letter 32   14-6-67   The car is now clean of grease but it cost £5-0-0! But it was well cleaned inside and out and also the engine was cleaned.

Richard tipped the two locals who cleaned it (before we got the bill) and we couldn't get away because they both flew around it, giving it the extra polish and opening doors and boot and things to show where it had been cleaned. They both directed me out backwards. In fact they were more of a hindrance than a help, and both were waving their arms in every direction. Obed wipes both cars down in the morning, as they are soaked in dew. They therefore don't need regular washing.

I am very much at home with the car and it is beautiful to drive and control. I have driven the big one a few times, but find it heavy to manoeuvre. Whereas with mine, I don't need any brake at stops on an incline, the big one needs the handbrake. I am getting used to parking and am no longer nervous of traffic.

The first week, I would avoid awkward traffic junctions and things, but now that I have more confidence in my ability to control the car, I no longer think of routes. I just go from A to B. I have given lifts home to two girls in the office who were stuck, and was pleased to be able to do this, and shall never mind giving lifts to anyone, knowing how reliant I was on other people's cars until I got my own.

Richard has gone to Lusaka today. I drove him to the airport this morning at seven. This was not a VC 10! This plane needed a shove to get off the ground. I am going along later to meet him and shall probably see the plane go overhead.

With going on about Obed and the tennis, I forgot to mention that Richard played in a Unilever Golf tournament on Thursday afternoon and all Friday. Apparently, it's called the Dash Cup and all Unilever firms all over the world play. Richard was eighth out of 10 which was good considering that he only played about three times last year, and that the managing director was ninth.

The Levers' ladies (sounds like char women) were invited to lunch at the golf club and I got an extended lunch hour from work, but who should be at the next table, but half the top fellows from my office, who kept coming to me later in the day to see if I enjoyed the golf!

I'm sitting in the bedroom writing this looking at my view. There are some odd bods coming up the road. This morning, we passed the township on our way to the airport and the road was like Cammell Lairds letting out. Everyone going to work. Coming in single file out of the paths in the bush, along the railway line, from everywhere. All black faces and that easy lolloping walk. It was fascinating and far more colourful than Lairds.

The golf club looks down the hill over undulating golf course dotted with trees to the lake, which is covered in lilies at the moment and up the other side are trees and then the bush. So the clubhouse obscures the lake. I think we'll blow it up!

Talking of blowing things up, the Benguela railway line has been blown up again by 'Freedom Fighters' and will take up to a month to repair. We are hoping that our sea things are on this side of the damage! There is still no news, except "any day now" from the shipping people.

We had more bad luck with chocolate biscuits. We bought a completely sealed packet of Huntley & Palmers chocolate digestives but when we opened them, they were covered in maggot eggs. Who'd live in the jungle!

Times of Zambia

> 18th June   **Fire brigade loses its way. ZamTan's waste oil goes up in smoke.**

Letter 33   19.6.67

Received the May Illustrated News today. We are doing a swap with the News, after we have read it inside out, with Mrs Cross, Jill's mum, who has Cheshire Life sent out and a very snooty one called London Look, with nothing less than a princess and a couple of Rt. Hons. in the wedding column, and Country Life, which has houses for sale, complete with gatehouses and gamekeepers' cottages.

We have sacked Obed. We did the dirty deed on Saturday and neither of us could eat our lunch, we felt so rotten, and didn't know whether we had in fact, after all, done the right thing. He didn't argue when we said we couldn't keep him, and Richard told him how silly he was (he had acquired a brass medallion this week which he hung around his neck, and yet pinched our food) and he went to his cupboard and put his bits and pieces in a paper bag. Richard wrote a reference for him regarding his ability to work and his full month's money although he had worked only a fortnight, and a packet of tea and sugar. He stood there in the door way with his parcel, and said "Goodbye sir, thank you very much, sir" and off he went. I watched him go from the upstairs window and he just stood there outside for a bit and then went off.

Then, as I say, we felt too miserable for words. All I could think of was poor Obed going home to tell his wife. We spent half the evening trying to justify the sacking, but now two days later, I can see it in the proper light, but still feel rotten.

The new chap started on Sunday morning. He worked today and has done all the washing and ironing and has washed down all the paintwork in the kitchen. He seems proficient workwise, (his reference says that he makes nice egg & chips!). His ironing is excellent. He is about 40, with his own house in Chifubu, a township about five miles away (he walks here in the morning!) and has a wife and family. His clothes were very shabby and his shirt was in a pretty bad state of disrepair. Obed's uniforms fit him well, and he has gone off home in one tonight and looks very tidy. He is not dirty at all, and appears very clean and doesn't smell. He is very brisk and business-like, but his English isn't very good (not as good as Obed's – poor Andres, he will be compared always with Obed as he is the only yardstick we have). He doesn't smile at all; perhaps he wants to be efficient. He doesn't wait to be told what to do – he tells me! This morning he came in, picked up a cloth and announced 'Wash car' and he marched out and did just that. When I talk to him, he says, "N'yes'm" which Richard is imitating already.

Another trick of Richard's, is when I'm in the bath or in a state of undress, he comes up the stairs saying in Obed's voice "Can I go home now, Madame" – the fool.

It has been rather cool lately: midday is fine and warm, but we are wearing cardigans in the house and in the middle of the night it is very cold. I must invest in a thermometer to see what I now regard as 'very cold'.

I had a half-day on Friday and enjoyed it very much. I had a read. Went and did all my shopping that we do on Saturday as Richard was playing golf on Saturday morning and then I went on to Marlene's as Marlene was to take me to the workshop of the blind and disabled in a place about six miles out of town, five of which were down a dirt road in the bush. I was hoping Marlene wouldn't get lost. Anyway we found the right turnoff and came to a pleasant house and garden, beyond which were the actual workshops and the living quarters, rather like small prefabs but with only tiny windows high up under the roof.

These are where the disabled live, complete with families and relatives. They are very well off by African standards, and for disabled – extremely well off, as only 10% of the able population is employed. They also have wheelchairs and other such aids, which is a luxury. (One fellow in town has no legs and runs along on his hands – he wears sacking gloves on his hands and swings his body between his arms – horribly repulsive, poor chap, but at least he is getting about). So you can see how well off they are in the workshop.

The superintendent, a very pleasant African, who lives in the house and runs the place, took us past the workshops, just barn like sheds with the blind sitting on the floor making things with cane. There were children everywhere, and they ran ahead of us and hid in doorways, watching us, giggling – more like village children and not like the town 'gimme sixpence' children. We came to the warehouse where the finished goods were despatched and the raw materials were kept. The cane is imported as the local stuff, being little more than dried grass, of which my wastepaper basket was made, is far inferior. There were some beautifully made things. Marlene and I both liked a glass top cane table with cane braid edging the glass, very modern and not a bit wicker-wonky. We asked the price, but were told it was new and hadn't been costed, and it had been made for the trade fair, which is to be held from the 31st June to 3rd of July, over the Bank Holidays, Monday and Tuesday. (Heroes Day and Unity Day) Marlene wanted a chair for Sally as they are not like the normal child's wicker chair, but have straight arms and legs and are very smart. Sally was a bit small, but didn't mind the chair at all, and sat there quite happily while we looked around. There were some huge dog baskets for Alsatians, which were like great armchairs and Marlene and I drooled over the cradles. They were beautiful, and are very practical out here, as they are cool. Marlene brought Sally out at 6 weeks in a carrycot, which was plastic and far too hot. There was one like the one I think I had – on a stand with half hoops for the drapery.

The disabled men seem to check stock and make up orders. Marlene had to order Sally's chair, as the one she liked was reserved for the show. I picked a dog basket with a highish back and 14" base, which was 28/2, and well made at the price. I now have to find a cover. Marlene got Pinky's cover (their bulldog) from an Indian shop. It was a cot blanket and was £1 (sort of army blanket material) so I'll try there after pay day (it's set us back with the housekeeping paying Obed off). Last Friday I spotted two Prestige pie dishes for 1/9 each and bought them. They are about 6" across and 1" deep and will do for Pucci, as there are no dog bowls in town, despite the large dog population.

Joan from Ndola has written to us three girls at the office. She says Jill has been to see you and that she herself is very homesick and wishes she were back in Ndola – can you imagine that! Perhaps we should do a swap. So if you ask Jill again, can you ask Joan too? I got to know Joan better the month before she went and am sorry that she's not liking England. She said the people are very unfriendly.

By the way - Jill's mum is a dressmaking wizard – she can knock up allsorts. I think Jill is a bit on the lazy side!

Daddy said that dogs only need one meal a day. Well he's not a dog yet, only a baby dog and therefore is only on milky stuff and cereal and chopped meat. Did you know too that a puppy eats twice as much a day as a grown dog the same size? What do you think of my dog's name! You didn't say anything, just accepted it!

Times of Zambia

20th June 1967   One dentist for 160,000 people. World Health Organisation says it should be 1 for 30,000.

Chapter Thirteen   Trade Fair

21.6.67   Letter 34

We have just had a polite note from the P.O. to say that there was a letter with 1/3d to pay on it and that "as we were sure to want it" they had sent it on and would be obliged if we would affix a 1/3 stamp to their form. The letter will no doubt arrive tomorrow. So you needn't worry about things being held up because of shortage of stamps, as they do not hold them to wait for the balance.

Sue's boy told Sue that Obed came on Monday and tried to start a punch up with the boy next door but one, with whom he was quite friendly, and blamed him for his getting the sack for some unknown reason! Sue's boy said that he and Andres went inside and locked the doors until he had gone – not so soft were they? Perhaps Obed had been pinching things for his friend! Andres is shaping quite well and we have shown him how to make toast and put the Kellogg's out, which was pointless as I only have half a box left. I should have bought about half a dozen when they were in.

We have had some disturbing news about our sea things. Richard was asked to go and clear the customs documents, which he did. He then went to the railage people and asked where the truck was, as it was not yet in Levers' sidings. They told him that the truck was unaccounted for and should have come through and was the only one with goods from that particular ship that hadn't arrived, and they had no idea where it was.

The transport manager at Levers (he's Dutch and I can't spell his name – (Hank Van den Boes – so Richard tells me) was very good and took some men to the railway and checked every siding for truck no. 1917 for Levers, but could not trace it. He said not to worry as it was probably in the marshalling yard just over the Congo border waiting to be made up into the next Ndola train. Otherwise it is still in Angola, in front of the blown up bridge, which is, according to rumours, going to take anything from two to four months to repair. Also the train with food supplies from England was on the wrong side! So we will have been, if the truck is found, six to eight months without our stuff (I just daren't think of the stuff in the crate – everything we own, except the bits we have with us). Again I say – who'd live in the jungle. Richard says that by the time it arrives, will be time to just stick a return label on it to send it back. We are however, managing quite well without the things, but we can't keep the borrowed blanket for too long, can we. It gets warmer in August, thank goodness. All my kitchen utensils, Tupperware, pans, Pyrex, casseroles, crockery, clothes, tape recorder, golf clubs, baking tins, linen and so on and so on. Luckily we brought the right things by air, but it is so very annoying and frustrating not being able to do anything or find out anything.

There are only three sea routes to Zambia, via Lobito, which is out of service, via Beira, which is partly closed because of Suez, and Cape Town which is blocked because of the extra trade caused by this, so I, like everyone else, on pay day, will buy as much tinned stuff as possible.

It is probably not necessary at all, but things are made scarce by people panic buying more than shortage of goods, so either way, the shops are emptying. Anyway it's different! Makes you shop less haphazardly. When I come home I may go mad, dashing around supermarkets grabbing stuff from shelves. Talking about going mad, you know of Denis Bratton, who showed me around the factory? Well he has been here for five years and for ages has been trying to get to London, as he feels he is getting older without learning anything and although he was an advertising manager, he felt he had become out of touch with modern methods. Anyway, his transfer came through two weeks ago and this week he has been flown to Bulawayo mental hospital. He just went off his nut. I can't find anything more out, but you've never met a more normal bloke! They are keeping it very quiet at the office. We were going around to his flat this week to have a farewell drink too! Richard says that he is starting to talk to himself too! Gosh! I must keep my eye on him.

We haven't yet chosen a puppy, although the fellow asked which one we would like. I said I would leave it until we came to pick one up. If there are still two, they will have grown a lot and there may be no difference. If one has been taken, then our choice is made. I knew I should pick the bigger one, but the small one was curly and rather sweet so that is why I didn't decide there and then.

I had a nice day at work yesterday. There was a board meeting in the afternoon and everyone was polishing and dusting like mad and the best tea set was washed and serviettes aired etc. Cookie came in with two-dozen red, pink and white carnations and fern and heather, which cost £3! We had a large jardinière in the cupboard with wire in it, and Cookie proceeds to ram in the flowers, snapping stems off here and there. They were beautiful flowers and I was cringing. Anyway as I was hovering around she says, 'I give up – you have a bash,' which I did, post haste and when I had finished, it looked gorgeous. It was easy because they were lovely flowers with stiff stems and plenty of foliage to fill in. We put them on the table in reception and I was told I was official flower arranger from then on; I was very pleased, but they only have board meetings once a year!

Later in the morning, the manager's secretary came and asked if I would hand around the tea if she poured, during the meeting, so I put a clean uniform on and powdered my nose at lunchtime (Andres wouldn't be pleased – two dresses in one day). I was given strict instructions to serve a little bald man first, sitting in a red chair and work down the table from there. We went in at three with the teapot, and the sideboard was set out with cups and everything went smoothly. Our manager was sitting at the bottom of the table!

I duly served the fellow in the red chair first, as they were all oldish and baldish, but apparently he had swapped chairs with the right man! But I don't think they noticed who had their tea first. One fellow, as I went to put his cup down, said 'and this will involve between one and a half and two million pounds' and I nearly spilt it on him. We were in and out in about two minutes, after getting glammed up. Richard said I should have put fishnet stockings on and a pair of bunny ears.

.

Sue and Margie on the wall outside the office

A fellow from the Congo came around selling oil paintings for £1, which are very garish, but I shall buy one later on, just to bring home as they are locally (well near enough) made. He also has paintings done in watercolour on pieces of black paper. They are done in brush strokes and are like sketches, but are more attractive. They were 5/- each, but I was apparently diddled as you can buy 3 for 10/-. But I didn't like bargaining for a painting, like vegetables. It seemed like belittling his talent, and a bit insulting. They were worth 5/- each to me anyway.

Very popular here are the Boots pictures which are sold by a picture framing firm (who does a roaring trade of H.Ex. the President, as every shop and firm and hotel – anywhere public must display one). The Boots pictures are sold at terrible prices and everyone treats them like originals! Ugh! (Aren't I snobby?) I'm going to order a £5.10.0 original drawing (abut 6" x 4") by an English unknown artist in 1815 – of a seated child, from the London gallery, which sends its catalogues. It's the cheapest – the others run into hundreds of pounds. Last time I ordered one, I was beaten to the draw and it had gone, so I'll try again. I think it's more romantic to have an old small original than a print of the same price, although I think if you can get one a bit different like my 21st picture from the office –which I have just remembered, and my huge Beardsley black and white one (in a truck somewhere in Angola) it's ok, but a picture that everyone's got – no.

Anyway, although I could rattle on for a while yet, I'll close, I like writing to you both, as I feel as though I'm talking to you when I'm actually writing. Putting the pen down is rather like putting the phone down and then everything is still and quiet.

With x from Doodle, who is trying out Pucci's basket. He doesn't mind Pucci coming as Doodle is a lot bigger, but he just won't be able to stand it if Pucci won't leave him in peace, will he?

Times of Zambia

26th June   **Rhodesian Africans warned they will be sent home to fight Smith, says Mutemba.**

*   **Opposition party unnecessary says Choma. The necessity of forming an opposition party in a country comes only when the ruling party makes blunders, says the Minister for Presidential affairs Mr Matunga Choma.**

*   **All Western Province Assistant Ministers of State have been instructed to take the names of all Rhodesian Africans who came to Zambia after 1962 so that they could be sent home to fight.**

Letter 35   26.6.67

You must excuse me if I write on both sides today as only have four sheets left. However I shall number them.

On Thursday night we went to the pictures and saw Kaleidoscope, quite a good film about a fellow who alters the plates in the factory making playing cards for all the casinos. The alterations to the backs can only be seen by special glasses – all very far fetched but good fun. In the crucial game new cards are called for and a box of very old cards brought in, unaltered but the hero wins fairly. There were a lot of Italians in the audience who obviously knew their poker, and gasped and oohed at every turn of the card. In fact audience participation here is very good. The Africans love slapstick comedies, or anything relying on the actual picture and not the dialogue and literally roll about in their seats with delight, which greatly adds to our enjoyment of the film.

On Friday, the office had a film show in the evening, with a bit of a cocktail party beforehand. I wore my woollen dress and heavy coat (a cardigan would have done, but I thought my coat would be a bit different. I only have two 'fancier' dresses with my tunic and my blue dress that I wear with my linen coat. I am wearing my skirts very short, as all the girls do but I think I'll leave my best ones as they are and just wear my uniforms short. The film was called 'O for Oxygen' and was all about O^2 and its uses and manufacture. They showed Bristol and Newcastle and Port Talbot, which raised cheers from us, and in the next shot Kariba Dam, which raised cheers from everyone else. It lasted about an hour. They then showed a short film about the hurricane aeroplane, which showed a shot of Ndola airport and the exact view that I have from my window. There were about 30/40 of us, all the office staff and wives and husbands. Everyone was dressed up and we had sherry and beer and snacks and a chat and then had the film and then a little more of the former. We left about 10ish. Richard was impressed by the friendliness of everyone – I do seem to have been lucky with my job, don't I. My flowers were put on the reception counter, and were the first thing to be seen. And someone said that they had never seen the flowers done so nicely – and she didn't know who had done them – I was very chuffed.

On Saturday we went to Sally and Stuart's for dinner. They have a flat about 2 miles away. It isn't in a very good area, and the furniture is very old, but they have set to and had it painted and new curtains put up and have made it quite nice. They arrived about 2 months ago and like us, left a new house and most of the fittings. They have also left a lot in store, as they were told not to bring very much, which they now regret as they have had to buy a lot of expensive inferior goods. We had a nice meal and they, like us, had to wash the drinks glasses so we could use them for wine!

Anne Williamson, who is playing in the tennis with Richard, was playing with me in the ladies handicap doubles. We got a bye into the semi-finals and won our match which we played on Saturday morning. Anne and I are both the club's 'rabbits' and we are now into the finals! We had a 5 handicap in each game and played a good pair who were unbelievably off form. We won mainly on their faults (doesn't Wimbledon start about now?). However the other semi-final has yet to be played, and three of the four are the club's strongest lady players, so poor Anne and I will be hammered, well and truly, but everyone was pleased we won, particularly as one girl we played is a poor loser and is a bit snooty if she loses (which is hardly ever) and they were glad she had been sat on.

Richard also won his second round game with Anne, but I haven't played mine yet as one of the fellows we play against is on holiday.

Sue and John are off in four weeks' time! That was a short friendship. I'm hoping they will be in the UK for at least 6 months after we arrive.

I bought a blanket for Pucci. It is a single blanket and very, very poor quality but was only 11/6 so that was ok. I got it from an Indian shop rather like O'Kells. All the Indian women wear saris, but they love chiffon and brocades and they look a bit off in a shop especially as they are usually a bit on the grubby side, and they have to keep shoving the loose shoulder piece into place. The Indians wear loads of jewellery, even tiaras, and love those glam diamond brooches (like you get free on C&A dresses) and bangles and earrings. No modern stuff – all gilts and glam stones. Even girls who can just about walk wear lurex dresses, and only the most daring cut their hair. But it's the Indians who drive around in Dodges, Plymouths and Cadillacs, usually with about 6 children in the back. I must admit that the families are very close and everyone from granny to baby go out together. I've just realised that you don't see many old Africans. I've only seen a couple of old men but no women. Perhaps they retire to their villages on reaching old age, but with malnutrition and TB rampant, I don't suppose they even reach old age.

It is very cold in the evenings now and will be until nearing the end of July, but yesterday when Richard was fixing a burglar alarm onto the car, I sat on the garden chair in the hall as the sun shone directly into it, and my face got very red and I was knocking back iced orange juice as it was so hot, but in the dining room where the sun hadn't reached it was positively chilly. We are not very brown as everyone says we must be, in their letters. Our arms and legs are brown, but the rest is the same. Richard's face is a good colour. We are brown through playing tennis as I have a ring around my ankles where my socks stop. However in November I hope we shall look very healthy.

Richard would like a sports shirt for Christmas. Is this OK? He has socks and under clothes but not a short sleeved open necked shirt. A plain one with little or no pattern would be ideal. His collar size is 14 ½, and his chest size, so he says, is 38". His only shorts are olive green and at present he wears a hideous orange shirt that he's had since he was 16. We priced shirts and none were below £5, so he says he prefers to look hideous.

We are going to Luanshya in two weeks, on July 9th, to collect Pucci. Richard already has invented a voice for an invisible dog, as the basket is ready with a blanket and rubber ball and bone in it. He tells it to get out of its basket and he will give it a biscuit to which the invisible dog replies 'big deal'. I hope Pucci isn't like that.

I saw my first red Chinese last week. He came into the office. He is here for the Trade Fair.

He had a pyjama outfit on like this:

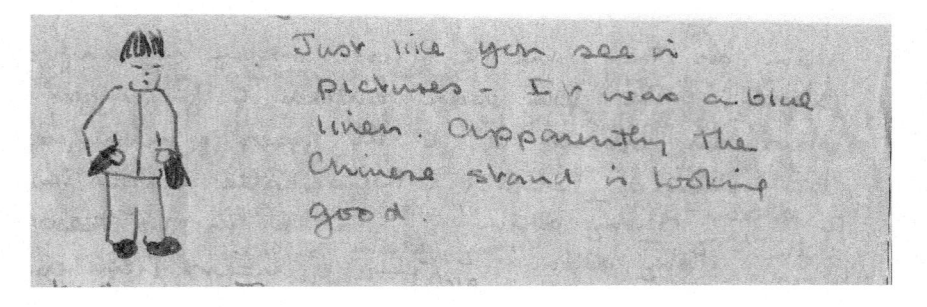

Just like you see in pictures – it was blue linen. Apparently the Chinese stand is looking good. Last time they got into trouble for handing out badges with pictures of Mao on, which the Africans went around wearing. Can you imagine the Government's consternation?

Talking of government, apparently the Minister of the Western Province who lives in a huge house by us, has just failed his 'O' levels for the third time. No comment!

My cold is better and Richard didn't even get a sniffle. His chest is fine. It was bad at the Rhodes Hotel, but there were loads of flowers and foliage around the windows.

How old is Nanny on the 7th? 72? and Gran? I must send them both cards, mustn't I? (*Nanny 72! I thought she was 90 when I got married!*)

Letter 36   28/6/67

This is a very brief letter but I know you'll excuse me when I tell you why. Our sea things have arrived! Not only that but they are now all away in cupboards and on shelves without, as far as we can see, any breakages or loss.

I have just had a bath and am in bed under an extra blanket. Richard rang up on the off chance for news and they said they had just rescued the truck on its way to Lusaka for the second time and they would unload it there and then, which they did. It was delivered to Levers where the outer crate was removed, as it was as big as our dining room table and half as high again. Inside were four tea chests of breakables and bits, and they were padded by parcels of linen and clothing and the tape recorder and golf clubs and odd cardboard boxes of things. Richard then brought the firm's minibus with the things and two men and unloaded at our house before lunch. I could hardly wait to get home after Richard rang me. I could hardly get in the door for things. We opened a few parcels and took everything except the tea chests into the spare room upstairs. We then went back to work and Andres cleaned up all the straw and stuff so we had a clear start tonight. Damp seems to have got into the clothes although the chest was bitumen coated and lined with wax paper, so everything has to be washed as it smells funny so I've made two piles – Andres washing and mine. I'll do the woollies and the things that don't need vigorous washing. When we had finished unpacking, I noticed the pottery spoon to my pineapple jam pot was missing so we sorted through the lot and found it and the rubber mat to my steel carving dish. The room looked like a bargain basement. Richard had first covered the hall shelves with stuff (Contact) in beige and this brightened the cupboard no end, and eventually we found homes for everything even the Christmas

Tree.

We have played the tape until we both had headaches, as it was the first music we have heard for four months. Your tape also sounds a lot better than on the little tape machine I have borrowed, and we will start ours this weekend.

Sue and John have got a new parrot. They have been waiting a while for him and they drove 80 miles last night to fetch him. They took about three hours. When they arrived back they called us in. The cage was empty, but there were scuffling noises coming from a cardboard box. The cage is about 3' high and 2' wide at the base. We held the cage and John covered his hands with cloth. When the parrot climbed up on to his arms and on up into the cage, we put the cage onto its base. They have called him 'Herb' and it is a present for Sue's mum, who surprisingly likes parrots. Herb is a West African grey parrot, and cost about £15! I went around this morning with grapes, but Herb was still unfriendly. Apparently he has been handled a lot recently, both vaccinations and travelling and is a bit wary of everyone. He has to be ignored for a week with just visits to feed him, and he will settle down.

Richard wants to know what the position would be if we brought a German car into the country from Germany, or a Swedish car from Sweden as regards Customs & Ex. He was thinking in particular of a Volvo. Another of his schemes!

Times of Zambia

30th June   Mining groups state plans for Zambianisation. "There will be more than five times as many Zambian shift bosses at Anglo American Corporation Copperbelt mines in 1971 than there are today, providing Zambians get to grips and learn the job."

Letter 37   2nd July 67

This is a new writing pad and is rather thin but I thought I'd try it as it was only 2/6 and the others are 4/1 to 4/3.

This is our long weekend – Monday and Tuesday off. Yesterday we played tennis as usual and went to see the Sand Pebbles in the evening, which was about the Chinese uprising and was filmed by the fellow who did Sound of Music and South Pacific. It was a bit gory in parts but very good visually – some splendid views of China. In one part a little coolie had to fight a big fat baddie, and he, the coolie was losing, but of course recovered and by some sly punches started to win. The cinema was in an uproar – the cheers and whistles and oohs and aahs as the punches fell. Tears were tripping us up laughing. Most enjoyable.

The office has been in an uproar this week, as all the stores departments have been preparing our stand. Outside were the usual displays of oxygen cylinders and a newly painted oxygen wagon (I know it has been specially painted as I got the invoice) and inside was a fully rigged operating theatre – most effective.

We headed off to the Trade Fair ourselves at 2.30. This included creeping up in a traffic jam and then queuing for tickets and then queuing at the entrance. It was 5/- each and no car park fee (space isn't so valuable as it's just a great expanse in the bush about 2 miles out of town). The whole area is corralled in and the wall has a name because it is so long. People came from all over the country, as it is a yearly National event and popular. I filmed like mad and took one whole film, mainly of the crowd. I hope I got some good shots.

The first pavilion was the Kenya one. There were some good exhibits but what we both loved was the stuffed head of an impala. This is a small deer with a beautiful long neck and big pointed ears.

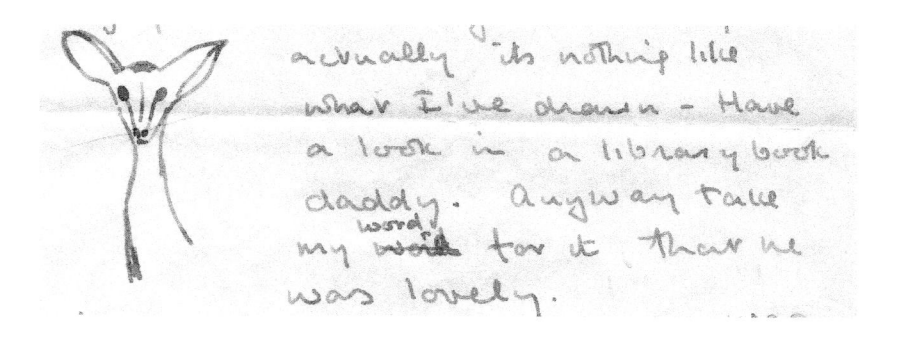

actually its nothing like what I've drawn – Have a look in a library book daddy. Anyway take my word for it, that he was lovely.

Actually it's nothing like what I've drawn – have a look in a library book Daddy. Anyway take my word for it that he was lovely. He was however £35. We enquired, but he had been sold already. We got the name of the people who deal with them as we will be hoping to pass through Mombasa or on our way home and could arrange to buy one then. Very extravagant but it was only small and would be a real African souvenir.

We found the British stand and went and stood under the flag for a bit. The theme was electricity and didn't interest me very much, but Richard wandered off, and I took a snap. Suddenly this terribly posh bloke comes up and asks me if I would take a photo of his display and he would pay for my film to be developed. I explained it was colour, but took one anyway and he gave me his card. He was from EverReady batteries and is here for one month just to sell at the show. I think I took it on the wrong speed too. Then he asked if I would like some champagne and off we trot to another part of the pavilion with a bar (how forward am I!) and I get my champagne, by which time Richard comes up, smelling the free booze no doubt, and we both had about three glasses of champagne and left the pavilion thinking how good it was to be British. We then passed two people we know, Bob and Naomi Dunkley with their two little girls, who were very miserable, as they couldn't get on the children's miniature train because it was full of African adults having rides. We went with them to find the children's zoo and play centre, which was very good, with rope bridges from tree platform to tree platform, and creepers and wigwams and huts and all sorts of pretend things – ideal!

Then we went to the Chinese pavilion, which frightened the life out of me. It was in a hangar like building and inside had a massive golden statue of Mao, and all his sayings in gold or red. There were pictures and slogans everywhere and hardly any products, just out and out propaganda. They were selling his red book, but we didn't buy one on principle, although we had a good look.

Every cliché of communism was there. We could just laugh at them but the locals just lapped it up. Such things as – "Here is a picture of happy mill workers singing their own mill song". At the door was a book marked – your comments are very welcome. We glanced through, and were amazed at the things that were written, supporting Mao and

Communism. Someone had even written – God bless the wonderful Mao Tse Tung. How utterly ridiculous – God bless a communist! This shows how the slogans had penetrated minds just ripe for it. I wasn't happy about it at all, and wanted to write in the book, but contented myself with writing 'rubbish' under one particularly ridiculous comment. How the Chinese must be chuckling. Another slogan was, "Here are some Chinese and Zambians happily working together for their country".

We then wandered around the smaller stands. Levers were sponsoring a pop show; another lager firm were doing 'Take your Pick' with beer bottles instead of boxes. There was some National Dancing, which I have photographed but could hardly see. At one point I held my camera in the air and just aimed and pressed the button. There were army bands and more national dancing in the avenues. I think I've got loads of photos of locals, in fact there were a hundred locals to every European I'm sure

It is absolutely super having all our things. All our clothes are now washed, and I have just to iron my silky dresses and my jerseys. I am also going mad baking. Yesterday, with Sue's help I made a three-egg sponge in two tins (one Sue's, the other Pucci's food tin). It's a very useful size; I must buy another.

On Friday night, I went mad in the supermarket, as they had a load of new stuff in. I bought icing sugar, breadcrumbs, Cornflakes – two packets (4/1 each!), castor sugar and cornflour. So I iced my sponge cake and put drinking chocolate in and made it chocolate icing and put jam and rum butter in the middle. It is a bit sickly, but as good as the local bakers. I made a meat and vegetable pie for lunch, and Richard on the spur of the moment invited the Rubners to tea on Tuesday afternoon, so I am just waiting for some scones to finish. Later I am going to make a proper chocolate cake and a sponge flan. For sponges, my mixer is great. Oh I nearly forgot, I did a lemon meringue pie for our evening meal, which wasn't as nice as I had hoped. I did shortcrust pastry, which didn't rise, but was otherwise fine, but my meringue wasn't crisp, but it was edible, nonetheless.

Andres didn't turn in on Saturday morning, the day after payday. Richard wanted some men in at the office for stock taking, so working on the principle that one in three turn up after payday and as he wanted ten men to come in, he asked thirty. Sure enough only twelve came in.

Anyway this morning Andres arrives and was very hoarse and has a cough, so he is pottering around sucking Dequadins, which I brought with me. It is 10 o'clock and I shall send him home after he has washed my baking things. (*Full of compassion, I am!*)

I have just looked at my scones and they haven't risen at all. I think a lot of it is the altitude. My cooker instructions say to use less sugar, but I just followed the recipe. I'll have to make them again, or we will have nothing for tea tomorrow.

Sunday afternoon. I am now sitting at the Bowls & Tennis Club watching, or half watching the Zambian bowls championships. Everywhere is hushed and the atmosphere is tense. I mustn't crackle the paper. It's quite interesting. I didn't realise it was such a complicated game.

Tony Wisdom called just on lunchtime today, with some office papers for Richard. I had bought some frozen plaice and we were having fish and chips and peas, so of course he stayed, which I didn't mind as he always clears his plate, and it's not much fun living and eating on your own, is it? The sun is lovely here at the club, which is one reason why we came to sit here, as it was rather chilly on our terrace. There is also no breeze here and altogether it is very pleasant and I feel very drowsy sitting here with just the click of the woods.

Later at home. Richard is at present experimenting with some veal chops in some Carrier concoction and I am banned from the kitchen. Spoke too soon, he just called me out to look for a jug and the kitchen is in a terrible state and he appears to have opened about six tins – this is going to be a very expensive meal!

This afternoon, he called me into the spare room, where he had made a table for my sewing machine with two tea chests and three planks from the sea chest, so we then covered the top with Contact and I'll make some sort of curtain to go around it. It's very makeshift, but just the job, and I can use my dressing table stool under it with plenty of legroom. However we are now rather cramped in our spare room, we will be taking the other two tea chests to Marlene's garage, leaving the airfreight chest, which I want to cover as I am using it as a blanket chest, it is so well made. (*We still have it although a builder has mixed cement on the lid. It holds the croquet set. Builders can be so insensitive.*)

Times of Zambia

July 1st   Three Congolese jailed, one for twenty years, for the murder of Harry Dunkerley. Clothing from the farm and Mr Dunkerley's wristwatch and fountain pen were found on them at Mokambo.

Chapter 14   Pucci Arrives.

Times of Zambia

July 2nd   Chairman Mao statue dominates the largest internal pavilion at Trade Fair.

July 3rd   Zambia is to drop its Commonwealth Day Public Holiday.

> The National Union of teachers has expressed concern over the increasing number of children who are sent to buy beer from taverns and bars by parents.

Letter 38   5.7.67

Yesterday morning, I made a sponge cake and a flan (4 eggs!) and both were dismal failures. They were an excellent colour but both hadn't risen and were as hard as bricks. Goodness knows why. I bought some rolls from the baker and ½ a dozen fancy cakes when he called with his van, and put apricots in the flan and soaked it in jelly, which softened it and made it edible. I then blobbed cream on that and chocolate bits, and it looked nice. In desperation I took the top off 4 oranges and scooped them clean, and made a fruit salad from bits of apple, banana, grape, orange and apricots (tinned – remainder of the tin that went in the flan and piled it back into the orange shells, dolloped cream on top and more chocolate bits and fortunately they were very tasty and looked most effective. I made egg and shrimp rolls and by the time we got to the cake, Marlene & Peter and Richard were full, which was just as well, as when I tasted the fancy cakes they were stale! With it being the long weekend, they had probably been baked on Saturday. As we still have meringue and chocolate cake and apricot flan to finish, I told Andres to throw the fancies out on his way home, but I note he has made a neat parcel of them. I hope he's not too disappointed when he finds they are so stale.

Richard has told me to have my letter written by the time he comes in, as he wants to list everything in the house for Insurance purposes. What a job. Anyway a list like that will be useful when we leave. I'm also taking art lessons and I go next Friday to see a woman who gives private lessons. It's expensive, but I might as well learn something or I'll get stale. I'm thinking of doing clay modelling and I can paint at home and take the paintings along for criticism.

Oh – some news. We have booked in to the Victoria Falls Hotel for August Bank Holiday – 7th August (is it later at home? I think it might be) so we shall see the Falls at a good time of year. In March they are too full and cover the islands and in November are very shallow, so August is a good time. The hotel has a heated pool and we have a double room and bathroom with shower, and I am quite excited about the whole idea. The weather too, should be good, nice and warm without being too hot. I must take loads of cine as the Falls are supposed to be too fantastic for words.

Last night we went to the pictures and saw Rotten to the Core, which was the usual Boulting Bros comedy. OK, but not really very funny.

We've been married 6 months on Friday 7th July. I seem to have been married for years but the wedding seems like yesterday.

We are also thinking of spending Christmas in a 'dress for dinner' type hotel in Salisbury as Christmas should be better there than here, and as hotels usually cater especially for Christmas, it won't make us so homesick.

Times of Zambia

July 5th All 85 tailors who went on strike are now back at work although their pay demand had not been granted. The strike caused a production loss of 72 dozen pairs of trousers and shorts.

July 6th An application by a Watch Tower sect member for a declaration by the court that his daughter's school suspension was unlawful. The 11year old was suspended for refusing to salute the national flag or sing the national anthem. Her lawyer asked for an adjournment so that he could study similar cases from other countries.

July 7th. **Fifteen more banned from Zambia. The government names 15 prohibited immigrants. Some were thought to have already left the country.**

Letter 39   9.7.67

Firstly before I forget, the 35/36" dress sounds fine and I'm sure it will fit. The dresses I brought with me ranged from size 10-14 and my office dresses are 34" hip!! I think 36 is about right. I do hope it hasn't gone or that you have bought it, but don't fret if it has gone as one new dress is just fine, two is a luxury indeed.

Richard says he wishes he had un-birthdays more often! The sort of shirt he needs is the short-sleeved open necked type in a cotton or cotton and Terylene mix or anything except nylon on its own. Go by the texture. If it's like nylon, then it won't breathe and will be hot.

Now, our news. Alongside me here is our new addition to the family, our Pucci. He is in his basket in the corner of our bedroom, where we thought we would bring him for the night in case he cries. I made a cushion from a length of spare material, from the stuff I brought with me, and stuffed it with nylons (old of course) and a pair of Richard's holey socks which were beyond repair. The blanket is doubled and spread out and the cushion in the middle and then Pucci and then I have folded one layer of the blanket over him and tucked him in. All you can see is his nose and ears, and he is fast asleep. We have also put the travelling alarm clock under his pillow, as the ticking is supposed to comfort him so that he won't cry.

He hasn't eaten much. The baby food that we bought as his breakfast, he didn't even look at, but I did some meat and gravy for lunch and supper, which he ate but didn't finish and there was hardly any of it. He has made two puddles, which I mopped up with tissue and then soaked in Sanpic. After the first puddle I put him into the garden, just before the second puddle, I opened the garden door as he has just got out of his basket after sleeping. Richard closed it not knowing why I opened it and Pucci dashes to the door and couldn't get out – 2nd puddle. I shouted at Richard for shutting the door and Pucci must have thought I was shouting at him and sat there whimpering, so I gave him a tickle and he was happy again (Pucci not Richard).

We took him out before coming upstairs but he ran in again and jumped in his basket, or rather clambered in. However we have a tin tray with newspaper on and have removed the rugs. He also refused his milk after I had warmed it.

He is very lively for about ½ an hour dashing around and then sleeps for an hour or so and then starts again. I put him into his basket as soon as we came in and he didn't even move. He just fell asleep there and then. Later after he had been playing, he curled up on the carpet and then as though the thought suddenly struck him, he bounded up and went into his basket and slept there – very quick, our Pucci!

<u>Monday</u>. Famous last words. Neither of us slept a wink last night. As I said about playing half an hour and sleeping an hour applied right through the night. He would wake up after an hour and whimpered until we couldn't ignore it any longer. At 5.30am I thought we could lock him in the kitchen with his basket but he howled even louder than ever and threatened to wake Dolphin Court, so we came down and tried to give him a worm pill, as he was scratching and giving symptoms of worms, which all puppies are born with. The pill was far too big, so Richard went to the chemist at eight, when he should have been at work and got some others and came back and administered them, and gave him some milk and the stuff that he had been fed on in Luanshya.

He is now asleep in his basket. Tonight he is staying down here, and we have bought a hot water bottle to put under his blanket and have dusted him with dusting insecticide to stop any scratching, so he should be more comfortable tonight and I am hoping we will be able to get some sleep! I'm worn out!

Yesterday on our way to Luanshya, we ran out of petrol. It wasn't our fault at all. The petrol gauge stuck at ¼ full. I had visions of us trekking through the bush for seven miles to Luanshya, but fortunately a motorist coming from Luanshya stopped, and siphoned petrol from his car into ours – and got his mouth full of petrol in the process. He wouldn't take any money or petrol coupons, wasn't he good? He had a piece of hose in his car especially for siphoning petrol, a common thing in these days of rationing.

Your Thornton's chocs sounded nice. My mouth is watering. I have just opened a Nestles Fruit & Nut and it had a big white maggot in! Enough to put you off chocolate for life. I'm going to take it back. The odd weevil is excusable, but this is too much. (I sound like a chip off the old block, don't I).

Andres, touch wood, seems to be fine and there were no signs of puddles when I came in tonight (from the dog, not Andres). We are taking the dog over with us to park the car and we can walk back again. He'll be worn out by the time we get back and will sleep all night. What a hope!

We went to the pictures on Saturday and saw Return of the Seven, a cowboy film, a sequel to the Magnificent Seven, and enjoyed it very much. Pucci better get trained quickly, or we will have to curtail our cinema habits. We seem to be going once a week and in the last week, we went 3 times, Saturday, Tuesday and Saturday again.

Richard came in tonight with a fan/convector heater, which would be just the job for your bedroom wall. We have a stand, but it can be mounted flat on the wall, and it's very slim and has a time switch incorporated. We are glad of it tonight but we have just realised that along the top of our French window is a grill with no glass just mesh, about three inches deep. As we are so open, we get a heck of a draught. So we are now off for our walk and a good night! (Aren't I tempting fate!)

Letter No. 40   12.7.67

I'm sitting exhausted on the floor here right in front of the electric fire. I have just played our mixed doubles match straight from work. We unfortunately lost – actually I'm rather glad (I hope my partner John isn't listening) because these matches are very strenuous and on the last games, I am on my knees and gasping for a drink and a wheelchair. It was a good game. We lost 6-3, 8-6 so you can see it was good. The majority of the games ran into deuce.

Guess who is fast asleep here on the floor beside me. Pucci. He sleeps quite well during the day it seems, but is averse to sleeping at night. On Monday he woke twice, not much it seems, but it takes about ¾ hour to get him to sleep. This by either playing with him so that he drops from exhaustion or shouting and saying 'stay' 'basket' 'lie down' 'stay' but on Monday at 5.20am we couldn't get him back to sleep, and got dressed about 6. At 7 o'clock as we were eating our breakfast, what did he do but climb into his basket. If we leave the room before he goes to sleep, he cries and this grows into yelps. If we were in a detached house we could stick cotton wool in our ears, but we must be careful here.

Tuesday he woke at 1 o'clock, 2.30 and 5. We take it in turns to go to him. At 5, Richard left him sitting in his basket and he whimpered a bit. When we came down at 7, he was playing with his duster and my old red clogs quite happily. We don't care if he never sleeps as long as he stays quietly downstairs. He is eating better now – mince, rice and gravy. Ugh. With a dollop of dried milk and puppy meal. He won't however drink his milk food that he was reared on in Luanshya. He also makes puddles outside at night to order, but won't as yet use the metal tray at night.

I've had my big Beardsley framed in black and went to call for it today but as it is 54" x 39" it wouldn't go into the car.

Pucci has just woken up and moved to another spot. Richard says that Pucci says "I don't mind waking up in the middle of the evening, but in the night, some fool keeps chasing me with a yellow duster." This is right because we drag the duster across the floor and he chases it to exhaustion. Lying here he looks so sweet, giving no indication of the devil he is. He has laddered two pairs of nylons this week (4 days) so at lunchtime I sit with my legs on the chair and in the evening take them off as soon as I come in (my stockings not my legs).

Our holiday in August has had to be scrapped. I'm disappointed. I thought that as we had booked nothing could stop it. We (Zambia Oxygen) have August Bank Holiday but Mr Mackie at Levers has decided that Levers will work, as it's not a definite public holiday. Miserable thing.

Some more unfortunate news. The Youngs have been "cleaned out".

The houseboy that came with the house was no good and they sacked him not knowing he had a key. So even if Andres is trustworthy, he isn't getting a key. Most of Mrs Young's clothes went, all the linen and Mr Young only had what he stood up in, not even a change of shoes. Just think of the lucky escape we have had! If we had moved into that house! I feel very sorry for them. It must be lousy. However they are lucky in that, as they are only temporary, all the household stuff was the company's. This has affected us in that I wanted Norman Ravenscroft's wife, who is coming out in a month, for a month, to bring out a suit or two, but Mrs Young has already asked her to bring some more of her clothes. I can't grumble because she needs them more than I do, but it was a waste of a golden opportunity.

We are picking up the Beardsley in the Minx tomorrow. I want to hang it for Friday, when I have the afternoon off and am inviting the girls to tea at 4.30 after work. I am going to try a chocolate cake and sausage rolls, but will buy a few bits from the bakers. I'll also have to provide sherry, as it is a late tea. About 9 to 11 will come. I have asked two old dears, but don't think they will come and Mrs Mhizha, the African telephonist. I don't know what her first name is, she only uses surnames, but she is very pleasant. A pity there weren't more like her.

Richard is downstairs making what seems an unsuccessful effort at putting Pucci to bed. I hope he settles and that if he wakes, it will be infrequent, and we hope the gaps will lengthen until he sleeps all night. I'm going to drink my orange juice and kip down before Richard comes upstairs. From the tone of Richard's voice, Pucci will be lucky not to find himself in a bucket of water tomorrow.

Times of Zambia

July 14th   Children should be protected from sex on the screen according to the President of the Teacher's Union. Many films these days place great emphasis on how to go about love affairs. Mr Nyendwas said he wanted films, which were based on building the nation. Children should be shown films on buildings, farming and the organisation of cooperatives. Films, which show

cowboys fighting and killing one another, encourage the Rhodesian type of life.

July 15th   Are these your children? Millie came from Kitwe to visit relatives in Ndola but could not find them. The other three were found penniless at a bus stop

Letter No. 41   16.7.67

Sunday morning. I thought I had better start my letter quite early because the last few have been pretty brief. Richard has popped up to the tennis club to check the ground, as yesterday morning we turned the courts around, which was quite a big job. The old markings can still be seen, but these will no doubt wear out in a few weeks. We have been up since six because guess who wasn't sleeping any more. He has been sleeping while I cleared away breakfast and did some washing but he is now wide awake and chewing my toes. This won't be bad in the week and after waking two to three times a night all week, is quite an achievement, but today was Sunday, the pest! He is eating well and runs up and down by the French window when he wants to go out, but we have to be very quick opening the door and showing him out. After all he's only eight weeks old. He still cries a lot but he now recognises us and jumps up and down at the front door when we come in at lunchtime. In the evening when I am cooking the supper, he curls up at the sink and watches me. He is very affectionate and when not chewing your fingers off, he licks your face. Last night we stayed later at the tennis club, and they started selling curry and salads, so Richard and I and Sally and Stuart had curry, and Pucci started sniffing and licking his lips, so I put some on a saucer, with a bowl of water in close proximity, and I thought he would turn his nose up at it, but no, he wolfed the lot, and wouldn't drink any water. I myself had to keep swigging coke to cool down my mouth. Richard, not liking curry very much had steak when we came in and Pucci had mince and kidney. What a pair of gluttons I've got. I had a bowl of Instant Whip!

We picked up the big Beardsley print on Friday and we only just got it into the big Hillman! It took both Andres and Richard to lift it and we had quite a job hanging it. We already have a big spider who has taken up residence behind it and who comes out at night (Fred and Joe have long since departed – probably perished in the cold).

Only six turned up to tea on Friday afternoon. Margie's girl was sick and Margie was at home looking after the baby and two others offered excuses. But Vivienne, Carol, a new girl, Mrs Kent, Mrs Giles, Cookie and Betty came along and we had a jolly good afternoon. I popped over to Mrs Cross to invite her but she had gone to stay with Jill's elder sister in Bulawayo. I had sherry, tea and coffee on the go and loads of snacks. At Cookie's, they cleared three to four bottles so I was prepared with three bottles but when everyone came in, they said how nice the coffee smelt perking away, and I made three fresh pots! And no one touched the sherry! On Thursday afternoon I made a sponge cake, with a new recipe of Sue's in which you boil up the milk and butter before adding. I also added drinking chocolate and it just rose and rose. Both halves sank a bit but I put peach jam and butter icing inside and chocolate icing on top and it was super. In fact I'm just going to get a piece right now. Please excuse me writing with my mouth full.

Richard and I are very taken with a Bernina sewing machine. It's called the Record 730. A lot of the girls here have them and we watched a demonstration of one at the trade fair. Cookie traded in her perfectly good machine, which did everything the Bernina did, for a Bernina, as it was so easy on the Bernina.

There are hardly any attachments and no extra feet and things, just a lever, which alters stitches, <u>as you sew</u>. This particular machine is £100 (ouch!), but is the same price here or even less than home. If there is a Bernina shop in Liverpool, ask how much this machine is, just for curiosity, when you are passing – there's no rush at all! Not at £100.

You say we've better pavements in Ndola than in Tranmere. You're joking. The only roads with pavements are the two main shopping roads and the streets joining them. Elsewhere the tar just runs to the grass and stops. Not even an edging stone or anything. Even the new modern library hasn't a pavement outside. Just a rutted mud track.

Dennis Bratton has happily fully recovered and is flying to London this afternoon. Lucky devil.

The Congo border is now closed. It's a good job our stuff got through, as we really would have been lucky to get it back.

I'm just looking at the ads in the paper for Zambia University. Assistant Information Officer to prepare news material, produce Univ. publications etc. 5 GCE or equivalent. Sports & Athletics Instructor. "Must have completed Secondary School" and "experience in sports and athletics is desirable".

Monday evening. I'm getting a lovely job to do – repairing one of the tennis nets! I went into the shop and asked for a bodkin. Oh no, they never had any of them – 'what's the biggest needle?' 'an embroidery needle'. 'Sorry but that's too small.' I then spotted another packet labelled Two Bodkins. Never mind, I got them in the end and also some nylon thread. It is just the netting at the top has parted from the webbing. It cost us £2 to have them repaired about two months ago and they fell apart about a week later. They were only sewn with cotton, which wasn't strong enough. When I've finished this I have two more to do!

To get Pucci away from nibbling my toes, I have just thrown the duster to the other side of the room and by coincidence instead of chewing it in the corner, he came belting back with it, so I threw it again and again yelling 'fetch' and he kept bringing it back so I hope it has sunk in. I hope he'll do it for Richard when he comes in, but he'll have probably forgotten by then.

Did I ever answer your question about Sally and Stuart? They are from London, and Stuart is designing and installing the air conditioning for the new hospital, and will be here for three years. They have been here about 2 ½ months. Stuart went into a partnership with another fellow, and for the first year the turnover was £10,000 and the second year £200,000, but the fellow he went in with did all the selling and Stuart did the designing of heating systems and as far as I can make out, most of the donkey work. However Stuart's shares were put up as security for a loan and Stuart lost everything as the other fellow pulled a fast one. They are not a bit bitter, but notch it down to experience. They traded in their new car, and moved to another house and for six weeks he worked as a labourer for one of his customers. Although they should have been miserable during these weeks, they said they enjoyed them, as he worked it out of his system on the building site, and he knew that it was only temporary. I don't know how he eventually got this job, but he has the necessary knowledge and qualifications. Sally has got a job as a secretary for Costains, and Stuart's firm is working in conjunction with Costains, and Sally has to take the minutes of the meetings where Stuart is. They both said they feel like giggling. That's the soft sort of pair they are.

Pucci slept until 5 this morning, and it was only because I went to the bathroom and creaked the door that he woke up. After about 10 mins, he was so noisy that I had to go down to him. I gave him some breakfast and a new hot water bottle by which time it was nearly six, and he wouldn't go back to sleep. Richard then came down and sent me upstairs, and he put Pucci in his basket, and everytime he got out of his basket he smacked him with a rolled newspaper. Richard then came to the bottom of the stairs and Pucci followed, but Richard turned round and raised the paper and Pucci belted back across the floor and into his basket, and there he stayed quietly until 7 o'clock. Richard says that Pucci must associate making a noise in the night with a rolled newspaper on his backside.

I am now going to do Pucci's bottle and walk him around the terrace and leave Richard to see him to sleep with the help of a newspaper, although I hope it won't be necessary.

I'm reading at the moment 'Memoirs of a Dutiful Daughter' by Simone de Beauvoir, which had extracts printed in one of the Sunday papers. It is well written and would perhaps appeal to you, but would be a bit too sniff-making for Daddy. It's only a new book, but is very worn and has been well read. The library is now giving four tickets for 25/-. Richard and I both have two each, and Richard only uses one, so I get four new tickets this week and rolled home on Saturday, with seven books! Can you imagine how much sewing I've done since then!

Times of Zambia

July 16th   **Two lions believed to be part of a pride, which has been killing cattle east of Lusaka, have been seen in Leopard's Hill Road.**

> The Chairman of Anglo American Corporation said the group was facing considerable difficulties because of increasing Zambianisation. "But it is going better than perhaps one might have feared.

July 17th The Minister of Labour Munu Sipalo said people did not want to wait until they were 60 for their retirement benefits. This Bill would give them a chance to buy a store or a farm before they were too old.

July 19th Zambia is commodity starved says CB trader group CBC. As a result of UDI, the traditional routes through Beira and Laurenco Marques were severely restricted.

Letter 42   19-7-67

Wednesday evening. I am sitting here by the fire. There is a howling gale at the back of the chair. On writing that, I realised that the draught was coming down the stairs. No wonder. The spare bedroom door was wide open and so were all the windows. You can see how lovely and warm it has been all day. The days are not always sunny – just warm and overcast. In the mornings on my way to work, there is always a heavy mist over the bush at the edge of the road. I go down a diversion to work as the main road is being repaired. It once had a row of trees down the centre but these have all been chopped down to widen the road and make parking space – it happens even here. However the centre island is to be planted with bushes and trees. The road I go along is an African shopping area. The shops are all run by Indians and are very seedy, like the outskirts of Liverpool combined with a Western town – you know the sort of thing, wooden frontages and platforms to the shops above the level of the dust. There is a bar, a market hall, quite new but shabby as the whitewashed walls are discoloured, and the bus station where hoards of people wait with a varied assortment of luggage. In fact they all look as though they are camping out. It's always very lively with plenty of colour, but I must remember to keep my eye on the road.

Richard is at present at the table balancing some sort of ledger. It is the end of the quarter and his time for working late, although it wasn't as bad as last quarter when he sometimes worked until 7.30ish. He gets home around 6.30, so I have had time to do a bit more cooking for the evening. Monday, a casserole, Tuesday steak and kidney pie (with fillet steak – what sacrilege!) and tonight I did pancakes and left them in the oven. I had no lemon, but someone at the tennis club gave Richard two limes. From pictures on fruit pastilles, I always thought limes were small, but they are the size of two grapefruit and the same shape and colour as lemons. We decided to slice these with our pancakes, but they taste so much like lemons, I think someone was pulling his leg, but they are so huge for lemons. Anyway, they served the purpose. Last week, I bought a lemon, only to slice it and find it was an orange!

Andres burnt the iron today. Last week Richard returned the firm's iron, which they lent us, and bought a new larger one for 30/- (at a third off from a wholesaler). Goodness knows how long Andres had had it on because the handle had melted and the house stank. He must have been outside on the step sunbathing. I didn't realise it was so bad until Richard showed me after examining it. The iron isn't a week old yet. My iron is upstairs in the packing chest and I have used it myself but have no intention of letting Andres use it. He can carry on with the burnt one.

The post is a bit cock-eyed at the moment as the VC10s are coming in at all times. There has been no mail, so I hope it will come as usual tomorrow. The planes are not allowed to fly over the Middle East or the Congo, so planes are making a 2,000 mile !!!!! detour via Persia!

I saw my first American missionary this week – what a weed. He was in the office paying the Mission gas bill. However, they fill the gap in education and training that the government cannot provide, but often they are troublemakers, so I have been told.

I was telling the girls, that I stuffed Pucci's pillow with stockings, and they all came out with what they used stockings for. Two of the most interesting were to save them as bandage coverings for the leprosariums.

They are put on as stockings or over arms to keep dressings cleaner longer, the other was to send them to the wildlife people. When Kariba Dam was built and all the animals rescued, the nylons were made into ropes to bind the animals' feet. They were as strong, but did less damage than rope.

Times of Zambia

July 20th   Shebeen queens continue to brew beer for illegal sales. Mounted police destroyed eight gallons of a local brew "nibote"or honey beer, which sold for 10/- a gallon.

July 21st   Typhoid hits Fort Roseberry. Thirty to forty cases were evacuated to Lusaka Hospital. There was an outbreak of rabies at the same township and police had shot one hundred and sixty dogs in two days.

Chapter 15   Sculpting

Letter 43   25/7/67

I'm writing this letter in a mad rush on Tuesday morning at work to catch the mid day post. Last night we went to John and Sue's farewell cocktail party, which was supposed to last from 6.30 to 8.30 but we didn't leave until 10. Marlene and Peter came back to us for coffee as they said it wasn't worth having a babysitter if they were to go home early and we chatted away until 12. We left Pucci in the house just after 6.30 and went through his bedtime procedure and every hour we popped out of Sue's French window and along to ours to listen and there wasn't a peep although he was very pleased to see us when we came in.

I took him to the vet yesterday to see about his injections. There was the vet with his African assistant and his three children, one of whom made out the cards and acted as receptionist while the other two, wearing bush hats, just cooed over Pucci. The young girl wrote on his card. Pucci Maltese Lapthorne d/birth May 67. The vet said it was OK to spoil Pucci and it was better to keep him in the bedroom rather than have him hysterical downstairs, as he is only a baby. So this morning, as he had slept until 6 without crying and had been very good in the evening we plonked him on the end of the bed where he curled up and slept until seven.

Ann and I lost our finals 6.0 6.3 but at least we won three. After tennis we had an Indian stew and a choice of three puddings for 3/-.

I was thrilled with your photos of Joan and Jill in your garden. The things that made me homesick were the mugs of coffee on the plastic tray and Dad's wonderful weeding stool thing. The new fence looks good. You look very suave, Daddy, leaning on it in that way. That's what I call confidence in your own work.

I was called into the accountant's office on Friday and told that my rise after three month's service had come through and that I had been put forward for an increase to £90.00 per month. I started on £75. I'm thrilled to pieces. I never thought I should break the £1000 a year mark. It's £1,080 actually... I was going to finish work well before I came home, but this is too good an opportunity to miss as my cheque goes straight home untouched, so if I work for a full year or more. Wow! But we have a £750 company loan outstanding for the car, to be paid by March, so most will be swallowed by that.

On Friday I saw a pair of pale mustard trousers with tiny flowers on them. Vivienne told me at the beginning the week that the shop had trousers in, so by Thursday I had persuaded Richard to let me have them. They were £5-7-6d and although not very good quality were unusual without being too mod. On Thursday, Vivienne and I went to the shop and saw them and I liked them so on Friday lunchtime Richard forked out and I went at 4.30 to buy them only to find that they had been sold. I was very disappointed. The saleswoman wanted me to buy a purple flowery pair, which weren't, I'm afraid, me at all. Anyway the weather is warming up so there will be no point in buying any when the next lot come in.

Letter No. 44   27.7.67

John and Sue left today at 6 o'clock. I went in at lunchtime and their house was chaotic, with last minute packing. They left here at 5 and I went to the airport at 5.30 and they had just gone through Customs. They took Herb with them hidden under Sue's coat in a tiny cage. There are no restrictions but the customs here can be a funny lot. Anyway Sue spotted me on the other side of the fence and we shouted cheerio. I shall miss her popping in and out. We often had coffee together after work, and we four were always first at tennis. However, we are friendlier with Sally and Stuart and they are coming on Saturday with Bob and Naomi Dunkerley. They will bring their two little girls with them and they will sleep or play in our bedroom. They live on a farm eight miles from here and two miles from the Congo border. They can't, as you can imagine, get babysitters. They have had a lousy time of it in the past two years. Just after UDI, Naomi's sister and two children happened to be the first European car to arrive accidentally on the scene of a riot outside Kitwe. A petrol tanker had blown up and the Africans said it was European sabotage of Zambian petrol, and they burnt her in her car. The children escaped into the bush. This was the only incident over UDI and the only murder of its kind for ten years, and it just happened to be Naomi's sister. Last year also, Bob's father was murdered by Congolese on a robbing expedition. He had just retired and had sold his farm to move down south, and came back for a week to wind up his affairs. He was one of the sort who has lived here all his life and trusted the Africans and never had his house locked. He was shot with his own shotgun.

The court case only closed last month. The murderers were found because they were wearing his clothes, with his nametags in, and one was caught wearing his hat.

However the Dunkeleys aren't as bitter about Zambia as you would think, but it's because it's the only country they know. Bob has however studied farming in Canada and they are thinking of moving there.

The Youngs are now staying until Christmas. Both they and Norman Ravenscroft said that they wouldn't stay an hour longer than their six month contract. Norman showed us his return ticket last month, but Bill Young just seems to be all wind.

My face has, for some unknown reason, broken out in spots, which I haven't had since I came here. I hadn't realised that my skin has been so good since I came until Sue said, when I moaned about my face, "and your skin is always so lovely" – do you wonder why she was my friend?

Pucci is still not sleeping and we both have rings under our eyes. We tried him on the end of the bed as the vet suggested but he chews your ears when he wakes up, etc and I'm not keen on a dog in the bedroom really, even if he is so small. I woke up to find him looking me in the face, and when I opened my eyes he licked my nose. This was the view I saw!

I have knotted three stockings together and he spends ages dragging it around and chewing the knots. He is OK with the furniture (so far) and chews only what is provided (except shoes & toes & fingers). We put his collar on yesterday for the first time and he went mad trying to get it off. We took it off at bedtime and put it on this morning and he was that miserable and didn't eat his breakfast or lunch. He just lies under the chair crying. It's not tight or too loose and is leather and isn't irritating. He's just a crybaby. Tonight I took it off him because he was so whingey. He is now climbing the stairs. He gets half way and loses his nerve, but if you run up, he runs up too. I went for a bath when I came in from work and usually he just plays downstairs but he now sits in the bathroom and chews the towels or shoes or whatever he can find. He is growing. He was 4lb when we got him. I'll weigh him again sometime when he sits still. He has just dragged my paper hanky from my bag and is shredding it. He also snatches my hanky from my sleeve when I bend down and stroke him, the naughty dog. I tell him he's a bad dog but all he does is look at me or runs and hides under a chair.

When I was combing my hair, he climbed into Richard's wardrobe and dragged out all his shoes. I shouted but he hid under the bed.

Letter 45 30.7.67

Yesterday morning I had my first sculpture lesson. I loved every second of it. On Thursday and Friday, I made a smock, the same pattern as one of my dresses but with darts only on the front so that it would be loose. I wore it over a dress but in the summer I shall have to wear it on its own, which doesn't matter as it just looks like a dress. I arrived at nine o'clock and she explained the basics. I build on a wooden frame – the base and pole are wood surrounded by a halo of lead

However this wobbled after I had been working for ½ an hour and we started again with the lead pressed into shape over the pole and this was steadier.

Richard arrived about 9.45 (he had to go into work) and I was just starting to model from his actual head, when it cracked across the middle and his nose and chin slid down the pole. This was because there had been air trapped behind some clay and the middle had been weak. She thought I would be discouraged but I wasn't. Remember me making umpteen pots in pottery to have them split on firing. So about 10.15 we started again.

Richard sat there while she poked his face saying – 'see this broad plane, and these subtle depressions' but he suffered in silence. Anyway, we were working in a beautiful garden and he was sitting on a deck chair; they also had a circular swimming pool, with fish painted on the side under the water. They looked very real with the water shimmering.

Our hi-fi arrived on Thursday. Richard ordered it direct from Telefunken. It is a radio and a record player with two speakers and it links with the tape recorder. It's all in teak and most impressive. However we were stung for £46-10-0 duty – a new regulation was brought in <u>after</u> we ordered the stuff; which slapped on extra duty. Also, it is not supplied with a needle. The needle would have been £4 if we had ordered it from Germany but here it is £14-10-0!! However we got discount but even then it was £12. As Richard says, it cost more than his first record player. (Later) Pucci has been out on his lead with me at the boat club. Richard walked ahead and Pucci ran after him and I followed on the other end of the lead. He wasn't as bad as I expected. I sat with the lead on my arm, and except for wanting to chase passers-by, he pottered around within lead's length and every time he got restless, we played with him. I expected him to sit and howl.

Our peculiar neighbours next door saw Pucci on the terrace and encouraged him to climb through to their terrace, and they then invited us over for drinks on their terrace and they were very polished. It must be 'be nice to the neighbours' week. Now the snag is that Pucci can realise he can climb over. It is a wall about the height of a stair with a trellis on top. I will try and put string along the bottom to discourage him. The trellis on the other side is covered with foliage and isn't a problem.

Monday evening. What an afternoon. At lunchtime after being paid Andres announced that he wanted an extra £2.15.0 a month to cover his house rent. Richard explained that he was getting the normal wage for a boy and more than Sue and John's boy who cooked and stayed until 8 or 9. He agreed with this but said that Kaffers (Sue's boy) had no house and therefore no rent. It's the same everywhere isn't it? People with big families wanting more Family Allowance and Tax Relief for something of their own doing. Anyway we offered him an extra pound, which he said was too small. So we told him to leave tonight, as we were not paying him that much extra. This would bring him into the category of a cook, and he only does breakfast and toast, and we have no children and a small house etc. Anyway he decided to leave. Aren't they more trouble than they are worth!

Richard and I went back to work and I was worried leaving him in the house after sacking him and I rang Richard and he agreed that I should go home and lock up the house. Mr Pawson, my boss, said I could go and also bring the dog to the office for the afternoon. When I got home Andres was ironing the weekly wash and there was loads so I cleared away the unfinished ironing and told him he could go home there and then. He then started to do the dishes, so I told him he could leave them (as I had to be back at work) and would he bring his uniform back tomorrow. He carried on wiping the sink and I repeated more slowly, that he was to bring his uniform back. He then said "I stay". I asked him what he meant and he said, "still work, Madame". So I pointed out we were only giving him £1.0.0 extra not £2.15.0 and repeated it a couple of times in pidgin English and he still said he would stay, so I left him to carry on with the dishes but took Pucci to the office in any case, as I had asked and to be on the safe side.

Pucci was so good in the office. I took his blanket, put it by my chair and hooked the loop of his lead under the chair leg. He wandered around sniffing and whimpering for a few seconds, but then spent the afternoon asleep or just sitting on his blanket. I took him outside at tea break and put him on the grass and he obligingly made a puddle and came back to his blanket. Everyone said how good and quiet he was. Little did they know his transformation at night. He travels well now in the car. I stick his basket on the back seat and formerly he used to stand and howl, now he sits and looks out of the window. It is surprising too, how many people speak to you with a dog. Numerous people stop me and ask his name and how old he is and have a pat. Even a little girl in the library with her mother, who could only just walk said, "Hello ickle puppydog." Pucci is very good with children. Whereas he gnaws adult's fingers he lets children poke him and at the most licks them. Isn't that uncanny.

On Saturday, Bob and Naomi and Sally and Stuart came for a meal, which was our most successful yet. I say 'our' because Richard did beef olives which take a lot of preparation and I did cauliflower cheese, fresh peas, croquet potatoes, new potatoes to go with them and I did fruit salad in oranges again but I bought a pineapple and hollowed that out and filled that too with fruit salad which served as seconds. Come to think of it, it wasn't very economical but it went down very well and looked super on a dish surrounded by the oranges. On top I usually put tinned thick cream, but the tin I opened was bad. I panicked for a moment and then made some pineapple instant whip and dolloped that on top with chocolate bits (grit, as Richard calls it) and cherries (recap. Pineapple 3/6, oranges 3/6, bananas 1/-, apples 3/-, tin of peaches 2/9 (cheating, but it adds colour) instant whip 1/3 so that's 15/- divided by 6, that's 2/6 a head, not bad, as I had enough left for Sunday tea for us).

Naomi had put a mattress in the back of the car and made up a bed and her two kids who are about 2 and 4 and a neighbour's little girl of about 5 slept in the back. They slept all evening, but when we came to break up, there was a honk on the horn as the baby had climbed on to the front seat and couldn't climb back into bed. They looked sweet in their pyjamas, all sleepy.

It's Mrs L's birthday on the 12 August and I'm having a terrible job finding a present. I'm trying to buy a brooch, but not having much luck. I know it sounds most un-Christmasy but it looks as though for the dads at least we will be sending a cheque, because what's the point of say, buying a £3.0.0 M&S Jersey here for £6 or £7 plus postage out and the risk of someone at the PO fancying it, I'd rather send the £6 and have you buy <u>two</u> M&S jerseys.

Chapter 16   Cooking

Times of Zambia   August 3rd

Electricity for every home in Ndola is the plan of the City Council. Already in two years more than 2,000 of the 200,000 homes without electricity had been connected.

Letter number 47   6.8.67

Richard and I are cross with Mrs L. From your letter, it seems that Richard is asking Joan to bring things back, but we had a letter from Mrs L, and she said that Joan had offered to take some things back for us, and would we say in our next letter what we wanted taking back. So Richard writes back accordingly, it seems that Mrs L intimated that the suggestion came from Richard. Joan took with her the maximum weight and I knew she couldn't bring anything back. Unaccompanied baggage is very expensive and we couldn't expect Joan to bring anything over. Also, Joan and I talked about this before she left, and we agreed she had enough of her own stuff to try and get through. Please tell Joan that it wasn't our suggestion or she will think us cheeky. I have had two letters from Joan and if she had had room, she would have let me know. I hope Richard suitably reprimands his mother in his letter.

On Friday, I rang Mrs Hall the music teacher and she said she would be delighted to take me and although she mainly did Associated Board Exams, she could put me through Trinity if I wished. She sounded just like Joyce Grenfell, and was very enthusiastic. However, she is going to England for three months and will be back in October, so this is not a snag, as it will give me more time to get a piano

Flour came in this week, after being out for about three weeks. I was OK, as I had about 6lb in. Two of Mrs Cross's friends both dashed around with flour they had bought and Mrs Cross had also bought some, so she did a pile of baking. I popped in from work and was there with

Pucci until six! As she kept pressing me to have more tea and more cake and mince pies, which of course I didn't refuse, particularly after my dismal baking efforts. My sponge cake continues to be a success. Last night I made a chocolate one and some scones and the scones were a flop once more, and I altered the recipe by adding more baking powder. How do you make yours? Also, I want the recipe for Eccles cakes and your maltless malt loaf, as I have a bread tin and would like to try it.

We went to the pictures on Friday night for the first time since we have had Pucci. We saw In Like Flint, which was a skit on Bond and it came off – it was clever and just as spectacular and as fabulous as a Bond film, but it exaggerated the hero's powers. We enjoyed it and when we came home Pucci was quiet. Richard put him in his basket and we left a light on and food and biscuits and a hot water bottle and he had apparently played on his own as his toys were all over the floor. But was he pleased to see us. He climbed all over us licking and tail wagging. If the film had been lousy, I would have felt mean leaving him, but he was used to us going out and I think he must only cry when he knows we are upstairs.

This morning was a Bank Holiday Monday. I sewed from 8 until 11am. It was one of the dresses I had started at home. It's an awful pattern. It has three pieces at the front and one at the back and bound buttonholes down the back and on the sleeves and pockets. I've had two or three sittings at it and have just got the sleeves and cuffs and cuff buttonholes and tidying up to do. I think I shall have to wait until next Bank Holiday to do anymore.

I have another woollen one cut out and two uncut dress lengths, one wool, the other cotton and a skirt length. When I feel the urge for something new, I shall buy a pattern instead of a new dress. I shall try and save them for next year when I will be tired of some of the things I have. I doubt if I will last for two years, though, without anything new.

This afternoon I went to the boat club with Vivienne and her 9-month-old baby Michael. We stopped from about 3 until 4:45 and I was home by 5 to get Richard's supper. He was working all day. Wasn't that crummy. This was the weekend we should have gone to Victoria Falls!

I am enclosing my Friday shopping list. I left my mincer at home, as it was so heavy but there is so much I can't do without it, so I bought another. Your mincer wouldn't work here, as it needs a table to screw on. The one I bought was a sucker type. However as I was finishing the meat for cottage pie at lunchtime it skidded as the cupboard top was wet and smashed my Pyrex measuring jug. My most useful utensil. I measure and mix and do allsorts with it. The glass went all in the meat so I had to waste it and start again. What an expensive lunch! It's not so much that I have to buy another but whether there are others to be bought.

My shopping list this week. *(I had enclosed a till receipt but it was now too faded to be legible)* The jam is tinned M&S jam. The three packets of crackers are because crackers have been out for two weeks. The 11d peas are the 6d size. The total of this was £7.0.5 less 49/6 for the mincer that's roughly £4.10.0. The two 4d spoons were for eggs as Andres melted my two. I also bought 6 packets of seeds for 4/6, 1 doz eggs, 1 bar of chocolate about 13/- that makes £5.3.0 which is about my weekly average for groceries. On top I usually buy something like the mincer, Last week was expensive as we had friends in, the week before I bought 6 glam fruit dishes for 12/-. Remember how I said sets were £5 ish. Well, I found these on a hardware shelf. They are thick and not too attractive but 12/- is different to £5. They are rather like Woollies quality, which, come to think of it, is pretty good now though isn't it? The week before was Pucci's gear and before that I had been buying Prestige baking tins, ordinary ones, not non-stick, as their price is prohibitive but Sue told me to grease them and then put sieved flour over and shake out the surplus. This works fine and is as good as non-stick.

Then there is green veg and fruit – about 15/- a week and potatoes about 9/- two to three weeks (wholesale) and meat about £2 to £2.10. You will note I haven't bought sugar or tea or fruit. I have enough sugar and tea (stockpiled) and tinned fruit is out at the moment. With petrol and pictures and tennis and soft drinks we easily get rid of £15 a week, but our car insurance is £100 a year and electricity is £5-£6 a month (with no heat, just light and water and stove and fridge). If I wasn't working we wouldn't be able to save anything to come home. Any spare of Richard's is going towards a piano, which I am looking for avidly in the paper each day.

Times of Zambia   August 9th.

> Civil servants who did not develop a sufficient sense of urgency would have to be replaced by people who did, said the Minister of State for Western province.

Letter 48   7.8.67

We are going to the pictures tomorrow to see the Pumpkin Eater, which we have already seen two years ago, but which I thought was tremendous.

As Pucci's tray was unsuccessful, I have one of the tea chest lids and have bound the edges with sellotape where they were rough and will try and get him to use this. He is OK when we are in, as he goes and sits by the door, but at night he makes puddles all over the place.

I have just now spotted a pool by his basket but when I went to investigate his hot water bottle had leaked and his blanket and basket are soaked. I have hung the blanket over the stepladders on the patio (out of view of the road as it's miles to the washing line and at this time of night with no boys around and therefore no one to keep an eye on the lines, it could get swiped. Pucci is now lying on the lid chewing the sellotape. That's not at all what he is supposed to do. The flowers that I have planted in my boxes are portulaca, pansies, primula and zinnias all straight from the packets into the soil. They will probably all choke on one another as I threw the seeds between existing plants but pansies and zinnias are hardy enough. I've never heard of porttulaca that's why I bought them. I've also bought aquilegia as they were so pretty and I'm going to rear these in a pot, if I can get hold of a pot.

There is a strong wind blowing at the moment. A day or two ago I was passing down the road on the edge of the bush going to work and a miniature whirlwind passed across the road in front of me. It was the classic shape and about six feet across and twenty odd feet high. It was higher than the trees. It was completely red dust and leaves. What surprised me was its perfect shape, just as in illustrations. Yesterday I hit a smaller column, less well formed about ten feet high. It felt just like a sudden gust of wind, but the car swerved.

Today an African turned right on a bicycle in front of me. Luckily I was going between 20 and 25. I slammed on my brake and stopped in about six feet, screeching and squealing. I was about two feet from him. The brakes startled him and he overbalanced and stumbled off. He then pushed his bike to the other side of the road to the bar, while I started up again. Had he been European I would have got out and yelled at him, but as he was African I did not as here, it seems, the African is always right, and as there were other Africans around I just went on. Africans have been known to mob drivers in accidents and police arrive anything up to half an hour after an incident. Wasn't it a good job I was going slowly and that nothing going faster was behind me. I had slowed down because cyclists swerve a lot. Usually you can tell they are turning right because they look around, but sometimes as this chap did, they just turn the handlebars. I am always wary of them and pass as wide and as slowly as conditions permit. Cookie in our office was 6' behind a lorry at a Halt sign and all of a sudden it backed straight into her. The driver got out and apologised and gave his firm's name and phone number and cleared off. Cookie went and reported the accident to the police. When she rang the firm, and spoke to the firm manager, he asked her if she was paying for the damage to the truck as she had run into the back of the lorry and he wouldn't listen to her story. When she came off the phone she was most upset. The fellow had said that as there were no witnesses, it was her word against the driver's, and Cookie said it looked bad, as it was far more believable that she had run into him. Anyway, the next day she sat at the halt sign and lucky for her, the African who was behind her at the Halt sign came along and she flagged him down. She asked him if he saw what happened and he said "Yes, the chap backed right into you". Phew, relief and he is something at the council and therefore a reliable witness.

Our double bed arrived yesterday. Someone else had had it before us and it wasn't new like our twin beds, and although 5' it looked so small! The previous bed was huge as it was the two single ones together. However, it is very comfortable and we can at last fit the headboard to the side tables. The bedding fits better and we both have enough blanket.

I saw a piano advertised in the paper "£25, suitable for a beginner", in other words pretty crummy, but I rang so we could have a look and see what it was like, but it was sold and this was at 10 o'clock this morning. Richard is taking me to see another piano at six, any minute now.

Well, brace yourselves. We have just bought a £55 piano. We intended to pay up to £65. There is nothing wrong with it that a good tune won't put right. Isn't it a terrible price though! However, this is average, and you can understand the cost of shipping pianos out here. The piano is not as high as mine, the tone is thinner, and there are three notes not sounding, but these can be tuned, as I could see nothing actually wrong with it. The tone is clear, and will be adequate to practice on. Pianos go out of tune very quickly here with the heat and humidity. One consolation, as there is such a demand, we will be able to sell it for roughly the same price. Even if we don't, what we lose will be less than the cost of hiring one. Do I sound as though I'm trying to justify spending so much? I am! I'm trying to ease my conscience. It will be lovely being able to play again. I haven't played for nearly eight months!

The little girl whose piano it was, had been taught by Mrs Hall and won a cup at the convent for her exam results and says Mrs Hall is "a super teacher – she's lovely", so she sounds fine.

The piano is ornate but is a light mottled wood and not heavy looking, so it won't darken the room. The keys are white and not yellowed, surprisingly. But my piano at home has a beautiful tone, and I have been spoilt with it. It is even better than Miss Adamson's grand. *(My old piano teacher)*

Just had a note from mother-in-law to say you will post our things. <u>No!!</u> You must not send them. We only wanted them if Joan had room. The risk of loss and the expense is far too great. And we do have adequate warm clothing. Many thanks for the thought, but please don't send them; I'll have something different to wear when I get home then.

Times of Zambia   August 10th

The Reverend Ben Zulu has been appointed Manager of The Broadway Cinema, Ndola, completing the Zambianisation of the cinema. Other posts such as cashiers, ushers and projection officers have long been Zambianised.

Letter 49   13.8.67

We went to see Genghis Khan last night, an epic, which wasn't too good. All blood and battles and not much else, except huge cardboard sets.

We have cancelled the piano! The following day, we went to see some in an auction room (Richard was in town, so my boss, Pawson, let me off to go and have a quick look, as the girls had said there were three in the auction room). When we got there, it was like that Irish second hand dealer's by Birkenhead market. One piano was in pieces, one was up for £15 but the girl said it was only worth £5 (and it was) and a baby grand for £150. The tone on this was lovely and by Ndola standards was good for £150, it was a pity we had neither money nor space for it, but it showed that there were better buys to be had, so when we got back, he rang and told the woman we had seen a better one and had decided to wait until we could get one of better quality, which she accepted.

Mrs King, in the office asked whom we were buying it from and when I told her she nearly fell off her chair. When she came from Rhodesia, just after UDI, their removal van was blown up and all her furniture burnt, so she went to the same woman who was advertising furniture for sale. This woman wanted £125 for a double bed and dressing table. They were big and dark and old too! She also wanted £115 for a large but chipped fridge! Mrs King bought a smaller but new one for less. The woman buys up departing ex.pats furniture. So it looks as though we were nearly had. Not knowing the prices here, we are wide open to sharks. What a narrow escape! I hope we don't have to wait so very long for another.

I have put away until Friday (Richard's pay day) three paperbacks 9/-, 11/- and 24/9. The 9/- is a 7/6 Penguin and the other two are larger with maps. They are all about Africa, geographically, economically and politically. One is about the whole of Africa, the other this area, and the third is on the break-up of the federation.

On Friday, Vivienne was going to the dentist and Pawson said I was to wait with her, as she was scared. Some boss! Last time she had all her back teeth out in hospital, and this time was a right bag of nerves. The dentist's is on the far side of town by a bookshop, which is only open office hours and Saturday mornings, so when Vivienne was suffering, I had a lovely browse around the bookshop. I saw these and asked if she would hold them until Friday, which she did. This is normal practice. If you see something, any shop will stick your name on it and even leave it on display, for a while. If I had gone back on Friday and they had gone, they would have taken months to get new ones. I have had a cookery book on order since May-ish. I learnt my lesson with those trousers I went back for, to find them gone.

Jack Pawson, the best boss ever.

Richard is doing the meal tonight. He is making Hungarian goulash. It smells good. We intended having it last night, but we played bowls with Sally and Stuart in the afternoon and they invited us back for dinner and we had steak and salad. Yum, yum. We took Pucci with us, but he was naughty and kept running around and sniffing everywhere.

We went to the library on Saturday morning as usual, and we found the book that I wanted ages ago in the bookshop but was too expensive. It is called "The World of Children" and is chocabloc with tremendous photos of children from all over the world, and articles by famous authors on childhood. All the famous Sunday newspaper photographers had taken the photos, even Snowdon. Richard, found me the cookery book that is on order at the bookshop, and between us we have by far enough reading. The good thing about having four tickets each and the library so close, is that we can pick books just to look at, like flower arrangement books.

People here keep their soap powder and Lux liquid and Vim on the window ledge, and Andre started putting mine up and I dashed in and whipped them off and said "It looks awful from outside, most untidy"! In fact, all the things you shouted at me for doing, I now shout at Richard or Andre or even myself. So things have sunk in at last, so take heart, it only took twenty-three years. I've heard later that the boys like displaying the amount and quality of their cleaning equipment.

Pucci's sleeping better at night. If, as he usually does, he comes upstairs, we take him down and say "stay" and usually at the third time he stays. He may come up about 5 o'clock but we take him down and say "stay" and he does, but about six he comes up and we put him on the end of the bed and he dozes until we get up. He has just finished the most fantastic game. He has been chasing and attacking a tennis ball, and belting around the room like mad, leaping on it and stalking it and growling at it. He took about three drinks of water in between and has just collapsed exhausted at Richard's feet. He made me tired just to watch him.

I was just having another look at the photos. Have you lost weight? You look very trim. I got weighed on the firm's scales in the stores. I am now 117lbs (no stones and lbs) i.e. 8 stone 5lbs, which is just the same as before, so the change of climate hasn't done me any harm, has it? *(8 stone 5 lbs. Oh bliss)*

Letter number 50   15.8.67

Thanks for the newspaper pictures. Hasn't Borough Road altered? Did I tell you that just after they pulled the houses down, I was on the bus and a woman in front of me looked out of the window and said "and to think that I scrubbed that front step for forty years for it to be pulled down".

Today has been dull at work. I have been just adding statements and putting them into envelopes as my own work is clear and the weather is gorgeous. But then I think of my pay and am happy again. I think the weather now is perfect. I have cast off my cardigan and am going to work in my dress. It is warm and very fresh and dewy in the morning, like the start of a "scorcher" and it is a scorcher until now, 5:30ish when it is cool. We have cast off the blanket and it is warm at night.

Pucci was a pest last night, but we realised he is teething! He wouldn't stay downstairs and in the end after taking him down for the umpteenth time we ignored him when we heard him come in and curl up on the rug. But at 4 he woke again and was whimpering and rubbing his mouth on the floor and sucking on his jaw and making funny noises. He slept again but was very miserable. When I looked in his mouth this morning there are white lumps just below the surface of his gums so they must be coming through. Our dog book says that ½ an aspirin is permissible and will help him sleep. It's worse than having a baby in the house.

I have my next art lesson on Saturday and we are having Ravenscrofts and Youngs to dinner in the evening. Norman Ravenscroft's wife arrived for his final month and I would like to invite them, and therefore I must invite Youngs. Mrs Young is a harmless enough body and they haven't been invited out much, so it can't be much fun for her.

Richard has just come in with your Thursday letter, a day early. I know Andres' wages seem poor but we are paying the rate recommended by the Labour Board. On the nights he comes for dinner, we give him overtime. The labourers in Richard's factory get the same and they have trade unions etc. We must do the same as everyone else. Some poor chaps work all hours. Sue's boy, who is working for the new fellow, Jim, does all the shopping and cooking. The thing is I suppose, that as there are so many unemployed the employers can name a price. I know this is all wrong. If wages were compulsorily increased, people would just buy floor polishers and washing machines and the ranks of unemployed would be increased. However, I am no sociologist. I see that poverty and unemployment are wrong, but the country has one heck of a problem. Ignorance is the first. Half of the Africans have no use for money. They live in villages and grow their own food. With education and knowledge comes the need for money. It's a case of spreading knowledge. The labourers in Richard's place don't improve their standard of living with higher wages, just drink more and spend their money on transistors and loud shirts and winkle pickers rather than cabbages and meat and things. They are no different from blokes who give their children money for fish and chips, whether they are on the dole or on £40 a week.

The more I think about it, the more out of perspective it becomes. I think the first thing is to educate this generation of children then I change my mind and think that it is better to educate mothers re malnutrition believing that healthy bodies breed healthy minds. The trouble is that too much is expected too soon. You can't expect to take a primitive people out of the bush and expect after a year or two to have them living a European type existence. The African civilisation is the oldest in the world yet they are still living a stone-age type existence. Yet the European races have forged ahead. This, I think must mean that there is basically something lacking. Adequate nutrition? How two civilisations growing in different parts of the world can grow or advance at different rates to such an extent is extraordinary.

Its more than twelve months since we saw The Birthday Party, and we were going again ever so quickly weren't we. I'm reading the play, "Waiting for Godot", this week. I'd heard a lot about it in the Sunday papers reviews, but it seems at the moment just an excuse to be crude and lewd, just a dirty play. However, as I read on, it may improve, but I should hate to sit in an audience and listen to it – I should find it embarrassing.

Cookie in the office brought in a kitten this morning. She had bought it to console her little girl as their dog was run over, but the other cat was attacking it, so it needed a new home. She found someone to take it, so as her car was in the garage, I ran her home. Her house is beautiful. All open plan with huge plate glass windows. The whole front of the lounge is a sliding glass door onto a patio (a stoep – pronounced stoop). Her bedroom also had a stoep and so did the dining room where they had their braaivleis. The garden was huge and full of flowers and a lawn with banks and hollows in it. The view was across the Dambo looking north i.e. facing the sun. Lovely.

Not only do we have dogs and children in the office but kittens as well! Betty, another woman had a kitten and it had been bitten on the head by a dog. It didn't break the skin, but the kitten hadn't eaten for three days and although it was alive and would stretch, it was otherwise motionless. She brought it in to see the vet, who said that it had bad bruising and concussion and it had damaged its sight, but it was too early to say. Betty is feeding it on her desk through a dropper with milk and egg. It is such a sweet little kitten too.

Times of Zambia

August 14th — **A portrait of Queen Elizabeth of Britain has been removed from an ex servicemen's club because it hangs alongside that of President Kaunda and the club cannot be an "island of colonial practices".**

Upon opening the new Matero Girls' Secondary School, Education Minister said that over half of the girls who had registered initially had to withdraw because of pregnancy and appealed to parents to be more responsible.

Chapter 17   Dog Training

Times of Zambia

August 15th   Drinking Hits Kitwe Literacy Drive. The majority of students were women. The men appeared to be too busy drinking.

August 17th.   The Suez Canal could be open for ships within three months, though it may take a year or so to be fully operational.

Two Lusaka shantytowns with round thatched huts will disappear within two years. Modern houses will be built instead.

Reported cases of TB have trebled.

Letter number 51   21.8.67

I've not had a letter from you this weekend. The fellow who empties the PO Box and brings the post to the tennis club has gone to S. Africa for the week but no-one opened the box in his place and whereas there was mail today there was too much for the box and the rest was on the floor at the back of the post office.

Pucci, as I have probably told you, has taken to coming upstairs at night, so we decided to be strict with him and risk Friday nights sleep for future nights sleep. We blocked the stairs with the tea tables after he refused to stay downstairs and he cried and cried, but not as loud or as much as we expected. He slept until 5 ish and then cried for a bit, got no response and slept 'til dawn, so we tried it last night and Saturday. We give him the chance of staying down and if he comes up more than twice, we block the stairs. Last night he only cried a little bit and then slept until 6:20. This is fine as the alarm goes off at 6:30 and we lie awake until Andre rings the bell.

On Saturday morning we asked Andre for his full name and address. We understood his address "1490 Chifubur". The house number and township, but couldn't decipher his name. Richard gave him the form (a government one) to put in his own name, but Andre can't even write his own name. He then said he would ask Kaffers – next door but one. The name sounds like Potchusimbele, but he came today with his identity card showing Potias Mbewe. Goodness knows were Andre comes in! The form is for a tax, which he himself has to pay, but which we will pay as it will cut down his salary too much. Anyway it's only once a year.

On Saturday morning, we went to Browns, our shop, for eight o'clock and I bought a pair of green and pink flowery trousers! They aren't as nice as the original ones I saw, but I spotted them on Friday and they were my size and the only ones not plain so I bought them £4-7-6! You can tell Richard was paid on Friday! They are only cotton too. Then we went to the bottle store (gosh aren't I slipping into the lingo – it's an off licence) and bought cokes and Lion (the local beer – more a lager) and then we bought some tennis balls for the club, and were at my art lesson for 9 o'clock. Richard's head is now built up and I have to do the features. It doesn't seem to be much progress but after you do the core, and it hardens, the rest must be built up by tiny clay pellets put on with your thumbs, with the completed likeness in mind. Mrs Mills is going on leave at the end of September for 2 months, so I am having two lessons before she goes, and will try and do as much as possible, before she goes.

At 11, after sculpture, we went to the office to pick up the milk and to Marlene's for the meat. It was gorgeous in her garden, roasting hot, so Marlene asked if I would like to sit out in the afternoon. So, Richard and Peter went to tennis and I went to Marlene's. It was a nice change. Sally has a paddling pool (a rubber one) and she sits outside it, puts all her toys in it. At four, I went to the cinema and bought the tickets for the 6 o'clock performance of "Deadlier than the Male". I picked Richard up and we came home to change.

Pucci was funny with Marlene's boxer Pinky, who is a placid old dog. Pinky would sit in the sun and Pucci would dash to about three feet from Pinky and tease her. Barking and dancing backwards and forwards until Pinky chased Pucci round and round the garden. Pucci would then hide under a chair and Pinky would collapse in the shade only to have Pucci come again and nudge her and start all over again.

Anyway, this made Pucci good and tired for when we went out. Tony came just as we were going out to see if we were going to the pictures for the 9 o'clock show, but decided to come along with us to the 6 o'clock. On arriving there we met some friends who had previously bought us coffee, so in the interval which is ludicrously about 15 minutes after the start of the performance and lasts for about 15 minutes, we bought them coffee. We invited Tony back, as I had some sliced ham (big treat) and I did peas and chips and put my hors d'oevres dish out with pickles, chutney, gherkins and tomatoes in salad oil. It's surprising how the little bits and pieces poshed up an ordinary meal. We had fruit and Birds Eye Dream Topping, which is gruesome stuff, and cheese. When Tony had gone I spotted a box of chocs on the fridge. Wasn't that nice. I'm not opening them yet. Let's hope we can get to them before the weevils do.

Sunday morning, Tony had invited Richard to play golf so off they went. In my absence on Saturday, a busybody dear who plays tennis at the club decided that as we were always served last, the tennis section should make their own tea. We are all on a rota together with bowlers and take it in turns to make tea and provide sandwiches, the club providing cake. I've been there 5 months and my turn hasn't cropped up yet, so it's no trouble. All the tennis girls do is collect the trays when it's made, and bring it to the courts, also not much bother. The 6ds we collect goes into one fund. I was given 10/- on arriving to collect Richard on Saturday and asked if I would buy teabags, sugar and milk and start off making the tea on Sunday morning. I agreed, being in a hurry and not thinking much. I was also asked if I would mind keeping the tea and sugar at home.

The tea is normally kept in a locked cupboard at the club, the next person on the rota being given the key. This I didn't fancy as it meant that if I didn't feel like going, as on Sunday, I would still have to appear with the tea and should no one else be willing, have to make it. Even having a rota, I would have to remind the next person, in case I got lumbered. The tea money also buys crockery, so if we split it fully it's only fair for us to buy our own crockery etc. What a storm in a teacup!

Sunday afternoon it was cool, so we stayed in and read and read right though until bedtime. Lovely. (We ate in the middle). A minute ago there was a flutey tune on the radio and Richard started skipping with the dog and I joined in and we skipped round until we were out of breath. The dog was skipping too; we went round and round one after the other. Must be the sun.

The Congo border opened last week and the managers and families of a Lever's company came through and were entertained before being evacuated via Ndola and VC10. We didn't meet them. I would have liked to. Ndola airport is the nearest main airport and the managers here put them up. The Congo managers were concerned that the border should remain open so they could go back, after seeing their families off home.

Richard says that the order of evacuation from a trouble spot is, private firm, the government staff, the army and in the rear, Levers squirting Lux liquid in the faces of the enemies. Richard says that if we were in the Congo, it would be Lapthornes out first.

Times of Zambia   August 18th

*   Rationing of regular petrol is over. Premium and Diesel will continue.

*   **The Ministry of Natural Resources and Tourism have declared that jackets and ties need no longer be compulsory in hotels**

Letter 52   23.8.67

I was doing a crossword in the office yesterday and wasn't doing very well. I didn't have a "Thinker" that's what it was. *Dad had stubby pencils and always had one behind his ear when doing the crossword or DIY. These were 'thinkers" as he reckoned he couldn't think without them. He was buried with a supply.*

Re my shopping list – the cauliflower is frozen not fresh. Fresh are 3/6 each and you need two, as they are only as big as your fist.

You also asked if I'd finished my dress. I finished my smock for art, but not my dress. It had an awful yoke and bound buttonholes and buttonholes on the sleeves. Sally is using my machine to reinforce her curtains as the poor girl made them all by hand when she came and they are now feeling strained around the Rufflette tape.

I'm reading a thick book called Fame is the Spur by Howard Spring about a boy from the slums of Manchester who grows up to be a famous then disillusioned MP. It's also about the birth of the Labour Party. It brings in people like Engels and Keir Hardy as characters and it is difficult to know how much is fiction and whether any is fact other than the vague outlines, so I'll have to get a book like your "50 Years March, The Rise of the Labour Party" but I suppose with Richard around, I'll have to put a paper back on it. Poor Richard. I think I have adapted better than he has. He is so English and comes in for a lot of ribbing. It is easier for me, working amongst the local girls. I try not to mention the high cost of living and how much better England is and am accepted as "one of them". In fact, Vivienne is so friendly that I'm almost glad she's leaving. I don't mind being friendly with anyone but the chummy "best friend" type of thing makes me shudder. I like Marlene and going there as we both lounge in chairs with our books and mags and papers and hardly utter a word except "Listen to this", "Look at this". "Yes thanks I'd love a drink of coke". Exchanging confidences is not my line. That's why I like Joan W at home. We were always disagreeing about education and social services and corporal punishment, things that we knew little about but I prefer a friendship with a bit of spirit to it. To enlarge on Vivienne, she is full of "Try my lipstick, these shoes would suit you, let me do your hair nicely". Etc. It's odd to think she's married with a baby 10 months. She is however very sweet and thoughtful. Maybe if I had not been an only child, I might be more comfortable with sisterly behaviour. I find the girls on the whole very nice and friendly but have been educated differently. I think I've mentioned that none had read Wuthering Heights or heard of Yehuedi Menuhin. But what relevance would such stuff be. Life revolves around the TV. All the children have modern names. Margie's baby is Michelle Yvette and Vivenne's is

Michael Heath; a Damien and Samantha and such like names abound. Can you imagine when I said I liked Kate and Emma and Catherine? How old fashioned they thought me!

I'm drying my hair at the moment and Rich is too! He had his cut today and I could have cried when I saw him. He's not had it cut for ages and it was gorgeous and curly and long to his collar and boy, has the barber shorn him. He looks awful. I hope it will grow quickly. He has given up half way with his letter. He also has trouble on Wednesdays. He is now examining the dog's gums for new "toofipegs" and said "I just can't wait for him to talk". I suppose we do treat him as the baby in the family. After all he's only 12 weeks old.

Times of Zambia   August 23rd

*   Since the new Nakaputa cemetery was opened, residents have complained that it is against Zambian custom to take coffins through a township or let children watch burial ceremonies.

*   A State House spokesman denies Salisbury's allegation that Zambia was harbouring freedom fighters and was actively encouraging and helping their incursions into Rhodesia.

Letter 53   27.8.67

Norman Ravenscroft and his wife came on Saturday for dinner. Mrs Young was ill again and so they didn't come but Alan Williams, the fellow living with Norman came instead! The meat was tough again but the rest of the meal was OK, although Alan said that they had had beef olives in the army to use up the leftovers!

We've had a lovely lazy day today. We slept until 10. We didn't go to bed last night until way after 12 and the dog woke us up at six and I pushed him outside and he then played noisily in the bedroom for half an hour and he must have fallen asleep on the rug as when we woke at 10 o'clock he was still asleep. We had some toast and coffee and popped along to the tennis club but there was no mail for us in the UK stuff! So we came back. I made an apple pie yesterday and we had that for our lunch and had our main meal tonight, which, was mainly leftovers from last night. I roasted some beef, but there was half a casserole of cauliflower cheese left over and I made a ring of mashed potatoes (I sieve it and then cook it with an egg – takes hours) and filled the centre with peas. We heated all this up again. I hate wasting stuff like that. Pucci had mince and cauliflower cheese.

I felt clever yesterday as Richard had fitted an immobiliser to my car and I couldn't switch it off so I disconnected the immobiliser's wires from the coil and the distributor and hooked the correct wires back. Andre was most impressed

Yesterday I shampooed my carpet with Surf and Sanpic. Richard went out at 7:30 to play golf and as Andre arrives at 7:30 I had to get up so after my breakfast I rolled up the carpet and Andre and I rolled it out <u>in front</u> of the house and I got cracking. I didn't allow Andre to wash it as I only used the suds and he would probably have soaked it. I expected the woman next door to come over and complain but she didn't and it was too early for many people to be out. It was dry and back in the house by the time Andre had polished the floor. I am hoping Pucci will make more puddles outside and that the Sanpic smell of the carpet will discourage him. Actually two out of three puddles are now outside and all his mess, and all his "accidents" are by the door, when I have failed to open the door or when it has swung to.

I have read another Howard Spring book today called "A Sunset Touch". I enjoyed it although it is not a taxing read. I like his style of writing. My knowledge of Africa from my books isn't coming along too well. They are so crammed with facts that I'm having trouble sorting them out, and they are out of date.

I can find little about the origins of Ndola, Daddy. Ndola originally was a couple of miles from here so perhaps that is why. I'll still ask around. On my way to work is the slave tree, a huge tree whose roots start a good way up, and here it was that the slave buyers did their dealings from the north. I thought what a funny tree it was and knew which one it was as soon as I was told about it. . *(I glean from Mary E Fuller's Travel guide to Zambia that the Slave Tree was a mahogany tree, Afzelia quanzensis, at the end of Makoli Avenue Ndola and shaded a stockade where Swahili slave traders conducted their business. Ndola started off as a trading post for the Copperbelt.)*

Apparently that Mrs Williams, the local councillor who visited, wrote an article for the Bebington News on her visit to Levers, Zambia and said she was pleased that so many remembered her from when she was Mayoress! No one knew her from Adam!

Oh Mummy – how can you ask if Richard received his shirt. I'm sure I thanked you as soon as it came, and I'm sure too, that I mentioned in a later letter that it was never off his back at the weekend. Please skim back over my letters. We were so pleased with it that I'm positive I have thanked you. But if not, and I hope it isn't the case, I assure you it arrived safely and that Richard is delighted with it.

Doodle is OK, but hates the mosquitoes in the bedroom and hates the fly spray even more.

Times of Zambia   August 29th

Stricter Dress in Hotels, appeals the spokesman for the Hotel and Catering Worker's Union, referring to reports of teenagers rampaging through Ndola's Savoy Hotel, smashing glasses and beating up staff. He said that members could be protected by admitting only gentlemen who wore ties and jackets or national dress.

Letter number 54   30.8.67

Well, quite a hectic day. I rang the airport at 11 and the plane Joan was arriving on was on time, so at 12, Margie and I went off to the airport to be told by Joan's mum that the plane was only arriving at 12:45 not 12:05, so back we went to town. As our lunch hour is from 12:45 to 1:45, at 12:45 I rang again and was told the plane was due in, in three minutes, so Margie, Vivienne and I dashed back to the airport (in my car) and the VC10 was coming in on top of us. It looked marvellous. We met up again with Joan's mum and clung to the netting around the airport. Joan was one of the last to come off and the excitement – "There she is in the blue", "No, that's her in the red" etc. We waited an hour and quarter until 2 o'clock but then decided that we ought to go back to the office. Apparently Joan got out of customs at three – more than 2 hours!

After work, at Joan's mum's suggestion, we went up to Joan's. First we went to Margie's and picked up her daughter, Michelle and sent her nanny and boy home and then to Vivienne's crèche and picked up Michael and then to our house to send Andre home and pick up Pucci. What a carload! Three adults, two babies and a dog.

Joan was in with just her Mum and Dad. Her boyfriend had just left her and her Mum went into town so on the arrival of two more friends, we had a look at all Joan's new dresses. Some of them are super. Then to my embarrassment she hauls out half a dozen or so of Richard's shirts. I'm so cross with Mrs L. After Richard writing too. Not only that, but he has plenty of shirts still unopened. I can't understand it and neither can Richard. The only shirts he mentioned were his Bri-Nylon ones (the light jerseys) and she must have been confused. But one was past it. It had paint all over it and I had already turned the collar and cuffs. I felt awful. Joan said she didn't mind bringing them. I'll take her a box of chocs or something. Luckily, although Joan's things were overweight, the customs bloke let her off. She said that she had messages from you, but she couldn't remember them all, and said she would pop over when she got herself all sorted out. As you can imagine, she was still all of a dither.

We stayed until six then I came home and dropped the dog with Richard who was cooking our tea! I then ran the girls home and have just got in. We have just had a storm and have had thunder and some <u>rain</u>! It is very sultry out and what with that and the dashing around, I have a lovely headache.

Still nothing from Joan Wilson! *(my best friend)* It's nearly four months since I heard from her.

We had cakes at work today. Yum, yum. Not as nice as Sayers, but cakes nevertheless and one's taste adjusts anyway. I found a huge live maggot in my flour and I just picked it out and carried on sieving.

Richard has told his mother that I am taking my A levels. As Richard always jumps the gun, this isn't yet so. I've got all the gear from the Metropolitan Correspondence College in London, and have now sent for the overseas syllabus from London University who can tell me what syllabus can be taken in which country and at what time, so you can see I'm a long way from studying yet. If I get the two I want, English and

Geography I may be able to get a better job when I get back, as I couldn't face a basic clerical job, especially after doing what I have been doing (a dead easy but boring job) for the pay I have been getting. But that's a long way off. Coming home isn't so far off now. Six months gone on Saturday. Only eighteen to go.

Pucci was still awake at 11:15 after going to bed at 10 and he was whimpering and crying. I came down and gave him a Disprin in jam, and as Richard said, he wasn't to come upstairs; I stayed with him until nearly 12 when he dozed off. I tiptoed upstairs but he started off again. Richard gave in and we brought him upstairs and he slept until 6:30 under the bed, when the alarm woke him. It must be his teeth because he has been no trouble

Times of Zambia

August 31st   KK addressing UNIP said he was deeply hurt by what had happened at the Mulungushi conference. "I must admit publicly that I have never experienced in the life of this young country, such a spate of hate based entirely on tribe, province, race, colour and religion, which is the negation of all that we stand for in this party and government."

Chapter 18 Office dresses

Letter 55   3.9.67

Six months completed this weekend

Yesterday we hired a projector for 12/6 and fortunately it was a Eumig like mine, only a good bit more antiquated. As they gave no instruction booklet it was just as well I was familiar with it, as the frame switch needed a twiddle. I had three films and I have joined them all on to one reel. I have spliced them together but have left the leader on so there are two white gaps. We also made a commentary on the second side of our letter tape. It is quite tricky playing it back trying to synchro it but if the film was a second ahead of the commentary we switched the projector off for a second and then switched it on. On the tape we say, "switch on now" but I will put a note in the box about operating it. The films are a little bit bitty so the commentary is useful even if not synchronised. Anyway Daddy I'm sure you'll enjoy fiddling with them. We had fun doing them last night. On the whole I think you find the films interesting, as the surroundings are so unusual - and the drive in the storm turned out well too. It lasts for just over 12 minutes.

On Saturday, I went to Marlene's in the afternoon to lounge in her garden and took Pucci, who slept in the shade in the soil under a bush, instead of making the most of the space, although he did have a belt around, but it was too scorching hot. We had ice cream milk shakes and I took along some sponge cake.

On Thursday I decided to do a flan, a normal sponge and put raspberries and jelly and cream on top. Richard said he had seen a good recipe for a chocolate flan with mousse inside. I said I would try one but it came out like a brick. He insisted it looked good and so we decided to do our chosen recipes each. I measured his flour and stuff and got on with mine. I was beating and getting air bubbles in and stuck it in the oven. Richard was stirring his cement mixture like porridge. Mine came out quite normally but it broke in half coming out of the tin. I pieced it together and put Richard's cake in the oven and much to my chagrin, his came out beautifully, it had risen to twice the size of mine and fell out of the tin. We then proceeded to make our respective jellies. Richard put ice cubes in instead of water and I told him not to be so daft, but his jelly set in about ½ an hour and mine hadn't set next morning and I had to put another jelly in it. Richard whipped his up with cream and poured it into the flan. While I was making fresh jelly, he was decorating his flan. Even that was nice, chocolate grit one way and cherries the other. I was putting blobs of cream on mine and one blob ran into another and I had to cover the whole top with cream, like trifle.

We went to Marlene's at 10ish after shopping and had coffee, but the butcher had delivered the wrong meat order, so as the order we had seemed to be stewing steak and dog bones, we decided to take it back to Marsala. This is the African township where the butcher is. I didn't really fancy it, but Richard had been before and it was only a road or so inside the township.

Anyway, it wasn't half as seedy as I had imagined. The houses are all something like this rather like prefabs and are row upon row like this

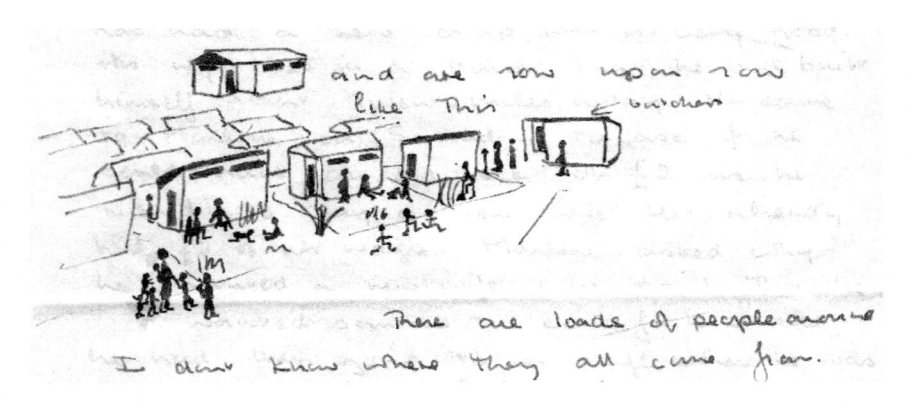

There are loads of people around. I don't know where they all come from. A lot seem to be making social calls as they sit very formally on straight chairs outside their houses. The piccanins run alongside the car. When Richard went into the butcher's, he locked me in the car, but there was no need as no one took much notice. Some piccanins peered in the window but only to look at Pucci not at me.

You will see from the managers' list that some of the African managers live there. Although their wages are good, they prefer to live here and run brand new cars. One, Richard says, has a new Viva!

I must tell you the tale of Marlene's new domestic. Banda has gone back home, so for a few weeks now Marlene has had a new chap, who is very good. His wife lives in a house that he has built himself about twenty miles away. He came to Marlene on Saturday to ask if he could have an advance of £2 as he wished to buy a new wife. He had already had £2 of his wages. Marlene asked why he wanted a new wife and he said that he wanted someone to cook for him and he had been going to a café where he was charged 3/- a day for mealie porridge. His own wife didn't want to leave home. Marlene offered to let him have food from the house that they themselves were eating, but he said he couldn't eat their food, as he needed mealie to make him strong. Marlene asked if there were any children (as Sally played in the khia with Banda's baby, and it's not the healthiest of places to play) and he said there was only one baby, a tiny one. So, at lunchtime on Saturday, a chap arrives at Marlene's with a bicycle and loans it to her new chap who rides off. I would have loved to have been there on the return of the procession. The fellow would ride the bike while wife followed with the baby on her back, her luggage on her head (even a mattress if she had one) or if she had no luggage, she would ride on the cross bar. Marlene pities the new wife, as there is only a mattress and chair for furniture in the khia, as the chap's furniture is with his chief wife.

All the girls in the office are getting new dresses in October, but I miss out, as mine have been bought recently. I will have to wait until next October. I was the last to get the old style. The three who joined after me haven't got uniforms yet so will get the new style which will probably be flowery. I told Mr. Pawson that I was sulking and that it would be his own fault when next year people said, See that shabby girl there, the poor thing works for Zambia Oxygen, that's one of their uniforms", so he asked me how long I'd had mine and if I was the only one who didn't qualify, so I'm keeping my fingers crossed. If I still don't qualify, I'll have them made anyway with the rest, as they will be about the £3 mark, and if they are invoiced together, they might not have the heart to charge me. I'm not complaining really, as I do very well and it's only four months ago that they forked out £10 for the dresses I have now.

Joan popped in to the office again. She is now missing Liverpool! She is going to save to go away again, as she now says she is sorry she didn't stay longer! I told her it was very well to talk bravely when she is back home again.

Times of Zambia

September 1st 1967

*   Railman, listed as British Resident, accused of Spying for Rhodesia.

*   First Export Elephants Fly Out. Two baby elephants captured in Zambezi River Valley will go to New York Zoo and two caught in the Luangwa Valley would go to London. The game department said it was intending to export fifty to seventy baby elephants a year.

Letter number 56   6.9.67

We just have Radio South Africa News on. We also have on during the evening, Radio Rhodesia and Zambia News so you can imagine that we get a full or at least varied picture of the border skirmishes, and the variety of figures of the numbers injured on both sides.

We pick out the plays if we can, sometimes reception is stormy - we still haven't an aerial. Zambia has a lot of BBC quizzes with Dennis Norden and Frank Muir and its nice to hear familiar programmes. Rhodesia and SA have reasonable plays, but they vary as can be expected. They have American plays, which are rather like TV series quality, full of corny emotion and elementary psychology. The thrillers and mysteries are best even if they do have the same actors week after week. RBC, which is on now, has some music called Dinner Music. It's 7:20. Richard has come in late and as compensation is making the tea. It's worth a grumble. I didn't like him having to work too late as we don't finish eating until after eight and the evening is gone. I can't start anything much before dinner as I'm waiting for him to come in.

Although you say Joan was excited to be going home, she is having trouble getting a machinist job and says she wishes she were back in Liverpool! She's also gone off her boyfriend.

Our iron has broken. I took it in to where we bought it and he said the element had gone and it would cost too much to replace it, so Richard went and bought a new one. We intended getting another cheap one but the man said that a thermostat was much better as overheating was the main trouble, so instead of a 35/- one, we bought a £4/10/- one. We then spent our lunch hour explaining to Andres how to use it.

We had the dial on cool and said "Cold" and then as we turned it round we said, "Here hot, here hot, hot, here hot, hot, hot". Then the light - "Look Andres, light gone, now ready, now hot". We then switched it off, and all stood watching it until the light went out and shouted altogether in jubilation when it did and all made frantic ironing motions as "iron ready". What a pantomime.

We are going to Marlene's for a meal on Friday. Peter's passport has expired and he sent it to Lusaka for renewal, but they won't renew it without Peter's father's birth certificate, as he is Austrian and Peter lived in Austria until he was nine. It's funny to think of Peter as Austrian originally, as he is so British. He had a very refugee type childhood. His father came to the UK before the war and shoved Peter off somewhere outside the war area, and sent for him after the war. He lets snips drop now and again, like we were talking about the filthy Dambo for swimming in and Peter said he used to swim in the Danube and you couldn't get filthier than that. Peter is also bothered about getting a renewed work permit for his second two years. I certainly hope there is no trouble in this respect as I, or rather we, would miss them both very, very, much, although we would probably take over their house. I couldn't imagine Ndola without the Rubners. They said they would have liked to have seen you in their three months leave, but Marlene's parents are retired in Devon and Peter's father is in London and all their relatives are in the London area and Peter has to attend a course in London and then they cruise back.

I don't want them to try and fit you in as well. You wouldn't be keen if we went off when only home for two months, would you? Marlene has been talking about her leave since she arrived. They leave in March and are back in June, when we will only have nine months to do. She has already knitted Sally three quick knit cardigans, a jumper and woolly matching hat and a knitted mod dress in stripes. I'll buy Sally another jersey for Christmas and make her a pinafore dress to go home with as her birthday is in April. I am starting my Christmas shopping at the end of this month, with my back pay. Mrs. Hall is back from leave next month and there is still no sign of our piano. There were three in the paper today, Kitwe, Bancroft and Chingola, all too far away to have them delivered.

Last night, I shortened two dresses, my green silk one and my pink spotty one, that you hate with the puffed sleeves, and I took them up <u>four inches </u>each. I had not worn them since last summer and they were mid-knee length - how I ever wore them I don't know. My dresses for work are about 4 inches above my knees, my own an inch or so longer - the length of my tunic, and I am antwacky. A few girls wear them just below their bums. It's as though they're determined to show that fashion is still existent in the jungle.

Chapter 19   The Hoskyns- Abrahals

Times of Zambia

September 8th.

Zambia is not alone in having too many pregnant schoolgirls. Mr. Nyendwas said parents should do their best to stop their children from becoming pregnant. He did not support those who wanted to give pregnant schoolgirls maternity leave from school. "Who would be looking after the children?" he asked.

New decimal coin samples are being made. All coins would bear the head of President Kaunda.

Letter 57   11.9.67

Well things are hotting up socially during the next week. On Thursday we have a cocktail party at Mackie's and on Friday one with Graeme, the commercial director. This is because on Wednesday with a fanfare of trumpets, arrive Mr. Hoskyns-Abrahal and his wife. He is a director of that holiest of holies, Unilever. A list has even been circulated enumerating his likes and dislikes e.g. coffee rather than tea and his favourite wines etc.

On Tuesday lunchtime Marlene has to entertain Mrs. H-A and I have been invited. Marlene was given a list of people from whom to choose to invite and luckily I was one. She has also invited Naomi Dunkerley. Marlene can invite two Lever's wives and two outsiders; she has picked Cecily and Dolores from the tennis club. Marlene and Chessy Muirhead are to split the commercial managers wives between them. Luckily, Marlene grabbed me first, as Esme Rowlands and Moira Dunsmuir are two stuffy dears.

I pity Mrs. H-A. She has a week full of coffee mornings, lunches, afternoon teas, cocktail parties and dinners. Mr. Pawson has given me an extra hour for lunch. Yippee! I am also getting my hair cut and set on Thursday lunchtime and if necessary, as it probably will be, will have a comb out on Friday lunchtime.

Richard has just come in and went to switch the light on and nothing happened. We checked and all the electricity is off, even the stove and I was using the mixer only half an hour ago. I might have to leave off writing as in 15 mins it will be pitch black. This isn't uncommon. Luckily we have candles.

Later. Just as we lit our candles in coke bottles around the room and watched glimmering candles in other windows, the lights came on again. A fellow who lives opposite went past and shouted "Happy Christmas" because we were lighting candles on the kitchen window ledge, about eight of them. Would have been twenty if it hadn't been for Obed.

On Friday night we went to Marlene and Peter for a meal and had a chatty night. They were going to invite someone else, but said they couldn't think of anyone else to invite as well so it was just the four of us, We had a very nice chicken paprika.

On Saturday, we went to sculpture in the morning. It was beautifully warm and I finished the back of his head and his ears, but I only have one lesson before she goes away for two months, on leave, so she is giving me the head and the bucket of clay. Lovely. All to go in our spare room. It can stand on an upturned tea chest. I have to keep it covered with a wet cloth otherwise it will dry out.

Pucci now brings his ball in his mouth and stands and puts his front paws on the edge of the chair and drops the ball on you. Richard is just trying to start his letter and Pucci wants to play.

We had beef tonight, roasted and I made a Yorkshire pud. and when we took the dishes out we realised that the pud was still in the oven. What a waste. We couldn't eat it on its own with no gravy. My sherry trifle was OK, but half a cup of sherry didn't seem to make it taste. I made another trifle tonight without the sherry, because we can't keep on using sherry like that!

I washed Pucci's ears as they were filthy. It's not surprising as they flop in his dinner and his milk and the soil. No wonder that none of my seeds have come up. But those in the back haven't come up either. The soil may be sour, being in a window box and not changed for years.

We are on the phone! It came on Saturday morning. We are Ndola 4987 so I'll ring you Mondays. Wednesdays and Fridays and you ring me Tuesdays, Thursdays and Sundays. We won't bother on Saturdays as we are usually out.

I rang Marlene to tell her our number, but I'll be interested to see what our phone bill will be because we've no-one to ring.

There has been a big train crash here. Two of the new diesels pulling a passenger train crashed into a stationary train, which had broken down, and a lot have been killed. The radio has announced that wooden coaches were pulped and railway lines twisted and broken by the impact. Must have been going at some speed.

Ravenscrofts went home this weekend. They were due to leave Ndola at four o'clock but Tony called to see us at 5:30ish and said the plane had been delayed and wasn't leaving until 8. We were on our way to a braaivleis at the tennis club so we decided to pop up to the airport to say Cheerio, but when we arrived there was only a porter on duty and he said the plane wasn't going until 6 o'clock on Sunday. They were going to spend the night in Nairobi and sightsee there until the London connection and that messed all that up. We didn't see them again, but at eight o'clock saw a plane take off. If they call and see you, tell them that we went to see them at the airport.

Sally and Stuart had a wonderful week's holiday in Livingstone. We called to see them on our way to the pictures on Sunday night, as we forgot they were on holiday, and wondered why they hadn't been to the tennis club. They had just arrived having driven 600 miles non-stop. They were exhausted and we were in a hurry, which was just as well. They were so pleased to know we had missed them, so I was glad we went. We saw "Viva Maria" on Sunday night.

PS I said in my last letter - Hope you liked the enclosed cutting but I think I forgot to enclose it and now can't find it but roughly said - A delegate from Brafia was asked if he had seen President Kaunda, and he replied "I cannot answer you that question", "But it would have been nice to have seen him".

Letter 58   13/9/67

As usual, mid-week and not much news. It was decided that if the girls in the office would have to pay to have their dresses made, we would be able to have four lots of material each and not two, and I can have mine this October with everyone else. The material we chose was an American linen. We could have four different colours, but we must have the same four colours, one of each and the same pattern. We were all asked to submit patterns. I put forward a Weldom's pattern that I brought with me. It had a yoke with sleeves and darts to the side seams. The skirt is slightly flared and the sleeves are dolman. It seemed just the job.

Mr. Pawson wanted low necks and short skirts. Mrs. Kent and Mrs. King were in fits as I said that perhaps we should also have thigh boots, fish net stockings, leather jerkins to the hip with a chain and medallion round the middle. Mrs. King is about 5'2 and about the same round the middle, so you can imagine that tears were rolling down her face at the thought of herself in this get-up. But she said she would compromise with a bell-bottom trouser suit.

Out of seven patterns, mine was chosen. It was popular even though the Weldom's packet isn't at all exciting, but it will suit Mrs. King better than the shift that we wear now. And Pawson said we could leave the sleeves out of two. I shall try and make mine, but if I have no time, I will have them made. We are also having contrasting yokes too. The material is 17/11 a yard and we are allowed £8.00 each.

We get the material in October. It has been cut and put away, but October is the new financial year.

Pucci has started bringing in bits and pieces of twigs and leaves from the garden and yesterday I was sitting reading and he comes out from under the settee, and drops between my feet a brown grass hopper about 4" long and as thick as a cigar. I was up in a flash and dropped a cushion on it and went for the dustpan and brush and held it down like Daddy does with the spiders and dropped it in the waste bucket and sprayed it as, unfortunately, Pucci had already taken off its wings and half its back legs, as otherwise I would have put it in the garden. But I looked around and couldn't for the life of me find its lost legs. Now when he bounds in, I watch his mouth. I just hope the lizards are too quick for him. I just couldn't pick up a mangled lizard.

Richard was sitting here struggling to write his letter, when Pucci stands with his front paws on Richard's knees and drops his ball on his writing pad and then sat waiting for Richard to throw it. Any old excuse for Richard to stop writing.

Two weeks ago, I sent away for the G.C.E syllabus and yesterday got a note to say I had sent insufficient postage. If it were a private firm I am sure they would have sent it with a request for the excess. Anyway, I sent the extra, which means another delay. Even if everyone replies by return as they usually do, that's two months from my original enquiry.

Richard put his letter on the coffee table and Pucci ran off with it and chewed it before I could catch it. Richard was that mad. He had to start again.

I took Pucci to the vet's for his booster distemper injection last night. The vet asked if I had had him aclipped and I said No, and then the receptionist came in and said "Oh you've had him clipped?" I said No and then she said, "Did you do it yourself then?" and again I said "No". What it was was that I brushed him thoroughly at lunchtime and again before I took him. I brushed his fur up from the back so that it stood up and he looked like a little snowball.

Pucci turns his nose up at mince and meal at lunchtime and wolfs down his liver and kidney stuff at night. He will now only eat meat. I put oat stuff on his liver and steak tonight and he picked out the meat, yet he eats my soil and seeds. Horror of a dog!

Answers to questions- 1. Vivienne left because she was a typist and she was put on an accounting machine with her consent, and couldn't master it and was behind with her work and working Saturdays to catch up. She was offered a job as a copy-typist with more money, so now a new girl called Susan is on the machine and doing very well.

    2. Our neighbours are funny in that she is the general manager of the property firm owning the flats and is always peering through the curtains and issuing letters of complaint on the strength of what she sees. They are, I think, South African, but have been here fifteen years and when you've been here that long you start getting a bit provincial.

    3, Why not get some cutlery like mine? I think its one of the nicest designs and not too modern, unless you have seen something you have your eye on. Have you?

    4. Would you get nanny some slippers for me for Christmas? I'll send £2. If you got some from the market £2 would be enough?

Its funny how I looked forward to you coming home from your hols and hearing your tales. Never mind, just think how much more exciting it will be to share tales in seventeen and a half months.

Times of Zambia

September 9th. **Thought Rape was a Chief's Privilege.- Chief Fwambo was sentenced to five year's hard labour. He believed, by his act, that he had made her his wife. If he believed she was his wife, he could not be guilty of rape.**

    Thirty workers of Lusaka branch of Zambia Oxygen went on strike over alleged racialism. A night watchman was sacked for smoking in a no-smoking area. The workers claim that whites are allowed to smoke in the non-smoking area.

Letter number 59   **17.9.67**

We have had quite a hectic end to this week. On Thursday there was a cocktail party at Mackies from 6:30 to 8:00 to meet this Hoskyns-Abrahal and his wife. I'm enclosing a picture of him in which he looks rather like a pixie (I've lost it and will have to send it later). The party was OK but when the two guests went on to a dinner party it livened up. We have loads of photos taken talking and dancing and Richard has instructions to order all those with the tiniest glimpse of us on them if they are orderable.

Buchanan, Marlene and me

I wore my gold skirt and beaded top, and had my hair done in curls and things at lunchtime. On Friday morning it was so thick with setting stuff, pins and lacquer that I couldn't do anything with it and when I got to the office, Pawson said "Good Grief, go and do something with it", so I bombed up to the hairdressers who re-combed and brushed it up again for 3/6d which was well worth it. I was then tidy too for Friday evening when I wore my green silk dress to dinner at Muirheads. The visitors were coming from a cocktail party to the dinner at eight. There was a gorgeous cold buffet, a baked ham, lamb, beef, tongue, chicken, salads, a salmon mould, shrimps, rice, every kind of pickle and bit and pieces and caviar. I tried some caviar and it was bitter and the little egg things didn't break easily. They were hard and squeaked in between your teeth. Ugh! I could have slept all day Saturday, but on Saturday I was at my sculpture lesson for nine o'clock. I have started on the actual facial features, not that I have finished the main bone structure. It doesn't look a bit like Richard. He's OK when the teacher is around, but when she moves away, he sits with his nose screwed up or his tongue out, so it's no wonder it's not like him.

She, my teacher, is on leave for 2 months and has given me the bucket of clay and I am to pick up the head on Tuesday, when it will be dry after Saturday's effort, and I will have to work on it on my own. Richard has agreed to sit for an hour or so each weekend and has promised to be still and sensible. Some hope. I hope Andres doesn't think I'm a witch making effigies.

After my lesson, we went to Truworth's, the most decent dress shop and I bought a pair of denim shorts and a jersey - a skinny one with no sleeves and a polo neck in a silky wool. This came to £5.15.6! I had to buy them because the three pairs of shorts I had were ever so antwacky. No wonder, as the newest pair I had, you bought for me to go to St. Ives when I was about twelve.

On Saturday afternoon, although now rigged out for the boat club, it was too gusty and instead we went to the Ndola Motor Show! This was arranged by the local motor club. They have made a racing circuit in the bush and have built a club house and now want to develop it into a commercial venture. It was 5/- each entrance fee! So already they have the right idea. There were a few stands and all the local car firms had loaned their cars and they had tests of skill in cars and a fashion parade in cars and it wasn't bad for an amateur effort and was somewhere to go.

In the late afternoon, we went to the pictures to see "Battle of the Bulge" which was good and quite impressive. Tony was there and guess what, we invited him back for spaghetti bolognaise.

This morning, Sunday, we went and played tennis and this afternoon from 12 o'clock I walked around the golf course with Richard and Tony. I took my time as I could dawdle while they played their shots. The course was huge, as space is one thing that isn't short, and is in excellent condition and I saw lots of pretty birds and a live anthill as big as a house. The ant tracks were about an inch wide and have been used so much they were about half an inch deep in the clay with millions of big ants belting up and down them.

No snakes however. I was rather disappointed but when I saw a hole with an entrance as big as a tennis ball with something in it, I fled to the fairway, after the boys. I then kept strictly to the centre of the fairway and the paths and never ventured near any longer grass.

We are getting our new uniforms next month. The material has been bought and we decided to have four dresses and make them ourselves or have them made rather than have two each and the company pay for the making of them.

MONDAY. I went to Marlene's after work with my table mats and wooden napkin rings, for the lunch tomorrow. Marlene has some beautiful huge linen napkins, all monogrammed and some serving ladles also monogrammed, which were Peter's father's from Austria and part of a bigger set. Peter said the napkins are to be tied around the neck and demonstrated. They still hang over your lap. Magnificent things. Marlene's mats however were all odd ones. I shall say tomorrow, "Your table mats are beautiful. What exquisite taste you have".

We are just now going to listen to a play for an hour.

Letter 60   20.9.67

On Tuesday lunchtime we went to Marlene's for lunch with Mrs H.A. She was quite a character when you got to know her. She is about 60 and has blonde hair in a very glam bouffant style slightly pink tinted. She also wears false eyelashes, which I examined from the side and just couldn't believe they were false even when she told us. She said, "At my age your face needs a little furniture".

Marlene had made a lovely lunch. We started off with shrimp cocktail and then had half chickens with pineapple and salads and fancy sauces and cold asparagus. I wolfed it down. For pud, Marlene had hollowed out a melon as big as a football and filled it with melon balls and fresh strawberries from Naomi Dunkerley's farm. Marlene had put bright yellow daisyheads into the outside of the melon and it looked great. We had cream, and then I had some yummy trifle and there was cheese and biscuits. We all had wine glasses and Marlene asked Mrs. H.A if she wanted wine and she said she didn't, so none of us could have any. It was the same throughout the meal, all waiting for her to sit or stand or eat.

Mrs. H.A brought the proofs of the photos that were taken on Thursday and there is a good one of me and one of Richard side faced and a few good groupy ones that I would like as they have all our friends and acquaintances on them. I still don't know if us mere employees can order any. If I don't hear anything I shall ring up Mrs. Mackie (brave creature that I am).

Richard and Peter went and had ham sandwiches in a place that sells ale and snacks. The only one in this roaring metropolis.

I got back to the office at nearly three, just in time for tea. As it was, I had to down my coffee in two minutes. At the lunch were Naomi Dunkeley (Cecily couldn't come), Jean Bowen, a bank manager's wife whose garden backs on to Marlene's. She is nice but Marlene says she has three horrible children, one of whom said when they visited Marlene "Let's run through the house and open all the cupboards", which they did, until Marlene booted them out of the bedroom. Jean was telling me that her youngest little girl had been difficult that morning, and that in town when they got out of the car, the child sat on the floor and refused to move. "I just left her there screaming", she said. Just imagine! I find that all the children with nannies are all a bit bratty.

Anyway, back to the guest list. There was Dolores from the tennis club who is very lively and who has just had a swimming pool installed. Unfortunately she arrived with her husband who is very nice. His name is Julius Yodakien and he is the town's electrical engineer. He was all dressed up and he looked around the room and said "I'm not supposed to be here am I" and Marlene said "well actually – " and there was a bit of confusion with everyone apologizing. Apparently Julius has a swim at lunchtime and he said "it's too hot for lunch and I won't miss my swim after all" so off he went. He made a very charming and discreet exit.

Last night I went to pick up my head from Mrs Mills, but when I unwrapped its damp cloth at home, all the clay from Saturday had dried away from the week before's effort and could be picked off in lumps. I don't know whether to patch it or give it up as a bad job. Pucci was scared stiff of it and kept backing around the table growling with his tail straight up in the air.

Today I got a postcard from the library saying that a book I ordered in May – Shelagh Delaney's, A Taste of Honey-, had arrived, so I took back a Thelwell cartoon book on children (horrors) and their ponies, and have just read it in about 1 ½ hours. It wasn't a novel as I thought, but a play, and a very slim book. But I enjoyed it. The film was a lot nicer though, but you can do more with a film script than a play.

I have opened a new file for your letters from 51 up. I'll keep 50 in each, so as each one finishes, it's six months gone. How do you keep my letters? There is a red or a blue file in my magazine rack, or used to be, that you can use if you haven't anything else.

Tomorrow there are a lot of celebrations; there are standards and flags in the streets all ready for Kaunda to declare the town a city. All African staff are off, so I've given Andres the day off. All the shops will be closed too.

We have a horrible bill of £129 to pay for car insurance. The penalty of being a two-car family. Petrol only costs me 25/- a month. The insurance is loaded because of age (under 25) and Richard can only get no-claims bonus on one. Ah well, sardines on toast for a bit, or as Auntie Elsie would say "plus fours but no breakfast".

Letter 61 24/7/67

Well not a busy weekend but I enjoyed it better than our last weekend full of parties. On Thursday, The President came to declare Ndola a city and there have been flags and standards in the street and the place had quite a festive air. On Wednesday, we were teasing Pawson about having the afternoon off to celebrate as the shops were closing as was the civil service. On Thursday, he informed us we had the afternoon off. On Thursday morning, I was given two material lengths and cotrasts to make up two uniforms together with two reels of white, red and brown cotton, and two zips so I will not be out of pocket, so I thought I would start on these in the afternoon. I had already given Andries the afternoon off, before I knew mine was off too. But when 12.30 came, it was roasting so I thought I would love a swim, so off I went to the boat club when Richard went disgruntedly back to work. As there were a lot of small children in the pool like little fish, I didn't get my swim, but I lay on my towel reading and dozing until 4.30. I was disappointed to find I wasn't a bit tanned. Richard says there is a slight line on my back, but that's that. It must be the sea that does the tanning. Most of the girls here are a lovely colour.

On Saturday I started the dresses while Richard went golfing. At 10.30, I had got on very well, so went into the office to pick up my milk and then treated myself to a Homes and Gardens. It was three months out of date but as it has articles, it didn't matter. However it had advertisements for my lovely cooker and fridge!

Naomi Dunkerley came round to invite us to swim in her pool on Sunday.. She said it wasn't a proper pool, only a converted reservoir. After golf, we went to the boating club to sit and read. Pucci found a dead frog and I had to take him to Richard to prise his teeth off it as he refused to release his hold on it. We walked Pucci by the lake, and then he is happy to sleep under our chairs. Until a child runs past and he wants to chase it. He also barks at other dogs, especially very big dogs. So if I see a big dog coming I pick Pucci up and cover his eyes until it is past.

Pucci was crying when Richard was in the bath, so when Richard got out, he held Pucci over the water and Pucci did mad doggy paddle with his front paws and a breaststroke with his back legs. How did he know to do that?

At last, he now cries to go out, so no more puddles, although sometimes he just wants to go outside to play. He is also better when we go out. He just sits looking at us soulfully at us as we say "Stay" and shut the door. He has a biscuit and a bowl of milk before we go out and we never leave him for more than a few hours and not twice in one day.

Bob and Naomi live a few miles from the Congolese border. Bob runs his father's farm now his father is dead as well as working at Levers. They have huge chicken houses and mainly deal in eggs on a large scale. On a smaller scale they grow carrots and strawberries and dahlias, which are not yet profitable. They have a tennis court and the pool/reservoir is surrounded by a thickly thatched fence and is in a lovely spot. I wouldn't have known the pool was a reservoir. It was round and the walls were tin coated with a plastic and painted white. The water was beautifully clear and blue and it took me all my time to swim across it. They had a lilo and rubber inner-tubes. There was enough room for the six of us (two other guests). We had a great time, and were doubled up with laughter fooling around like kids.. the boys were trying to see who could reach the inner tube by running along the lilo. Of course no-one got further than the lilo, except Peter who fell into the inner tube bottom first and got stuck. They then had a pillow fight sitting either end of the lilo and using the inner tubes as pillows. What a childish way to spend an afternoon, but I love having a good laugh. Naomi has two lovely children, both very blonde haired and bronze-skinned. One is about two and the other five. The two year old is tanned all over as Naomi says she refuses to wear any clothes when it is hot. She dresses her in swimming pants, but finds them abandoned on the back door step and Robyn playing in the sand without them. Both children are little cherubs. The elder child Linda went to a party and we went with Bob to pick her up and drove along the Congolese border, so now we can say we have seen the Congo.

The local Kodak office says that my slides should have arrived by now and said to write to Kodak, UK with a description of them in case they had become separated from the label. How annoying to lose them.

Chapter 20   Christmas shopping

Letter 62   27.9.67

As I said, I think at the end of my last letter, your tape arrived. The case was in terrible condition and tied up with string and the reel was broken and the middle warped as though it had been heated. Fortunately we had a spare reel and transferred it very, very slowly and except for a little blurring in the centre it is fine and we certainly enjoyed it as I hope you did our film and tape. I'm dying to know how you got on with it and whether you enjoyed it. Norman was very prompt in coming to visit you and I'm pleased with him.

Hurray, hurray. After writing yesterday to Kodak about my slides, they arrived today in good condition, and with the odd exception, have turned out OK. We have decided to send two per letter, rather than together and then you'll still stand a chance of getting some of them, as I'm afraid you may not get the box intact. Two per letter takes two months to complete the set, but your tape took nearly that long airmail.

I wore my new dress to the office (the brown one) on Monday and today I have nearly finished my navy one. Richard and I were both ill last night. Richard was very sick, most unlike him and so was I, but we are both OK now although not recovered our appetites. Richard played golf after work, but I feel as though I've been kicked around. I made a Hungarian Goulash last night, but I have made it lots of times before and have never been affected. Pucci had a plateful too and he was fine so I can't think what it was. We boil and freeze our water and soak our vegetables in permanganate before eating. We both had frozen plaice tonight, on its own.

You must excuse me therefore if I shorten my letter, as we are both off to bed early to get a little more sleep.

I think I am doing too much with A levels, so I'm afraid my music must be held over, at least the serious study of it. I'll see how I manage A levels.

One geography study is the study of the local area with survey maps etc. Rich and I will go and do our field work together so we will learn a bit about Ndola. I hope the fieldwork will be OK by correspondence, but then Richard did surveying in one school holiday, so I'm lucky. (Turns his hand to anything, wouldn't he make you sick – anyway he can't do clay heads). (Neither can I).

Times of Zambia   5/10/67

Charcoal burners have been warned by their Union not to display their bags of charcoal too close to the roads because this could be hazardous to motorists.

Letter 63   1.10.67

Another new month. I tried to do some Christmas shopping yesterday! It was useless. I wanted something for you, Mrs L, Stephanie and Joan's baby boy, Simon. I looked at small teddies for Simon, but they were too dear in one shop, too dirty (not just grubby) in another, and in another the foam stuffing was dropping out. I got a 6/6 book for Stephanie, but will have to try and buy something else. The bookshop is the only civilised place. The books are beautiful, but the children's books are so few although they are a good quality and standard. There were books called "This is Hong Kong" or Paris or Rome, which were travel guides with a funny commentary especially for eightish year olds. They were very educational, but lots of fun. Children's books are so adventurous and exciting these days.

It seems so odd shopping for Christmas in this heat and dust. Are Christmas cards and things starting to come into the shops? Is it cold again? I feel very nostalgic about Christmas. Apparently here Christmas doesn't exist. The shops don't decorate or anything. Most miserable.

I went to the office for the milk and Cookie said she had an unused teddy she had for Cathie but didn't give her, as she had so much for last Christmas. She invited us for drinks at 12. Cookie had lent me her pinking shears, as when I went to use mine I remembered they were yours and that I hadn't got any!

We went to Marlene's for the meat to find Peter in the midst of opening his birthday presents, so we had coffee. At eight o'clock yesterday morning we took Pucci for his rabies injection. At five past eight there were about eight dogs waiting plus six police Alsatians with handlers all in a line at attention. Pucci was first but another bloke pushed in front and I'm glad he did as the livestock officer (not the vet) who gives the injections missed and had to do it twice. I was holding Pucci and this bloke charges at us with this great big syringe. I hung on to Pucci and shut my eyes when he jabbed him up the backside. Did Pucci squeal! I thought the needle was coming into me! There was a huge Great Dane with his owner astride him hanging onto his collar with his heels dug in to the ground. When the first dog squealed this thing nearly threw its owner and he and his wife could hardly hold it. Fancy having a dog so big. Smacking him with a newspaper wouldn't have much effect.

We went to Cookie's at 12. She has just acquired a dog, which can sit on your palm. Their hamster is bigger! They also have a Siamese kitten about the same size, and you should see the two of them fight.

This afternoon two auditors are arriving on the VC10 and we, and Rubners, have to meet them and see them to their hotel.

Monday after work. We met the auditors; one is German and the other Swedish and speak with strong accents. Richard says imagine them saying to a local – "Und vat system employ you here?" with "yes please boss" or "no please" as a reply. Richard has enough trouble explaining what he wants and he speaks reasonable English!

On coming home at 5.30 it was still hot although cooler than the mid afternoon so we decided to go for a swim at the boat club. As Richard won't even take his shirt off with people around, we waited until everyone had gone from the pool by which time it was dusk. Even then he needed a lot of persuasion, and we went in. I had a lovely splash around and tried to teach Richard to float, but he won't relax and hates, as I do, his head going under. He is far too stiff and won't float and even holding on to the side, he can't let his feet float up. He tries to put them up, but of course this is no good.

On our way home we got caught in a football final match traffic. I was in my swimsuit with a wet towel around me and dripping wet hair and Richard was in his wet trunks with a shirt on. The policeman stopped the main road traffic to let the entire car park out. No filtering or alternating lanes. Nothing so complicated. Richard shouted out, "How long will this take" and one policeman said, "Its alright, they'll all be out by seven.". It was then 6.25. We couldn't turn back as we were hemmed in. At twenty to seven, a higher policeman came along, and let our stream move. The lane was probably blocking town traffic. By the time we got home I was perished. We got dried and changed and were soon sweltering again. At night, I am sleeping in my nothings under a sheet. The sheet is only a protection against the mossies).

Today I went to work in my new office dress (I have finished all four now) and just pants and bra underneath – not petticoat nor stockings, and my slip-on mules and I was still sweltered. It's getting hotter too! Richard's office is cold as it's air-conditioned but ours only has fans and all your papers must be well anchored down.

Mrs L wrote to us today "I was hurt and disappointed that Norman visited Mrs W. It's not much good giving our address when he didn't even bother to see us" and such ravings. I am very cross. The poor bloke was decent enough to see you, without dashing around seeing everyone. "After waiting so long to see him," she also said. He called on you four days after I said you would be available. You can't expect better than that. In fact, I was livid. If she's nothing more important to be hurt and disappointed about, she's damn lucky. And why rant at us. We can't control everything from this distance. Right, grumble over.

But first, a grumble at you. Why on earth don't you buy cutlery like mine if you like it. Why compromise? Don't be so martyred. Richard says you must buy some, as he was reckoning on completing our set when visiting you for tea.

I agree with you about Dr Zhivago. In the book, he lives with another woman after Lara, nowhere near his intellectual equal, and has children, and then just disintegrates, goes a bit mad and dies. Before he dies he received letters from his wife, but made no attempt at reconciliation and after his death, Lara clears up his affairs (business). Perhaps it was to show how revolution and hardship rot a character. Zhivago wasn't a revolutionary was he? He just got swept along by it.

Don't make an effort to get Nanny very cheap slippers. Get her some with a decent sole and a good heel, which will take a lot of wear, which no doubt they will get.

Do keep your eye open in T.J. Hughes sales, especially for a sleeveless sporty blouse to go with my blue denim shorts. All they have here are frilly flowery ones. Plain or stripes or check. You know what will go with denim. Remember when looking, that out here I'm as mod as they come!

Times of Zambia   6/10/67

We killed people and burned shops during the struggle and we shall continue to do this if necessary to defend our freedom, said UNIP Youth General Secretary, Leo Katekwe.

Letter Number 64   4.10.67

I'm glad you liked the film, but I thought you would have commented more on it, Mummy. Did you like the shot of the two boys reading the comic and how about Richard's long socks? And what did you think of the rain and the lizards?

Talking of lizards. On Sunday afternoon, I drew the curtain and a horrible <u>thing</u> fell down the back of my dress, which had a lowish neck. Boy, did I scream. It fell almost straight through and plonked on the floor and ran behind the coffee table and we lost it (it was about 5" long). We then went out to meet the auditors and when we came in we still couldn't find it. Later when I put Pucci's basket out, it was hiding in the blanket and it ran out. I ran and jumped on the settee picking up Pucci, and Richard chased the poor thing round and round until it ran outside. I had visions of Pucci jumping on my knee with it. Ugh. They are nice from a distance but down a dress, no thank you! I now stand well back when drawing the curtains.

We had the auditors to dinner last night. We also invited Jim who lives next door, who took John Gibbon's place. Jim is the only one who has heard from the Gibbons, and then it was a letter from John asking Jim for the money for some things he had left with Jim to sell for him! I'm disappointed. They were so fussy about insisting on collecting everyone's addresses too!

The auditors are very nice and we had a real international evening. A German, a Swede, a South African, a Rhodesian and us two. It could have been an explosive group. The main subject was Apartheid and both sides and the middle and back and front of it were very thoroughly debated, and a lot learnt all round of the different viewpoints although no-one veered from their original views, but understood better the other side's views, and the reasons for them. I did manage to get a word in occasionally and, surprisingly, I cooled things down occasionally with coffee and drinks. We also heard a lot of tales, some a bit embroidered, no doubt, but that's storytellers' license. I only have four pages in this pad, so will have to write on the back if need be.

I went along to Vivienne's tonight. I didn't really want to be bothered but felt mean not going. So I went, and I was glad I did, as she was miserable. With her husband moving jobs, they are living in a one-room bachelor flat that goes with her new job. It has one room and a separate bathroom and a kitchen. The whole flat is smaller than our lounge. Anyway, we had a gossip and played with her baby, who is ever so bonny. He was one yesterday and both her mother and mother-in-law forgot his birthday, so that didn't make her any happier.

Betty in the office has gone to Bulawayo for her divorce today, and last night her six-year-old son was taken to hospital with malaria. The doctor said she should not worry about leaving him. Anyway, I'll go up tomorrow with some comics. So she was happier going away!

On Saturday, we are playing tennis with the auditors and Rubners at Mackies at four o'clock. Honoured aren't we! I couldn't find out about the photos at Mackies party, and rang the photographer who said the proofs had been returned so on Saturday we went to order some but all the good ones weren't there, so I was disappointed. However, on Monday, Richard came home with them from the office where they were being passed around for orders, so I've ordered mine. We are only on about three, but the rest are people we talk about and whom you might want to look at.

I promise we won't open our present before Christmas, as when we got to Kariba, we won't have any to open and that would be miserable for Christmas, wouldn't it.

Chapter 21   Study books arrive

Times of Zambia   11/10/67

Zambia would not accept the machinations of political idiots who thought that God was wrong in creating people of different colours, President Kaunda replied to Chief Jonathan yesterday.

Letter 66   10.10.67

Last week I spent £2 something on Christmas cards. They were on two shelves and I picked 5 packets of the best ones. They are all UK Hallmark brand and the usual ones that I buy. There is nothing African except 17/6 elephant calendars like big postcards.

Today too I got a card from John and Sue from Holland, posted in Italy over a month ago. They have been all over the north of Europe and now say that they just have Italy, France and Spain to do! They bought a car in London and went over to Sweden. So at least they have written and I didn't really think that they would.

On Saturday playing tennis I slid on one knee on the gravel court. I did feel daft. I carried on playing and looked down to see blood pouring down my leg and into my sock. Nobody seemed to notice so we carried on playing but when I came off they already had a big first aid box out. When it was cleaned up it was only a graze but it has gravel in it, so I've a plaster on it at the moment. It was nostalgic having scabby knees again.

Our phone is still not in proper working order and I have reported the fault four times. People, like Marlene, have told me they have given up trying to get through. As it's not been right since we got it. It's a pity we can't refuse to pay for rental until it works. Ah well, this is Zambia.

I'm glad to hear the squash are OK. That's the colour they should be. You boil them cut in half and eat the fleshy middles. Tasted rather like mushy turnip and I don't recommend it. Any signs of the eggplants or have they given up the ghost?

I have done some more of my sculpture. The bits which really came away I chipped off, but even as I was doing it, it was drying and flaking and even pouring cups of water over the top didn't help much, it just got soaked in and dried out. Anyway, I'm getting good practice. Richard isn't very good sitting at home. He wanders away "just for a minute" for all sorts of odd reasons.

Are the children collecting bonfire wood yet?

Thank you for the stamps. They are super ones. I've been offered swaps, but am keeping them.

Times of Zambia   11/10/67

TV might improve once the rains start, said Zambia Broadcasting's chief engineer.

Letter number 67   5.10.67

I received our Christmas parcel on Wednesday and went white at the stamps. We paid 13/- duty

on your declaration, each item being given a code and then a percentage charge. We will work out which is cheapest. Possibly you can send lots of tennis shoes. The parcel was undamaged and we opened it and had a feel, but no peeping, honest! I've put them back in the brown paper and they are on the top shelf of the bedroom cupboard where I can't even see them. I did open the calendar though; the picture of Chester made me homesick. I'm going to hang it by my office desk as I can look at it all day. The girls laugh at me because on the first of every month, I dash in and rip a page off each of the two calendars.

We have been busy entertaining this weekend. We had the two auditors again and Sally, but no Stuart. Sally staggered in with her projector and slides on her own. Stuart was ill. He had come home from work with flu, and had gone to bed dosed with Disprins. Anyway it evened us up a bit regarding ladies. We had a good natter and the slides went down very well and I enjoyed seeing them again. We put the projector on the fourth stair up and show it onto the opposite wall which gives a picture of about 6'x4' and is very big and clear. I gave the auditors paw-paw, a big fruit like a melon, and ice cream. I scooped out little balls with a special utensil and it tasted good.

On Friday afternoon it was my half-day, and I went to the boat club and met Marlene by arrangement. I took Pucci along and tied him by string onto his lead to a tree, making a lead about 12 ft long, and he played around and slept all afternoon while we swam. The afternoon was hot and humid but overcast and so there was no sun to tan me.

In the evening we went to the pictures and saw the Hallelujah Trail, a send up Western. It could have been condensed into half the time. It was quite funny but made the jokes spin out, but I enjoyed the night out.

Yesterday (Saturday) morning, Richard was up at 6:30 to play golf with Tony and Jim, so at 7:30 I went out to do the shopping. I picked up a sack of potatoes at the wholesaler and went along to the bakery at 7:45ish but it was still shut. I thought it opened at 7:30. All the other shops open at 8. So as I couldn't do any other shopping before 8 and as the bakery is on the opposite side of town, I waited. At 8:10 it still hadn't opened. I collared someone going through the side door and asked when it opened and was told that it might open at half eightish! All I wanted was a Swiss roll for a trifle and I could see them on the counter, all four of them! So I went and did the rest of my shopping and went back later.

Today a chap came round selling bulrushes. Do you remember the ones I bought for 1/6 each? They were, or still are, under my bed. I asked how much they were and he said 1/- which I thought was a bit dear, but seeing he had been in the Dambo for them I said I would have three, "But Madame", he said, "I only have two bunches". They were 1/- for a bunch of six, so I bought the two bunches. (I couldn't very well ask for 6 pennorth). They are green stemmed and I hope they will dry without going to seed. I hope too that they're not covered in bilharzia germs. There is a tiny snag – I'll have to buy a big vase! (I haven't told Richard that bit yet).

On Sunday morning, at 7:30, we three went to the boat club for a swim, although we were in bed late Saturday. We swam around until 8:15 but Pucci was miserable and sat on the edge crying because we were in the water, so we came away earlier than we would have liked. By 9:30 I had finished breakfast and all the odd jobs and we put the armchairs on the terrace and sat there and midday Tony called to see if Richard wanted to play golf, so off he went and played 18 holes until 5 o'clock and I alternately dozed, read about Philby in the Times and read one and a half books. The sun disappears from the terrace at about 10 but its lovely sitting outside. Whereas if I stay in, I get a headache.

I bought a fresh chicken for 12/- (2 ¾ lbs) and we had that in the evening. The vet's wife reared them. They were unclaimed from the airport and half were dead, so the vet was called in to dispose of them. She had over a hundred. It was a bit roughly cleaned and the bits were in the middle, so Richard emptied it out for me.

Coincidence! Marlene told me that boys sold bulrushes and commented on those in the Dambo, but I have looked everywhere for a boy selling them, and just now another one has come to the door selling them. Two in one day after none for months. It must be bulrush season. Perhaps, as it is the end of the dry season.

Many thanks too for the new series of stamps, which are envied in the office.

Now your letters. Did you like my new trousers? Did I look well? Even if not as brown as Richard. Doesn't Pucci look like a teddy. We call him teddy-dog.

What a mad night you had on your Spanish evening. I miss daft things like that. What are you doing to the box room? You had better put my bike in the shed, with the lock on the wheel; the combination is I think 5352 or 5354. The lock is in the side pocket of the saddlebag. Are you taking all the junk off the top of the wardrobes? If you find anything of mine that you think is useless, throw it out. What I don't know about I won't grieve over and why should you store it if I shouldn't want to. (Don't throw my teaching reading books out though).

I am now listening to our Monday serial. It's very dull and very fantastic science fiction. Not half as good as "Journey into Space" on the radio, with Lemme and Jock was it? Or was that Dick Barton?

Our new uniforms are super compared with the blue ones. I am not wearing them anymore, only two are practically unused. I shall wear them in the house when I get home. They will make good overalls to clean in. (What does "to clean" mean?)

Times of Zambia

11/10   All but one of four villagers who claimed that their chief had manacled them to a wheelbarrow at night lost their claim for damages in Lusaka High Court yesterday.

16/10   The bad state of Zambia's locomotives was attributed to "mishandling, negligence and lack of experienced staff" when the inquiry into the Kasiki rail crash resumed yesterday.

Letter No 68   8.10.67

We had a tiny shower of rain. It smelled gorgeous. If the rainy season is starting, it is too early. It usually starts about the 15th November. It smelled just as nice as English rain and the air was so lovely and cool afterwards, although within half an hour it was just as oppressive.

Yesterday I received my booklist from the Metropolitan College in London, the books I need amount to £9.15.0. Ouch. The biggest is a £2 atlas, which I thought would be dearer. The English Lit. Books are all paperbacks and the hardbacks are all geog. ones. Today I received the first book of study notes and test papers by air. The main notes are coming by sea. However, the first notes also refer to the textbooks, which I haven't yet got. I went to the library this evening and saw a good atlas, which unfortunately is a reference book, which however I can borrow on Saturday if I return it on Monday.

Richard read my notes and says he may take my examination too, if he has time to see all the notes and things. It would help me if Richard was conversant with my subject too, but you know how good Richard's memory is! I'll have to work hard to equal him.

It's nice of you, daddy, to offer my book as a present, but if I should want anything else, then I would not like to ask in case you thought I was fishing for a buckshee present. It was a present enough that you took the trouble to order it and send it to me.

It is eight now and I am going to have my bath and read my study notes in bed. Richard isn't too well; (don't tell Mrs L). It is quarter end and he has been having bad headaches. It's no wonder – working until 7 and then brings work home, what does he expect. He made an appointment on Tuesday to see the doctor tomorrow (the 1st appointment available) Thursday. He must be feeling crummy, as you know how many times he has seen the doctor in the 4-½ years I've known him. Nil.

Oh Mummy! I'm so sad that you lost your watch, and here am I with your little Oris all done up in a new strap. How do you know you lost it between Custom House and home? Did you last look at it at the office before coming home? Did you leave it in the cloakroom?

Times of Zambia   20/10/67

Fifteen time bombs found at Livingstone Railhead

"The TanZam Railway must be built", says Simon Kapepwe

Letter No 69   23.10.67

Well, I'm having a lovely restful day. Tomorrow, Tuesday is Independence Day and Pawson said there wasn't much point in coming in today! So we're not disagreeing. We slept with the curtains wide open last night to try and let some breeze in. It's even too hot sleeping in my skin. The result was that by half five we were wide-awake with the sun scorching through the window. It was a pleasure to get up and have a soak in cold water.

Andre has now disturbed my peace, as I'm sitting here on the terrace, by watering the window box. I've felt sorry for him, as he has done all the washing and ironing today. It's now three and I'll send him home. I think the watering is just to let me see that he has finished everything else.

I went in to work after visiting the bottle store. We were both broke at the end of the weekend and last night we ran out of oranges and cokes. Calamity. We sorted out our bottles and I went to see what I could get. I raised £1.5.9 on empties, bought six family cokes and a concentrated orange and a lime and got 8/11 change, so I bought another plastic water bottle; the one we have holds three pints which we go through quickly and as we boil the water, it takes 3-4 hours to go cool, by which time we have drunk a couple of coke bottles (more expensive) so I bought another three pint water bottle.

Richard is now better. He went to the quack, who diagnosed sinusitis, probably caused by going under too much while swimming. He's not to swim for at least another two months. Richard said he's fated not to swim. The doctor gave him nose drops and things.

I stayed at work dishing out milk (it was my turn) until 9 when the library opened and I got out 6 books. One for Richard and the rest geography books!

Richard saw a snakeskin about 6 feet long on the golf course. He was going to bring a piece of it home, but thought the snake might want it back and come after him.

I was going to the boat club this afternoon, but it's too hot and very quiet and pleasant here on my stoep. I don't sit on a garden chair. I put out the armchair and tea tables and sit in comfort only moving to get some lunch (I did keep Andre supplied with plenty of orange. It can't be much fun watching someone sit gulping gallons of the stuff, can it). This sort of weather makes me want to do mornings only, but I'll do full days until this time next year, i.e. if he will agree ("he" being Richard and Mr Pawson).

Your new coat sounds super, but the thought of a fur coat – excuse me I'm just getting up for another pint of cold, cold orange.

Your new colour schemes sound super too. My carpet here is green with leaves and things and I think it looks fine. My carpet also has leaves and twigs on it. Pucci brings them in from the garden and chews them up. Richard says it's like sitting in Storeton Woods.

Pucci has just drunk my orange! The table is full of books so I put it alongside the chair and the next thing schlurp, schlurp and it's gone. However, it made his nose tickle as he is sneezing like mad.

We shall, I think post this letter tonight, as there is no work for Richard tomorrow, and with it being Independence Day, no European goes out tomorrow as the booze flows freely and it can get nasty, so it's best to avoid town.

We went to the tennis club on Saturday at two and stayed until three, but no one else arrived. I'm glad, as it was really far too hot to play.

On Friday night, we went to Bob and Naomi's for a braaivleis given for the auditors. It was good, but the same old people. I went in my flowery trousers and skinny sweater. My meat was a bit tough to say the least, and when I disposed of it discreetly, the dog followed me around all evening, and it was a great big watchdog too.

Daddy, I don't think you'll find "Bleak House" much kop. I have never gone further than the first chapter. You'd be better reading a good modern novel from the library; at least you'd enjoy it more.

I'm not blasé about spiders. I don't like them, but they are harmless and run away not towards you. I've had a few spider bites on my arms after being asleep and can't bear to think they had been running on my arms while I'd been asleep. We've had a lot of cockroaches in the kitchen. One species is red and about three inches, four including feelers. I thought it was a mouse when I first saw it. Richard sprayed the kitchen and next thing, he just caught one before it went up the leg of his shorts. He knocked it off with a yell, but the thing was doped with spray.

Betty's little boy has recovered, but he now has chicken pox. Betty is going to Salisbury to be nearer the rest of the children. who are at boarding school and who set off on bicycles after her divorce to find their father, so the head advised her to move nearer so she could at least see them more often while they were so unsettled.

I've almost forgotten what Bournie tastes like. We have drinking chocolate but only use it in cakes and things. We also dream of fresh sliced bread, and crusty cobs and cakes and buns, and Walls sausage and nice eggs and chickens and turkey and Richard says gammon, bacon, new potatoes, cabbage, English apples, plums *[and in Richard's writing]* and walnuts and brazil nuts and your dodgy nutcrackers. Cheek!

Chapter 22   Independence Day

Times of Zambia

24/10   A woman who attacked and killed a leopard with a piece of wood was in a list of 24 honoured by President Kaunda.

25/10   CARS stops services through the pedicle road. The last straw was the difficulty encountered with the pontoons at the Chobe Ferry, which broke down from time to time. CARS and other transport companies have been hard hit by tolls introduced by Congolese Customs.

Letter No. 70   **25th October 1967**

You can tell how hot it is by the fact that my fountain pen is empty at the start of every letter, instead of at every fourth or fifth letter.

Tuesday, Independence Day, was a holiday and at 6:30 Richard went out to play golf and I put out the armchair on the stoep and sat there with my breakfast. It is so hot that at 6:30 it's like midday and it's too hot to sleep anyway. The sun disappears over the house at 10-11-ish although by nine it has half gone. But even so my legs got a good tan even in that short time and by 11 it's so hot anyway that the shade is good. On Monday I was going to the boat club, but it was too nice at home here with plenty of orange and no other sweaty bodies about.

This is me at 2pm

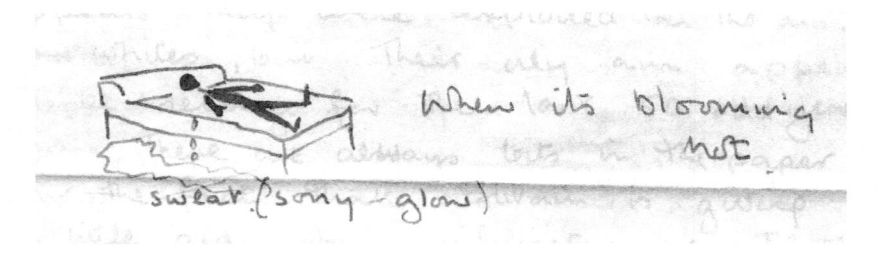

Whew it's blooming hot.

On Sunday night we filled a hot water bottle with cold water but it wouldn't stay cold. Cooking is agony at night. Richard loves his evening meal and the oven is on nearly every night.

Seven towns here have been renamed with African names, even Livingstone, which is part of their history even if colonialist history, but colonialism did exist, so why eradicate all traces. Whereas tourists will visit Livingstone, no-one is going to visit Umbilungilungiboo or whatever, so they are cutting their own noses etc.

Do you know that the Stone Age, not even the Iron Age, existed here in the last century, so local archaeologists have just discovered. Only 150 years ago! These people have had to jump 10,000 odd years. No wonder there is trouble. It's a pity they weren't left alone. Admittedly it appears they were exploited on the arrival of the whites, but their only aim appears to be revenge for the last 50 odd years.

There are always bits in the paper about the fact that Britain is giving too little aid, which infuriates me. If they are so keen to be independent, let it be really independent, and if they can't manage it, well! Let them stew in their own juice. This is the second richest country in Africa. Look at the distribution of the biggest copper mines in the world. The majority appear to be in South Africa, but Broken Hill South, Nchanga, New Broken Hill, Rhokana, [Roam Selection Trust], Zam Anglo, and Zam Broken Hill, are all here in this country. None are nationalised but the towns up here have all been built by the mines and are the only source of employment for hundreds of thousands of people.

My arguments are a bit ranting and lack logic, but it is so irritating reading one-sided opinions in the paper, including the letter page. At least if the British press is biased left or right, the letter page is varied.

One article in the women's page today says about Christmas gifts in the shops being tantalizing and being spoilt for choice. I think she's been shopping in another country. If the things are not grubby, then they are fantastically expensive and poor quality, usually all three together. I give up. It's a good job the weather's good.

We had a tremendous storm last night, which cooled things down a lot. It's the first big storm we have viewed from our bedroom. The sky was black, not the magnificent reds and oranges it normally is at dusk.

Pucci couldn't make out the rain at all. He went to the terrace and ran back in and hid under a chair, eventually going out and approaching the bouncing spots cautiously. Richard said he probably thought the terrace was getting its own back and piddling on him for a change.

Times of Zambia

26/10 Mr. Justice Whelan yesterday ordered a villager to be detained at The President's pleasure after a High Court inquiry involving leprosy, madness, witchcraft and murder.

27/10 Mini-skirts are as dangerous to children as dagga, smoking and beer drinking, a spokesman for the Teachers' Union said yesterday.

Letter 71   30/10/67

I have received your letter 69, with the Christmas stamp, which is lovely and I now have a waiting list of about half a dozen for duplicates.

On Saturday night we went to the pictures and saw "The Trap" with Rita Tushingham and Oliver Reed, a story about a trapper buying a wife and how she grows to love him. Not perhaps as mushy as it sounds. If it comes try and see it as I think you would like it, and Daddy, you would like the scenery and the wolf fight if nothing else.

It was a miserable day on Saturday, cool with drizzle all day. Not hot and sunny at intervals, just like a drizzly English summer day. Yesterday, Sunday, was our day to entertain the auditors and we had intended to go on a picnic, but Sunday morning came and it was too drizzly. We had some steak so I did steak and salad, which is popular, or steak and salad<u>s</u>, as it is called here. I bought a lettuce, a real, proper lettuce and put it in my Spanish bowl, just plain and in big leaves and then used my long Ecoware tray with sliced tomatoes in vinaigrette dressing, pickles, chutney, CELERY, that Richard bought. (I daren't ask how much). I halved eight eggs and mixed half the yolks with anchovy paste and half with tomato paste and put it back in the eggs. For a roughly unplanned meal, it looked very good, and both chaps ate heartily and it amused me the way they helped themselves to more when they fancied it. Eating buffet style is a bit continental though, isn't it? I found it so in Germany.

At two it was still damp, but our neighbour Jim, had suggested we visit the Dag Hammerschoeld memorial, where his plane crashed, but they had already seen it, not surprising since they have had four Sundays out with other people. However they wanted to look at the Congo border as this was the nearest to the Congo they would ever be. They picked a rather awkward day, as the army and police were looking for an Alice Lenshina, a rebel leader who has a 75,000 strong anti-Zambia government movement. When they last rose, they were chased out. They had no arms, and a fellow in Richard's office, who was once in the army, led the Zambians to fight these Lumba, who only had spears and axes and he said the Zambian army fled. When they re-assembled, the officers said that this time they would go in the rear and shoot anyone who turned back. This time, when the Zambians found they were winning, started filling the Lumbas with bullets and after the cease fire, the officers had to threaten to shoot any Zambian who carried on shooting. This Alice escaped from the Congo and Zambia believes she is trying to rouse up her followers.

On the way to Mufulira, we were stopped at a roadblock by police with rifles who examined the car. We got to Mufulira and took the Mokambo road and were stopped again by armed police, who told us it was O.K. to visit the border and come back. We then passed machine gun posts at the side of the road and rolled barbed wire barriers ready to be thrown across the road. It was slacker at the border than along the roads. People wandering everywhere. There is a stretch of no-man's land between the two posts and the difference with the Congo is marked. The border uniforms are very French with Gendarme type hats with back flaps and there were Citroens, and just coming through the border were two police cars with plain-clothes police in them. In the paper today, I read that "two car loads of police were last night in Mufulira, but wouldn't state their business." About 100 yards back from the border post, we spotted a camouflaged lorry and on looking closer, and slowing down slightly, we saw a whole encampment, lorries, trucks, tents, soldiers, the lot, but had we not spotted the one truck we would have missed the lot.

On the way back, we stopped at the Tudor Inn, six miles from Ndola and had drinks. It has just reopened and has fountains and a pool and a bar and served afternoon tea, rather like a civilised pub. We arrived back at six and I put a leg of pork in and did roasties and stuffing and the trimmings. As I had made a rhubarb pie, (tinned rhubarb, not fresh, but pleasant nevertheless.), I did Instant Whip with bananas in and chocolate grit on top.

It has annoyed us that Mackie said no-one must claim expenses for entertaining these chaps, even though the entertaining was compulsory, but he has put in his own claims and so have a couple of other directors. (Richard passes them so he sees them all). Although we have enjoyed having them, four meals and 130 miles worth of petrol doesn't cost nothing, plus the bottle of whiskey we bought. However, the auditors brought us a bottle of Harvey's Bristol Cream for our hospitality, and they were very appreciative of our efforts, exclaiming over the food, e.g. "This is superb" "Oh yes how I agree, most definitely" Very continental, but I appreciated it. When I apologised for the evening meal being late, they both said how nice it was being in a home and reading the papers,

While we were out we saw a bird about two feet high, like a swan crossed with a dodo. It was black with a red plume. It was walking on the edge of the bush. Only the Swedish chap and I had seen it and as we were telling the others it grew and grew, until Jutter, the Swede said it ran alongside the car shouting at us and it wasn't a red beak, it was breathing fire, and so on. We came across a clearing with three or four thatched huts and tacked onto a tree was "Lifebuoy" and a picture. Both chaps took photos to show at home how the sales had spread to the jungle. We didn't linger as there were people cooking around a fire.

Peter told Richard that the auditors had said what a good day they had had.

Our Monday play is now on. Part 5 already. At the end of last week's episode, they were being chased by a mammoth. Reception was unfortunately very poor. Must have been a storm somewhere.

Times of Zambia

28/10 A nationwide hunt is on for Alice Lenshina, plump, 43-year-old leader of the fanatical Lumpa Church who escaped from her lightly guarded camp at Kalebo.

Letter 72   01.10.67

Wednesday. Please excuse biro but my pen has run out and I can't open the ink and Richard's not here with his lid openers. Andre is quite good at pickle jars but he's not here either. We had a good night last night at the Ndola club, the food was OK and the company was OK, Mackie, (his wife is in the UK looking after her mother), Rubners and the auditors. But after the meal the company fizzled out because the bar isn't much good and it closed at 10:30 and long before then they were trying to throw us out.

The auditors went home today in separate planes. One went via Hamburg to visit his relatives but the other went straight home. After seeing the last off on the plane, Marlene popped around to see me and Pucci laddered her stocking! Was I embarrassed? Luckily I had a new pair unopened and after protests Marlene took them as she was out in the evening and hadn't any. Now our room. It's a lot lighter. A Valerie blueprint coming.

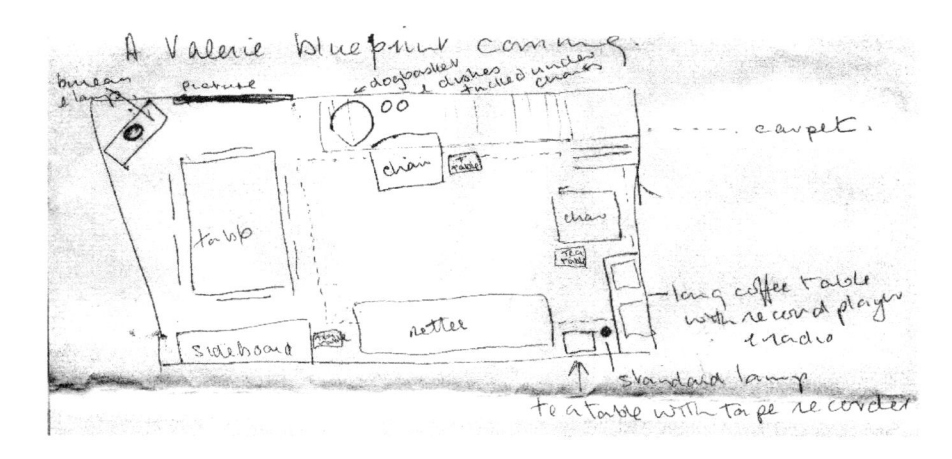

There was a dreadful storm last night and we were nearly flooded before realizing it. We didn't remember the upstairs windows were open and the floors and chairs were soaked. When we had finished mopping that lot up, we came downstairs to find the hall flooded from rain blown under the back door, so we had no time to film any lightening although the thunder was the spectacular thing in this storm. Pucci was terrified and he ran and hid under the bed but Richard got him out and for the remainder of the storm, Pucci sat on his knee licking Richard's fingers, his heart beating ten to the dozen.

Mackie has decided to give us £10 towards entertaining the auditors. This will fill the hole in our housekeeping. We bought a bottle of whiskey and a crate of ale that we would otherwise not have bought, plus what we spent on petrol and extra food, although we did enjoy entertaining them.

I met Joan at the cinema. She is working now and asked after you and asked to be remembered to you.

If UK National Insurance stamps are going up any more they should bring in some sort of no claims rebate, although the cost of administering such a thing would outweigh any gains from increases, and what government is keen on giving money back anyway. Perhaps an increase on the eventual pension for those who have claimed least, but I suppose that's not a very socialist type scheme.

The studying is going OK. I can only read the study notes at the moment and I have got some vaguely relevant books from the library, which help slightly, but can't do much until the proper books arrive.

The music teacher came back from her leave and rang me but I had to tell her that I hadn't been able to get a piano, and we agreed that until I could get a piano it wasn't much good taking lessons. I suppose I've got enough to do anyway.

African pants may be a good idea, but they only are sold in the wrong quarter of town and although I've passed through in the car, I've not been there nor have I seen another white face in that end of town but I'll pop to a shop on the end and have a look at the quality of the material. It's probably all made in Hong Kong anyway.

I must ask Peter about his work permit. I don't think he would be much bothered if he didn't get a renewal.

We have been getting the airmail edition of the Daily Telegraph in batches of seven, a week late from Levers. We are last of three to get them and I'm just going to start on this week's lot. Lovely.

Times of Zambia

31/10   **It is understood that half of the two hundred girls attending Seskale Secondary School are being treated for hookworm as a result of the school's poor drainage systems.**

Letter number 73   06.11.67

We had a quiet weekend this weekend. The weather is better now. The sun comes out hot enough for sunbathing and then comes a heavy shower, so our terrace is just the job for nipping in and out between showers, and it is sheltered and doesn't get too wet.

Jim came round for a meal on Saturday and the poor chap had rather charcoaled pork. We left it in the oven while we went and had a game of tennis and stayed out a little too long. The tennis court dries out reasonably quickly, but if it rains at 3:30ish, it's not dry enough again to play on, in the afternoon.

Pucci has lost another bottom tooth and is rather gummy. I hope he's not going to start chewing things all over again. Pucci is good in the mornings now. He now cries to go outside. Usually he was too quick for us.

Bonfire night was odd last night. We put the tape on loud so that Pucci wouldn't hear too many bangs. It wasn't quite the same. It was far too hot. We didn't see many fireworks as our house faces away from town.

Marlene had brought Sally a 10/- box of fireworks and they were going to have them before she went to bed as its dark at six. Marlene and Sally were to sit on the step and Peter had instructions to go to the other end of the garden and set them off.

We had a cup of tea and cake at Marlene's yesterday afternoon. She makes super cakes although she said it took her a long time to adjust her recipes to the altitude.

I've tried your fruit loaf and some recipes without much success. They end up like bricks, so I'll have to ask her for her recipes.

I shall post my Christmas cards by sea in the next week or so; I've still another packet of 10 to buy! Every now and then I think of someone else I must send one to.

No letter at lunchtime unless Richard fetches one home this evening.

I may have told you that Woodworth, our manager was having a braai at his house by a lake, but the idea has changed to Christmas dinner at the Tudor Inn in the middle of December, which I dare say will be just as enjoyable.

We have a raffle every week for a bottle of Champagne, the proceeds to go to a children's party, but I've not been lucky as yet. Perhaps I should draw a ticket in your name and see what happens.

Nancy Carter, the local scandalmonger, who is at the tennis club, is coming to live in Dolphin Court. She says, "My dear, you must come round and chat". Not flipping likely. She is friendly - very friendly with our funny neighbours, so the less she knows about our business, the better.

Times of Zambia

2/11 **The United Party plans to make a formal protest to the government over the illegal ban on party meetings**

Letter 74   8th November 1967

On arriving home yesterday afternoon, I found Richard at home supervising the installation of burglar bars, which I'm glad is being done before we go away for Christmas.

On going upstairs, I went into my bedroom and found the pillars for the dressing table had arrived and now instead of one mirror propped against the wall, we have three mirrors properly fitted.

Also in the corner was the chest of drawers to match the headboard and dressing table. It had a huge piece as big as your fist chipped out of the front, and two drawer handles missing. A new chest too. Fancy having the nerve to deliver it like that. The top drawer won't open either, as the key is jammed.

Unknown to me, Richard had already ordered a Bernina sewing machine for Christmas, and as usual, he couldn't wait to have it installed at Christmas, and when he told me to go into the backroom, there it was, complete with a loose flap table. The table came from a recently vacated Lever's house and Richard had covered the top with Contact. ALSO, laid out across the airfreight chest and a tea chest was a Scalextric racing car set. I just sat on the bed stunned and when I recovered I proceeded to shout at Richard, "Do you think we're made of money? How can we afford this? He was quite crestfallen. Apparently he received a sizable tax refund and £10.00 for entertaining the auditors, so decided to get the Bernina now, and he also found that he could buy the Scalextric wholesale. It was £5.15.00. He said it was his Christmas present from me and the back bedroom was now the recreation room.

When I cooled down, I read through the instruction book and cautiously had a go. It's wonderful. It just hums and I even worked out how to do the embroidery stitches. They are very simple. A special foot is clicked on, the lever set to embroidery and an indicator set to whichever stitch is required. I can have proper lessons on a Saturday morning, working through a manual and making samples. It even hems so that you can't see the stitches from the right side.

I am going to find out how much it would be to ship my own machine home for you to have. I don't want to sell it, as it was the first thing of value I bought and you know how long it took me to pay for it, and I know your little old faithful machine deserves a rest. One thing about my machine is that it has never given the slightest mechanical trouble. If the freight charge is too great, we shall just bring it home at the end of our tour.

This account is slewed somewhat. Richard bought the sewing machine to cheer me up after coming out of hospital having had a miscarriage. So he brought me home and asked me to go and see the surprise upstairs. I had lost loads of weight and felt so weak I just wanted to sit downstairs, but he was so convinced that it would make me feel better that he insisted I try. I made it on all fours a few stairs at a time, sitting down in between efforts. So being fragile, I just burst into tears because I knew we didn't have that sort of bank balance. Hence the tale of the tax refund. I later found out that he had taken out a bank loan, but the knowledge was softened by the fact that I was making great use of the machine and the loan had been paid off when I found out about it.

Mum's old machine was a German one which she bought pre war. Her Aunt with whom she lived wouldn't have it in the house. Mine was passed down and mum's went to an Africa charity in 1970 being a robust hand machine.

My two books arrived today by airmail and cost £2-4-0. The books themselves only cost half that, but at least I can start my studying in earnest.

I have a lovely creeper covering the trellis dividing us from next door. I've been training it to grow to the top, but it has been cut or accidentally broken at the bottom. I didn't realise until it began to wither. Am I mad?

Richard has found three of his shirts in shreds down the front. Two good white ones and a green sports shirt. We asked Andre and he said they were OK when he ironed them. I think it must be moths but they were only washed at the weekend. There are circles missing and strips out. It looks as though the strips have been cut out with a knife, but that doesn't explain the circles, so it must be a grub. The shirts are ruined as the damage is on the fronts and collars. I am going to buy some smoking insecticide and fumigate the cupboards.

We have a new messenger at the office and I wrote in his shopping book "a 2/6 AIRMAIL WRITING PAD FROM THE GOLDEN RAY (a shop). He comes back with 60 airmail letters from the Post Office. He said he gave the note to the fellow in the Post Office and that's what he was given. So neither could read properly. So we now have over a hundred airmail letters, which should keep us going until we leave, and after.

The enclosed slide is of me sculpting Richard's head. Richard says he looks like a toothless gnome, so he must agree that it's a good likeness.

Valerie Lapthorne

Chapter 23 *Molly*

What I didn't include in letter 74 to Mum and Dad, when I was 23 and newly pregnant. I had had stomach pains in the middle of the night and was on the doctor's doorstep when he arrived first thing next morning. Go home to bed, he said, and keep your feet up. If it gets worse, go to the hospital, or just stay at home and see what happens.

I went in to the office to tell the boss that I was going to have a few days off, to avoid a miscarriage. So far, so sensible. This would be the first they knew about me being pregnant. I knocked on the boss's door and opened it, as we did. He was at his desk with his assistant accountant standing at his shoulder perusing papers on the desk. There were two visitors in the room with their backs to me. I blurted out my set piece but spoilt it all by bursting into tears. There was an embarrassed flurry while I was ushered from the room by the deputy accountant. He must have summoned Cookie, because I found myself in the ladies' cloakroom, being provided with hankies, and Richard appeared, as he always does when I need rescuing.

We went home, but by late afternoon, doubled up with stomach cramps, I decided I would feel safer in hospital, not knowing precisely what "miscarrying" would entail.

I was put in the first section of a much-partitioned long ward. There were eight beds, grouped in two fours on either side of the central passage down the ward. My bed was alongside the central passage facing the main double doors of the ward, through which were a short corridor and a further pair of double doors. Matron's office and the bathrooms and utility rooms were in this no-man's land. To my right was an empty bed and opposite were a further two empty beds. The four beds to my left on the opposite side of the passage were also empty and between them a pair of open French windows. The sunlight was so bright outside compared to the dim light inside that it bleached out any view. Above my head was a knotted mosquito net and above my feet a languidly turning ceiling fan.

The nurse who had ordered me into bed appeared with a tray and drew the bed curtains around the bed. "Have you aborted yet?" I had heard vaguely of abortions. Seedy things done clandestinely with gin and knitting needles. I thought she was implying that I had tried to self inflict an abortion so vehemently denied this and was somewhat offended by the suggestion. She slapped a cloth covered enamel kidney dish on the bedside table with a *"change your dressing for inspection"* and left me. I meekly did as ordered and then didn't know what to do with the bowl. It didn't seem to be the thing to do to leave it and its contents on the bedside locker like a cup of tea or dish of fruit, so I lowered it to the floor and shoved it slightly under the metal bedstead and pulled my curtains back open.

I lay there a while watching the ceiling fan. It would spin slower and slower until it stopped and then would gyrate like a mad thing until it ran out of impetus and would again slowly grind to a halt. These cycles were irregular and I started to count the seconds between each and was about to doze off when a slight movement caught my eye. In the bed diagonally opposite, I saw what had escaped me before. A hump in the bedclothes, a tiny mop of tight black curls and two big eyes peering at me over the edge of the blanket. As our eyes made contact, the eyes and head disappeared under the covers. As they tentatively reappeared, I smiled and they disappeared again. The next time they appeared I had pulled my blanket up to my eyes and when they looked at me again, I pulled the blanket up over my head. I could hear giggles from the bed opposite. We played this game, without any diminution of the giggles on the other side and with increasing amusement on mine, until interrupted by an older nurse, with a friendly smile, a cup of tea and a sandwich.

"Who is the little boy over there?"

"Oh, that's Molly. She's six. She's just got boy's pyjamas on. That's all we could find for her. She's in for some tests on her kidneys. She should be out in a few days if she gets the all clear."

Richard arrived for visiting at the same time as Molly's parents, who were both barefoot. Father wore the khaki uniform of a domestic, removing his trilby as he entered. His wife sported a floral frock with a floor length kitenje tied around her ribs. Mother went to the French windows leading to the garden and retrieved an enamel bowl from a smiling, waving group peering in. Molly was delighted with this gift. It seemed to be a bowl of spare ribs, which she ate with relish and much slurping. She had previously been admonished for not eating her sandwich tea.

Both offices had sent me fruit and flowers with Richard, who had also brought in a writing pad and pen so that I could fabricate my regular letter. Richard was going to the cinema and to eat with Marlene and Peter, so it wouldn't be difficult to pretend I was there too.

After he left, sourpuss nurse came to take my pulse and temperature. She spotted the enamel bowl under the bed.

"How disgusting," she sniffed, "Have you hidden any more?" She yanked open the door of the bedside locker and then the drawer. At the children's home I worked at, disturbed teenage girls would often hide sanitary towels in their rooms until the smell found them out. Boys were inclined to hide turds.

I was indignant, "What sort of loony do you think I am?"

She turned away from me having run out of steam and spotted Molly's enamel bowl. She leapt upon it. "Look at this disgusting mess!" She picked up the sucked bones one by one and pinged them back in the dish. " Disgusting. Disgusting" and with both enamel bowls she bounced off to the sluice room.

Both Molly and I in trouble over our enamel bowls. I put my hands over my mouth and rolled my eyes conspiratorially and she copied me and we both fell about. When she fell asleep, I couldn't tuck her in, as I had to stay put. I fell asleep counting the rotations of the fan.

Molly was braver the next day. She ventured over to my bed, holding up her boy's pyjamas by the waist so that she did not trip. Soon she was sitting on the end of my bed. She spoke no English. I lined up all my fruit and she named them in Chibemba and I copied her. She thought my efforts were hilarious. I named them in English for her to do likewise. We scribbled pictures on my writing pad. She drew her extensive family and named them and I drew us and the dog and tried to show how we had come from a long way away in an aeroplane. Then we tried drawing the flowers that I had pulled from the florist's arrangement and the time passed comfortably with the occasional interventions to do medical stuff and admonishments not to let Molly pester me.

Months before, Vivienne from the office had shown me her hideous scar from her Caesarean section. It spread in a huge smile from hip to hip and had stretched about three inches wide at the centre with the gathered stitch marks like grinning teeth. She said the gynaecologist was a vicious monster with a clubfoot.

My gynaecologist arrived in the afternoon. She was no taller than four foot six. She had thick pebble glasses, which magnified her eyes like a giant codfish, and she spoke with a thick Germanic accent. And she had an orthopaedic shoe on a clubfoot.

Her head was on a level with mine on the pillow as she interrogated me. A platform was brought for her to stand on and she donned a huge rubber glove that looked like a vet's calving glove. It probably was. I backed up the bed as she approached me barking instructions. As my head hit the bars at the head of the bed, the friendly nurse whispered urgently, "Just hang on to my arm as tightly as you need." The gynaecologist pronounced that my pregnancy was no longer viable and that she would remove the foetus in the operating theatre the following day. I thought, at this point, that she had already done so with her fist.

They left me miserable, uncomfortable and feeling a long way from home. I surfaced from my self-pitying doze to see a small face. Molly had my pen in her hand. There was no need now for me to lie flat, so I sat up in bed and she climbed up and we made rows of torn out dancing dolls. She sang songs to me and I to her. The tune she most liked to dance the dolls to was the signature tune to the BBC World Service.

Slowly rousing from the anaesthetic from my trip to the operating theatre the following day, I got the fright of my life. Peering down at me was The Grim Reaper and I thought my time had come, but it turned out to be the Catholic priest in his black cassock. I apologised for not being up to conversation, but he already knew. "Never mind, my dear. Just think of the fun you'll have trying again."

I thought it was somewhat inappropriate for a priest to even know about the process of procreation, let alone think it was something to be enjoyed. I was a prude even then.

That evening was the fifth of November and we could hear the sounds of fireworks. Why would Zambians want to celebrate Guy Fawkes Night? Any excuse for a barbeque, I suppose.

There was a flurry of activity in the ward, and a young girl was brought in, with her foot and ankle in a huge bandage. At a bonfire party, a snake had bitten her and they would be keeping her in overnight. She was a beautiful child with long black hair and dressed in a bright pink shalwar kameez. By the time her parents left, she was fast asleep on the top of the bed like a little doll. Molly's parents had been shown the day's drawings and the dancing dolls and when they too left, Molly took a lot of interest in this sleeping princess. She then climbed back into her own bed and disappeared under the covers. I knew she wasn't asleep as she kept fidgeting. The covers were then thrown back and she dropped naked out of bed, threw her pyjamas on the floor and set off through the double doors and down the corridor.

"Nurse, nurse. Molly's escaping."

A very sulky Molly is returned to her bed.

"It's the pyjamas. She says they are boys pyjamas and she wants pink ones."

The nurse, the friendly one, persuaded her back into the boy's pyjamas and rooted in the bedside cupboard.

"Her mother usually leaves her something"

She retrieved an enamel bowl.

"I don't know what it is tonight. Something fishy, I think."

Molly seemed consoled by her fishy take away.

The next morning, her father arrived with a paper bag. Inside were girl's pyjamas. Not quite the Asian ones she wanted, but pink, floral and definitely not boy's pyjamas. Resplendent, she lay on top of her bed and smirked at the girl in the bed next door.

I found out later that the father's boss was paying for her bed on this private side of the hospital. Patients on the public side had families who sat outside and cooked for them. I suspected her mother and relatives did something similar with the number of enamel bowls that were passed in during the day.

The afternoon saw us in high spirits. Me, because it was all over, and Molly because she had her new outfit and both me and a new girl to play with. She spent her time dashing between the beds with drawings and paper dolls.

Next day we were all due to go home. I sat in my bed waiting for Richard to bring my clothes. Molly sat beside me. Our arms were touching, side by side. Her black skin was dry and dull. I thought black skin would be shiny. At Sunday school, we had a dominant picture on the wall, of Jesus in flowing robes surrounded by what were supposed to be children of the world. It was a Methodist church, big on African missions. We were given books each year containing tear out pictures of shiny, cute African children to sell for a penny each, to raise money. A hymn we sang then was "Praise Him, praise Him, oily little children" which I thought referred to these shiny, black children. My friend Pam told me recently that she used to sing, "Gladly, the cross eyed bear", with the result that all teddy bears in the family subsequently, were called Gladly.

Molly wasn't oily or shiny. Perhaps she sensed my thoughts, for she stoked my arm and said in perfect English, "white lady" and looked up at me without smiling. Not for a few seconds anyway. I hoped my next effort would be like Molly. It would be fun.

Shortly afterwards, Molly's father arrived with her clothes. She dressed hastily, piled her sheaves of drawings into her father's hands and ran past the end of my bed to the French windows, where her family were waiting.

Wave to me Molly. Turn round and wave to me.

But she was gone. Swept up in a flurry of floral skirts into the searing sunlight.

Her father packed her pyjamas and the enamel bowls and the drawings into a paper bag. He hesitated at the end of my bed and, with his trilby clutched to his chest, he gives me a bow. I bow back. And then he too is gone.

Chapter 24   Thunderstorms

Letter 75   **13/11/67**

Tony came for dinner on Friday night and he and Richard disappeared into the "recreation" room. When they had rearranged the circuit, I had to go up and have a race. The only way I could eventually stop them was by making coffee and refusing to take it up to them, so they eventually came down. On Saturday, Richard played nine holes of golf from 7 until 8.45a.m. We then went for the shopping, the office for milk, the library, and Marlene's for the meat. Peter Hitchman who arranges the milk is not doing so at the end of the month. He says it is too much messing about and I agree with that. People forget their milk bottles and expect to get double the next day, or forget or cancel it and want their money back. The churn is delivered each day with the required number of gallons, which is paid for in advance. You take it for granted that if you can't get in for your milk, then it's too bad. Anyway, Peter is losing out on it in cash and goodwill, so he's fed up. Don't some people spoil a good thing? Tea is undrinkable with reconstituted milk, (locally called constipated milk) and can only be drunk plain with flavouring. I'm so mad, but you can't blame Peter. He was only doing it as a favour.

Went to the tennis club where it was very hot, but we had some lovely fruitcake, that someone had made and I had three pieces for my 6d tea money. Pig.

Peter told us Marlene had been given 3lbs of prawns and they would go off quickly and did we want a load. Someone had brought them back frozen from Dar-es-Salem. So we went back with Peter and of course then had some tea. While we were supping, the heavens opened and it sheeted down and we were stranded for another hour, and even then we had to run for the car and got drowned in the process.

We had supper and went to Sally and Stuart's for the evening. They are having teething problems with the new house. The rains have come before they have got the roof on, and have also hampered brick making and general progress. Also, the hole from where the clay has been dug, is collecting funny things that Sally doesn't like e.g. water scorpions, just as deadly as the ordinary ones. The pioneering spirit is fine in the sun, but the rain seems to have dampened it a bit. The site is just mud at the moment.

I have arranged my Bernina lessons on Saturday mornings. Richard is most unhappy, as he says he will have to stay on the golf course for another hour and a half, and that will be such a nuisance. He is also a bit sorry he bought the machine, because he had two holey vests that I wanted him to throw out, but I salvaged them and practised my darning stitch on them. There is also a zig-zag stitch to strengthen where the fabric is wearing thin, so I strengthened away like mad. He now has the most beautifully patterned vests in Ndola, and I can't see why he is so reluctant to wear them. One can't spend all that money on a machine and then not put it to the fullest use.

Yesterday I got down to some serious studying and started a two-hour paper. Two hours! More like two weeks it took me. I had two cross sections from the ordinance survey maps to transfer to graphs. I thoroughly enjoyed doing it, but it took ages trying to do it beautifully seeing that it was my first paper. I also had two essay questions including a map. All I have to do now is make a fair copy of the essays.

Did I tell you that I wrote to the Ordnance Survey Dept. in Surrey and they wrote back and said they would send the map I wanted, but not to send any money out, as they would invoice me. I'm using the map and have not yet received a bill. They are very trusting seeing that I am 5,000 miles away and if I don't send the money, they have no way of getting it, but then again, if someone writes all the way to Surrey for a special map, then perhaps they may be of satisfactory character.

I gave Andre the prawns and he peeled them. I couldn't face it. They are so huge and slug-like, not pink at all. After they were boiled, they shrank to a fraction of their size, and stink! Boy. So much that I couldn't face eating any. I did them in batter for Richard, and he had them with chips. I had ham.

The jacaranda tree is the last slide. You will be able to put the projector away now and dust the sideboard.

Times of Zambia

13/11   Eighteen Zambians are being groomed for top jobs in local government in newly introduced courses aimed at early Zambianisation of exclusively expatriate posts.

17/11   There should be enough meat to last through the Christmas season, said a spokesman of the Cold Storage Board.

Letter 76   **15.11.67**

On my way back to work, I called in at a certain office, which I shan't mention in case the letter is read. I wanted a copy of two maps of the district which were displayed on the wall, but I was informed that she was unable to sell copies, but that she did have a few spare ones and asked what I needed them for, and I told her and she rolled two up and another small general map, and snapped an elastic band around them and said " There, if anyone asks, say you found them by the wayside". Well they are just what I need, and I'm delighted with them. Whereas on my Ripon map, there are symbols of woods, on these are symbols for forests and mud hut villages.

Pucci's baby teeth have all come out except one. The new tooth has grown up alongside it and the baby tooth is still in. He is still chewing things, luckily mainly his toys and Richard's old sandals (newish before Pucci came but taken over since.)

A most terrific bang shook the house and I'm still shaking and Pucci ran outside barking. I thought a plane had crashed, but I think it was thunder, although the sky overhead is quite clear. I'll soon know if it's a storm as a terrific wind starts and that's the warning to go around shutting the windows. Yes, there's more thunder, although a lot quieter. Pucci is cowering behind the coffee table. I must go and pick him up. He hates thunder.

Another terrible bang. I ducked in my chair. The storm must be coming from the north. No. I've just looked out of the kitchen window and its sunny with light fluffy clouds, but over Marsala, its grey and I can't see the hills beyond.

On Saturday, we are going out to dinner with Marlene and Peter. (What extravagance!) They suggested it, so we didn't refuse-it saves cooking something. Its not the cooking I hate, it's the thinking what on earth to have to eat. When I feel like having a banana buttie, Richard wants a roast and vice versa.

Richard's watchstrap on the watch I bought him for his birthday has rotted at the fastener. He has had to buy an expanding bracelet, not half as nice.

My smart ice bucket has split again. (Here's the wind, the trees are swaying, and its howling like on the Yorkshire moors. Richard will have to park his car outside the house instead of miles away.

I've just realised that I\m working the Saturday before Christmas weekend so I'll be entitled to the Friday afternoon off before Christmas. Good. As from the first of Jan, I'll also be entitled to four weeks leave. Not bad hey? And two more weeks than Richard gets next year.

I've sent my first test paper off. It was supposed to take two hours, but it took me all day. I was so careful and did everything in rough first. Richard says that'll soon speed up, and won't be doing it so painstakingly by the twentieth paper. If I don't take the exam or fail, I'll have had fun and it won't harm me any.

Cookie has just informed me that my Saturday Bernina classes have been booked with her. She is demonstrating on Saturdays and she is very good. I've bought a pattern for Sally, which is a plain dress with smocking on the sleeves and neck with a pinafore dress over the top. I want to do the dress in a small flowery print and pinafore in plain wool, but the prints are too mod, and wool is non-existent. I'll have to keep looking.

Richard is playing cars again instead of writing his mother's letter (clat-tale). He will probably write it over breakfast tomorrow. He has great trouble writing. I waffle on for ages and he has written an inch. He only writes sensible things though.

Times of Zambia

23/1167 Reckless profiteering traders were more evident in remote parts of Zambia than on the line of rail where the Price Control Office had launched a campaign against over charging.

Letter 77   20.11.67

We went to see a film, "What did you do in the War Daddy?" It was funny and I actually enjoyed laughing at it. Usually when a film is labelled comedy, I sit there daring it to make me laugh, but this was a clever film with some good ideas.

I've called at the library on my way to my Bernina lesson and got a good book on Zambia, not political, just factual and published in 1967. It is called A Social Geography of Zambia, by George Kay. It's just the job for my local geography and it's a new book I reserved on seeing its cover pinned to the notice board. I shall renew it until I'm requested for it. And if it comes to the push, I'll treat myself. I'm just looking at the sources and references in the back and find it refers a lot to "Horizon". This is RST's (mining company)'s house magazine and it has good articles and photos from pioneering and prospecting days. My sculpture teacher's husband is the photographer, and on the cover this month are three merged views of one of Mrs. Mills' bronze heads. These magazines are 1/- a month on a twelve-month subscription, so I might lash out.

Pucci is sitting on my knee while I'm writing this. He has been pestering me with a tennis ball since I came in, and tired of waiting, he has jumped on my knee, so now, I'm leaning on the coffee table to write. Pest. Richard can just shout "Down" and he'll jump down and hide under the chair, but even though I've shouted 'Down", he has now curled up with his chin on my knees. He's getting heavy now too. He's oversized for a Maltese, but this makes hi more of a dog and less of a toy. He's a good watchdog and doesn't bark at the doorbell, but if someone walks past the stoep, he stiffens his tail and growls in his stomach, real savage like!

Don't be so rude about my sculpture. I must send you a photo of the finished product, as Mrs Mills is now back and I'll have to break it up and return the base.

On Friday, just as we were leaving for the cinema, a woman calls for a donation to the caretaker's retirement. Everyone else had given 10/- so Richard did. I was mad. I am sure it was the caretaker who cut, and it definitely was cut, my creeper.

One of those weavils has got into Richard's suit. Only a little hole, but right on the lapel. We have sprayed all the cupboards.

Pucci's last baby tooth has dropped out.

I enjoyed my sewing lesson, even though it was very basic. I did learn a few things that I hadn't deduced from the instruction book. Margie also has a Bernina and is frightened to use it, and I said it was wicked not to learn, after her husband bought her the machine, so she called in to Bernina on Saturday and booked lessons with me. I bought two hangars today and as they are rough, I will cover them. They are handmade and were only 6d each.

A fellow came around today trying to sell a tortoise. He was swinging it around and had another in a sack. The usual trick is to say that they will eat it, or kill it, if you don't buy it and this usually extracts money from soft things like me, but I said No, Thank you, and turned away. Crooks like that should be locked up, but I suppose they are on to a good thing.

When we arrived at tennis, Cheryl had slipped on the court and cut all her back on the gravel. As I was the only girl at that time, I had to get out the first aid kit and mop it up. Ugh! Anyway, I put on my best Florence Nightingale face and sloshed her with Dettol.

On Saturday evening we went out for dinner with Marlene and Peter. We all had good meals and enjoyed ourselves. Then up comes a chap from

Richard's factory at about eleven and says are we going dancing at the Savoy, to which we say No, as it's 10/- each. He then says not to worry, as he can get us in on his ticket. We didn't believe him, but as we were about to go home, decide to go along with him, as we could at worst be kicked out. The man at the door rises to take our tickets, and our fellow motions the man to sit, which he did, and we all trooped in. We were dancing until 1.30a.m. There was a good band, but there has been a government statement banning restrictions on dress. Normally it is jackets and ties only and was very pleasant. This is to promote "the Common Man". However, the few Africans there were well dressed in suits, but there was a horrible element of Europeans, who seemed to be Irishmen from the mines. One looked like Stan Ogden from Coronation Street, complete with check shirt, red boots and hairy gap of stomach above his belt. He and his friends were absolutely stoned. We were dancing away from these animals, but is it any wonder Africans despise Europeans, if this is the sample they see?

Richard is dancing for joy, as with his new aerial, we have just picked up "This is Radio Moscow broadcasting in English to South Africa. So as well as Rhodesian and South African propaganda we will be getting all the Russian gab as well. Ah well it'll widen our horizons and no doubt make us as mad as do some of the other things that are broadcast.

How about devaluation! We are OK here as Zambia isn't going to devalue and that means that every £85-14-3 we send to the UK will be converted to £100 in our bank account. So if something costs you £5.00, I need only send you 84/- and the bank will give you £5.0.0. Good for us, hey? But not for you. Every £100 in the bank will have less buying power, won't it?

Richard has just picked up BBC World Service, and we've had Big Ben (sounds lovely) and the time announced as 4.15 (its 6.15 here) Richard says you can get a free year programme from the British High Commission in Lusaka. So we can have British Propaganda now too.

Chapter 25   Puzzle of shredded clothes

Times of Zambia

25/11   "A woman's place is in the home, not in the beer halls" said UNIP's women's regional secretary.

Letter 78   22.11.67

We were up at 5.30 this morning to take Richard to the airport. The lucky thing was going to Fort Jamieson to have a look at the running of the depot there. Look at your map and see how far away it is by road. Richard and Mackie and Eric Hannaford Hill went in a four seater, chartered plane. Eric stayed overnight and we were in the airport restaurant (a Nissen Hut) and were sitting sipping coffee when Mackie arrives with his chauffeur and camera. I think Mackie just went for the ride. Richard had his (my!) camera. Richard said he saw elephant and rhino, but missed them with the camera as it ran out as they approached them. The pilot buzzed them to make them run. He said he wasn't allowed to go over the game reserve, so they saw nothing more.

I've had a good day at work today. Pawson, my boss, had so much junk in his office that he had a shelf built to put it on, about 12 feet long, the width of the room. Most of the work affects me. There were loads and loads of papers and the disorder was holding up my work, so I had a blitz. I marched in to his office and said, "Do you mind if I can see what I can do with this?" He grunts his consent and all day I have been sorting. Everything is now in five big files, taking up about a foot of space. Beside these is an in-tray. This had been full with stuff dating to 1966. The hard core of stuff I didn't know what to do with, I presented him with at four o'clock tonight and said. "What about this? Should I reply to this?" and he sat there saying Yes, No, OK. I think he has been stunned by the tidiness. Anyway, he was pleased and I hope it will make my job easier in the future.

Richard, now home, says that Fort Jamieson had a bank, some Indian shops, their depot, and that was that. He said that hippos looked like grey slugs, but the baby elephants were rather good. The flight was very noisy. He couldn't hear himself think.

We are plagued by ants at the moment, great big flying things. If we have the light on and don't draw the curtains, they come in by the crack under the bottom of the door.

I am reading another Howard Spring novel. I do enjoy them and they take ages to get through as they are so thick and usually childhood to old age type yarns.

I bought Andre a plastic mac this morning but it was too small and I'll have to take it back. I just picked the cheapest. We have been intending to buy him a mac as for the last two mornings it has rained early on and he arrives rather wet and says "Too much rain today Madam, Very Wet" I am starting to think like an employer now. I bought the mac to prevent him catching cold (so that he won't lose a days work) and to stop him giving in his notice (too far to walk in the wet.)

There is a play on South African radio at eight, usually corny, but last week was a suspense thriller and very good, so we will listen in tonight while I get on with my maps and things.

I got my prints back from the bloke who took them at the party, but they are very poor. He has used highly contrasty paper, but at least it will show you the people we know. I'll send one in each letter. Look after them as they cost 45/- for nine. Five shillings each! Isn't that scandalous? You can see that I am one of the most fashionable. My skirt was tripping me up, but with it being corded silk. I was apprehensive about shortening it. Actually it's not a bad length, but I had it pinned to my top at the waist.

I had them all saying "butties" in the office today. You should have heard Margie. Ever heard a Rhodesian whacker?

Times of Zambia

27/11 The Times of Zambia would be banned by UNIP if it continued to publish false and distorting news of party

activities

Letter 79   27/11/67

What a horrible weekend. We have found the gremlins that have been eating Richard's shirts. – RATS! Ugh.

On Saturday evening, we came to go to the pictures and Richard got out his good suit, only to find that the front and the lapel were in ribbons. We didn't know what on earth had done it. With that we took everything out of the wardrobe. His overcoat was shredded at the collar and so was the lining of his terylene mac, and one of the new pairs of trousers had a piece out of the knee as big as an orange. By this time Richard was flinging the clothes out. We started on the cupboard and his golf hat was ribboned, but none of his jerseys had been touched. Then I found a bit of black stuff on a shelf and thought-mice! as this is what we found in the office stationery cupboard. As we now knew it was not grubs, we shifted everything to the spare wardrobe and cupboards. We had hesitated to do this before, as if it were a grub, we didn't want to spread them.

We decided that nothing could be done except report to the caretaker that we had mice. This we did and, as he was not in, his wife said he would call in the morning. So out we went to the pictures, Richard in the least chewed of his suits. He only has three, one being his heavy English suit. I really liked his brown one, evidently so did the rat.

We came in from the pictures and switched on the light and this damn thing ran across the kitchen. It was about eight inches long, not including its tail. I screamed and fled outside. I had visions of them pouring down from the wardrobe upstairs. Richard opened the dining room door and the dog dashes out. I grabbed him and we decided to go and see Peter, as I didn't want to go into the house again. We arrived at Rubner's about nine and had coffee and a reviving drink and then set off back, with Marlene saying we could stay there if we didn't fancy stopping at home.

We arrived back and Richard went around the house inspecting and declared it OK. I came in with Pucci.

The rat appeared to have only visited the kitchen, but what a mess. There was dirt all over the pine cupboards, fridge, stove and even my stool and a shelf on the wall, which was not connected to anything. The kitchen had been clean except for a frying pan, in which I had cooked Pucci's liver, and there were teeth marks in this in the cold fat, and a tomato ripening on the window ledge had been chewed and all my spice jars had been disturbed. We decided to stop, as it was obviously afraid of us and while we were in the house we hoped it would stay at bay. We slept together in the middle of the bed with a hockey stick and golf club propped at the side of the bed and Pucci on the rug at the foot of the bed. I slept but Richard said he was lying awake all night listening for scufflings.

Next morning, the caretaker examined the mess and declared it to be a mouse. I said it was a pretty huge mouse and that it had a very big appetite. He then said that we must move our clothes about more as they nest in clothes. Richard wore his suit on Wednesday and his trousers on Thursday and all the other clothes are worn once a week, as we have no old clothes. The only things that are not used are our big, heavy overcoats. He tried to insinuate that it was our fault.

The day passed uneventfully until evening. Richard went for a coke and saw a mess in the sink. We had deliberately left the kitchen spotless. We decided to wait half an hour then Richard went back and there it was, but it was too quick and dived under the sink. We examined under the sink and found a small hole in the corner leading to the water pipes. On examining this cupboard, we found dirt and also in two empty drawers, one only housing a hot water bottle. Luckily the food cupboard was untouched and all the food is in Tupperware boxes anyway, even the packets.

The caretaker said we couldn't call in the health department, and that we should put poison and traps down. Ugh! I always associated mice with dirt and as you can imagine, our house is spotless, even the cupboards, as, with not stopping here long, we were deliberately not accumulating any junk, or excess luggage. As we have a lot of cupboards and minimum clothes, things are spread out and believe it or not, very tidy.

At lunchtime today, Monday, Alan Phillips, a new chap from Richard's office, in charge of housing, came along. He found the hole in the wardrobe. Between the wardrobe and the ceiling is a gap of about an inch or two, where he said it had not been fitted properly and there is access from the loft. This is so in all the wardrobes and he reckons his report should go to the firm leasing the flat.

Our "fully comprehensive" insurance policy says in small letters "no claims for mildew, moth or vermin" and appears to only cover fire and theft.

Alan says it is definitely a rat, not a cane rat or a sewer rat, but a smaller version he just called a roof rat.

We went out after work to someone's farewell drink and set traps before going. We got back and one trap had its cheese taken but had not sprung. We left them on the draining board well out of Pucci's way. We had our meal, washed and polished and reset the traps. Richard had also bought twelve plastic bags at 3/9 each (Ouch) and covered his remaining clothes and my two coats and a suit.

Alan has called the health department and he will have all the holes around the pipes cemented and the wardrobes repaired and men will put poison down in the roof. The loft is communal, so others may have had them too.

Times of Zambia

28/11 **Measles kills fifty in Mpika. The Ministry of Health was not notified of the epidemic.**

30/11 **The Pink Peril. Little pink caterpillars are chewing their way in farmlands in parts of Zambia leaving behind a destructive trail of dead and dying food crops.**

Letter 80   28/11/67

We had Enid and Pat for supper with a secondment called Percy Furlinger. We had spaghetti bolognaise with a side salad and I bought small cucumbers and cut them in half and scooped out the middles in balls then mixed the middle with shrimps and filled them up and put sails made out of a cross section of the top on a cocktail stick. The meal didn't take long to prepare which was lucky as it was a Friday. Richard and the two men disappeared up to the recreation room for an hour, and all we could hear were cries and groans, and we eventually followed them up, but I refused to take them coffee and made them come down for it.

Saturday, Richard played tennis and I cut out Sally's dress and then took the tacked up dress to Marlene's and tried it on her while she was half asleep. I cut it smaller and it fits well. I then went to buy cinema tickets and back to Marlene's for afternoon tea as she had another Lever wife coming, but who didn't turn up. All the more cake for me. Marlene makes super cakes.

The picture we saw in the evening was Tubruck and was about a battle in Egypt and was the usual war film, but it was in colour and had some good moments.

Sunday at home. Richard pottering and Scalextricing and me making Sally's dress. It was more involved than I thought, as it had a frill around the neck and sleeves and the sleeves are gathered into smocking. I did a mock smocking and everything on the machine even the tacking and gathering.

I spent until tea break today doing the flowers for the office. Super.

All my text books have arrived from Foyle's today, all ten of them, two of them quite hefty ones, but no sign of my study notes. The college sent the study notes on the ninth of October, but Foyle's only sent these by sea on third of November and I received them today. They are good books but Wow, Chaucer and Marlowe. They are like a foreign language. Not a good novel amongst them.

Weds. Vivienne has just called for an hour after work. Her husband is now working freelance window dressing, but judging by the number of windows to be dressed, I don't think he can be doing so much, and Vivienne seems to be supporting him, not vice versa, and it's about time he got down to some work. Vivienne is getting put out of her bachelor flat as it is only a concession until they got another one as Vivienne's firm don't give flats to married women, unless they are on their own.

We are off to the pictures to see "Bunny Lake is Missing" Richard is wearing his UK suit until I can patch the other that's not so damaged.

We've still not caught the rat. This morning, the trap was on the floor, sprung. I had tied the cheese on it with a piece of cotton, so he couldn't sneak off with it, but a big mouthful with teeth marks had gone. Ugh. But I am making sure there is not the slightest thing to attract it and all the clothes are in plastic bags. We still hope we can claim from someone.

Richard has just pulled the curtains and a big lizard dropped out and the three of us chased it around the room and outside.

My English textbooks are Edward Second, a play by Marlowe, Rasselas by Johnson. The Tempest, Othello. Milton's poems, Spencer's Faery Queen and two by Chaucer. Not a good yarn amongst them. Every one full of Ye's and Thou's. Last year there was Wuthering Heights and a John Osborne and D H Lawrence. Never mind. It's a new field.

I am writing this in the middle of the dining table. I am sitting on it, as there is a moving lump in the curtains. It may be the lizard from under the door, but I am not taking any chances. I heard scratching and saw the lump moving. Pucci came with me and didn't even raise an ear. He's sitting looking at me as though I am mad. Richard has gone for the cinema tickets and should be back in ten minutes.

Pucci now takes cod liver oil from a spoon. The dog book says to disguise it in his food, but half is usually left on the spoon, so I gave it to him to lick and he loves it and licks the spoon all over.

Chapter 26   Budgeting

Times of Zambia   December 1967

2/12   1. President Kaunda said that the British bulldog still has teeth but they are made of rubber.

2. Zambia has been facing a serious shortage of sulphuric acid resulting in a number of garages being unable to change batteries.

Letter No. 81   4/12/67

Happy Birthday Daddy xxxxx

Well we're into December and who would think it. I can say this year with truth "it doesn't feel a bit like Christmas."

Andres didn't turn up on Wednesday so I popped home at my tea break to let Pucci out for a run round and see if Andres had arrived which he had. He then announced that he was late because "wife have new baby". After a third degree, he says that it's a boy and his third child and both his wife and baby were well, so we gave him an extra £1 on his wages for the new addition. At least he can't produce another one for 9 months at least.

At last we have managed to buy him a mac, which was 25/6 for the bigger size. When I came home at night he had washed and ironed Richard's golf hat which the rats had got at, and which I had given Pucci to play with. He hovered around for a bit and then came in with the hat. He asks, "What is madame to do with this?" Madame replies, "Why?

Do you want it for the rain?" "Yes, for the rain" he replies and jams it on his head. I could hardly keep my face straight to point out that he could have it but that the rats had chewed it a bit. Anyway he needed it as it rained solidly from 4.30 yesterday afternoon until 11 this morning.

On Saturday, it was dull and Richard went up to the tennis club to see if there was a game and I, with a precious jar of mincemeat (normal size 4/) made a flat tart (I've no pie tins). Then a storm started, and what a storm. At a big peal of thunder, Pucci dashes from under the settee and jumps on my lap and puts his head under my arm. I felt like jumping on someone's lap myself. Richard got stranded at the club, and as there was tea and cake and butties on the go, I'm sure he didn't try too hard to dash for it. A flash of lightening struck the telephone wire and rang the bell, and another flash flashed and there was a terrible crash upstairs and then a tremendous thunderclap overhead. I thought the house was coming down on top of me. Anyway when it had subsided I went upstairs and the light bulb in the spare room had been hit and there wasn't an inch without glass on the floor. I left it for Richard to see, as I couldn't clear it up without Richard around to keep Pucci out of the way.

Richard comes in when the rain became lighter and he didn't notice the lovely smell of mincies. I produced some slices with coffee and he said, "No thanks, I'm not keen on mince pies." I could have hit him over the head with them. What sort of bloke is this I've married that doesn't like mince pies! But I noticed that he has since matched me slice for slice.

I went for my Bernina lesson and did some flowery patterns. Quite tricky but good fun.

We are also trying to work to a new budget and to stick to it strictly. So we are buying the non-perishable items once a month. We bought ¾ of a month's supplies on Saturday (one week in Richard's pay month had already gone). It was murder shopping as it was the end of the month, but normally Richard's pay day is the week before the end of the month i.e. the 21st so we should be shopping at the quietest time. But the Saturday after next payday is 23rd December! Richard will then just draw out per week enough for eggs, milk, meat and our spends.

We have been buying what is called whole milk, which isn't reconstituted but is not normal. It's like thin condensed milk and very sweet and a bit sickly in coffee but OK on cornflakes. We don't drink tea anyway as I drink so much at work.

Did I tell you that because of a suggested tax that is rumoured to be coming out in April, that I shall have to stop work? Married women are to be taxed at 10/8 in the pound so my pay will be reduced by more than half. I now pay £5.18.0 a month pension and £2 for something else, both of which I get back. The first on leaving, and the second on leaving the country. Personal levy, normally £2.0.0 per year is to be increased to £10 per year so that's roughly another £1 a month. If I stop work, Richard will gain £10 per month in tax, so I will be working for less than £6 per week.

The idea is to stop European women working and introduce Zambian men, which is, I suppose, a good idea from the government's point of view, but I think it will be too drastic, as most of the shops and banks and businesses are still employing large numbers of married women.

In our firm out of 11 girls, seven are affected, Cookie, me, Margie, the secretary, the copy typist and our African receptionist and Mrs King, leaving Mrs Kent, Mrs Bailey and Mrs Giles who are widows and Susan who is single. Cookie who runs the office would probably have her salary doubled but the rest of us, being clerks would have to go. This means there would be no staff to train new ones, and even a month's notice is too short to train a new one, and who anyway would fancy training someone who was shoving them out of a job.

Mrs Kent and Mrs Giles say that they would leave and go south as they couldn't work with a new staff, whose habits e.g. blowing their noses without handkerchiefs, would make it too unpleasant to stay. Susan said she would stick with it until she married and Mrs Bailey, who is a wonderful 70, will probably retire.

If all the reactions are the same, there will be many vacancies for local people, but at what a cost!

Also shopping in shops with untrained staff would be unpleasant. It's bad enough now, another reason for making a shopping trip once a month.

Richard's place would be in a mess too. A local man would be Mackie's secretary.

Your Monday letter arrived Saturday and your tape on Sunday 3rd. Good going hey? Peter Rubner delivered them as he has the postbox key. I loved the tape, especially the children. What was Sharon saying? Is she attending hospital for speech therapy? I liked Paul's seagull. It frightened the life out of me, and Neill's "Poly pu da kekkle ON" with a broad Yorkshire accent.

Fancy Alan smashing the piano. It was in a better state than the one we were going to pay £55 for.

We've not been to the boat club for three reasons.

1. Dogs are no longer allowed and we used to take Pucci there for a walk. He was always on the lead.
2. Richard is not advised to swim.
3. Our membership has expired and we haven't the current funds to renew it.

We only hear of Jill when I see her mum.

I still love driving. I hope I shall drive OK at home. Here one has to cope with lousy drivers, busy roads and parking in town and ton-up kids in fast cars on the longer roads.

Daddy, how long has the strike been on altogether?

Stuart called with a pad of graph paper for me, and Marlene has given me some old stuff of hers and Richard brought me a roll. I'm doing well. This was after I moaned that it was so expensive a sheet.

Times of Zambia

5/12 So drunk he did not realize the girl in the bed was his daughter.

6/12 Lusaka Mayor, Whitson Banda has offered to resign if charges of corruption, bribery, inefficiency, and nepotism against the City Council are proved.

Letter No. 82   6.12.67

Our Monday serial has now finished. It was good for episode 1, 2, 3, dull 4-9 and had a good twist to the end, which we nearly missed, as the reception is awful.

Marlene and Peter and we decided to go halves on a New Year's Eve party (or Old Year's Night as they call it here) but everyone is going somewhere and it looks just like being maybe six or so of us! I think we'd be better going to one of the parties everyone else is going to.

I've finished Sally's dress but for the tidying up and the hem. I'm not finishing off the seams until I try it on her at the weekend.

We are opening our tin of sausages tonight. Richard has said I must not heat them but wait for him to cook them, as he doesn't want them spoiled!

Still no sign of any study notes, my Museum Book, Birkenhead Newses or Liverpool Illustrateds. Perhaps it's something to do with the dock strike and I think the Benguela railway is closed again. I'll probably get them altogether in six months' time.

Everyone in the office is getting new outfits for the office dance. Margie and Cookie have new dresses and Margie wants me to go and buy shoes and bag with her. I would like new shoes and a bag as my one bag that I bought for my 'going away' outfit has had it, as I use it for work and it is a bit shabby, but whereas Margie thinks nothing of paying £10 for shoes and bag, I go white at the thought. The shoes I like are £5.19.6 and bags are all over £4. They are not leather either, just moddy straw and plastic ones. I don't like suggesting such frivolous things, with Richard wearing his smelly old corduroy jacket with his suit trousers. Mackie met Richard today and said 'That's a smart jacket Richard' Ha! Ha!" And Peter Rubner said 'It's the only one the rats left'. Good for him because Mackie thought the fact that we had rats was rather amusing. I want to patch Richard's coat and make him wear it to the next cocktail party.

The rat (or rats) is still around. The men came and put fresh poison down, and it's wolfed another pile and left dirt and mess in the pan cupboard. It's a good job we covered the shelves in Contact as Andres can wash out the cupboards every few days, which he couldn't have done with the chipboard. The first time they came to put poison down, they put it in the bottom of the wardrobe and all around the spare room floor and on every shelf and even in the airing cupboard. I went into the spare room and Pucci bounds in after me and I grabbed him as soon as I spotted it. Wasn't that stupid of them. It must have been obvious we had a puppy. We brushed it up from the floor and the bottom shelves of the wardrobes where Pucci can get, but blow me if they didn't come again on Monday and put more down. And they didn't put any in the loft where they are scampering around. I should have thought that a couple of doses up there by the holes into the house would have been better than little piles around the house which means that they have to come into the house to eat it (it's mixed with a bran).

I've just thought. I'll wear my blue backless dress with the lacy top with my patent leather shoes and maybe buy some mad earrings or a bangle or something to go with it. I've got a black evening purse (not very mod but very much manager's wifey. It's probably better to go smart, than to make a poor attempt at being with it. Actually I'm at a good age for clothes. I can still wear short, short mod dresses but can also wear smart things too.

It has been dull again today with heavy rain all morning. Now and January are the wettest. We must book our holidays soon, but we can't decide on dates. It's got to be after June. Richard's contract says that local leave must be taken in the year in which long leave isn't taken, which we take to be March 67/68 but the firm say is after June, because long leave is taken in 1969 (Mar-June). Our local leave must be in 1968 after June. Some reasoning! Anyway Peter is on leave until June. I don't mind because the later they are the better, because after our holidays it will be so much nearer to coming home. In fact there'll not be much point in unpacking!

Everywhere is beautifully green here and the locals are starting to plant the mealies, which once they get started will grow like beanstalks.

Later. Richard has just come in at six in a bad temper. Levers have had a letter from our next door neighbour in her capacity as manageress of the firm who owns the flats complaining that we have been parking two cars outside our house, which on two or three nights in the last month we had done. She said we had parked outside for the last fortnight. I am mad. I feel like writing saying that if she looked out of her door instead of peeping behind her curtains she would see that it was only two or three times. These times have been twice when we came in very late, once after the Savoy, which was at two in the morning, and as there were six parking spaces outside we left the car outside. Once was after the pictures and Richard went to play golf at seven in the morning and took the car away. The other time was when it was raining and we were drowned running from the car to the house let alone, three blocks of flats away. The woman herself parks in a handy space around the corner of her house and I suggested that I park my car there until Richard comes in to keep the space and stop her getting it (aren't I awkward). As I have said before, Richard is now forced to park as far away Auntie Elsie's is from you and this is useless in our sort of rain. I've just remembered that Richard parked outside after tennis on Saturday during that storm, but he moved the car after the rain, but she probably was watching her TV then.

Enclosed also was a circular which was issued to all tenants. "No radios after 10 o'clock" "No articles to be left on the terrace". She has just sold her aviary – coincidence that the circular only came afterwards? She has an oil drum with a rose in it. I wonder if she'll move that! Mutter, mutter.

Peter told Richard that Nick Mengel, who lived here before us, had a motorbike, which broke down, and as he wasn't allowed to mend it on the car park, he sneaked it round onto the terrace on the Saturday and stripped it and mended it over the weekend. On the Tuesday there was a letter at Levers from her threatening eviction! No one overlooks our terrace and she could only see the terrace if she came onto the lawn and looked up. Oh well. If we find any of our rats I'm going to put them under her door. Nasty aren't I? Ah well. It's all experience and very character building.

Those sausages were lovely. We may get some more but at 5/2 a time! The sausage I used to buy were 1/7 for eight and they were skinless.

Times of Zambia

8/12/1967 Railway Pact. Congo-Kinshasa has agreed to put its railway at Zambia's disposal to free Zambia from its reliance on Rhodesia's railways

Letter No. 83   11.12.67

No letter today, probably because of the pilots' strike, because the VC10 didn't arrive at all yesterday. However we have received loads of other stuff. We got our cine back, which must remain unseen for a while, a few Christmas cards, an October Nova, a Liverpool Illustrated News, the first for a while, and the next load of my study notes. I have my second test paper back – I've never seen so many red lines on one page. Never mind. The comments were all helpful and reasonable. My two lots have been 67% and 53%.

I am writing this sitting at Marlene and Peter's. We are babysitting while they are at a cocktail party and we are eating with them when they come in. Poor old Pucci is on his own, but we are not stopping very late. It depends of course when they come in and how merry they are.

On Dec 14th last year was our office dance when Richard came back late from London with our 'good' news. Twelve months to the night, Dec 15th is our office dance here. Who would have thought I would be going to another office dance so different. And yet I feel as though I have known our office staff for years.

Brian and Billy in the office (have I mentioned them?) were in a horrible smash up on Friday. They killed a man who was mending a tyre in the middle of the road. It was on the Bull & Bush road, so you can imagine what driving conditions are at night. Brian is still unconscious with a broken skull, shoulder and damaged spine. As you can imagine we are all holding our breath for him. One of our chaps is always at the hospital. Billy escaped with face lacerations and bruises and shock. Even if Brian recovers fully, there'll be court proceedings etc. His mum is hoping to come up from Rhodesia to him. With being in the office on Saturday morning, I had the job of trying to contact his mother in Bulawayo for our manager, who has done as much as he can. It's funny how the office rallies round like a family, because most of the people are on their own and the office is the only source of friends.

Brian is such a jolly chap, he taught me my job, and the dance on Friday won't be the same without him.

I've stuck my cards onto the bars on the stairs. It's surprising how attractive it looks with the various shapes and sizes and the graded stairs. I felt all miserable because I remembered that I didn't have an Advent calendar, and that very evening, looking for a nice card for Joan, I spotted one in the newsagents. The girl informed me it was the last one. I now have it in the centre of my cards, but it's not the same, having no-one to compete with to open the doors. Richard doesn't even know it's there, I'm sure.

We still have rats. Richard saw it run across the kitchen last night. Most of the poison has been eaten, but they are apparently thriving on it. Perhaps it's supposed to feed them up so that they can't get through the holes. Richard is renewing his efforts to get the workmen to block up the holes.

Sally and Stuart were to come last night after their call from home. But they rang at 8.30 to say they were still waiting. So they are now coming on Wednesday. Apparently the call had come through, but neither end could hear the other. Sally could recognise her mum's voice but couldn't hear what she was saying, and she said it was so frustrating and disappointing after staying in all day, on edge, waiting for the phone to ring. At 8.30 they were still waiting to be reconnected as they were cut off after about thirty seconds! We will decide on Wednesday when we see them, whether it is worth ringing home at any time.

At the office we dragged out a box of Christmas decorations, but we were too hot to put them up and have left them there.

We have just started ordering polish and stuff for the office, wholesale. Previously we have bought retail! Anyway I suggested we make up orders for cases and split them amongst us, to save money. We got £36 worth of stuff for £26.13.5. The only things people required enough of to order complete cases were pet food, orange juice for children, Sanpic, floor polish, Jik (bleach) and fly spray (7/1 instead of 9/-). I only ordered stuff I buy normally, otherwise it wouldn't have been a bargain if I were spending what I saved. This afternoon I made invoices out for everyone and made up the orders into the boxes the stuff came in and delivered it all on a trolley. It depends on how easily we collect the money whether we do it again.

Mackie is on leave in the UK (2 months leave every Christmas!!) and a couple are living in his house here and it's been burgled. With Mackie away it's not known how much is missing, but it is believed he'll claim from the company for double his loss, that's for sure.

Chapter 27   Sewing and Post

Times of Zambia

12/12/67   The Minister of Transport, Power and Communications is expected to make a statement in Parliament today concerning the breakup of Central African Airways

Letter No. 84   13/12/67

(New pen – the one you bought Richard) I'm just waiting for Vivienne to arrive. She should have been here by now.

Poor Nanny. But at least it solves a problem. The hospital now knows that she is not fit to live alone and depending on how fit she becomes, she will either go to the annexe or a home. I suppose pneumonia and shock are a big danger too. But however things go, it's out of your hands. Your biggest job is sorting out her house (and what a job – probably best to burn most of the stuff and pass the rest to a saleroom) Proceeds, if any, will bring her some decent clothes if she stays in hospital. Don't whatever you do, wear yourself out visiting. Take it in turns with Auntie Ve.

How was Uncle Charlie taken ill? What did he die of? Sounds as if they both went on an almighty binge.

When Nanny, my grandmother was widowed, her brother came to live with her. He was a bit simple and had been since he returned from the trenches at the age of nineteen with his toes lost to gangrene. He shuffled round for the rest of his life whistling tunelessly. One night he collapsed and died in the street after a night out at the pub. When the police arrived to tell Nanny, she was unconscious at the back of the front door having fallen downstairs. She had broken her leg.

Daddy, you make sure Mummy doesn't go worrying about things that might not happen, or such like.

I had a lovely letter from Gran, written just as she would tell the tale e.g. "and the postman said, I've had to be careful with these, they're flowers from Cape Town and I said to him, "I don't know anyone from there" and then our Fred says, "Oh look it's from Val & Richard." She was obviously pleased and I'm very glad I sent them.

I've not heard from Mrs L about hers. I hope she gets hers safely. I'm glad they're ok. I ordered them through a shop here and all three names were on the same form, so if two lots arrive, the third should. I thought white flowers might be a bit insipid. I just bought some flame lilies today from a boy who had picked them wild. They were 2/- and I beat him down to 1/6. I was disappointed because they are only about the size on the enclosed postcard. I thought they would be huge. They are rather like aquilegia. Richard says I can treat myself to a vase. Goody! They are in the kitchen at the moment in a Nescafe jar! Talking of flowers. The ones that I planted and thought were coming up, have been weeded! Cookie says that if Andres weeded them, then they would have been grass, but I'm not sure as he weeded my primula!

I've got a small card to send you. The boy selling it said it was 1/-. It was a bit grubby but I gave him a shilling, as it seems insulting bargaining for something he has painted. He had a selection in an exercise book, and it's painted on paper that looks as though it's from an exercise book. I'll enclose it after Christmas when the post has regulated itself.

We are talking holidays. Richard brought more brochures home on Mauritius and it looks a real paradise island. He wants to go in May, but this is their cold season. September, October and November are the warmest and driest. I fancy going in November as it would give us longer to save up and all next year we would be looking forward to it and then no sooner had we came back then we would be packing up, to come home. It is £115 for a double room and I've a horrible feeling that that is each! So you can see we will need to save. Prices are also going up because Zambia Airways have broken away from Central African Airways and we must fly to Salisbury and from there to Mauritius instead of direct to Mauritius from Ndola as before.

Eventually made it to Mauritius in 1997, thirty years on.

Brian, from the office, is a lot better, and is now off the danger list. He is recognising his visitors and can move all his limbs, so his spine isn't damaged. But he remembers nothing of the accident, except that there was one, and was most concerned over the state of his car. It may be a safety device of his brain, shutting off his memory until he recovers physically. He doesn't yet know that the other chap, who was a friend of his, is dead.

Vivienne hasn't turned up; it's now six o'clock. Jill's mum and dad are leaving here on the 10th of Jan for Liverpool, after all these years. The only snag is that Jill's elder sister has married a Rhodesian boy and is well settled in Bulawayo.

Later. Sally and Stuart are due now 7.30. We have just cleared up after supper. I didn't mention supper so I hope they have eaten. Wouldn't it be awful if they haven't!

We put the decorations up in the office today. There were a few super ones. Three in fact. Apparently there were more, but after last year's party held in the office they disappeared. I just put the whole lot around one doorway in a big splash and left the rest of the room plain.

P.S. The men came to block up the rat holes today. We can still hear and see dirty signs of him!

P.P.S. Happy Christmas

Times of Zambia

14/12/1967   **Lusaka magistrate warned yesterday that anyone appearing in future in cases relating to the anti mini skirt campaign, would be dealt with severely, probably by caning.**

Letter 85

Well we have had a very fun weekend.

On Friday I had my half-day, and in the morning coming back from the bank I bought a pair of pale green patent shoes (£5.9.6!). I've had my eye on them since the day when I went with Margie to buy shoes. Very mod. When I went, all my size had gone but I got a half size larger as with the strap across, they won't slip. I bought them to match my dark green dress, the silky one. Remember. But when I got them home, they clashed horribly. I was in a panic, as I wanted to wear them, having bought pale green stockings too. So after lunch I went and bought three yards of material from an Indian shop in the seedy part of town. It is an African print the sort the Africans wind around for skirts with a broad pattern along the bottom. The Indian didn't want me to buy it and just shrugged his shoulders. It is maroon and white and was 7/- a yard (compared with the other stuff, that's cheap). It is a lineny cotton. Just a mo, I'll go cut a bit.

You can see I've opened my pinking shears. Having just the afternoon to make the dress, rather than go and borrow Cookie's I cheated. They are super. Had to cut the pattern across like this.

> to cut the pattern across like this. As is only 36" wide, you can imagine that its shar shart. The style is like this [sketch of dress] ← Tent. I sewed & sewed & in between I washed my hair. At 7.10 I ironed it & as you can see, it ironed beautifully.

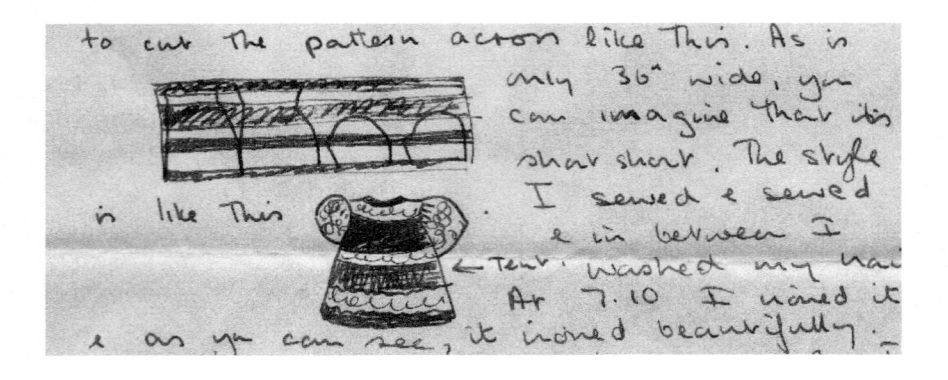

I sewed and sewed and in between I washed my hair. At 7.10 I ironed the dress and as you can see, it ironed beautifully being stiff, and it stuck out. Mind you when I just tried it on it was more like a marquee than a tent but with Richard sticking pins in it, the finished result was one of the most striking dresses I've made. In fact Cookie met someone who said, "Who was the girl with the long dark hair and that gorgeous dress." (I'm doing an Auntie Nance.) *Auntie Nance was a friend of Nana's who was always boasting.*) Anyway, believe it or not we arrived at the Tudor Inn at eight, complete with my hair curled and contact lenses and tights, as my dress was so short you could see my stocking tops when I stood up!! We had a jolly good meal and paper hats and crackers and cigars on the table and loads of wine and champagne. Our next-door neighbour was in the band. We now realise why he falls up the stairs at three in the morning! And pees loudly and long. We had an excellent night – the best party I've ever been to. At about 3a.m., there were only about five couples left, and Pawson went mad and with what was left, bought the five girls a 4lb box of chocolates each. I've never had such a huge box and the picture on the box was so good, I'm going to hang it in the bedroom! Despite the heat it really felt like Christmas, what with party frocks, turkey and beautiful decorations. There was a rainstorm just before we left and the road to the Inn was steaming creating a mist about 6 feet high. This in the dark with the bush and our headlamps was very eerie.

Saturday morning having got to bed at four, Richard was on the golf course at seven, and I was sitting on the terrace. That's the trouble with servants coming in. When Andres had done the bedroom at about nine,

I got back into bed and woke with a lousy head at 10. My Bernina lesson was at 9.30 so when Richard came in at 10.15, we crawled down there and I arrived to see Cookie giving a lesson with her sunglasses on. Margie had just been and gone, saying she felt lousy. The other women at the class were laughing at us saying it must have been a good party.

At two, after some soup Richard went to play tennis and Marlene and Sally called. When they left, I went up to the tennis club. We both came home at five and proceeded to get ready for our "night out" at the theatre, seeing the Gala Performance of the Sound of Music. I was falling asleep getting ready. When we arrived, me in my green shoes and green stockings and long dress, we sat in the car until we saw someone arrive (we were half an hour early) in evening togs. Then we went in. We were presented with special Gala night programmes, a flower for me for my dress and 20 cigarettes for Richard. (*Who has never smoked, I must add, in case you think this was a youthful secret.*) Gradually everyone arrived, and I have never seen such gorgeous long dresses. Nine out of ten were long and some were most elaborate. The show was good and the children were excellent. We met the mother of the youngest child beforehand (I've met her before at Cookie's). Her daughter was five and was super, and of course, stole everyone's hearts with her little lisped solos. It's surprising to see how much talent there is in a small community. We saw on the programme, a couple, whom Mike had told to contact us; they are his friends from Birkenhead Operatic. Richard met her afterwards getting drinks and introduced himself. We then had supper, tongue, ham, chicken and salads and rolls and things. Very welcome. We sat at a table on the lawn, and munched away. It was a very picturesque sight. There was dancing in the ballroom-cum-foyer to a band, but Richard and I just sat and ate. About two o'clock it was chilly so having no jerseys, we came away, dropped into bed and slept until one, waking only at six to let Pucci out.

Sunday was spent very quietly indeed! I wrapped the Christmas presents I bought on Saturday – long mod gold earrings for Marlene (did you see her silver ones in the photo?), a pinafore dress (St Michael) for Sally – (I did tell you the dress I made was too small didn't I?), plasticine and mould set for Cookie's little girl, Cathy. Plasticine and bubble soap for Margie's Michelle and cigars for Peter. I bought a barbeque cookbook for Sally for 35/- so as it was expensive, and it looked mean putting it for both of them, I bought a tin of bubble soap for Stuart. We can play with it in Kariba. It's complete with blowpipe!

I went to see Vivienne tonight. I rang on Thursday to see what happened and while I was waiting for her she was sitting waiting for me! I took Michael some bubble soap too and he loved it, sitting on the rug poking them and squealing. I bought some for Richard too (no, there wasn't a bargain offer on) and we had a laugh with them before tea. Pucci kept eating them and they would burst on his nose and make him sneeze.

I'm afraid your 1/- card has had it! Richard tore it in half to make a shopping list. He didn't notice the picture! Fool.

I was going to say I hope Nanny is better, but, it seems a wicked thing to say, but I hope she recovers, but only sufficiently to go into a home, where she could have a few years with good food and clean surroundings and company as dotty as herself and a TV. But this wouldn't seem much of a life to her probably. It's a problem. I shall just say therefore that I hope things turn out for the best, and that you don't worry and rush yourself off your feet.

Thank you for your long portion of letter, Daddy. You have excelled yourself and should be on strike more often. I loved your description of Uncle Charlie's funeral, poor dotty old chap. Quite a dramatic send off!

(My father was there on his own with the vicar and it was snowing. He made it sound funny, but what a life the poor chap must have had after WW1, aged only 19. My mother rescued his medals from his vandalised house, which seemed to be the only personal possessions he had. I still have them.)

Times of Zambia

20/12/1967   **Petrol filling stations on the Copperbelt were yesterday hit by a shortage of fuel and oil.**

Letter No. 86

It's Wednesday morning, 11 o'clock and I'm stretched out on my terrace, having done my 'work'. It's my Christmas shopping day, so at eight this morning I went out to the Indian shop and bought some more material for a dress for New Year. At 21/- Richard can't really complain. It's the same as the other stuff only green. It's also, I notice, "Made in Japan"! This time I'll use the same pattern only with long sleeves gathered above the elbow.

I came home at half eight with the remains of my Christmas groceries and cut out the dress. The gathering thing on the machine is fine for shearing elastic. It zig zags over the elastic and there is hardly anything to be seen on the other side. Remember how I laboriously gathered those sleeves in that navy chiffon!! I hope it's a success. After that at half nine I went and licensed the dog (what a procedure!) and went on to the office for my ten o'clock cup of tea. So at half ten I was back home. I then made a huge mince pie to take away with us. Then I told Andres to scrub the kitchen floor. I don't think it's been done since we arrived. He just puts polish on over the muck. When it was finished it didn't look like the same floor. I then got out the tree that I bought last year and put it up and put the presents I have bought around it. We are taking Rubners' presents to them tonight so there will only be four left. On Stuart's bubble soap I put "from Father Christmas". Richard's bubble soap is nearly gone. Its very relaxing blowing bubbles and watching them float away.

The tree and cards look nice. There is a sort of Christmas atmosphere about, with the shops full of people (but the shelves almost empty).

We had a blow yesterday. All the garages in Ndola are out of petrol. So is Broken Hill out. Richard managed to fill up with eleven gallons of lousy 10th grade stuff and this will get us to Lusaka. We also have to take the dog to Mufulira, which is 160 miles for two journeys so that's 5 gallons! However there is just over two in my car and with a gallon of crude stuff in the can it might take us there and back on Thursday night. Richard is going to try and get a few hours off, to go to Muff in the daylight. Lusaka isn't yet out of petrol so we must fill up there, to get to Kariba and back to Lusaka. Richard's going to try and get a 5 gallon can.

We have also saved our coupons but they are worthless if there's no petrol. Eric Hannaford Hill says he can fill us up in Lusaka on the return journey. I hope it all works out. We think it's just to stop people going to Rhodesia for Christmas. I should be so disappointed if we had to cancel this holiday too! I hope to get a good tan, although Kariba is reputedly too hot to even sit out!

There are three little African boys on the tree over the hedge. It has fruit rather like applies and they are all sitting up there quite at home and seem to be taking bites out of the apples before picking them to eat.

I have three roses out. They are a bit feeble but smell OK. The leaves do fall in the winter but it seems to be only for a short time. As soon as the rains start everything recovers. My creeper is back to normal again. Flowers flower all year round, dying off a little in winter. The only things that seem to be seasonal are the jacarandas, which bloom in August, September and now are covered in green. Ndola, as far as I can see from my maps and observation is in a flat depression with a ridge and gentle hills around. This gives the feeling of being enclosed, but I'd like to climb one of these hills for a better view and maybe get some snaps of the thousands of miles of African nothingness.

One little African's head is now out of the top of the tree. Goodness knows what he's standing on. He seems completely fearless.

Our office now appears to be preparing for the future as an African chap was interviewed for the vacant job. He seems quite smart and in his early twenties, so maybe he'll make a good job of his job. He'll have to be brave to put up with 5 women. If Cookie leaves for Lusaka, it will be in Feb., so we will be shifted around then and maybe will get another. I would rather, as Richard would, have a good trained African, than a procession of European women who only work a few weeks and have no interest in the job. I should be far happier to train an African and know that when I left, my job was being well done, especially after building it up by trial and error. If I'm sacked or taxed to the hilt, I won't feel inclined to train a newcomer, but if I leave before I come home, I should like to train someone to do the job. My job only came into existence after the UDI because stocks had to be held locally.

Did I tell you that I had seen a fairy? One night a while ago, this little spark was flitting around, only going out when it landed. Last night we saw one on the ground. It was fluttering a green light on and off. We put it on a piece of paper and brought it inside where its light went out. There was a little patch on its back, and this was like the luminous stuff on a clock, and this is what flashed on and off. We put him back outside and he fell down a crack on the step and the whole crack was lit up with the flashing.

Hope you have a good Christmas. Pucci goes into kennels today and we are both feeling sad, because he'll cry when we leave without him.

Soon be the New Year and then, here's hoping, time should fly.

Chapter 28   Christmas 1967

Times of Zambia

22/12/1967   Panic buying by housewives and wholesalers and inadequate transport has resulted in a shortage of white sugar in Lusaka now for three weeks.

Letter No. 87   23/12/67

Kariba, Zambia

Dear Mummy & Daddy,   Having a wonderful time. Wish you were here. It's Christmas Eve at 4 o'clock and I am stretched out by the side of the lake on the terrace of our chalet, on my lounging chair in my bikini. We've done so much. I'll go back to Friday or further Thursday.

Richard set off to Mufulira with Pucci but before he was out of town, he decided we hadn't the petrol to take him and go to Lusaka so he came back. We then desperately rang Ndola kennels, who said they might have had a cancellation on Friday. Friday I rang again but they hadn't anything but recommended a kennel this side of Kitwe. On the way to work I passed three garages and outside the third there was a queue, so being English, I joined it, and got my tank filled, making six gallons, enough to go to the Kitwe kennels and at 12.30 on Friday off we went with Pucci and his bone, slipper and ball to Kitwe. He was good in the car and sat on my knee all the way looking out of the window. We turned off the road before Kitwe and went four miles down a dirt road, and arrived at the kennels. The young woman came out and hugged Pucci, so I reckon he'll be OK.

He went into his run and had a look in the little house and I went in and had a look and put his luggage in. I then came out and the woman locked the door and poor Pucci, he cried and cried and I wanted to take him away again, but the woman said they all settle down in half an hour, but you know Pucci. Most dogs settle down in a night or two, but Pucci took about six weeks! The woman was very pleasant and the food looked OK. When I got home at night, the house seemed so quiet! We are now geared to having a dog, and I was keeping some vegetables for him from supper and opening the oven so he couldn't get in it and it was funny not tripping over him or his bone or cushion and not finding twigs on the carpet. And I didn't enjoy reading the paper in peace either. Never mind he'll be back on Tuesday. However on Friday I nearly tripped over the rat, so it's still around, and has the house to itself this weekend.

We were up at 4.30 yesterday and Sally and Stuart arrived just after half five. We locked up the house as securely as possible and will have to keep our fingers crossed as Christmas is a real high day (or hey day) for our light-fingered friends. It was dull all through the journey, but not unpleasant, either weather or the journey. We stopped at Eric's for coffee in Lusaka, and sat in his garden for half an hour. Then off we set again and stopped just after Kafue for a coke and then at the turn off to Kariba there is 42 miles of dirt road, just mud and millions of stones. This was the slowest part of the journey, as we couldn't go very quickly. The total mileage was 324 miles and we arrived just before 2. We unpacked, had a quick salady lunch and on to the beach where we dozed until six o'clock.

It's a super place as regards situation although the chalets are rough. Our chalet is on the very end.

Under the open bit is a sink, fridge, working table, four dining chairs and table (Formica) and four lattice armchairs. The entire top is open under the roof and all four of us were bitten near to death last night. The only thing is to pull the sheet over your head and to switch out the light as soon as poss. Sally's nightdress was in shreds, as she had fought with the mozzies in her sleep Her body was one big itchy blister.

We bought "Scrabble" in Lusaka and spent until 10.30 playing it, in between being bitten. We sat outside and saw the most horrible of creatures, beetles, spiders, and long black worms with bushy legs. Sally and I kept jumping up and knocking our Scrabble letters on the floor.

The showers and toilets are two chalets along and after dark we are escorted there with a torch and jump at every rustle in the grass.

This morning I lay in my bed and watched the sun light up the lake. We then made breakfast on a Calor gas stove. It tasted great. Afterwards we went along and hired a motorboat and driver for the morning and spent the morning cruising down the Zambezi looking for game, but did we see any? Not on your life. We saw a white headed eagle and a man in a wooden canoe and some villages but not a single croc or hippo (on the way down there was elephant spoor about 2 miles from here). The lake is fantastically large; you can see across it to the mountains, but the other way it just fills the horizon. It's as wide as the English Channel, and 150 miles long. In the middle as you can imagine, the fiercest storms can develop. We kept to the creeks and islands along the coast and on the way back as we were crossing an immense stretch of water it started to rain and we were tossed up and down most fiercely and I hung on to the front and kept my eye on the life jackets. However we came back and went on towards the dam (still in the boat). It was most impressive. We could only go to the boom, which was quite a way away. We came back to the chalet for lunch.

After lunch, we went off to the dam to see the other side. Unfortunately however, the Zambian customs post is about a mile up the road from the dam and the dam itself is no man's land. We therefore needed passports, which Richard and I had forgotten!! Fancy coming all this way and not seeing the dam properly! However the Customs man was very pleasant and when we produced driving licenses and car papers, he confiscated the lot and Sally and Stuart's passports as security for our return. And I'm very glad we went. It's the most fantastic and awesome piece of engineering in the world. It was so huge it was breathtaking. We walked across to the middle. If a double decker bus were placed at the bottom, it wouldn't have been seen. There were men at the bottom who looked like ants, their shapes couldn't be distinguished properly, only the movement. A film or description could never do justice to the tremendous sight. I wouldn't have missed seeing it for anything.

We are now lazing before supper. Sally and I are going for showers and

Richard and Stuart are doing the fire. So I'll continue tomorrow.

December 25th – HAPPY CHRISTMAS

We are having a super Christmas Day. We got up and had breakfast and set up our tree with the presents around it and we all sat around and opened our presents. It was great fun. Well, a lot has happened since I wrote "fun". I got up to get some drinks and nearly put my foot on a puff adder. My foot was poised in the air when I spotted it and I couldn't believe my eyes. It was only about 10 to 12 inches long. I yelled but fortunately stayed still. It looked at me and when it looked the other way I backed away. Sally said I sounded more excited than frightened. Stuart got two long sticks and he held it. It coiled and hissed and spat and the chap in the next chalet, one of a group of Finnish people got hold of its head with the steak barbeque tongs and held it on a rock while Stuart bashed it and killed it. It was a shame to kill it but we couldn't have moved it without it biting.

In the evening the next door cabin started singing carols. All the nationalities joined in with their own carols with a Silent Night in umpteen languages as a finale. We couldn't see everyone clearly just the singing from each little group on the lake, lit by candle light. Lovely. I also missed out Christmas lunch. We had taken everything in tins except the duck, which we cooked on Christmas Eve at home, thinking it would keep better in the cooler box with an ice pack. We heated it up on the barbeque. Big mistake. All the way home on the following day we were all horribly ill and had to stop urgently while one or other of us dived into the bush. However, the planning with the petrol worked and we were able to reach home with some still in the tank.

Pucci was so pleased to see us. When we collected him it was pouring with rain and he was sitting in the doorway of his little hut looking so mournful. When I called him he came to me slowly, and out of the door while I collected his toys. Richard picked him up and said 'Hello Pucci' and then it clicked and he did his nut. In the car he didn't know which of us to lick first, and fell asleep, with exhaustion probably, on my knee and was quiet until we arrived home, when he went berserk, under the chairs, up the stairs, round and round, and now he won't leave us alone. And did he eat! He wolfed down a plate of liver and a refill of spaghetti Bolognese.

Received your letter and tape today, and this evening Sally and Stuart called and we all had a giggle with Doddy. I loved all my super presents and my jiggy. Doodle said it's not a very flattering picture, not being of his best side.

Mrs L sent me a swimsuit, size 36" bust! *(I was then a 32)* After saying she had got the smallest possible. And it was very grubby. I think she got it in bargain week. Anyway, it's a nice style and I have altered it as best I could and have washed it and it now looks presentable. Isn't she a funny woman?

My tennis dress fits perfectly and as Sally says, "Doesn't your mum buy super presents." Sally bought me a lovely vase in blue glass, after seeing my flame lilies in a Nescafe jar, and she was delighted with her cookery book. In fact she spent most of Christmas Day reading it, and Stuart was delighted with his bubbles. Richard took his with him and Stuart said he was pleased that he could now have his own bubbles. If anyone touches his bubble tin he would stamp his feet and start "They're my bubbles!" And, all in all, they created a lot of fun.

Times of Zambia

27/12/1967 Eight Chinese engineers have arrived here to make a preliminary report for the 1,000 mile Zambia-Tanzania railway that the Peking government has promised to build.

1st Jan 1968 **Zambia Airways, the country's first independent national airline since Independence was born today.**

Letter No 88   1.1.68

Happy New Year! At our party last night we sang Auld Lang Syne at 2 o'clock as well as 12 o'clock and drank to you. I'd never thought that people all around the world would be welcoming in the New Year at hourly intervals. Just think, we can now say that we are coming home next year.

Our joint party wasn't a great success. Only half the people who were invited turned up. It was such a disappointment. There were only twenty of us at one time and when we were using the sun lounge for dancing the other room was empty. We had loads of luscious foods. Richard and I made four sweets in big dishes and Marlene roasted six chickens and we had ham and sausage and salami and salads and rolls and it took us all morning to do the puds and from 4 until 7 at Marlene's laying the dishes etc. It's the last time I give a party. However the ones who did arrive, tried to do double work in enjoying themselves. Seven of us were left drinking coffee at 4 o'clock. All the crockery and cutlery and glasses and a huge coca cola ice cream fridge were on loan from Levers, and we had loads of drink over. It cost us both a lot to put on, which would not have been begrudged had people arrived.

This morning we had some people in for drinks at 12. However at 11 just when I was preparing snacks, five arrived. Panic! However it was Eric Hill and his wife and Enid and Pat Case, and Eric's sister who was visiting them. They were going out for lunch at 12 and left at 12.20 and as they left, Marlene and Peter and Sally arrived, and stayed until 2.30. It is now 4 and the other four we invited still haven't arrived. We have had our lunch however and Richard is sleeping in the chair having written two lines of his letter.

I have also written to the Dog Kennels in Liverpool enquiring about accommodation for Pucci from next December. That makes us feel we are nearer to coming home!

While we were out last night, Lindiques, the flat's managers next door, had an attempted burglary and they were upstairs with the light on! Our dog barked and may have chased them off, but they had gouged out the putty around the window catch to undo the screws and had ripped the gauze from a fanlight! We have decided we want bars for the upstairs back as the terrace divider lattice is metal and a perfect ladder particularly as there is a ledge a foot wide three foot under the bedroom window, that we hadn't noticed before.

On Friday, I took Pucci to the vet as, after coming from the kennels, he was licking at a boil thing on his backside that grew bigger. The vet said it was a putsi, and extracted a maggot as big as my little finger end. He asked if I'd seen one before, and before showing me, said, "You won't pass out will you?" He then examined Pucci all over and found another in his elbow joint which I couldn't have seen while I was brushing him. He said it was caused by sleeping on damp ground or bedding. Poor old Pucci. He didn't have much of a Christmas holiday, did he? It cost us 25/- for kennels and 21/- for vets bill! Anyway he's better now. The big holes the maggots left have healed over. This is what Sally Rubner had on her arm from something that hadn't been ironed properly.

Daddy, does your new watch wind on its own and what happens at the end of the month with the date, can that be wound on too? I've never looked closely at a date watch. Very posh!

I have bought a plant pot not much bigger than a teacup for 12/11! However it is brown pottery and will take the African violet which is now flowering and up to now has been in an oil can wrapped in a brown paper bag, in the kitchen.

I'm just going to check on my leg of pork and if it's OK, I'm nipping upstairs for an hour's kip. Tonight I want to get back into routine with my studies, as they have been neglected over the holidays. Have you started on a new diary? I haven't been able to get one. The cheapest is 17/- so Richard is trying to get me a desk diary by the end of this week. I'm already writing on the 'memoranda' pages of last year's.

Times of Zambia

2nd Jan 1968   Expats' exodus will hit councils. A complete breakdown of efficiency threatens Zambian local governments as expat officers plan to leave for good at the end of their contracts

3rd Jan   Zambia will have its own postal orders after decimalisation date on January 16th. British

> Postal Orders, which were being used, were dropped after Britain devalued the pound in December.

5th Jan   Lack of coal hits copper output

Letter No 89   3.1.68

I'm writing with great difficulty as Pucci and his sandal are on my knee, and he keeps joggling my elbow. I've only just come in and he normally won't leave me alone for about half an hour and just as he settles down, Richard will come in and he will be plagued too.

There's a pretty bird outside, a beige one with a brown plumed head, as big as a starling. We've also had two birds around that look like kingfishers.

Many thanks for your tape received yesterday complete with beautiful rendering of Auld Lang Syne. On the tape, you must talk to us more. We feel as though we are eavesdropping on your conversation, so do include us in the conversation as though we were listening. It sounds funny hearing you say, "I wonder if they enjoyed Christmas" as though we are thousands of miles away!

Sally and Stuart enjoyed Doddy too and you laughing on the tape made us laugh even more. Your laughs sound just like you both and it was like sitting with you on Sundays eating chocolate and watching TV.

I've worked out a timetable that all my household jobs and letters must be finished by the time Richard comes home and anything unfinished (except your letter) must go by the board, as after supper, I must study, or the whole thing will be a waste of time. I must do a paper a week which will take 9 months, but this is probably too strict, as apart from my study notes for the third paper I have to read 210 pages of a stuffy book and digest the information to do the test paper. Last night all I managed was one chapter! Must buck my ideas up.

Daddy, what a horrible couple of books you are reading. I bet you get no further than the first pages! I picked a book from the new bookshelf called Art in the Primary school, and was fascinated to learn of all the tremendous ways of teaching art. Children have never had such fun at school. No one else in Ndola has read this as I have renewed it. This book led me to the education section (one shelf of about 15 books) and I brought home seven more super books. One was recommended by the new book I first chose, and is called Experiment in Education by Sybil Marshall, a village school mistress with only one class of 4-11 yr. olds who taught just what they were interested in. "Unobtrusive guidance" to the utmost, Daddy! Do you remember that short story? When her school was closed, she went to university and now lectures in art education. Also another book called Biology for the teacher, which is an illustrated handbook on all sorts of experiments including keeping ants. Remember my effort to keep ants in the fish tank? I must try again the proper way.

I now firmly believe in not teaching a child reading before school, as the schools have different teaching methods. Apparently the thing to do is provide books and painting facilities and things to promote the urge to read on reaching school.

Can't you tell this is a Wednesday letter? I'm rambling again. If and when we have children, I know who's going to have the most fun playing with all the "educational" toys!

This Sybil Marshall book was a tremendous influence. It was what made me get so involved with the Pre School Playgroup Association and apply for Teachers Training College, just before Richard got posted to Paris so I never followed it through. She worked in an idyllic rural school, teaching all ages together. I'd like to read her theories after working in an inner city, seventy languages primary school. Looking at her biography, www.guardian.co.uk/news/2005/aug/31/guardianobituaries.schools the book must have been new when I read it and it was the basis for so much future child education, She wrote her first novel when she was eighty. Hope for me yet!

Chessie Muirhead has just had a miscarriage on her holidays, and is in hospital in Salisbury. I reckon it's all the travelling they have done, by air and road. It's wearying at the best of times.

You say on the tape that we didn't say much about Kariba before we went. Well out here, things are so uncertain that I thought I would tell you afterwards. After telling you about Victoria Falls over August Bank Holiday, it was cancelled, and as it turned out, Kariba was touch and go on the last day too. I don't mention it as I get all enthusiastic and am disappointed and will make you the same. I don't think this is a bad idea, as if I told you the times we were going, you would only wonder if we had arrived safely, wouldn't you? It also prevents disappointments like Mrs L's phone call that fell through, do you see?

I bet Richard will forget our anniversary despite the cards. Is 1st paper or wood?

Here he is now. Pucci heard him before I did.

Later, after supper. Andre made coffee at lunchtime and put it by the armchairs and flapped around no end, and I asked Richard what he was after. Anyway Richard said that after I had gone he asked for £6. He had paid £6 of his £12 fine on Friday (pay day) and was given until this Friday to pay the balance. Isn't that ridiculous. It's the equivalent of us paying about £100 in a week! Anyway rather than have him go to prison, we'll give it him and deduct it gradually from his pay. If he doesn't reappear then it's our hard luck. We've seen his fine papers so he's not pulling a fast one.

Chapter 29   Decimalisation

Times of Zambia

3rd January 1968

Zambia will have its own postal orders after decimalisation date on January 16th. British postal orders which were being used were dropped after Britain devalued the pound in December.

Letter No 90   8.1.68

Richard used the last of my pad without telling me. Twit! It's Monday after work again. Well, how about our phone call, wasn't it super. I never thought it would be so clear. It was just like an ordinary trunk call! I forgot everything I was going to say, but it didn't really matter.

When we rang at 1.00 to see what had happened to our call, due at 12.10. The operator had no record of it although we booked at 6 o'clock Friday, the earliest time possible. She then said she would tag us on the end. On Saturday we had booked a call to Mrs L, which didn't come through and was rebooked for tonight.

At 5 o'clock the phone rang and the operator said "I'll try Birkenhead now". She came back straight away and said, "Mr Waring is at work but Mrs Waring is there. Will she do?" Well I could hardly say no! Next time Daddy, we'll make sure you are in. All the time you have been off work and you are out at work when we ring. I reckoned Sunday was the best bet too. If I had let you know beforehand, it might not have gone through and that would have been frustrating. I'd made a list of things to say, but forgot to look at it, although it was in my hand!

I'm glad you liked your cheques. It seemed a bit odd sending cheques and Richard didn't think his parents would be so pleased, but I said that you couldn't be offended by being given money, because you would take so long spending it, having changed your mind twenty times first. Wasn't Daddy's card smashing? Fancy someone else putting flowers in a wellie. I must say Daddy, that you'll be posh in your boudoir in new pyjamas, slippers <u>and</u> a tie! And black socks too?

On Friday the office had another do. This time it was for Cookie, as she and George are off to Lusaka. We went to the Bull and Bush where they do steak and chips. They have improved the place since the time we went in the rain. There is a thatched building with an open front. (Isn't that a cue for a picture?)

Right. one coming up.

← Thatch.
Bar
Smaller bar covered in
Rustic dining room.

The inside of the roof is open like an Anglo Saxon building.

It went with a real swing. The meal was a bit rough, but the dancing was great and there was just our crowd in the place. At one stage I danced outside into the garden with Susan dancing behind me, and the next thing the place was empty with everyone tagging on. I couldn't dance for laughing. I left Richard who wasn't dancing, but was talking shop with our accountant, sitting at our table, but as I completed a circle and went to go back inside, who should come dancing but Richard with a string of people behind him! I ached with dancing and laughing, and the lousy steak. Lever's do's never go off half as well.

Pucci is in a "let's get all my toys out and make everywhere untidy" mood. He's flying around throwing his old sandal in the air.

Times of Zambia

5th January 1968   Kapepwe praises expat experts

Letter No 91   10.1.67

I've just got in before one heck of a storm. It's 8 o'clock and I've been to a farewell party given by Marge Pawson, my boss' wife, for Cookie. The lightening is magnificent but if we had a cellar I'd be in it.

I went to the party straight from work and took Margie. Cookie didn't know it was a party. It was one of those "surprise, surprise!" efforts. She was up to her ears in packing and was going to ring and say she wasn't coming but Margie rang and said, "Come on round for coffee" and as she was sick of packing she came, fortunately. It was a good party with loads to eat. When I came in Richard had the supper on the go.

Our third attempt to ring Richard's mother is tonight, but the storm is so bad that I hope it doesn't come through. The calls are in any case 2hrs behind, so that makes it 10 o'clock at the earliest.

We have the tape on the pause button to record the call, and it keeps whirring with the vibrations it keeps picking up.

We bought Cookie a rotissamat thing, quite like the spit on our cooker in Chester, but an electric one on a stand as in barbeque shops. Cookie said before we left that nine months ago she didn't like Ndola, but then she moved into her super house, and the catty girls left the office and a new crowd built up (me!) and she didn't want to go back to Lusaka. I don't blame her. She has a beautiful house, which they have spent a lot of time and money on, and the crowd in the office are a good lot and we were held together by Cookie who knows everything. Margie is going on leave for a month on the 18th; two days after the country goes decimal (and chaotic too!) and so yours truly is in charge! Goodness knows how I'll cope.

We have a new woman, the boss' new secretary, who has refused invites to all the current parties and is going to be a horror. She is very full of her own importance (she ordered 12 boxes of carbon paper (£225 worth!!) when we had 10 boxes in stationery and the other typist says she only uses ½ a box in 6 months. This woman has just adopted her granddaughter, who her daughter abandoned at three years old to open a nightclub in Gibraltar with the jet set. The husband wrote to the grandmother, to say that the child had been in six foster homes in 11 months and was sick. Fancy the grandmother not getting wind of this. Anyway she flew over and collected the child. She roused the foster mother from a pub and found the child was locked with three others in a bedroom! She brought her home and says she is doing very well, and has settled down, and insists on calling her Mum although she started off with Granny. Do you now know what this Granny is doing? She is sending her to boarding school in Salisbury a week on Friday!! She is just turned five. This strikes me as being just as callous as her mother. No wonder the daughter is hard. She herself was sent to boarding school at seven and is now only 25. She brought the little girl into the office and she is blonde and pretty although a little precocious, but how she could part with her I don't know at all. Granny said to me today that the holidays are going to be such a bother while she is working! She has also had "such trouble getting a uniform small enough". I get madder and madder when I think of it. I hope that if you were ever landed with a child of mine, that you wouldn't hesitate to bring it up as you did me, whatever the cost or inconvenience.

Enough.

I have painfully finished my third paper and must copy it out (when, I don't know). We are going out to dinner tomorrow, to Linda and Graham's, whom we met at the Gala Night of the Sound of Music, with Sally and Stuart. On Friday we are going to my boss's for dinner with Margie and Calvin Coleman. On Saturday, Sally and Stuart have invited us to spend the afternoon at Misundu for a braai in the evening and Pucci is coming too. They said they have a new game for us to play by the light of their hurricane lamps. It should be good.

A bit more about Linda and Graham. He is a very Liverpudlian journalist with a blonde beard, and she is a teacher. She scraped in to St Caths TT College with English and Theology! She has blonde hair and pins her fringe with a clip, but they are an entertaining pair and have just bought a guitar and a book of folk songs and are struggling to learn the guitar, so that will keep me happy all night.

The storm has not yet abated (sounds like a third rate novel) and it is nine o'clock and no call has yet come through. We will go to bed at 10ish and when the line closes altogether they will ring us to rebook the call.

I dash home to do the lunch now as we take Pucci a walk on the golf course from 1.10 to 1.30. Ten minutes out and ten minutes back. Halfway we let him off the lead and he runs wild but only in figures of eight around us. Although he sleeps all afternoon (if he's the same as when I'm at home) I feel he'll sleep better after a good run around, and already today, he led the way and on reaching the point where on Monday and Tuesday, we let him off the lead, he started pulling to be off. I thought he might run off, or be difficult to catch but if we walk out of sight behind an anthill, he comes bounding to where he can see us, and if he runs on ahead, he sits and waits for us to catch up before going off again.

When we come in we all have cool drinks, but whereas Pucci flops under the settee to sleep, we have to go back to work. I'd love to flop down in the shade on the cold tiles too!

Times of Zambia

11th January 1968   **President Kaunda has condemned as an idiot, a fool and nincompoop anyone who behaves like a tribalist or copies a tribalist.**

Letter No 92   **15-1-68**

It's 6 o'clock and I'm falling asleep already, we've had such a busy weekend.

On Thursday night we went to Linda and Graham's with Sally and Stuart and they have a dreadful flat. It's like a barn with rooms put up inside any old way. To reach the bathroom you have to cross a veranda enclosed only in mosquito netting. There is a huge kitchen with a table, solid fuel cooker, ordinary cooker and a sink with no hot water. And we complain! We had a reasonable meal however and a good laugh.

On Friday we went to Marge and Jack Pawson's. Pawson has got a super new Zambia Oxygen house and we had an evening just as Richard likes it. A super meal and a good bottle of red wine and we talked into the early hours. Jack has some smashing stories, as he has always lived in Central Africa, and is very fond of the hunting and fishing life.

They have two monstrous Alsatians and three cats and a little dog half the size of Pucci and this little dog hangs onto the tails of the Alsatians and swings on them and the big dogs don't bat an eyelid.

On Saturday we went out to Sally and Stuart's for the afternoon and evening. Their chalet is very good. They even have a proper lav. at the end of the garden with a pit underneath. The chalet is like this:

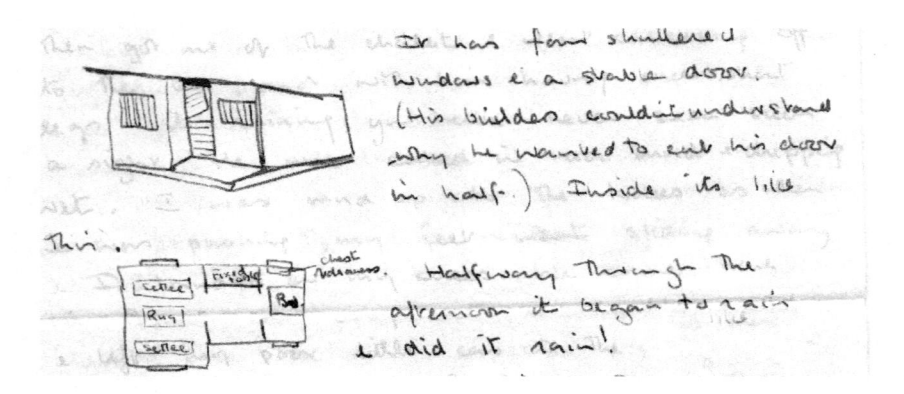

It has four shuttered windows and a stable door (his builders couldn't understand why he wanted to cut his door in half).

Halfway through the afternoon it began to rain and did it rain! Soon the whole ground was swimming in water. Anyway Sally and I decided we wanted to go down the garden to the privy and so we wouldn't get wet, Richard said he would drive us there and proceeded to bring the car around, but about 20' from the chalet, it stuck and the more he accelerated the more it dug in. The only thing to do was to wait until the water drained away, so we had our barbeque supper and tried again. In fact we tried until 11 o'clock. Richard and Stuart were digging and sticking planks and board under the wheels but the mud was up to the back axle. I was driving and Sally sat in their car with the engine running and the headlights on our car. At one stage we jumped out of our skins as this hysterical chuckle came from behind us; we think it was a monkey. Pucci then got out of the chalet and went careering off to the car, and with him having such short legs and it raining, you have never seen such a sight. He was caked in red mud and dripping wet. I was muddy up to the knees as when I as pushing, my feet went sliding away and I landed on my knees. We came home in Stuart's car very wet and miserable and cold and left my poor little car in the mud. When we got in we put Pucci in the bath and he's never had such a sponging. We dried him off with a couple of shabbier tea towels and he slept on the rug under the bed. I was frightened of him catching cold. We then had our baths and dropped into bed.

On Sunday at eight o'clock we went to Misundu, but Stuart had already dug the car out. He jacked up both sides, putting his and our jacks on planks and then as it came out of the hole, he put planks across the wheel holes and back out and sideways. But the car inside and out is caked with clay.

On Friday, this chap rang Richard and said he was Sandy McKay (pronounced MacEye). and that Mrs L had asked his mother to ask him to get in touch with us, so would we like to pop over for lunch. He lives in Chingola and this is like popping to Yorkshire for lunch. Anyway Richard said yes and we set off at 10 o'clock on Sunday morning leaving Pucci at home. We arrived at 12 and they made us very welcome, but Richard's mother said he went to school with Richard, but he is 32 and left in 1953 and Richard started in 1954!

When the two chaps met there was a lot of handshaking and slapping on backs as though both hadn't seen each other for years, but during the course of the meal, they gradually realised that they had never met. It was a brother who had been in Richard's year.

He and his wife Betty have two very nice children, Clare and Ben, 6 and 3 respectively. Ben lives and sleeps "open pit". His father is a construction engineer on the open pit mine, and after a very nice lunch we went to see the open mine, and what a wonderful site it was. Sandy said he would arrange for us to go underground sometime. Sandy is a very keen cine photographer and has just won the Zambian Amateur Photographer cup for a novice's cine film. (Mr

Mills, my sculpting teacher's husband was one of the judges) He also uses a tape accompaniment hit or miss method, and has an LP with special types of music (chasing, heavenly angels, Christmassy), which you are allowed to tape according to the film. They pressed us to stay for tea, which we did but as it was then seven and I was worried about Pucci, we left and were home for nine. Poor old Pucci; he was sleeping on the bed when we came in as the bed was warm. He had only made on puddle by the door, and we fed him and played with him for an hour before going to bed. The McKays also took us up the Solwezi road to look for elephants, but I was glad we didn't see any. Last time they went up this road, one did a bluff charge at them, tail waving, ears flapping, trumpeting, the lot.

They are coming to us in a few weeks. I must stop now as it's 7.30 and I've got my study paper to put in the post tomorrow.

Times of Zambia,

12th January 1968   UNIP men living in fear after Barotsi swing to UP

Letter No 93   **17.1.68**

Yesterday was 'D' day for decimalisation and we are now using Kwacha and ngwee. There are 100 ngwee in a kwacha. The banks closed for three days and opened yesterday. One bank's staff stayed until 1.a.m. sorting out discrepancies.

We had high jinks in the office. I do all the English invoices and now must convert for decimalisation and kwacha. Mrs Kent just couldn't get the hang of her cash. She changes her money at the bank and had £79.3.9d from the cash box, split into various amounts. This is K158.38n, but she was counting her cash like this: - I have £55 for canteen money so that's K110.00. Right (counting out loud) 2, 4, 6, 8, 10, Kwacha, that's £5 (counting 21, now 20 – coins) 2, 4, 6, 8, 10, that's 10. (instead of 20, 40, 60, 80 Kwacha. She just couldn't forget sterling and went on until she had £55 of new money.

It's easy when you forget sterling as quickly as possible and try and think in the new money. I've got the hang of it, and Richard knows it upside down as he has been giving lectures at work. I think he should write a paper for his accounting journal on the problems in accounting on decimalisation, seeing as England is going Kwacha.

The two and one have no equivalents. There are K2 notes (£1), K1 notes (10/-_) and 50n notes (5/). All my money isn't yet changed. I'll trace them for you when I get some.

The 1n coin is like a farthing and as big as a tickey (3d) only copper. The 2n coin is about the size of ½d (which we don't have here). Mrs Kent was calling the 1n coins "those tickey things" and the 2n coins "those pennies" which didn't help at all. I shouted at her each time she mentioned sterling, and she is slowly but begrudgingly getting used to it.

Poor Andre, he is going to be muddled right, left and centre. Richard said their K1 was 10/- and 1/- was 10 ngwee, and said, if 1/- is 10ng what is 6d? Andre rubbed his chin, and scratched his head and said hum, and mmmm don't know. Well if K1 is 10/-, how many Kwacha in £13 – hum, um, or don't know bwana. However he knows the colours of the notes, and K1 is the same colour as 10/- and 20n is the same as 2/-, but it's the pennies that are disappearing. Five ngwee is the same as 6d. Andre was given 20n to buy bread, which is 1/8 and was given 5 pennies change. It is illegal to give sterling as change now. 1/8 is 17ngwee so he should have got 3ng change, which is 4d, so the poor old bread boy was having trouble too.

Most people are like the chap I rang to order stationery. He said "That comes to 9 Kwacha, ha!ha!ha! 9 Kwacha ha!ha!ha!

Balancing the day's accounts is difficult this week as half are £ s d and half are K, and ng. I suppose things will work out. However prices are zooming. For example, I buy milk at 9d a pint in coupon bundles of 30, which is £1-2-6. I bought 30 yesterday for K2.40, which is £1-4.0. You see 9d_=8ng. 10 pints at 9d = 7/6. 10 pints at 8 ng= 80 ngwe and 80 ngwe is 8/-, so they make 6d on every 10 pints. Things would be OK if 2 ½ng were introduced giving an exact conversion to 3d and 7ngwe to 8d but the smallest convertible unit is 6d. After the transitional period, the 2 ½ units could be gradually dropped.

Now your last letters. Would you not now think of renting a TV? How much is TV rental now? I believe colour TV is £6.00.0 a month. That's what black and white TV is here.

We look as though our dream holiday in Mauritius is on its way out, as Central African Airways has been displaced by Zambian Airways. They still go to Mauritius, but CAA has all the hotel contracts and therefore all the all-inclusive holidays. We would have to go to Salisbury by car (a day's journey), as there are no longer flights to Salisbury. We are down here with opportunities to see this part of the world and I can see us arriving back having seen nothing. It's most disheartening. Suez is still closed, which ruins our boat trip home.

Richard's mother makes us laugh in her letters. She writes, "Dear Valerie & Richard, How are you. I had a letter today. Please tell Valerie to" etc., as though I live miles away from Richard. I read her letters first anyway, as Richard doesn't even bother opening them.

Chapter 30   No petrol

Times of Zambia

13th January 1968   Kaunda warns Watchtower against foreign leadership. He has ordered the Watchtower sect in Zambia to Zambianise its clergy

16th January 1968   Tribesmen flock to see leader. Big welcome for chief. He reported that he lost four of his subjects who were devoured by a man-eating lion last month. His visit to the Copperbelt was due to one of his wives absconding

Letter No 94   22.1.67

The Lindiques are the ones who invited us for a drink, <u>and</u> the ones who complain about the cars, and also now about Pucci. They said he barked while we were out on Saturday afternoon. We were away from 2 until 4.30 and he sleeps during this time. We left him asleep under the bed and he came downstairs when we came in, but we shall not be able to leave him alone in the day. She probably was peering in our French window while we were out and disturbed him. We went for a game of tennis and I wore my new dress. It's a very nice one (vain, aren't I?)

Someone will be moving into Marlene's while she is away, although they will still pay rent for it. They will lock all their personal things in the spare room and just leave the company things there. Lots of people here just live in "leave houses" especially newlyweds. People advertise they require tenants and some people just live for 3 months at a time in other people's houses. Sue Gibbon did this before she and John came to live next to us.

You say I don't mention Ratty. Did I not tell you Andre found him dead behind the pressure cooker? Ugh !

I'm glad Nanny is happy in hospital. She's never had it so good with all the attention and food and TV. Let's hope they forget to discharge her. Can't you cut down your visits to once a week? With you and Vera going, it should be enough, especially if she doesn't notice you.

I have just checked on the dinner, and found that I left Pucci's to cool and forgot about it and have stuck it in the oven to reheat. Tonight he's having chopped liver, puppy meal and gravy. Yum, yum. Richard always pinches a piece or two of liver before I put the meal and gravy on.

We have three nights out this week. Tomorrow, The Savoy for cocktails and buffet 7 to 10 to meet someone or other (all Levers), and Thursday also at The Savoy 7 until 8, for someone else (a retiring director). I don't mind Tuesday when there are eats, but Thursday is a waste of time as we don't eat and you have to get all dolled up and then come home after one hour. Marlene and Peter either stay out for dinner or come to us, as it's expensive and difficult getting a babysitter so they make the most of their night out.

We have been invited to someone's farewell party, also a Unilever bloke. I hope the food's good, as I don't know the chap, but Richard does.

Sally and Stuart came around on Friday at 6.30, and I had made a goulash and we ate straight away, and then got down to business. They have bought a Waddington's game called Risk, which is a map of the world with territories and armies and it's a lot of fun. In fact 12 o'clock came and we still hadn't finished the first game. We then found a rule that made all the difference and we finished at 1 o'clock. Phew. But we laughed and cursed and generally enjoyed it. It's a wonder old moaner next door didn't write to complain! We nearly banged on her wall this week. Her TV is so loud we can hear odd words in the news, and recognise most of the other programmes. What with her and the chap next door's TV, it's like living in a stereogramme.

Richard is now in and tells me that it was decided to clear the grease from the warehouse floor for when the visiting director came. They covered it in soda ash and rinsed it and scraped the grease. A chap on duty decided this was too slow and used a pressure hose to clean it, and soaked all the finished crates of soap powder. He also rubbed off the storage lines painted on the floor, and another man was ordered to repair them. This he did, but where a crate or obstacle was in the way, he painted the line around it. These are the people Richard is training, so you can see that it's stiff going.

P.S. Richard has got a rise. However it is not permanent and will be knocked off when we go home. It is given the title of "extra responsibility rise". A quarter will go in tax however. Most importantly though, Mackie said Richard's progress had not been just very good, but excellent and when he was in London, he had mentioned this. However, Richard's audit boss says he wants Richard back. I hope he can get out of this.

Times of Zambia   17th January 1968

Decimalisation. There was confusion because many shop owners are under the ignorant impression that the old money was no longer valid after today, packed the banks as they thrust their pounds, shillings and pence across the counter demanding crisp, new notes and shiny coins.

18th January 1968

Livingstone, Zambia's Cinderella town, which relies on buses run by the Rhodesian Omnibus Company in Bulawayo, is being heavily hit by the inadequacy of the service. Only one bus is in use at the moment.

20th January 1968

Zambia Railways' train guards will no longer issue 1st or 2nd class tickets to passengers who fail to obtain them four days before their journey, as a measure to reduce overcrowding the two coaches.

23rd January 1968

The Tan Zam pipeline from Dar es Salaam to Mbeya, and Mbeya to Ndola has reached the halfway mark. Zambia will at last have her own direct source of fuel and will stop relying on the notorious Hell Run. Three hundred vehicles are currently stranded, many of them tankers.

Letter No. 95   24.1.68

Pucci is playing with the cardboard middle of an adding machine roll, with a leaf on his head. I always bring the middles home, as he chews them and rolls them about and kills them. The leaf is on his head because he's been routing around in my garden and he doesn't know it's there. It's well worth picking up the bits to have him quiet while I'm writing my letter.

It's quite hectic at work being jack-of-all-trades, but I'm enjoying it. I hope there will be a board meeting so that I can buy the flowers as well as arrange them. Tonight at 4.25, McCarthy (the engineer) wanted some pocket files, which we hadn't got, so I immediately rang the stationers who said they had manila wallets, which sounded like the things, so I ordered a packet of 50. I wasn't even too sure which place to telephone. I then had an order made out and at 4.29 took it in for him to sign and said they would be delivered first thing, so how's that for speed. It's nice having a bash on your own, but there are so many little jobs to do e.g. the toilet rolls are finished, the milk coupons are out, and someone is pinching the soap from the ladies, for the past two days at 4 o'clock so I'm trying to watch that too.

We went to the Savoy last night and it was a "help yourself meal and then sit down". I had a plate of cold meats and salads and then a small helping of chicken a la crème (done on a stove at the table) with rice. I then had strawberries and cream. Richard was seated miles from me, so Tony got about 12 strawberries for me, and when Richard came to get his there were only two left. He went round and got one from everyone!

(Pucci is stalking the adding machine roll from behind the chair!)

Naomi grew hundreds of gladioli last year and the florists snapped them up, she sold them to the florists for 15/- a dozen. She asked me if I was any good at making up bouquets as she was thinking of starting selling them direct and wanted someone to do this. I had seen a book called "a florist's guide" in the library and recommended her to read that.

Funny that I didn't offer to help, when you think that later in the UK, I spent ten years making up flaming hanging baskets.

Pucci ran to the top of the stoep steps when I came in and kept whingeing, so that was when I gave him the roll. He just went out again and as he was crying there, I asked him what was the matter and he said Mon-Mon! Squeak, squeak and shoved his nose through the netting, and there in the middle of the lawn was his favourite toy, his yellow ball. So he's now got it and is happy.

He usually rolls his ball under the coffee table (once he could slide under the coffee table, but now he can only get his head under) and then he cries until we get up. We then have a conversation with him. Every time we pause, he squeaks and it's as though he's talking. I wish we could get it on tape.

The director last night was quite chatty and very sharp e.g. they were talking about charter flights and Richard said they were cheaper in the long run and he said, "Why is that?" Fortunately Richard could substantiate his statement, but I held my breath. He was quite a character.

He is against foreign aid, and told us the Dutch government sent 100 water pumps to a certain country, which I won't name, to help their irrigation problems. These pumps sat in customs for 5 months as the government of the country wanted to charge 100% import duty! He had other tales too. When he was in Bombay his wife helped a doctor distributing the contraceptive pill to Indian women. However they found that the men were taking the pills, as they explained that they were the important ones in the family and therefore they should have them.

As this director left, another arrived and it's his 'do' we're going to tomorrow, unfortunately. What a waste of an evening – cocktails 7 to 8. We either rush to eat before we go, or spend until 11 cooking when we get in (grumble, grumble!) I wish we could get out of going.

Mrs Mhiza, the African girl in our office asked me to make her a dress at Christmas and I said that I was busy, and to see after Christmas. I thought that was that but today she comes in with the material and a pattern. I could hardly say no. Anyway, luckily it is a shift dress, with sleeves and easy. I'll do it on Saturday mornings between 7.30-9.20 before my Bernina lesson. This girl makes crocheted tablemats, so I'll get her to crochet me one. I haven't told Richard yet. He'll do his nut.

However this girl hasn't a machine and she bought the material when Cookie said she would make one for her, but Cookie found she wasn't going to have time before going to Lusaka and gave her it back, so it is a big job hand sewing a dress isn't it. But people who don't sew, don't realise the work involved do they, like Auntie Molly.

Molly had Mum make sets of curtains for her new house. Mum bought all the header tape and cottons, and Molly, bless her, bought Mum a pair of stockings for her materials, time and effort.

Times of Zambia   24th January 1968

Police from Masaili were yesterday patrolling the village of 5,000 members of The Watchtower Bible and Tract Society "Police sought to know if this year we sent any children to schools. We told them that the Roman Catholic Priests at St. Theresa's have turned away our children from their school".

25th January 1968

Full scale war looms in South Vietnam.

25th January 1968

More than 600 charcoal burners have abandoned their market stalls in Luanshya in a counter protest against the public's resentment of the new currency prices. The town's charcoal suppliers had increased their prices from K1.25 to K1.75 when Zambia switched to the new currency.

Letter no. 96   29/1/68

Phew! I'm whacked. I've just walked in from town, from the office. There isn't a drop of petrol in the place. All the tankers are bogged down, as the road bringing petrol in from Tanzania is dirt and under water this time of year. The rationing was increased to 16 or 18 a month and has now been cut to 4 gallons a month. I use about 3 a month and Richard about 10, so all our petrol will have to go into Richard's. Susan can't get in to work from Luanshya, as no-one there has petrol either. There were 2 gallons in my car when it ran out and an oz. in Richard's, which he must save to get it to a garage, as no cans are filled.

Richard took me into town and to Peter's to pick up Peter. Tomorrow they will continue in Peter's car. At lunchtime I came home but it took me 25 minutes each way. Richard said he has walked it in 8mins. It is only just about 1½ miles, but at lunchtime it was scorching hot. Tonight it is cooler but it still took me until 4.55 to get home. More or less everyone is in the same boat. We're lucky enough to have filled up just before everyone ran out. Next door, the caretaker/managers have a 45 gallon drum in the house, which I feel like objecting to as a fire hazard in the flats (sour grapes!) This same neighbour (yes them again) drove past me in the street into town.

Tonight I'm all covered in red dust to the knees, and one section of road is long grass that I have to walk through.

Even if petrol comes in before Wednesday, it won't be released until the 1st when the 4 gallon ration comes in.

Richard has booked air tickets to the Falls, as on this ration, we will not be able to go by road. This boosts up our holiday to £100 for the four days and we won't have a car when we are down there! But we can't leave without seeing Victoria Falls now can we?

I have a filling coming out of my front tooth and a hole that gets bigger every day. Touch wood, it doesn't ache yet but I hope he fills it nicely as you couldn't see the filling before, and as my teeth are the only decent thing about my face, I don't want to have an ugly filling.

I'm looking forward to my navy jumper, but you shouldn't have told me, as it now won't be so much of a surprise. However as I know the colour, I'll look out for a skirt. I wonder if skirts really will go down.

I've got one of the three films back and it looks ok. How I see them is that I thread the spool on to a pencil and hold the pencil in my knees and roll it onto an empty spool holding it up to the light. My arms and knees ache afterwards but I can see the film.

The fact that my bulbs are sprouting makes me feel as though I shall soon be home ! Only one more sprouting and I *will* be home.

Meat has gone up 38% and is now scarce. The cheaper meat was the saving grace for this place.

Peter Rubner says that the firm will pay to send Pucci home, although not his kennel fees. If that's correct, won't that be super. We are quite prepared to pay as we didn't bring him out here, but Peter reckons that if that applied then the firm wouldn't pay for the larger amount of luggage sent home!

We went to the golf club on Saturday evening at 5.30, for Richard to be introduced to the committee and we smelled cooking, so asked, and were told they were doing steak & egg & chips, so we decided to have a plate each. It is only in a bar and a check cloth was put on the next coffee table and cutlery and sauce bottle, and when the steak was brought out, the waiter came over and said – "Dinner is served." It sounded funny.

Richard then went belatedly to the tennis club AGM, just after the voting and he wasn't re-elected, but he would have turned it down. Apparently the chairman congratulated the tennis side, on the way the courts were transformed with so little cost. Richard says that he wished he could have been there, as he would have said that not a soul helped him. I too think it was a magnificent achievement. As Richard said, someone else can order the lime and molasses and go down to see that the court is marked and rolled, and someone else can be moaned at if new balls aren't on the court at the start of play etc. I shall see that neither Richard nor I ever sit on committees. Richard isn't bothered. He says that now there are three courts, he never sits out waiting, which was the whole idea of a third court. Richard also tried to arrange a team to play Rhokana on Sunday, as Rhokana have been pestering for a while. Only six men volunteered! Rhokana is an African team. If they play, this will ensure the club's licence for the next year. Richard asked the last chairman about providing refreshments, and he said it was nothing to do with him. Such co-operation!

Marlene and Peter leave on Feb the 24th for their 3 months leave. Lucky things. We are treating them to a night out the Friday before. If the films and tape are ready, they will take them to London and post them to you

Chapter 31   Chameleon

Times of Zambia   25th January 1968

An old man from Luspula Province has fallen victim to a confidence trick. He hitchhiked to Mansa to change his life's savings. He had K220, which he had dug up from the ground at his home. Three men approached him and he gave them money in exchange for a wad of notes. Later at the market, he found they had been scissored from the Decimal Board's promotion posters.

26th January 1968

Hell Run to be closed for a week for repairs.

27th January 1968

Most of Ndola's 175 streets are to have new names. This follows a trend to do away with names from the Colonial era and names of people living, wherever possible.

Letter no. 97   **31/1/68**

What a hurried letter this is! All today I have been thinking it was Thursday and I came in and got the meal on, and got settled down to some studying. I have just had a bath and made coffee when it dawned on me that it was Wednesday. So I am writing this in bed. Richard says there is no guarantee that it will go tomorrow, as with no petrol, the firm can't get any more stamps. Everywhere is chaos. Richard has enough petrol for tomorrow and that's that. He is already taking Tony (who walks two miles to our house) and Peter. I walk. We have cut down the lunch hour to ½ an hour and come home at four.

Today I brought a chameleon home with me. It was on the bougainvillea in the office garden and was only a little one, about four inches long, half of that being tail. They are fascinating. I put him in a stationery box and sellotaped a paper lid on, put holes in and put a string handle on it. When I arrived home I put him on the sideboard, and let him out when Richard came in and we watched him while we were eating. He went brown on the deer, green on a twig and grey on a red table napkin. We lost him at one stage but he was brown grained and sitting on the wooden ice bucket lid! We then put him on my bush in the garden, which has loads of ants on it. They can become tame, and little boys play with them like white mice.

The two Africans in the office were terrified of him and said he was "evil" and if you touched him when he was green you got leprosy, and if it bit you, you died. I said that if it bit me, I'd bite it back, and they rolled their eyes horrified. Chameleons are completely harmless but have horny feet, which can scratch; thus originated the leprosy story. Nevertheless just in case, I only handled him on a twig. I hope he keeps some of the mozzies out of the house.

Everything is impossible with this petrol situation. People are buying bicycles like mad. The Africans of course think it's a huge joke. However supplies and deliveries are held up. And we can't bring shopping in from town in any quantity, and in any case it's too hot to carry much.

I'm loving my extra jobs at work and Mr Pawson is taking on an African to do the mundane bits of the job which are now running very smoothly as I have developed a method which I have written out and which can be taught to someone. Mr P says that I can then do some more interesting bits, but I think I'll still have enough to do. The job the African will do is the job I was taken on to do, but I am also doing the 'before' and 'after' action of the same job instead of the accountant, and have taken half of Cookie's job (the other half going to Margie) and this month I'm doing that half too! It will be nice to know that I'm training someone myself to do my own job. When Mr P suggested an assistant, I said that he was trying to Zambianize me and that anyway I would be leaving in 12 months so it was just as well. And he clapped his hands to his head and said 'Don't depress me!' Wasn't that nice.

Our boss has a new secretary because there are no Zambians with the required qualifications. In a year or two maybe, but not yet. Clerical staff is about the highest yet. The other African has started and is making satisfactory progress although some things take a bit of explaining. Once a routine is established things will go smoothly.

Glad Nanny is physically well. How do you mean you are having difficulty with the hospital? Do they want her to go home?

The woman who has sent her granddaughter to school has just won £1,000 on Ernie. It will stay in England to ensure the grandchild's boarding education, so perhaps she was meant to go to school, after all! We all had cakes to celebrate. Wasn't that exciting!

I'll reply more fully to your letters in my next and less rushed letter. Half a loaf is better than none! Talking of bread, that's in short supply too with bakers unable to deliver. Once again, who'd live in the jungle

Times of Zambia

28th January 1968   Armed bandits suspected to have entered Zambia from The Congo, have struck again.

31st January 1968   Thirty-three members of Watch Tower, who have been declared Prohibited Immigrants are leaving and returning to their countries of origin.

" Wanted. Tea Chests, Boxes and Cases always required"

Biddulph Removals, Lusaka

Letter 98   3/2/68

We took Pucci to the dog groomer's at eight o'clock this morning as he looked like this

He looked like a teddy bear, but he was such a scruffy teddy. We left him and Richard collected him at one o'clock and didn't even recognise him as he now looks like this.

His hair had been cut to one inch all over leaving him with long glossy ears and a puffed head and tail. He is beautifully glossy, but doesn't look a bit like our Pucci. She has cut him like a poodle. We hope his hair will

grow as silky as his ears. She has made a super job of him, cutting his toenails and cleaning his teeth. Richard keeps calling him a cissie and a powder puff. I hope I'll be able to keep him smart while his hair is growing so that he'll not get into such a scruffy state again. He is that white and shiny!

We are looking for alternatives to Mauritius for our short leave. It may now be Mombassa. I'd set my heart on Mauritius. It seemed so romantic.

I am thrilled and delighted that Nanny is in a nice home, and sorry to hear about her vandalised house. Did you salvage nothing? Not even the family photographs off the sideboard or her brass trivets from the kitchen range? I bet she has never had 18 shillings just to spend on herself, has she? I hope it works out O.K.

On Saturday night, Sally and Stuart and Linda and Graham came round for dinner at 6.30. We had a cine film show beforehand and played "Risk" afterwards. Sally would like a copy of the Christmas bit of the film, but I have already edited it and don't wish to delay sending it. Perhaps you could enquire sometime, whether it can be copied and if so at what cost.

We taped all the comments on the film. This film is 220 feet and not 100 feet like the last one and the tape runs out half way through, so there will be silence for the interesting bits. I've found that the picture is clearer the smaller the screen size, as when I stuck it all together I reviewed it about three feet from the projector, the resulting picture being about 10 inches by 6 inches. I'm afraid my little puff adder is out of focus, as are a few other bits, which I'll cut out when I get home, but I've left them in for now.

I was working on Saturday and so missed my Bernina lesson. I am still walking from work, but Susan walks with me as her boyfriend picks her up at five. It saves him going into town and saves her waiting from 4 o'clock. However maybe I'll get slim. Fancy having two cars and only being able to use one. Perhaps it will make me realise how lucky I am.

I have written again to the vet about Pucci. It would be so convenient to get him in to a Liverpool kennels.

On Sunday, Richard and five others formed a team to play Rhokana, a team who have been pestering us for a match. And we are glad we gave them a game. They have written to all the clubs on the Copperbelt, (there are five of us in Ndola alone.) and received only five replies, four refusals and one acceptance-ours. They had a good game and it was enjoyed by us all, although some people were deliberately awkward- like the ex secretary who said to be sure to keep them out of the bar until the bowlers were out. Anyway they mostly had Cokes on the grass outside. If I were an educated African like these chaps, I'd be slaphappy with a gun, rioting, causing trouble for the Europeans. It's a wonder they stand for it, although it is more the other way since Independence. The worst whites here are those who have a lot here, yet if they were put in a competitive European country environment they would be starving within a week, as half haven't the brains of mice. They are very narrow and "common". One woman who commented on these Africans never takes a fag out of her mouth, even when she's talking. Anyway our club has been invited to a return match. Richard said to the new committee member as he handed over the ball fund, " You see to the buying of new balls, and the marking of the courts at weekends now" and he replied, "You've a ******** hope". Richard left it at that, although he is bothered his tennis might be spoiled and the courts go to pot after all his hard work.

Times of Zambia   1st February 1968

Tanzanian Government is considering massive convoys of two to three hundred tankers to keep the oil flowing to the Copperbelt, and a ban on non-fuel traffic.

The pedicle link road between the Copperbelt and Luapula Province, (which crosses a peninsula of the Congo), has become another Hell Run as Zambians are swindled by Congolese officials who have been unpaid for months. Travellers are charged a "fee". Fines are imposed for

possessing dagga, which has been planted in suitcases and Zambians imprisoned and charged a release fee.

Times of Zambia   2nd February 1968

A farmer of fifteen years residence, who was given twenty-four hours to leave his farm and quit the country, in the middle of the maize planting season, was back in Lusaka to sue the government for damages for the loss of livelihood and the upset of his life, peace of mind and reputation. On November 5th 1966, immigration officials and police arrived at the farm with a document declaring him to be an undesired inhabitant. If he did not agree to go, he would be forcibly removed. The land bank then foreclosed on the crop loan and sold the farm to the government for K1 (50p) per acre. In January, Major Paton flew back to Lusaka to appeal, but was transported to and left at the Rhodesian border.

Letter no. 99   7/2/68

It's a whole month since I rang you. Let's hope the next thirteen go as quickly.

I am writing this in my half hour lunch break whilst drinking my cup of tea. Not going home for lunch does make the day long.

Richard, yesterday afternoon, went through to the Congo with Tony and Bob Dunckley and some of his staff and got enough petrol for our holidays although it was nine shillings a gallon. We are to keep the cans at Sally's "country house". You can appreciate that I can't go into details in print. This is a tale that will have to be told when we get home. However it is still worth the price if it means our holiday is saved. It's just one obstacle after another. I've just had a very unCornish pasty, but it was very tasty and hot.

The trip for petrol in Richard"s words.

It was Mr. Njamba who came up with the idea, "Why not buy petroleum on the Congolese black market?" Mr. Njamba was my salaries supervisor, a competent organizer and capable member of my staff. A few months previously he had invited us to choose one of his ducks for Christmas lunch. Now we were faced with getting to Livingstone, a twelve hundred mile round trip, using our monthly petrol coupon ration. Mr. Njamba heard of the problem and proposed this strategy. "I have a friend who is a sergeant with the Zambian police. He can organize for drums of petrol to be sold to you by the Congolese, who will deliver it to you in no-man's land between the Zambian and the Congolese borders."

Four of us set off in Bob Dunckerly's truck, Tony Wisdom, Mr. Njamba, me, and Bob driving. We drove onto the dirt road between the two borders and met the Congolese suppliers with their truck. Both the Congolese had black berets and horizontally striped tee shirts, caricatures of French onion sellers. They had the petrol in ten gallon drums. We were manhandling these onto our truck when the Zambian Police Land Rover came racing down the road and stopped alongside us. A burly sergeant climbed out. " Everything O.K? They aren't ripping you off?" We assured him we were fine. All the time one of the Congolese had a lit cigarette in his mouth. Everything loaded, we handed over four hundred kwacha and headed back to Bob's where we buried the drums, to await our calling for them before we set of on our trip to Kariba.

We are getting used to Pucci now. He certainly looks clean and he is so easy to brush. It's only his topknot ears and tail that are long. I want to get him into the habit of liking to be brushed again. Before going into kennels he used to sit on my knee eating biscuits while I brushed him, but when he got all tangled and matted at kennels, I had to tug and pull him, so that instead of running to me when he saw the brush, he fled under the chair and it took Richard and me to hold him.

Yesterday when Susan was at home with me, I was saying to Pucci, "Fetch your ball, which he normally does when told. He looked under the chairs and I pointed to his ball in his basket and said again and again, "Fetch your ball". But he ran outside. Wouldn't he shame you? However in he trots with his ball in his mouth. It had been outside on the terrace. He was forgiven.

However he will still only sit to command when you push his bottom to the floor and still gets terribly excited when we have visitors, particularly Tony. He piddles all over the place with excitement. Apparently, they are just an excitable breed. *Unfortunately Tony always wore suede shoes.*

I've had a letter from Cookie and she's not too happy in Lusaka. Margie is still on holiday and doesn't come back until 26th. I'm coping with my job at the moment, but will be glad when she's back to alleviate the quantity.

Our office has just sacked a man as he was stealing used cylinders and taking them back to stores for the twenty five shilling rebate on returned cylinders. After he had come back for the second time, he was caught stealing and was dismissed. The Labour Office has rung to say that this is no reason to sack him. We have also had trouble with the Labour Office when we sack chaps for smoking in the plant. There is a mess room for smoking, and notices are everywhere and in every dialect about smoking, which is absolutely taboo as some of the gases, such as hydrogen, are very sensitive. One spark and half of Ndola could go sky high. This just doesn't sink in at the Labour Office. They say smoking is no reason to sack someone, which it isn't anywhere else.

Richard is having trouble deciding on a birthday present. He says he is still thinking. He thinks he would like another sports shirt. He was very pleased indeed with his Christmas one. The two you bought are the only ones he has had since he went to Newquay at sixteen.

I must hurry and eat my cornflakes before Andre brings in the boiled "eggies" as he calls them. Most words in Bemba end in a vowel which links them to the next word, so every word that ends in a consonant has an "i" tagged on.

Chapter 32   Rain and Mud

Times of Zambia

3rd February 1968 — The Minister for Transport, Solomon Kalulu, pointed out that the Zambian Railways waiting rooms were filthy, trains were never on time, drunkenness is rife and goods are mislaid. Some conductors were cashing in by issuing pieces of paper for tickets.

5th February 1968 — On returning from his father's funeral, Gerald Manda found that his wife Gladys had vanished. He appealed for her to come back within seven days or he would bring her back by force.

Letter 100   12/2/68

I am very grumpy today. It's pouring down, and has been all day. This morning I set off to work in my car, going the longer way round, as I ran Richard over to his car first, as it was dropping down in buckets full.

I was one third of the way to work and my car just dies. I changed to bottom gear but it had no effect and the engine just conked. I revved and revved but nothing happened. I tried for ten minutes but it still wouldn't turn over, so I got out and put my mac on. Richard's mac that is. Its down to my ankles and covers my hands and although I look barmy, it keeps me dry. I pushed the car into a more convenient place and stomped back home, swearing and cursing. As you know there are no pavements and in one spot you can't walk on the road, as it is lower and busy. I was squelching along in the mud. One girl, out of the hundreds who passed, offered me a lift, but I was just about to turn in home. I rang

Richard and he said, "Have you tried he choke?" and I said, "No". Happily, he said he would come in and have a bash himself, which he did.

However, he couldn't get it started either, and also found his towrope had been left at Bob's, where we went on Saturday. So we borrowed a rope from the tennis club, outside of which I had conked out, but couldn't find a suitable place to satisfactorily anchor it, so we pushed. Three little piccanins appeared from nowhere and got at the back pushing. I walked back and fetched the big car and drove it home and then trudged back to Richard. We forked out 4/- for the kids. Richard said he couldn't have pushed it all that way without them. All this time remember it is raining. Richard is cursing the petrol, the country, the weather, everything.

He then ran me to work. My feet were caked in mud. Richard says that the carburettor will need cleaning, whatever that means. He also says my battery is dry. I didn't know it had to be wet. I have been given the instruction book on maintenance as a result.

Tonight Sue and I walked back to our house, and it looked like rain again. Sue took off her stockings and I asked her why. She said, "You'll see". We didn't get home before the rain as we had hoped. It just dropped down and Sue took off her shoes and walked barefooted through the mud. Her shoes are mod patent leather. When we got in, she just washed her feet and was all tidy again, whereas my sandals after two soakings needed drying and major cleaning. Half way along a fellow gave us a lift. It turned out he lives opposite to us and is a Unilever Merseyside man. He doesn't work for Levers Zambia, but on his own. He handles all the other Levers products that Zambia doesn't make or import. You can tell he was English. No South African nor Rhodesian would have stopped for us.

Friday, we saw Thoroughly Modern Millie. You would love the super dresses. Saturday, I learnt patching at Bernina, so maybe I can have a go at some of the rat holes in Richard's things.

At lunchtime, we went to Bob's to shift our petrol can to Sally's house, as it is outside the town boundary and it is therefore legal to store it there.

We ended up having a lovely salad lunch and then to Sally's. She has bought a piano for £46. It is a bit tinny, but it was super to play again. I had a go with my music and although rusty, they made me play all sorts, and I've been roped in to play folksongs at the party there on Saturday as another chap is bringing a guitar. Richard is delighted. He loves singing folk songs. I could feel him wince.

When we arrived home at four, Marlene rang to say the meat had come and would we like to come for afternoon tea. Pucci was exhausted when we got back from Sally's, so we left him on going to Marlene's and he was still flat out when we got back.

Sunday, we asked Marlene and Peter for coffee on their way back from the delicatessen. We were just into our snacks when Linda and Graham arrived to take us for a swim, so they joined us. Linda is now teaching at an Indian school, where there is a pool that teachers can use at the weekends, and it is usually deserted. When we came to go two hours later, down came the rain, which put an end to that idea.

I bought a yard of material and two cane rings as big as saucers. It is navy and I am making a bag, as my brown leather handbag, which I use everyday for work and for when I go out, is falling to bits. It will double as a beach type bag. I have halved the material after doing an appliqué pattern, with my Bernina of course, on the front.

The cat is in navy check left from my office dress and the mouse is just stitching like this.

I washed my hair when Susan left at 5.15 and now at 7.30 it is dry without the hairdryer, so it can't be all that cold.

Times of Zambia

7th February 1968   No petrol so telephone repairmen are on bikes. Some of the Kitwe street names, which have been scrapped, are Stanley, Livingstone, Rhodes, Moffatt, Jameson, Oppenheimer and Beit. New names are Chushamwamba, Kaluagushi, Hippo, Mwenda and Baobab.

14th February 1968   Lozis and Tangas were the target of a number of stoning incidents, which swept Kalushi township. Victims claim they have been listed as United party sympathisers.

Letter 101 or should I start at 1 again.

14/2/68

Happy Valentine's Day. Richard doesn't even know the date, unromantic thing.

No sign of Vera's parcel. That's four months now. Oh, the thought of all that lovely snow. On second thoughts, I'll keep our sunshine. What on earth were you doing digging snow? Or did you just feel all gay and made digging an excuse for playing in the snow. Talking about bulbs under the snow, Mrs Mhizha (the African girl) wanted to know if the snow didn't squash all the flowers. I explained that, in winter, there weren't many flowers out and that snow fell quite gently and wasn't so heavy. Doesn't it seem funny not knowing about winter and snow.

On Saturday, I bought a blanket for £2.10.0. It is only ¾ size, but is a kingfisher blue and bound with ribbon, and made in Zambia But for £2.10.0! The others were £9. Apparently they fall apart after washing, but I'd rather pay £2.10.0 (sorry K5) than £9 (K18.) for a £5.00.0 imported one. A blanket even if threadbare has its uses.

Still perfect and well used after nearly fifty years. (Just like me.)

At least we won't be cold this winter. When you send my birthday present, can you send my beige knitted stockings, if they don't weigh much, that is.

My car is OK. Richard cleaned the carburettor and it's going, but I wince at some of the noises the poor little engine makes. As the African girl in the office says, "Where is your baby car? (or bebbie ca as she pronounces it.)

Just think. I have had no Bournvita for twelve months. And no TV.

The chameleon has disappeared, but he has the whole golf course and the bush beckoning.

Our horrible next-door neighbour was on the telephone, so Sally says, (she works in the same office) and she was struck by lightening. At least the phone was. She went one way and the phone the other. Chuckle, chuckle. Aren't I horrid?

You ask how our letters will be affected by the petrol shortage. They are probably collected from the plane on a bike anyway

Times of Zambia

15th February 1968   **Forty pupils from Chileshi Primary School in Ndola were expelled this week after an unexpected visit by schools' inspectors. The pupils claimed that although they had paid**

16th February 1968

school fees for the present term, they were given no receipts. The school's headmaster was not available for comment.

A Kitwe man with three children at Chileshi School drove to investigate. He claimed that the reason for expulsion was tribalism. Lamba tribesmen had protested at the enrolment of non-Lamba pupils. The Chief Education Officer commented that Mr Sata's claims were untrue and if he continues to claim so, he may be in trouble.

Letter 102   19/2/68

Monday lunchtime and I've just had a loganberry trifle. Yum Yum. It was meant to be a flan, but it stuck in the tin when I turned it out, so I made it into a trifle.

Your Courtelle fabric sample is marvellous. I've not seen it in patterns like that, only plain. I'll be so shabby when I come home. Last night, I dreamt I went to C & A's who were having a closing down sale and I was buying alsorts of clothes for 10/- each. The shop girl said that the clothes were all out of date, but I said that was O.K. as I had just come from Africa. What difference that would make, I don't know. I was quite worn out when I woke up.

We went to Misundu on Saturday night to Linda and Graham's folk singing party. I put on my pink jersey, flowery trousers and my Christmas pink shirt and did my hair in pigtails. We weren't looking forward to it but it turned out to be very good indeed.

The only fly in the ointment was Pucci. He was so naughty. When we went out, he howled and howled. We went back and smacked him and he still howled. Not just whimpering but baying to the moon. We decided we couldn't go to the party, but we had promised to take some stuff over, so we bundled him into the car and set off. However Sally and Stuart persuaded us to stop, leaving him in the car, where he whined all evening before falling asleep.

He has also been making efforts to get out and has been very restless, so we think maybe that the little Maltese around the corner is on heat. Pucci is usually so good when we go out. This is not a very good development. We are thinking of seeing the vet to enquire whether we can have him doctored. This might quieten him down, although we didn't want to have him done, but we can't let him tie us to the house. We'll need a babysitter. Perhaps he misses us at lunchtime, because we can't take him for his walk, although Andre is with him all day. Never mind. I am going to ask if I can go onto mornings soon, sometime after Margie comes back. But I'll have to judge my moment.

On Saturday, I went to my Bernina lesson and learnt buttonholing. It's ever so easy and clever. I came home and showed Richard and I shouted at him because he wasn't interested and I said I was going to ring you, because you would appreciate how good they were. Later, I said that I had finished my bag and left it on the chair for him to see. He went over and thoroughly examined it and was asking what stitches I had used, and was trying so hard to be interested in how I had made it. I felt so sorry for him. Aren't I an awful natterer?

Fancy it being too cold for you to try your dress on. I am really going to miss this heat, aren't I?

We have had a reply from the vet. It is an RSPA place and is £2.10.0 a week for six months! Pucci just better mend his ways. Richard said on Saturday that he was going to sell him, but on Sunday, they were rolling all over the carpet together. One look at his little face and you couldn't contemplate giving him away to someone else, naughty as he is. (Pucci, not Richard).

We have just finished painting a poster with "Hello Dolly" on it on two big sheets with a row of cut-out dolls underneath. It's for Margie. The only song she knows is "Hello Dolly" and every morning she bounces in and shouts "Hello Dolly" instead of Good Morning and we all groan and say Look who's here! We are going to hang it over the door to our office when she comes back from leave on Monday.

The weather is beautiful today, roasting hot with no sign of rain. The rain is starting to thin out now..

Sunday Marlene rang to see if we wanted anything from the deli and we said, some milk, so round they came and had coffee. As if they needed an excuse! Richard had to decant some petrol, so asked if he could do it at Peter's, so we went there after going to the airport where we had some tea and watched the plane leave.

Pucci went mad around their garden. He loved it. Fortunately he only ran on the lawn and not the flowerbeds. Pinky, Marlene's ageing dog went gambolling about too. Pinky makes six of Pucci and they did make us laugh.

I used my new bag today and everyone said 'Ooh! Did you really make it yourself'?

Susan got engaged at Christmas, but her parents weren't happy about it, although she has known George for four years. However, today, her parents have agreed to December 7th for their wedding day. She says this morning that she's glad as I'll still be here. It looks as though we might get an invite then. That will be nice.

Richard has arrived with a letter from Cookie. She is dead miserable in Lusaka and has given me directions to her new house "in case we feel like going down when the petrol is better." She has written four pages so she must be feeling fed up. So I must try and squeeze her a line tonight.

Chapter Thirty Three   Marlene and Peter leave

Times of Zambia

17th February 1968   The riddle of the expelled pupils. The expelled pupils were repeaters, who were waiting to see if there were places, as priority was given to first time pupils. Their fees were returned by the head teacher and the parent withdrew his complaints.

* Chibuluma mine officials found that 80% of complaints about mosquitoes were traced back to the gardens of the residents. Mosquitoes have been found breeding in wheelbarrows, old tyres, choked gutters, discarded cans and bottles and ordinary puddles.

* Kaunda in resignation shock. The President briefly resigned his leadership at the UNIP party conference " I was upset by what was a terribly provincial and tribal approach to our national problems."

19th February 1968   Hundreds of bags of maize were just lying about in Northern Province, The Minister of State said that there was no use giving farmers loans to produce more maize if there was no means of transport. They should be given oxen and scotch carts.

22nd February 1968   Zambia Airways is to stop its BAC1-11 flights to Ndola as pilots considered the landing conditions unsafe.

24th February 1968   Plans for resettling many thousands of squatters in Ndola were afoot. The operation would take place before the rains.

26th February 1968   Lusaka's Airline offices were flooded with enquiries from Asians about flights to London, following President Kaunda's call to them to identify with the country in which they had chosen to settle.

Letter 104   26.2.68

I have got a very pink nose and very red legs. Yesterday Richard went to play a tennis match at the club, and I was doing my studying. At about 11.30, Linda called to take us for a swim at her school pool, and I said No as I was busy, but she said she was only going for an hour, so as Richard was due in at One, Pucci and I went off. There was only another couple at this huge pool and we had a super swim and I arrived back at 12.50 to find Richard at home. He had telephoned at 11.35 to see if I was O.K. and to give me a report on the match and he didn't get a reply so he came home and had been pacing around until I got in. I hadn't left a note as I was expecting to be home before him. Oh dear me.

The sun must have been very strong as my legs are burnt and my face is brown. On my stomach, where the lace of my swimsuit is, I have a red lacey pattern. People in the office were saying my job had been

Zambianised.

On Sunday afternoon, we took Marlene, Peter and Sally to the airport. They looked ever so funny, as Marlene had a suit on and Peter had his overcoat. Even Sally's teddy had a pom pom hat and scarf especially for the occasion. It was sad seeing them go, but when they come back, we'll only have nine months to go.

Richard's tennis game was lousy. He wanted to go early to see if the courts had been marked out, but I wouldn't let him. I said it was the new chap's job, so he went for the start at nine o'clock to find that the new chap hadn't even turned up. And when he did, he had forgotten to bring new balls. The visiting club were disgusted. Richard ended up organising the teams, as this chap didn't even know how many were playing, let alone who was to play with whom. Our club members were embarrassed by the disorganisation, but I was glad, as it showed them how much Richard did for them.

On Friday, we went to the Ndola Club for Marlene and Peter's farewell do and it was crummy. There was Tony and his fiancée, (they are getting married in June and he only met her at the beginning of this month) Gary Rowlands and his wife, Muirhead and wife, Rubners and us. Muirhead and Rowlands being South African, dominated the conversation with crude jokes, and snide remarks about the U.K. I didn't make myself very popular by saying their jokes were more suited to a men's club than mixed company. But I'm blowed if I want to spend an evening listening to blue jokes. The food too was lousy.

However, the next night, Saturday, we went to the Coppers with Marlene and Peter and had an excellent meal and lots of laughs and they readily came back to us for coffee and stopped until one, although they had intended to have an early night. We shall really miss them for the next three months.

At my Bernina lesson, I did tears and darns and we had tea and cherry cake. We then went to Marlene's to take their parrot and fish to their new lodgings.

Times of Zambia

27th February 1968	Four Rhodesian Africans declared prohibited immigrants were refused entry into Rhodesia having been left at Churundu. The Rhodesians feared they might be freedom fighters and not deportees. The men were in a bad state as they had been in no man's land with no shelter or food.
28th February 1968	Officials of the Hindu Association denied allegations that Asians were rushing out of Zambia. New Delhi has told Britain that the proposed new immigration laws to check the flood of Asians from east Africa contain "elements of racialism".
29th February 1968	Two men claimed in court yesterday that they were sent by UNIP's Chairman for Marapodi branch, to destroy the roof of Mr Beni Mumba's house. The trial was adjourned.

Letter 105

Last night, I was roped in to go to a meeting of the Zambia Children's Homes Association. It was very interesting, but it is a bit dormant at the moment as they have wound up their home in Rhodesia and are in the process of looking for land for a holiday home. However, much to Richard's relief, I didn't get involved on any committees. (*which was a bit odd given my involvement with Overchurch Children's Home before I married*).

Andre didn't turn up for work yesterday, so I took the dog to work, but had to take him home after an hour as he went for the Africans. I can't explain why, except that the Africans were nervous of him. He wagged his tail and settled down under my desk, until an African came in and he went for them, teeth bared. He was tied to my chair leg fortunately. I couldn't leave him as Africans are in and out all day. However, when I went home at lunchtime, Andre had arrived. After suitable rantings from me, he scuttles off upstairs with his dustpan and dusters.

When I came in after work, Richard was home and had made a stew with beer and tomatoes, which Sally made and had given me the recipe. It wasn't a bit like Sally's. It was horrible. The beer took all the taste from the meat. I kept on eating until Richard himself gave up. As he says, his meals are either splendid or dreadful.

I tried on my Crimpelene suit, but it looks so antwacky. I can take up the skirt however and wear that with a jersey. What a shame. Do throw out my jerseys and shoes or anything that you think I won't wear. Keep my pink Humpty Dumpty skirt, but I've forgotten everything else, so you can throw out willy-nilly, that is if willy-nilly doesn't mind.

If I win on my bonds, you must telephone straight away. Mrs Cleveley has just won another £25 this month. She has won something every month for the past five months!! She has £1,000 in bonds. Anyway, with winning £1,000 last month, she has more than recovered her lost interest.

I am up to date at work, now that Margie is back. So up to date that I'm bored, but I shall let Jack know in the afternoons, as I shall go in and ask for more work. I hope this will pave the way for mornings only.

I am starting to struggle doing my No 6 geography paper and have made a couple of ineffective bashes at it, and Richard says that I am spending most of my time gazing at the wall.

Pucci is behaving himself and is a lot of fun at home. We are making arrangements to send him in December, and we will buy a travelling box early and let him get used to it, so that it won't be strange. The RSPC say on the agreement that the travelling box must be removed within two days after arrival or will become RSPCA property. You can all go and visit him and see his new lodgings and that he is not hungry or anything. We shall miss him but will be so busy that maybe it will go quickly for us at least.

Times of Zambia

1st March 1968 — President Kaunda warned yesterday that it would be disastrous if Britain turned down the £27,700,000 aid package to meet the cost of the sanctions against Rhodesia. "To the British people, a rebel is not a rebel if he is white, only if he is black.

1st March 1968 — Trade Union and UNIP supporter Elias Mwanza was beaten up by a gang of youths at his home for being "uncooperative."

2nd March 1968 — People in Ndola who do not carry UNIP membership cards claimed yesterday

that they were living in fear because of threats from UNIP members who had begun a hunt for those who belong to rival parties. UNIP this weekend conducted a massive house-to-house campaign in which two hundred members checked the cards of people in Chifubu. UNIP's regional secretary refused to apologise to the Trade Unionist who was beaten up. " My enquiries show that Mr Mwanza got what he asked for."

Letter 106   4/3/68

On Friday, Sally and Stuart, Derek Glover, a personnel man here for six weeks, and Jack and Marge Pawson came to supper. We had the meal on our laps on trays, as there were seven of us. Richard borrowed the fibreglass trays from work and we had beef stroganoff and egg noodles with cheese sauce. It tasted good. It should have. We put four pound of fillet steak in it and fresh cream. The evening went with a swing. Sally and Stuart and Derek went at one and Jack and Marge stayed until two, so they must have enjoyed it.

Saturday morning, I was doing darning at Bernina. I had a cup of coffee and a cake. I enjoy my hour there and I am learning something at the same time.

Good news. This morning, I went in to see Mr Pawson and asked if he were in a good mood. I then asked if I could do mornings in April and May prior to my exams. He thought a bit and said, Yes, but that if I fell behind with my work, I would be expected to stay.

Anyway, as he said, barring mishaps, I should be able to keep the work in hand. At least I will be able to go into the exams having completed the course. The mornings only, is on condition that I take the exams. I haven't mentioned pay, but as its only two months, it won't matter so very much. We'll have to live on mealie meal and kapenta. So Mr Pawson is my pin-up today, and I've flogged myself all morning and I was up to date by lunchtime, in rehearsal for next month.

I'm worried about the cine film, as you should have it by now easily. I would hate for it to be lost.

The photograph I am enclosing is of us all at Kariba. We are sitting on the steps of our chalet. See how close the lake is! The tree decorated is a paw paw. See our tinsel tree behind and all our unopened presents. Richard and I look malnourished, but I've got horrid fat legs and a potbelly and Richard appears to have more bosom than I. The Finnish crowd in the next chalet put the streamers on their tree. We added our tree and tied Christmas Crackers to their tree.

Margie and I have just visited Bracaire as Richard has asked me what I would like for my birthday. I had spotted some cushions about a foot square. They were £2.5.0 each and that is just for the cover, not the stuffing. I'll have to admire them from afar.

I just can't understand why you aren't getting any mail. Your mail is coming through quite normally. If ever we couldn't write, we would get in touch somehow by telegram or phone, so don't worry if you don't hear.

Do you realise that the next birthday I celebrate at home will be my 26th. Good grief, I don't feel 18 let alone nearly 24, but I suppose you both only feel 18 too.

I've just bought Margie a card for her birthday tomorrow. Susan and I had both picked it up at the same time as the little girl has a mop of beautiful red hair and looks just like Margie. Susan however had half chosen another, so let me pick this one.

I also bought a flea shampoo (for Pucci, not a flea) and will give Pucci a bath at the weekend.

Have you tried the sun lamp on your leg? Would it do any good? Africans do suffer from rheumatism. I think it is the damp in the rainy season. Bronchitis and all damp caused diseases are also common.

Richard says that Unilever House, London reports that all mail for the ninth is missing, if that's any consolation.

Chapter 34   Missing post

Times of Zambia   6th March 1968

The government is going to take tough measures against undisciplined recklessness and drunkenness by train crews in view of the appalling railway derailments, collisions and other mishaps.

*Deputy Leader of the ANC Edward Liso was arrested for allegedly insulting the President.

*The Ndola Branch of ANC has warned it will revenge itself, tooth for a tooth, if rival parties molest its followers.

*Lusaka City Council has lost valuable qualified staff, said The Government Chief Staff inspector. There were indications that the appointment of former UNIP officials to key positions was to the possible detriment of the Council's efficiency.

7th March 1968

The staff of Hansard, who were criticized for alleged incorrect presentations, were defended by Vice President Simon Kapepwe. He pointed out that they were "transcribers in training" and their efforts were admirable. The reasons, which led to some white transcribers quitting, were much better left undisclosed for the good of the public and the people concerned.

Letter 107   7/3/68

I have had to write to the correspondence college for some more study notes and textbooks, as they seem to have taken the same route as Vera's Christmas present. I'm so cross. Richard's golf club however arrived safely and he spent a good part of the evening chipping from the tiles onto the carpet. He even had an imaginary golf ball.

Your letter has just arrived and you are getting nothing from us. I just don't know what to do, whether to post them myself in case someone in Richard's post room is stealing them. I'll send no more photographs until this is sorted out.

I went to the dentist yesterday and dare I say it, there was nothing wrong, except that front tooth, which he said only had a hole in the previous filling and not worth bothering with. The dentist was very careful and not the rough butcher I expected.

We are just listening to the news reports about Rhodesia. I reckon Britain should pull out and let them fight it out amongst themselves. I wonder what will come next.

I'm not writing any more until I hear that your letters are getting through. Maybe my letters are being censored.

Lever's had a minister close down the factory and lose a day's production so that he could give a lecture on productivity. It could only happen here. It turned into a tub-thumping political meeting and a witch-hunt for non UNIP members, who were named, for belonging to one of the opposing parties. Presumably over the next few weeks they will all be beaten up. Some democracy. The whole country stinks of corruption. If this letter doesn't get through, maybe I'll be deported. However even in the press here there are articles about corruption and concern over it.

I've decided to make a dress for Tony's wedding and I haven't even been invited! Maybe he now doesn't fancy Pommies at a Rhodesian wedding.

We went to see "Woman times Seven, seven little sketches all with Shirley McLaine and all very different and all showing her to be an excellent actress.

Times of Zambia   8th March 1968

A Times reporter who noticed Indian shopkeepers buying reduced goods in bulk at a Kitwe department store followed them to their shop and found them putting up "Bumper Sale" notices and selling the goods at up to 75% more.

* The Minister for State hit out at Lusaka's Asian traders for lagging behind in Zambianisation. Their wives and children stand behind the counters and Africans were only "water drawers and firewood choppers".

* A top UNIP official is to go on tour of Western Province to ensure that all opposition parties in his area are suppressed.

* Police at Ndola applied to withdraw a case against the men who attacked Elias Mwanza, as Mr. Mwanza did not wish to proceed.

8th March

1,000 Ndola women yesterday expressed their concern at the increasing number of drinking places and the limited number of clinics in the city's townships.

9th March..

Petrol rationing has drastically reduced the number of visitors to Munda Wanga Botanical Gardens.

Letter 108   11/3/68

Well here we go again. This time this letter is being given to my friend whose husband works in the Post Office He will put it directly into the London mail sack. I can't get closer than that without delivering it myself.

TOTI

EMUL

ESTO

Daddy, who is going to use your rock with a ring? I don't know anyone with mules. There, see? I guessed. It's just that I know your sense of humour and having ruled out Latin and Spanish and having spelt it backwards…. Even Richard had to have it pointed out to him, even when written out TOTIEMULESTO. Very clever. *(I still have it in the garden)*

I spent from 7.30 Sunday morning until 8 at night, studying. I read a play in the morning and answered the questions on it in the afternoon. I like the reading, but it is overshadowed by the hard work to come after it.

At seven, I came downstairs, and let the dog out and went into the kitchen and started breakfast. As I was doing it, I heard the distant murmur of lots of voices, and as I proceeded with breakfast, it grew louder. On looking out of the window, I saw hoards of Africans swelling up the road. Hundreds of them. I called the dog in and locked the door, ensured that the windows were all shut, drew the curtains and went upstairs and told Richard, who was snoring, to look out of the window. I thought, well this is it, a mob and a riot. Richard looked out of the window and realised they were mainly children. They all had flags and appeared to be lining up. At 7.30, they all seemed to be in class groups. By eight, they had torn up all the surrounding palm trees to make palm banners. By eight thirty, they were cheering everything that passed. By nine they were wandering into the bush and fighting with their palm leaves. By ten there were just a few lying around the roadside. At about ten thirty, a police car went through and the children all came scurrying out of the bush to take their places. About five minutes later, His Excellency The President came though in an open jeep, smiling and waving. He looks just like his pictures.

Well I am not writing any more. Why should I, if it's just to amuse the censors, or the boys in the post room, the PO clerks, or Zambian air stewards?

Times of Zambia   11th March 1968

*President Kaunda bitterly attacked tribal divisions and ambitions in UNIP. In next year's general election no UNIP parliamentary candidate will be allowed to stand in his own tribal area.

*An 1100ton landing craft bought by the Zambian Government arrived at Dar Es Salaam. It is the second vessel to join the Zambian Navy. Its proper use will be announced later.

*   Deputy President of the ANC, Edward Liso was jailed for eighteen months for insulting the President. A Zambian MP loses his seat if he is jailed for more than six months.

*   More than 100 dogs have been shot in a rabies outbreak in Kabwe. Twenty-five rabies cases have been reported.

16th March 1968

The National Union of Local Government has called for the cancellation of all ex-pats contracts when they end and has deplored the recruitment of Asians.

Letter 109   16th March 1968

Hurray-letters arriving at last. I can't explain their hold up and think myself that maybe someone in Lever's post room is hanging on to them. Anyway I'm posting this in an hour's time on my way to my Bernina lesson.

I gave our cine film to Bob Dunckley three weeks ago to post in London on his way to Switzerland and he thinks he must have forgotten it. Anyway wherever it is, it's as safe as with the postal service. Do the letters look as though they have been tampered with?

Margie liked her welcome back poster. She came back from leave early and we saw the car draw up and had it at the ready and stuck it across her cupboards. She was pleased and took it home and her husband said she was all weepy when she came home, as it was nice to be back.

Tony is marrying Beverley Allen who lives here and trained at Addington Nursing School in S.A. with Susan in the office. Tony is that mushy! Its not credible- and him a confirmed bachelor.

We still haven't bought Pucci's dog box although we have reserved it. At £8 it will have to wait.

We are still trying to get news of the slump and further devaluation. All we know is that all foreign exchange stopped at 8.30 yesterday, only 25minutes after Richard had transferred a good sum to Unilever from Levers, in the nick of time.

Andre is brushing my car out and singing, all on about two notes. I want it cleaned before I go to Bernina. I'll pop into the office first and see

Margie as she's on the switchboard and no-one will pop and see her as all the fellows are in for stocktaking in the stores. Normally on Saturdays it's not too bad, as the salesmen are popping in and out and having cups of tea and a chat. One fellow came in when I was there and there were three other fellows writing out reports and drinking tea, and he said. "It's never like this on Mrs Giles' Saturday". Mrs Giles must be about 70 and she's a great grandmother!

We went to a cocktail party on Thursday night at Muirhead's, a farewell to Rowlands. Richard is taking on Rowland's job, and Enid Case has been promoted to take on work as a supervisor. Richard says it will be difficult for anyone else to follow him as he now has 76 staff. They are thinking of taking on just a cost and works accountant in Richard's place, who will eventually replace Peter. Richard reckons that this chap won't have the scope required. However Mackie says to Richard last week that he is doing a great job (I think so too) and that they will have a job lined up for him and will have the red carpet out on his return.

I wish he'd back his pep talk with either a rise or an extra week's leave or a house with a garden. It's too late now for a garden, I suppose. We would just spend a lot of money on plants and not reap the benefit, although Pucci would love a garden, I'm sure.

Pucci's latest game is to run upstairs with a ball and lie by the top of the stairs and push it over the edge with his nose and watch it bounce down.

We've booked a kennels in Halewood, which is out of Liverpool but the nearest we could get.

Chapter 35   Work and Study

Times of Zambia   20th March,

* A complete clampdown on Police Information to the press has been imposed throughout Zambia.

*Police are still searching for 6-year-old Emmanuel Mumbo who disappeared last Sunday. He was among a party of schoolchildren who were taken to Ndola airport to see President Kaunda.

Letter 110   18/3/68

We want to visit Nairobi on our holidays and as Alan and Eva lived in Nairobi, they invited us to lunch, followed by an afternoon at their tennis club and tea. Alan and Richard drove to the tennis club and we followed on foot to give Pucci a walk. When he was thoroughly worn out, I drove him home and then returned for tea and an evening of very good cine films of Nairobi.

On Sunday morning, our next-door neighbour complained that Pucci had howled on Thursday while we were at the cocktail party. We asked about Saturday and she said he had been quiet. Perhaps it was because he was too lively at 6.30 and we should have taken him for a run. I can't understand why he has these howling bouts. When we go out on Wednesday, I'll take him for a walk and feed him. We don't go out until eight, by which time he is usually asleep. We will also tell Mrs Lindique that we are going out and leave her with our phone number in case he starts howling. At least this will show her that we are concerned. Alan and Eva's dog is just as lively and barks like mad for no reason, but because they are in a house you can't hear him from the gate. Ah well never mind.

Richard took Derek to play golf and then I provided them with steak, jacket potatoes and salads, baked apple with mincemeat in, instead of raisins, as I didn't have any. We then took him to see The Dag Hammarskjold memorial, a tiny stone with flowers, which is in a clearing in the bush where the plane crashed. We went on to Monkey Fountain Zoo, and parked the car behind a hedge where we could leave Pucci and go into the zoo. The zoo was a bit flea bitten, but Derek hadn't seen it and took photos. By the aviary was a cage and I couldn't see anything in it: there was sacking to chest height right around it. I was peering up into the tree, when I got the fright of my life, as right up against my chest was a huge, huge python. Did I squeal! It had just been fed and had a lump as big as a sheep in it. Its head was looking right at me .It was as thick as my thighs. We read the notice at the side, which frightened me even more. The python had been found in the zoo. They had noticed geese and ducks disappearing and then two deer disappeared and they found the python asleep digesting its lunch. It had come from the swamp behind the zoo. We decided to return home as we had seen all we wanted to see. I did roast leg of lamb and had the rhubarb crumble I had made in the morning. At least we eat well when we have visitors.

Derek and another chap are living in Marlene and Peter's house and looking after Pinky. To stop her pining too much, the two of them play ball with her when they return from work.

What a shame your manager is making you so miserable in the new branch. Anyway, at least the typist's room is nice and you always enjoyed yourself there didn't you? There's no point in making yourself miserable. Who knows, some knight might come along and sweep old Mrs Whatsit from her Collector's Secretary desk and take her to his castle, and there will be a cushy vacancy there. I feel like coming in and bopping that old mentally deranged nit on the nose. Maybe I'll save it up, so you can tell him that he's got that to look forward to. No, I'll go and squirt him with a water pistol and make all his staff laugh. He would hate to be laughed at. *Mum was being groomed for the post of Collector's Secretary, when the present post holder retired. Unfortunately, although she was typing pool supervisor, this post needed clerical experience in one of the other departments, so she was transferred. Unfortunately, the boss there thought married women should be at home preparing their husbands' suppers, not working, and he bullied her horribly. To avoid a nervous breakdown, Mum applied to go back to the bottom of the typing pool rather than stay. Happily, after a couple of years back in this post, the Collector decided that the six months as a clerk was adequate and she became an excellent Collector's Secretary until she retired. I still owe her previous misogynist boss a punch.*

Richard said that on his last trip, Bob lost his traveller's cheques and was in a right pickle, but on coming home he found them in his suitcase, so perhaps there is hope for our ciné films yet.

Must close. I am half way through the first question on a test paper. The question is "Do the masques and fantasies in the Tempest detract from the story as a whole?" No wonder I am procrastinating.

Letter 111   21/3/68

I like the sound of your hygrometer, Daddy. I'd like something to record our rainfall. I have a temperature chart on the wall and the temperature for this month has been 66-68° and 78-79° at 2 o'clock.

After we had bathed Pucci last week he was all snowy white. We washed him in the bath in a flea killing shampoo and then we had to sit and pick all the fleas and ticks off him. Ticks are horrid as they are difficult to spot, but when he is wet he is almost bald and you can see them easily. He had them inside his paws and one claw was so sore as there were three fat ones inside his toenail. He was a lot happier after all that grooming. However they have started to come back and within this week he has hundreds of fleas, so Richard bought more shampoo, flea powder and a soft plastic flea repelling collar. As the shampoo is so strong that it can only be used after a gap of three weeks and as bathing is such a performance anyway, we tried the collar and lo and behold, the fleas are keeling over and dying. Happily the smell isn't strong, but the fleas are not impressed.

Had a super evening with Derek and David Crawford, an engineer from Port Sunlight here for six months, along with Tony and Beverley. Good meal and back to us for coffee. Derek left this lunchtime and thanked

Richard for our attention, and said we had made his trip for him. Wasn't that nice. I intended to go and see him off but Woodworth, our big boss, was leaving for London on the same plane, and I didn't fancy bumping into him. Richard apologised for me, and said we will call in at Unilever House to see him on our return, but he said we must go and stay with him and his wife and family. *Neither happened.*

We had a postcard from Marlene today- a huge Union Jack. She can write anything on it, coming the other way. She wrote "Have reached Devon at last and it is gloriously cold. Sally doesn't think much of this country and hasn't really taken to many people." (Lets hope this doesn't include Granny) "As you can see, we are backing Britain." Peter has also written on the bottom about the b.weather.

I have just repaired Richard's pyjamas by fitting new waist elastic and buttons, and all by machine with no hand sewing. On one pair, they had ripped down the front, so I had strengthened the front with a square of lovely embroidery. He now informs me, upon trying them on, that he doesn't fancy embroidery decorating his whoogy. He's never satisfied.

Times of Zambia   21st March 1968

*A band of invading African nationalist guerrillas, estimated to be 50 strong, was reliably reported to be slowly fighting its way south.

*Lusaka Mayor, Whitson Banda paid K2 for a plot of land in Matero and sold it for K1, 200.

Letter 112   26/3/68

You haven't commented on my starting mornings. Perhaps this was in the missing letters. I am working mornings for April and May to study for my exams, which are the first two weeks in June, when I am taking leave. At least this will ensure I will read all the books.

I am now in the Advanced Bernina class. This means I can come and go as I please and learn whatever I like, Last Saturday, I darned socks! I also took up a few hems by machine AND sewed on a button.

I am doing little but going to work and studying. I do hope I pass in January, because just think of the lazing around I could have done with some decent books, if not studying.

Foyles have not sent my Othello despite a letter from me. Can you try around for me It's a Signet Classic Shakespeare. No other edition will do. It is 3/6d so I am sending 10/- to cover postage. If you can send it in the next week, I will still have a few weeks to cram it.

Chapter 36   MyBirthday

Times of Zambia   21st March 1968

Mrs Bidwell was cooling her feet on the edge of Hippo Pools when her husband shouted "Look Out" as a crocodile skimmed across the water towards her. In a flash, Zimba, their Alsatian leaped into the water between the crocodile and Mrs. Bidwell. As he snarled at the crocodile it clamped its jaws onto the dogs legs. The last they saw of the dog, as his wife scrambled up the bank, was its tail disappearing under the water.

Letter 113   29/3/68

I am feeling nice and mellow. With it being my birthday tomorrow, Saturday, I had birthday celebrations today at work, and Margie and Susan decided we should celebrate and have a drink at The Coppers, which has a nice terrace and garden, so at four o'clock off we went. We all had to leave at 4.30 as Margie's nanny leaves at five, and Andre would be wanting his ration money and George picks Sue up at 5.45ish. We had two thimbles full of sherry and a good giggle. The place was empty, as most people finish at half four so it was very pleasant. We arrived at Dolphin Court seconds before George arrived.

I got five cards from the office, from Mrs King, Margie, Susan, Sharmaine, Margie's cousin who joins us at lunchtime and Mrs Mhizha, the African girl I made the dress for. Susan bought me a beautiful "Intimate" Revlon spray on a posh crystal decanter, for having her round in the evenings, and Mrs Mhizha bought me a copper plaque with an outline of Zambia on it and she had had it engraved "To V Lapthorne From E Mhizha." Wasn't that sweet. She said it would remind me of her when I was back home with my Mummy.

So we had cakes today. I bought two-dozen sausage rolls, a lemon meringue pie, an apple pie and an egg custard. Guess what Richard had for his supper- sausage rolls and chips and apple pie and cream. We girls had eaten the rest.

Everyone has been chaffing me today. (that means "pulling my leg". I started to write it before I thought on.) It's funny, but I, deliberately at first and now by habit, used the lingo that the girls did. At first I felt awkward, but found that they didn't look at me oddly, but were more aware that I was strange when I talked my own lingo, so now it's habit. Yet when I talk to Richard I find I speak quite normally. Richard hasn't picked up an accent, but he has picked up a few expressions, some from me like "I reckon" suffixed after sentences, e.g. she went home at about four, I reckon" and some blue profanities, NOT I hasten to add from me, but I correct him when I think on, and I reckon he will drop them on the boat home.

Richard said I might buy a dress, because Sharmaine is modelling in the local shop on Saturday and she brought the dresses to the office to try on, which we did and I like a silky Tricel one (St. Michael) for K6.99 £3.9.11. It is yellow and green with a high waist, or a dropped yoke and is pretty. I tried on the more mod ones-black with lace, but the girls agreed it wasn't me. I don't know whether I am considered a bit staid, but I am glad they thought the other was best for me, as I liked it best too. Is that Irish-or maybe it's the sherries. I went for it yesterday but they only had 14 and 16 and I wanted the 12. They said they will keep the one Sharmaine is modelling so I have warned her not to dirty it. Here they wouldn't sell it off cheap if it were dirty, as there are dozens who would pay twice the price for it. I've done very well as I've not had a new dress for fourteen months, other than the two African print dresses I made for Christmas at a pound each.

It is becoming cold at night. We have put another blanket on last night. Now we have two. Soon we will have to close the windows. We have them all wide open to catch any breeze, but now the curtains are starting to sway with the breeze. *All opening windows had burglar bars and mosquito screens.*

I have put all my cards up, but will put them away now, to see if Richard remembers my birthday without being reminded. Then I can be pleasantly surprised, or I can play the martyr if he forgets and he can do the dishes all weekend. Aren't I awful!

Letter 114   30/3/68

Happy Birthday to me. Thank you for my super presents. I am going to wear my new dress for town this morning. I know that seems like sacrilege, but I am meeting Margie and Susan to see Sharmaine do her modelling. On Saturday mornings, all the latest fashions are on display- although I've yet to see a maxi, so we shall not be outdone. Margie will probably wear her orange trouser suit in silk with the cutaway top and Susan her new tent dress. I will surely outshine them both! It's unlike any of my other dresses, because it has such a pretty neckline. Thank you too for my sweater, which is a super fit. It is loose at the top and fits snugly round my hips. Do I sound like Veronica Papworth? Thank you too for my super slides, the velvet one is gorgeous and I am wearing the Woollies one today to town.

It is just getting on for eight o'clock and I am sitting on the terrace in my loungey chair with a coffee table at the side with all my essay writing equipment on it and a big glass of orange. Andre arrived early today. Usually he comes at eightish and I have time to snatch my breakfast, but he was here at seven and as Richard goes out to play golf, I had to sit out here until he announced breakfast was ready and then eat in state on my own. He shouts from the depths of the lounge, "Isready, mdm"

Richard did remember. He wished me Happy Birthday and made Pucci kiss me Happy Birthday and he (Richard not Pucci) sang, "She's 23 today". Isn't he useless? Perhaps he's decided to start knocking the years off now.

We had been disappointed with our proposed round the world tour next year. It doesn't leave Cape Town until May 3rd. The February boat is only going to Australia. It would have compensated for our Suez cancellation. Surely nothing else can go wrong.

Letter 115   4.4.68

Bob Dunckley came back yesterday and can't find our film. He forgot to take it with him, he thinks, and it is somewhere in his house, he thinks! I could clobber him. Well at least there's still hope for it.

I am waiting for Sally & Stuart to come for a planning meeting and Richard prepared a curry last night and it has been simmering since 2.30 and I have been smelling it all afternoon and it is making me so hungry! I've a horrible feeling they may forget, as I rang Sally to confirm and the switchboard said she had gone home sick, and they are living in someone's house at the moment and I don't know where it is! And there's such a load of curry!

Sunday. Well I've certainly boobed with my letter writing this week. I started this on Thursday to post on Friday, but Sally and Stuart arrived and I was under the impression that I'd sent it, but Richard asked me what happened to my Friday letter and here it is still, on Sunday. Well I'll post this a day early tomorrow and post another on Thursday before we go on our hols, and another the following Tuesday on our return.

We had a good laugh on Thursday with the noisy Parkers and did hardly any holiday planning!!

On Friday, Richard came home and said we had been invited to drinks to people opposite who are Levers (but indirectly - he is investigating further trade possibilities and his job is hush-hushish to avoid speculation). I wasn't keen as I was doing supper, but Richard said the wife had had trouble with getting a domestic, and would Andre wash sheets and shirts and polish floors once a week, for the 6 months they are here.

Some weeks there would be no work and they may be away for a month or so in between, and couldn't retain a regular servant. However in the end we went after supper because Richard popped over to say we were in the middle of supper preparations, but saw that they had changed and he had been out to buy glasses! So we went at eight, telling Mrs Lindique where we were in case our monster howled (he was as good as gold, as I kept going to their front door and listening, and we didn't hear a single squeak from him!)

His wife informs me she was a teacher of Eng Lit and offered her services if I got stuck!! She further endeared herself to me when she gave me four thrillers she had read, and I saw her coffee table crammed with books – from paper backs to painting books and allsorts.

They also offered £4.0.0 a month for Andre's services, but we thought he wouldn't take kindly to a drop in salary when they left. Also £4.0.0 was a lot for floor polishing and shirt washing – I'd do it myself for that. They said we should take three and give him what we liked, but we reckoned this would be unfair. We decided to give him £1 a month and keep £2.0.0 and save it for the six months (£12.0.0) and buy him a bicycle putting the extra ourselves (they are about £15). Anyway it rested with Andre. Richard put it to him on Saturday morning and he was very pleased, especially as another baby is on its way! (We now have 4 adults and 3 ½ babies and a dog to keep) We could also afford to keep on with the extra £1 for the 3 or 4 months (yippee) after the Whites (Ron and Elizabeth – for your book) left.

Saturday was my morning in the office and I took my homework in, but there were so many visitors I never did any. At 5 to 10 Mrs King came to relieve me while I went to see Margie's cousins' wedding (Sharmaine's sister – the one we went to see her wedding dress), and I saw her arrive and I went into the church – a lovely building with lousy acoustics. Margie's husband gave her away and there were only about twenty people there – and none of his people. The only adults were Margie's mum and Sandra, the bride's mum, and a granny. All the rest were friends. There were no hymnbooks and only one hymn – which only the vicar sang. It hardly seemed as though they had been married – and no ushers or proper photographer, but the outfits were all nice. I took a photo of Michelle giving a horseshoe and one of Calvin, Margie and Michelle. This is a 20 print film I am trying. They will be nice to keep in an album.

Bob still hasn't found our film. I am cross. If the film doesn't turn up we'll have to go to Kariba next Christmas, but will not replace the film of our puppy taking his first jumps down steps and the bit where we picked him up. Ah well!

Times of Zambia   5th April 1968

Opposition leader, Harry Nkumbuk said it was quicker to drive than to make a telephone call.

6th April

The rise in incidents of rabies has been attributed to the increase in the number of jackals. The police have shot 50 stray dogs following a tie up order in Lusaka last Thursday.

Letter 116   9/4/68

Did I say nothing could go wrong with our holiday? Stuart rang today to say that Sally had gone down with a stomach bug, and has been sent to bed until the weekend, and therefore their holiday is off! Stuart is very disappointed but says Sally is too poorly to come. Isn't that a shame? It affects us in that we have no one to share our expensive petrol with and we did have fun together at Christmas. Anyway, it will be nice with just the two of us. It's the first time we have been away on our own since we've been married.

Pucci goes into kennels from Thursday morning until Tuesday morning. He won't like it but will be fed and looked after. Ah poor little chap. The best part of our last holiday was going to fetch him home.

Richard went to Kitwe today to give evidence on a company case. He got £2.0.0 allowance and £4.0.0 petrol allowance, so he bought a £9.0.0 pair of binoculars for our holidays, and two magazines for me!! Can you beat that!

They are super binoculars. I have spotted nests in trees across the golf course and can see the people going into the golf club bar.

Sometimes it's the only way of spotting game and it's pretty wasteful going into a reserve without them and we intended buying a pair later on, but not yet!! Isn't he useless! We shall take them to Victoria Falls and I can do game spotting on the last bit of the road.

Our itinerary is as follows – so far. 11 o'clock Thursday – set off to reach Choma by evening and stop at a Choma motel (booked). Friday – set off from Choma to reach Livingstone by lunch and in afternoon view the Zambian side of the Falls, cross Customs into Rhodesia, book into Victoria Falls Hotel for dinner. Saturday and Sunday – laze around and view the Falls. The Hotel has pool, ballroom and goodness what else and it's 77/6 for bed and breakfast!! – each !! Monday – make our way back (all in one day!!) stopping at Cookie's in Lusaka midday for lunch we hope.

Stewart is coming tonight or tomorrow with some petrol coupons.

Andre is working his part time work well – in fact he never stops singing. However today at lunchtime he was in a state. He'd used a too hot iron on Ron White's white shirt (which said warm iron) and had yellowed it slightly. I said it couldn't be helped and to finish ironing it. However when he had finished he came and said it was finished so I said – well take it across – and he went on into a garbled – "not white, banana shirt, not white, gone bad on iron" etc. So I said shall I take it over and he nodded. So I went across and said we'd had an accident and she laughed and said she was used to it (coming from Nigeria) and Ron said he always wanted a cream shirt. I went and told Andre that the Madame had said perhaps it would wash better next time and he was relieved! He's not frightened of me like that. Mrs White is twice the size of me with a foghorn voice and being a schoolteacher you can imagine the effect she must have on Andre, especially as she is used to dealing with servants.

However Andre came at 5 tonight for K2.00 as his baby was sick and his wife was taking it to Mufulira mine hospital where her family work, to get it in to the hospital for treatment. When I asked what was the matter he made out that its stomach was big and churned up - it sounds like malnutrition to me – it can only be 6 months old. I bet she's not feeding it properly. Babies are breastfed until the next baby usually and as Mrs Andre is pregnant again, this baby is probably suffering.

Chapter 37   Rhodesia

Times of Zambia 10th April

*   Zambia's future 1,050-mile fuel line is now 300 miles from completion in Ndola.

*   Tie up order for dogs has now been made on the Copperbelt. Dogs not tied up will be shot on sight.

*   Rhodesian jets, spotter planes and helicopters are violating Zambia's air space at will, in their frantic effort to kill or capture Freedom Fighters, who are battling their way back to Zambia across the Zambezi.

*   A witchfinder who took three old men from their village and kept them prisoner at his home for two weeks, making them work in the fields by day and locking them up by night, in order to "cleanse them from witchcraft succeeded in his appeal against a two year jail sentence as such. Mr Justice Scott ruled that a slave is a person without any rights of his own, permanently owned and able to be sold to others. Since the intention of this detention was for a limited period only for the intention of "witchcraft cleansing" the accused could not be said to have been keeping slaves.

*   Passengers missed the train because it left on time. The train seems to have had no fixed time for departure, but usually leaves Lusaka around ten, but on this occasion it left at 7am. Kafue roundabout was bustling with people scrambling into any kind of transport to catch up with the train.

Letter 117   Rhodesia   Easter Sunday   4.68

Well we are having a lovely holiday. Richard took Pucci into kennels on Thursday morning, but this time he knew what was coming and he had a job getting him to go into his little house. Poor little chap. Last night Richard said he heard someone at the bedroom door and he opened it and said "There's a little white woolly fellow here asking for his Mummy, because he's tired as he's come a long way." I hope he's eating OK.

We set off at about 11 lunching on hot cross buns en route. We passed through some small towns, which consisted of a few chickens and garage (usually shut) and a trading store. We landed in Choma almost dry of petrol and pulled into the hotel, which was awful. There were drunken Africans sprawled all over the pavement and ladies of dubious morals holding up the walls. We didn't even get out of the car but drove to the police station where we were informed that the motel we wanted was outside of town for two miles. We then couldn't start the car. Apparently being so low on petrol had dragged up all the muck from the bottom of the tank. Anyway Richard and a policeman pushed it down a slope from the station and I let out the clutch sharply in second and it hit and Richard screams "keep it going" so I drive madly round a compound of police houses scattering chickens and back to Richard who climbs in while I'm still driving and takes over and we depart waving to a hoard of policemen who wave us on our way. We then arrive at the motel, which if a bit seedy, gave us a room and bathroom. There was a fight in the bar in the middle of the night with bottles and glasses flying but we were already in bed. *Although we remember the owner in broad Afrikaans yelling, "Get orff my property" we just checked the door bolts and hid under the bedding.*

At seven on Friday we were off again and were in Livingstone at 9.30. We went to a tourist craft centre and had a look around, and to the David Livingstone museum, which was notable. We next drove to an area known to have game, but unfortunately they go deep into the bush in the wet season. However just as we had given up a herd of bambis appeared on the road and on spotting us they ran away, leaping across the road..

We then went to a Zambian village, which is laid out for tourists, but which is occupied, mainly by fellows making things to sell, like woodcarvings. Lunch at a riverside restaurant, which was passable, and through customs (it took about an hour and a half) and to the hotel. It is a Rhodesia Railways Hotel and the best in Central Africa, the downstairs rooms are all very grand but the bedrooms are modern and comfortable. We have a bathroom and shower (lovely in this heat). I have no tan, as it is so hot, I shelter under a cotton hat and sit in the shade (you know me!). The pool is popular but we have not yet been able to find a spot between the cooking bodies.

We have posted two books to Richard's parents (because you get all the photos and Mrs L has complained). They are cartoon books on UDI and are banned in Zambia and are chock-a-block full of nationalistic propaganda.

Many thanks for my Othello which arrived very promptly and which I am now getting stuck into.

Friday late afternoon, we just wandered around and had an early night. Yesterday there was a dance in the evening and tonight a film show. Yesterday in the morning we sat outside and then went to see the Falls, which are magnificent, which I hope my films will show. We went through a rain forest (not rain but continuous drenching spray) but the volume of the Falls was so great that we could hardly see the main falls. The most thrilling were the gorges and spectacular plunges. We stood right at the edge. You would have hated it Mummy. We are now going for a stroll to try and photograph some monkeys, which we saw this morning and hope are still around.

I didn't mention from this trip the exciting flight in a three-seater plane zooming over the falls, which was absolutely thrilling. Perhaps I put it on a postcard. But I do remember being very queasy when I got off, which to me only indicated one thing…..

Monday night – home again - what a long drive 500 miles in one day – that's as far as London to Liverpool and back to London, so Richard says. We got in at 6 having started at 6.30 and having 2 ½ hours at Cookie's so that's good going. We are just off to the pictures.

Times of Zambia

April 16th

Start attending UNIP meetings or we will endorse your licenses, Asians told. People trying to disorganize Monsa township by canvassing for United Party would be evicted from their council houses, said UNIP's Mr Longoloshi.

April 18th

1,000 women march to police station in arrests protests as news got round that three men had been arrested after a fight between UNIP and UP members.

Letter 118   Thurs. 18/4/68

I have just finished two essays and I'm taking time off to write my letter.

I had one paper returned with "good, sound work" on it, (big head) but I am using my textbooks and have committed nothing to memory and am not likely to before these exams, but I am hoping to for next Jan. Mr L says he hopes I pass, but I have no intention of passing this time, as I haven't done the work. If I do pass, I'll have no faith in the English Education system. I can't really be expected in 4 months of evening work, and two months of half days to cover adequately a two-year school curriculum without personal tuition. There are six exams, not two. Three for each subject and one each day for six days from 10-17th June. I am taking them solely to do a practice paper under exam conditions so I will have a better chance of passing in January.

When does it go dark now? Here it's dark at 6-6.30 every night all year round, which is a shame with the weather being so ideal for sport. I don't even know if Australia is still on our route. We've had no dates offered that fit with what we want to do. Don't worry. I'll give you the dates and places as soon as it is I confirmed, which I hope is soon.

We have cut our losses and sold our excess fuel to Bob. We have enough for local use. Any other trips we go on we shall fly.

I have just been investigating a stink in the kitchen and was met by smoke. The butcher delivered an oxtail for some unknown reason and I decided to boil it for the dog – that was at 2 o'clock (the recipe said 2-3hrs). It is now six and there is a stinky charred oxtail in the bottom of the pan. I must get rid of the stink before his lordship comes home. Anyway the Whites have asked us for supper tonight so I'll just pop upstairs for a bath.

By the way, our Vic Falls Hotel had a shower in the bathroom, which worked properly and even Richard whom I refuse to sleep with to make him take his <u>weekly</u> bath, was under it every day and I was under it <u>three</u> times a day. Lovely. Mornings I sneaked in while he drank his coffee and at night while he was changing and midday by pretending to be cleaning my teeth. It got that so he wouldn't let me into the bathroom until I swore I was not getting into the shower again.

Times of Zambia   April 20th 1968

President Kaunda has announced sweeping measures to end foreign domination of the Zambian economy, by inviting them to sell the government at least 51% participation in their enterprises. He issued a stern warning against any attempts to abuse responsibilities over newly nationalized property and said there must be no scramble for a shop after a trade's license expired.

Letter 119   23/4/68

Have received your letters 118 and 119, so I'll start by answering questions. Bob lost the tape too as it was parcelled with the film. It was all packed for posting. Bob came this evening to borrow an accounting book, as he couldn't find his copy anywhere. I said he was pretty good at losing things! He's got 12 months in which to find it.

Re Andre – if he stays with us maybe whoever takes over from us will take him on; otherwise we will advertise for him.

There are quite a few churches with an assortment of ministers. The religions are the same and there are Hindu places for the Indians. There is Catholic, Anglican and Baptist (no Methodist – all the smaller ones combine into Baptist) and of course a strong Jehovah witness lot and Americans doing their Billy Graham bit out here.

How I miss Easter and home. I'm going to spend all my long weekends with you – Richard can stay with his mother!!

Nanny is certainly lucky – if she gets such treatment at Easter she'll have Father Christmas and allsorts at Christmas.

I don't think I continued about our Easter holiday. On the Sunday morning we went to another village and were shown around with a guide who had obviously learnt his speech from the guide book (as I confirmed when reading the book) and if interrupted, he had to start again from the beginning of his paragraph, but although the village itself wasn't as large as the Zambian one, the guide certainly made it live a bit, when you knew all the rituals that decided the size and position of huts and kitchens.

We walked around the hotel after lunch as there were monkeys about, so we headed down to the river and saw beautiful butterflies which I tried unsuccessfully to film and we saw some baboons which I filmed only afterwards realising I had it on 3ft focus for butterflies!! We then came back as neither of us fancied the thickness of the bush. Richard heard a funny snuffing noise and we froze. Anyway it didn't appear to move, so we stayed until it appeared. It was a wild pig. It was horrid, all hairy with a warty snout. Richard wanted to make it come into a good position for the camera, but I persuaded him that they could get nasty (which later we were told they could – very nasty in fact). Just as we approached the hotel, swarms of monkeys came down over the hotel vegetable patch, and I filmed like mad.

At 4.30 we had managed to take a drive in the game park (10/- per car) rather than a 3hr trip on the river, because the pilot of the plane we went in on our flip said the animals were in the bush not on the river as it was too marshy this time of year. We went about eight miles inside to a waterhole and resolved to sit there until something appeared, but the waterhole was dry! But we could see hundreds of huge and not so huge footprints in the mud. We waited until 5.45 when we had to move to be out for 6.30 (sunset – if you don't book out by then, they send a search party), and we had only been stopped 10mins. Anyway we tried to start the car and nothing happened. Exactly the same as the preceding Thursday. It wouldn't even kick, and we couldn't get out to push or even open the bonnet! We had two cokes and resolved to wait for the car to cool (and Richard's language and comments on cars and game parks in general).

However after cooking in the car for ages and afraid of being eaten by a lion if we got out, as the elephant grass was six feet on either side of the track, an African rides past on his bike, whereupon Richard gets out and fiddles around under the bonnet. Wonder why I didn't mention that, as it is one of our regular African reminiscences) Fortunately it started at about 3rd go, and was I relieved.

When we reached Broken Hill with a hundred miles to go we pulled into a garage nearly empty (it's impossible to reach anywhere with a lot in the tank, as the garages are few and far between and you can only have the number that your coupons will match (2 or 3 a go). Here the car refused to start when we moved into the queue, and we were blocking entrance and exit. I got out to push (it was pouring down), but Richard just sat there expounding on the beautiful petrol and the beautiful country. However two young people we vaguely knew came out of the caff and started to help me push and Richard got out. It was awful. The car was covered in red dust which had turned to mud, and way after a lot of pushing we got it going and we all jumped in and the muddy couple got out at the caff where we couldn't stop even to give them coffee and we went to another garage at the top of the hill, where we could free wheel away but we started OK and arrived home whacked at 6, having been travelling from 6am. However we washed and changed and went to see Grand Prix at the cinema, taking advantage of the fact that Pucci was in kennels, and what a film to see. It was all racing scenes, and views of views and whizzing road and more road, – the last thing we wanted to see!

Now George (a different George) Dumble and Susan Cranny. George works in transport at Levers and Susan is on an accounting machine with Zam. Ox. They got engaged at Christmas and are getting married on 7.12.68. They live in Luanshya, and as we now finish at 4.30 again, George picks Sue up from work. He only picked her up from here to save Sue waiting from 4.00 to 4.40 for him.

Well roll on Whit. I'll try and find time to write to Mrs L if Rich can't (he is ridiculously busy and works until bedtime and his eyes are all bloodshot.

Times of Zambia   April 25th

*   Unemployed squatters should return to rural areas to "face the challenge of the economic revolution" said Minister Of Works and Housing yesterday.

*   Hunt is still on for missing schoolboy.

*   Two baby elephants left for France yesterday. They brought the country K1,200 in revenue and are the first of 25 to be sent abroad this year.

Letter 120   26/4/68

On Wednesday, I made sweet and sour meatballs with soy sauce and pineapple from my new cookbook, which Richard bought me. It is super and has 1000 recipes each with a picture. The author is a Marguerite Patten and the recipes straightforward edible stuff – even to fish and chips and boiled eggs.

We have May Day as a public holiday as its Labour Day – yippee.

My rose here flowered on St. George's Day and had I thought on, I would have worn it on my dress!

Nationalisation won't affect us as yet although it may come when their new plant is built. It would probably be more economical for Levers to take 51% of Zambia than vice versa.

Richard is dashing back to work and wants this letter – or note rather.

Chapter 38   Holiday Plans

Times of Zambia   1st May 1968

While no official comment is available, Simon Kapepwe's statement that Zambia was thinking seriously about a ground to air missile system, London is clearly very interested. How it would be paid for is problematic.

*Petrol bomb thrown into house injures United Party official.

Letter No. 121   29/4/68

I am writing this a day early this week as we have a holiday on Wednesday (because it's your birthday). I also booked a call today for your birthday for 6.40 our time (5.40 yours). This was the latest I could get it. The last call is 7.40 our time. I just hope you are in and not visiting Nanny. The calls are normally an hour or two late anyway. If just you are in Daddy, that will make up for not getting in on the last one, but I know Mummy, you will be disappointed as the call is to say Happy Birthday. If you are both out celebrating, then it won't matter!

Your sideboard sounds nice and I certainly don't mind what you get, but are you sure a high one won't make the room darker? Anyway you know I like that old sideboard. You look after it Daddy, because I have designs on it as a playroom cupboard. However you might have to keep it in your shed for ages!

I used it as a playroom cupboard for years and then passed it on to be the grandchildren's playroom cupboard. I painted it with orange sunflowers on for the older three and then put the French Emilie characters on it for Sophie's room. And it was a 1940 utility sideboard. The V & A might want it.

Re nationalisation, Levers is a good firm and keeps to government policies about Zambianisation etc. The majority of firms that have been taken over deserved what they got. Both the copper mines and Lever can afford to quote terms too. The copper mines particularly as they hold the country's economy. However the mines are Zambianising as quickly as possible. I don't reckon that it's a bad thing having locals trained for good jobs even though the going is slow and thwart with difficulties, because they are less likely to move whereas the European population has less roots and can up and go.

We wouldn't be home any earlier as even if the company was nationalised Richard is still needed to train Zambians, and you can't just walk out of a job and leave 76 people without a boss and no-one doing the boss' job. The place would collapse. Even this government realises the need for 'imported brains'.

The dog has just run in with a length of spaghetti from the bucket and is really making a secret meal of it. However when I chop it up in his meat, he licks it clear of gravy and leaves it on his plate. He's just enjoying it because he thinks he shouldn't have it.

On Saturday we went to see 'Khartoum" about Jordan and the siege of Khartoum. It was very good, but I saw a play on TV ages ago and knew the whole yarn. Nevertheless, good spectacular film material.

Saturday, I didn't go to Bernina but took up hems on <u>8</u> dresses and one coat (three of the dresses were your cast offs). One of them was a pale blue and white shift which I ripped on the scooter (it's that old) I cut it across at hip level, and it now makes a super shift to go with my bathing costume, complete with belt.

One dress with a collar like this-I did embroidery around, and on that orange linen dress I did embroidery on the neck and sleeves in the same colour, so I will need no new dresses for our summer holidays, which are now finalised.

Yesterday afternoon we went to the resident ministers house, or rather walked along the road to his gate (through the golf course). I picked a lot of grasses and a bit of stuff like honeysuckle and have an unusual show in my vase. We then left Pucci asleep with exhaustion, and went to Sally's at Misundu for an hour, as she wanted us to see the progress that had been made. The house has certainly come on and is an impressive achievement but at the moment of course, very rough. They have also with the aid of a builder/gardener/watchman chap made a super vegetable garden which I would willingly buy vegetables from. Sally is growing everything from lettuce to aubergines. *The builder came out of the bush and introduced himself, saying Cementi, presumably indicating that he could build. He was hired and happy to answer to Cementi therafter.)*

Our holidays are now finally fixed up from the 4th to 21st of September. Time will probably fly when we get back from those hols.

Times of Zambia   2nd May

President Kaunda threatened to ban the country's two white run unions if their leaders don't disband and join their Zambian dominated counterparts.

Letter 122   2/5/68

How about that phone call for a surprise. I'm sorry to have missed you again Daddy. I don't seem to be able to catch you in, you gad-about, you. I hope you think it was worth the £3.0.0 – it seems to go so quickly and it's not as though we say anything very sensible! It is marvellous though.

I was looking at my atlas today and it's such a long way away and to think I can hear you schlurping your cup of tea and Sooty! I could almost smell banana butties and apple pie. It feels so funny sitting here after putting the phone down, knowing you are ringing Auntie Vera and popping up to tell Joyce. I had a treat and went to bed and started a forbidden paperback. Yesterday, it being a holiday, I did less work than I do in the afternoons, although I worked from 7.30 in the morning until 3 in the afternoon. I read a chapter without taking it in and have to start again. Whereas going a steady pace I enjoy working; now having 'a sense of urgency' it's too much like hard slog, especially as I will fail these June ones anyway. However it will give me a good ground on which to consolidate from June until next Jan.

No more developments in homecoming dates. I'm afraid whatever happens here we won't be home early. Remember that even at Independence not so many people moved out, and only a big split would cause an exodus, and even that should take longer than 10 months, so don't view every political move with the hope that we may be home. In fact, lots of cars were stoned yesterday, but all the cars involved were passing stadiums where rallies were being held, and were therefore asking for trouble, like going to a football match wearing opposition colours. They should have, like us, stayed at home and away from such places.

Richard really has been terribly busy and even I am up to my eyes as you can tell by the scrappy letters I have been sending to you. In six weeks I'll write to everyone. He is just coming out of his stiffest work, made worse by Peter's absence and by the absence of the salaries clerk and Richard had the abominable mundane job of doing the salaries and cheques and calculating pay just because there was no one else to whom he could entrust the knowledge of everyone's wages. It took him a week and weekend of evenings – even to putting the cheques in envelopes and he was getting madder and madder doing it. I couldn't even help, as I was busy. Roll on June. I don't regret doing my course but it is time consuming these last weeks. We both pitch in and cook and wash the dishes together. In fact that's the only time we speak until bedtime and "how about some coffee".

Tomorrow we are entertaining, paying off two debts, the Whites over the court opposite, and Alan and Eva for their day out, and Sally and Stuart are coming too. Eight to feed!! Our meat bill this week was £4.10.0!! This was because only half our order is supplied – sometimes only steak, so we always put down loads and this week he supplied the lot. From our meat book:

4lb fillet steak	£1.13.0	K 3.30
6 pork chops	10/-	(not a very nice cut)
1 leg lamb	1.2.0	(a nice one)
6 lamb chops	5.0	(not very nice)
2lb liver	8.0	} ox liver for
4lb chuck steak	<u>14.0</u>	} the dog
	4.12.0	

How did that happen? The butcher totals it to K9.00 i.e. £4.10.0 – perhaps it's discount. How does this compare? The lamb chops were a funny cut. The ox liver is O.K. casseroled for us, but the dog eats it. He prefers the chuck steak though. The dog today grabbed your letter from the coffee table and ran away with it. When I shouted at him, he dropped it and put his paws on it, which he normally does with his toys, but he was lying down and looked as if he was reading it. I had to laugh.

to laugh.

Pucci is good company

Pucci is good company in the afternoon. He is also a good watchdog, and won't even let a lizard on to the terrace. When Richard and I dance to the radio, he jumps up and down and cries until we pick him up and dance with him too. Isn't he ruined? We don't have an alarm anymore. At about 6.45 he bounces on to the bed and if you ignore him he brings up his toys and drops them over the edge of the bed. Perhaps the idea is to fill the bed with balls and rubber mice and old sandals so that there's no room for us.

Letter 123   7/5/68

Don't shout at Daddy for not writing pages, or you'll stop the good work in the garden (or is it the planning on the armchair that is time consuming?)

We had Alan and Eva Phillips, Sally and Stuart and Ron and Elizabeth White in. We had planned to do a buffet with a casserole that has previously been a success. However we cooked it on Thursday and left it overnight. On Friday afternoon we came to reheat it and panic! It had gone off. Don't ask me why. It just smelled odd. Quite inedible – 3 ½ lbs of fillet steak which had taken all evening to prepare. We pulled out our precious leg of lamb and defrosted it and Richard deboned it and stuffed it. It looked and smelled delicious. However instead of pasta, we had to do vegetables – loads of roasties and peas and cauliflower in cheese sauce. I used up my month's supply of spuds and two packets of our precious Sunday dinner cauliflower! Boy – did I begrudge it? What with the waste and the extra expense, we are living on mealies this week. I did three sweets. One a raspberry flan, one a sponge cake with cream and apricots inside and icing sugar on top, and the other a fruit loaf sliced with slices of ice cream in between and apricots on top. All the ice cream went and yesterday I threw away the remains of the sponges as the cream had gone off. The sponge was lovely though. The next dinner I give is going to be egg and chips and a tin of fruit! As I say every time – never again – until next time.

The evening, from the visitors' point of view however, was a great success.

Nothing exciting on Saturday. On Sunday we went to Mackies in the morning for tennis. It was good. Dwyers were there with their twins who are now five months old, and I had the opportunity to nurse the little girl, who just lay and gurgled for about two hours – very placid and not a bit of trouble. They carry them in carrycots stacked on top of each other and fling them in the back of the car quite haphazardly.

Our holiday dates are 4th Sept – fly to Dar-es-Salaam spend night at Kilimanjaro Hotel and fly to Mombasa on the following day. Spend 5th to 14th in Mombasa. Drive through Tsavo Game Park on the 14th staying the night at Kilagumi Lodge (£10 a night!) and on the following day travel leisurely through the game park and to Nairobi spending 16th to 20th in Nairobi flying home then. We hire a car from Mombasa to Nairobi at what appears to be reasonable rates. Hope to buy our impala head here and send it home direct to save duty back into Ndola, as these game things have to have a license. No more about our home trip. Richard has asked his father to find out what ships leave the vicinity of Cape Town anytime from the end of Jan. We haven't had much luck this end, as all local information is out of date. All P&O sailings are out. We have written to their head office. The round the world is £735 each!! And is in May. We had reckoned on £400 each, but they have highered the prices on devaluation to compensate, whereas we thought our money would be worth more. We had also knocked off our airfare, which the company give us. We had, in fact, planned to blow £1000. (Don't gasp, but this is what Richard gets on leaving – 3 months pay and a resettlement allowance and a percentage of this, that and the other). Sounds a lot in hard cash, sounds a lot any way, and we were working on the principle of what we never have we'll never miss and that it's worth the experience. It will in any case cost us £500 on a normal holiday coming home. Imagine how your two weeks holiday costs you and multiply it by 2 or 3 and add the Cape Town -Southampton fare and what do you get! Not far off that I'm sure!

However we will need the money to "resettle". I'll need loads of clothes, living so frugally here as regards clothes, and we will want to redecorate the house and invest in nice carpets and garden stuff – gosh can we afford to come home!!

We listened to David Symonds tonight but trust another Zambia request to get in first.

Went at half four tonight to Brian Behn's farewell drink. He has well recovered but is returning to his family in Bulawayo, where he will do TA (or the equivalent) training once a week, as do all the fit men, compulsorily. We are having trouble with mosquitos and wake four or five times a night, even with spraying the room thoroughly. On Sunday night, Richard went down in the middle of the night for a cool drink, and in his half-asleep state dropped the orange bottle from the fridge and overbalanced and put his bare foot into the broken glass. I heard the crash and a yell and came downstairs to find Richard, and patch up his foot.

Don't get a stamp album. There is one in my bookcase. Anyway, I would like to make a scrapbook on coming home and will put stamps and photos and cuttings into it.

I'm behind with my studies and am finding these later papers tough going, but I might as well press on, it's too late to give up now. Giving up is worse than failing by far, as I would lose my respect for myself, and call myself names like "chicken"!!

I've been thinking so much about banana butties that I toasted some bread and put banana on - the bread is far better toasted – not so doughy – and it was a fair compromise. Oh for a sausage!

Chapter 39   Fraud

Times of Zambia   5th May 1968

*   Southern Rhodesia kicks out 200 rail men with their families. They are now stranded in Livingstone.

*   The Minister for State for Technical Education escaped serious injury when his car hit a group of four lions and veered off into the bush. The injured lion was still alive, so the driver reversed back over it. Five miles further on the car broke down. The Minister was found by some game guards, who tried to go back to the scene of the accident, but immediately met the four lions, which had followed the car for four miles. The one that had been knocked down did not appear any the worse for its experience.

Letter 124   9/5/68

No letter today. I was looking forward to your comments on your birthday call. However we had an irate letter from Mrs L, saying not only have you had letters but a call as well and she hasn't had a letter for 3wks. However she should have had two by now as Richard is coming home at about 6.00 now. On Monday he was in at 8 and as we go to bed at nine there wasn't much evening left. However that was the final late night for a while. He goes back to work at 1.30 and I find the afternoons very long and get restless at 4.30 and usually make a cup of coffee, and start the supper.

On Tuesday, Richard was talking to Ron White about food and Rich said he didn't like mayonnaise, which was unfortunate as I do and also because it limited our recipes. Ron then invites us to supper last night and as he said he makes very good mayonnaise. We went over at seven and had a demonstration and had a crayfish salad followed by raspberry crumble. We came home at ten as they find it tiring having only been here six or so weeks and they usually go to bed at nine.

This started Richard's interest in proper cooking and why he prides himself on his mayonnaise and béarnaise sauces.

I was reading in my geography book that the altitude and heat in places like here and the Kenyan highlands are debilitating and the long-term effects on Europeans are dicey. I'm glad we are coming home. The boat trip will help us acclimatise and the holiday on the boat build up our resistance, I hope, otherwise we will be beset with colds and flu, which we have missed these last few months, after getting over the original upheaval.

We nearly had an invasion of red ants. They were spotted on the lawn by a fellow further along and the caretakers came with a poison to divert them from the houses, as when the red ants move in, you move out. They eat everything edible and move on leaving the house spotless. Apparently it's a good way of cleaning the stove and grime in the kitchen. They can move into a chicken house at night and eat all the chickens. The caretaker warned me to keep Pucci away from the grass, as they are partial to young animals. If they get on a human, the best thing is to jump into a bath. One just makes nasty bites, and you can see how they can eat away animals. Africans have been killed by them, but usually they have been drunk and unable to brush them off. Nasty little creatures.

Richard is very upset as he has a fraud on his hands, which he believes is his cashier. This man was a good clerk and to give him a chance Richard promoted him to cashier about four months ago and he has made good progress, and was one of Richard's examples of how Zambianisation works. However on pay day a pay packet was signed for by someone who turned up next day to claim it and Richard called in the police, and then on Tuesday a voucher for wages was signed by Richard and later amended. This was picked up at a routine wages reconciliation, which the culprit didn't know about. Of course, the sceptics have said to Richard, I told you so. However he has still some good clerks with promise. The one who found the error came to Richard in a dreadful state as he had discovered it and knew that the culprit was his friend.

Richard handed the two possible culprits to the personnel manager who is Zambian, who passed them to the CID, and this Zambian said the CID would know who it was by the morning as they would beat them up until one or the other confessed.

The firm has also had UNIP, the ruling party demanding the dismissal of four staff who are non-UNIP members and who belong to a small minority union UP. Richard reckons that these UP members are amongst the best staff and are an intellectual group who will eventually take over or give up and get out, because they are born leaders, and belong to tribes other than Bemba. There have been big fusses in the press lately about UP members being beaten up and their houses attacked by mobs of over 1,000 people. Such people are very brave being in a minority here, and deserve respect just for that. I, however, don't know the differences in creeds of the two parties.

Brian Behn went back to Bulawayo today. The office bought him a cine projector as his soccer club had bought him a camera. They had beer and champagne from 4 to 5 yesterday. I was invited back but I took time off the day before to go for a drink with the gang and couldn't afford to break into another afternoon. They apparently had a very good time.

It is now 8 o'clock and Richard is still working at the table. He half wrote a letter to his mother over breakfast and I must prod him to finish this. I would have thought she would have telephoned on Richard's birthday. When we gave her our number she was going to ring ever so quickly. Her next call will be her birthday (don't tell her). But two calls to both parents a year cost £12.0.0 which we don't mind, but she is a bit naughty moaning because we rang you and not her as well. She rather spoils the pleasure of us ringing. Probably when Richard rings on her birthday she will spend our 3 minutes moaning at him for not phoning sooner. If she does I'll reverse the charges!! I hope you enjoyed your call, because I did.

Times of Zambia

6th May 1968   UP official's house is stoned for a second time. Twenty windowpanes were smashed.

7th May 1968   UP supporters in Kalulushi have been told to fight back when they are attacked, or their houses are stoned by UNIP followers, so the world can see that UNIP is powerless in Kalulushi.

Letter 125   10.5.68

How do you like this typewriter? It's a micro-type machine and Richard has brought it home to do a bit of work on it. Fancy me writing eight pages in this sort of print. The amount that I've written already would have normally taken a page. Are you squinting yet? I'm not even attempting to read what I've done so far.

14.5.68. Well, still no Thursday letter No 124, but have received No 125 – this is the first letter that has actually gone missing from your end.

I don't know about you passing size 12 to me if you put on weight, I might put on weight too, but I hope you get more size 12s and then put on weight while I remain size 12. I am at present 118lbs. I have varied from 117 to 121 while I've been here and would like to be 115lbs eventually (that's 8st 3lbs). It's surprising how quickly one drops into the 'lbs' only bit. It's because I know my weight in comparison to the other girls and because of deliberately avoiding stones and lbs.

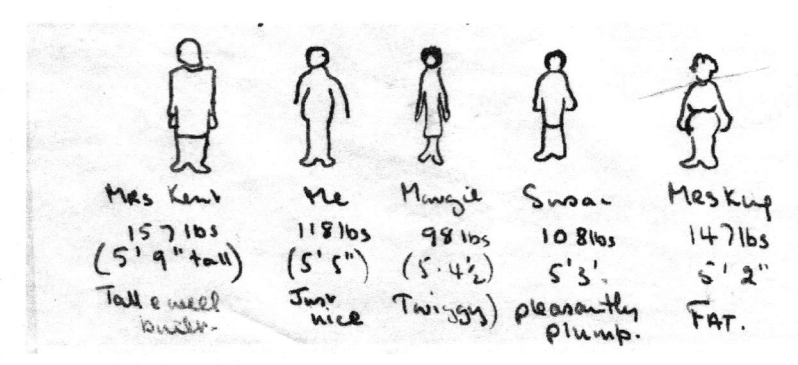

Mrs Kent — 157 lbs (5'9" tall) — Tall e well built.
Me — 118 lbs (5'5") — Just nice
Margie — 98 lbs (5.4½) — Twiggy
Susan — 108 lbs — 5'3' — pleasantly plump.
Mrs King — 147 lbs — 5'2" — FAT.

The graph started as a joke when Mrs King started to slim and is now treated very seriously. We all troop to the stores scale every Wednesday about 8 o'clock. Even the chaps in stores shout "up or down this week?" and offer suitable, although usually rude, advice. Margie is trying to put on weight and eats huge cheese rolls at 10 o'clock. Susan is very good and is the only one who is losing steadily. She is very firm with herself. I just eat normally and stay roughly the same, as does Mrs Kent. But poor Mrs King eats an apple for her lunch and then buys cream buns in the afternoon. She can lose or gain up to 4lbs a week and is like a yo-yo. We had one point when we forbade her to eat between meals and only salads for lunch, but we found her sneaking into the stationery room with bags of chocolates and ham rolls. She's useless. She then swears she is trying hard. I feel sorry for her daughter who is nine and very fat. She is already feeling conscious of it, but she has a craze for baking and eats all she bakes and always has a polythene bag of sweets with her. She is just greedy, because at one of Cookie's tea party everyone commented how she wolfed all the time. She is going to be so miserable in a few years' time.

How about this newspaper cutting.

PROWLER GRABS SLEEPING GIRL

Street chase— in underpants

Staff Reporter

NDOLA resident Calvin Coleman rushed out of his flat in the dead of night, picked up a brick and hurled it at a fleeing man along Kabelenga Avenue, past two streets, and up a hill. He was out of breath and gave up the chase . . .

. . . And it was only when a gust of cold wind hit him that Mr. Coleman, a lithographic foreman, realised he was only in his underpants!

Fortunately, there was no policeman around—otherwise he ran the risk of being booked for indecent exposure!

The chase started after the Colemans were awakened by screams from the bedroom of Mrs. Coleman's cousin, Sharman Meyer, 17.

At about 3.45 a.m. yesterday, a man broke into the flat through a back window and climbed into Miss Meyer's bedroom.

He grabbed Sharman's throat and threatened that if she screamed he would kill her.

"But she started screaming and woke all of us up," said Mr. Coleman.

It was then that he rushed into Sharman's bedroom. He saw a man dart out of the back window and make for the street. Mr. Coleman dashed after him — but in vain.

"I think the brick I threw at him must have landed below his ear," Mr. Coleman said.

Welders were busy at the flat yesterday morning putting up burglar-proof bars.

SHARMAN MEYER

MR. COLEMAN

I have written about Sharmaine haven't I? All Margie can think of is that she may have been on her own with Michelle, as Calvin often works nights. They had no burglar bars and the back window was on the catch. Calvin was going to Kitwe and Sharmaine offered to stay with Margie, but at the last minute he didn't go. Wasn't that a good thing? Sharmaine still has bruises down one side of her neck, and can't sleep at night without waking up scared stiff. Poor Sharmaine, she's only sixteen, or seventeen.

Times of Zambia   17th May 1968

No decision has yet been reached concerning the future of farms belonging to absentee landlords. Some farms whose owners, it is confirmed, will not be returning, have already been put to use by farming co-operative societies.

Letter 126   16/5/68

Sybil Routledge, who used to work in our office is leaving to go to South Africa. She actually left the office last September. Anyway she invited all the 'girls' to a tea party straight from work. I went to the hairdressers for the scond time since arriving here and had 4" trimmed off my hair so it's now about three inches below my shoulders, instead of in the middle of my back. I then called at the office and the whole gang trooped to Sybil's. Margie was the only one who knew the way so everyone followed us. She not only took us to the wrong house, but also got us lost. Anyway we arrived in the end. The house we went to first was Sybil's old house and was the woman surprised when this convoy arrived up her drive!

We had a good laugh and a good gorge. When I arrived home, Richard had put on some roast pork and roasties and cauliflower. And I was full up. However I did apple sauce and stuffing and at least Richard enjoyed it. I enjoyed it too but boy have I got a pot belly now! I'm bloated. When I served the meal I opened the window to let the air out and someone had parked with their headlamps blaring in my window. When I cleared the dishes afterwards the fool still hadn't switched the lights off, so I nipped out quickly and turned them off! Honestly, I only had one teeny, weeny sherry and loads of lemonade!

Oh! I haven't told you my best news! I've been promoted. Mr Pawson asked me to hand over my stock cards to the African who has the other half of the stock cards, and to teach him that bit of my job, which I did, and was happy to do because it was the routine bit of my job. I liked it sometimes when I was busy and needed something straightforward to do, but the bits that have been added to my job have overwhelmed it and made it too time taking. I thought this would relieve the pressure a good deal. However I am just now feeling the weight of mornings only. Last month they made a mistake and paid me my full pay, but said they would adjust it this month, which would leave me with next to nothing. Anyway, I was called into The Office and was asked if I could take on some personnel work including staff salaries, the job Peter Hitchman has been doing. The salaries take three or four days a month to do. It sounded reasonable, so I said I would give it a go, but that I thought it was a crummy swap for my stock cards, and they all laughed and that was that. Anyway, as I went through the door, Hitchman said – and we'll forget about dropping your salary for your mornings only! I nearly dropped. And he shut the door before I could say anything. He knows that I am only here for another 9 months so even if my basic salary isn't increased I have £60 less tax that we had counted on losing. I hope I can cope. In any case for that money I could spend evenings at home on it a couple of nights a month. You can imagine I am very pleased with their confidence in me. Richard uses the same wages system so I can always ask him. Actually he is now doing his own salaries, as his clerk doesn't come back until after payday!

We don't meet many miners here. There are further north in Kitwe, Mufulira and, Chingola . Here are mainly service industries: printing, packing, car assembly (Land Rover) and light engineering. The mines have a better standard of living for Richard's level in housing, pay and leave, but they are exceptional. Richard is getting a cost of living increase based on Derek's report to London. We don't know what percentage yet, but it is to be backdated. It will help us not to run into a big overdraft for our East Africa trip anyway. I'll not say no to extra. In any case Richard loses it on going home! Worse luck.

Times of Zambia   22nd May

UNIP's regional secretary for Ndola has threatened to take other measures if the Minister of Education sacks an Ndola school teacher for being a member of UP.

Letter 127   20/5/68

We had our first cauliflower this weekend. The packet stuff is frozen and insectless and does one or two meals depending on our appetite and is 30n (3/-). The fresh one was from someone in Richard's office for 20n (2/-), but needs a lot of cleaning for the odd bugs out here and needs a soak in potassium sulphate to get rid of bilharzia germs from soil or water that have been on it – so you see frozen is often simpler, and no need to poke around for crawlies.

Richard bought a book on Thursday for 35/- and when he got home he found it was out of date and I took it back and asked for another book. The books I chose were French cooking (very simple – lots of pictures 22/-) and a book called "The Flower Arranger and Her Garden" – just what I wanted – fancy that. It even gives shrubs and flowers to grow for foliage. It was 26/9. This makes 48/9 but I only paid 3/9 extra. Had it been dearer I would have had to wait 'til the end of the month or buy a cheaper cookbook.

The red ants have turned back – no further cause for alarm. The gardener comes around every day so they will catch them if they reappear. I don't think they make anthills. They are different. There are about six various types, some live in hills and some underground. Most are fascinating though. Sally & Stuart spend hours watching them out in Misundu. Sally came out to find a discarded snakeskin hanging on a branch of a tree above their door. Ugh! They also want to come to East Africa with us. However it looks as though they will only stay at the hotel at the same time and will go back after 2 weeks whereas we move on after 10 days.

I'm nowhere near the end of my syllabus and it looks as though I'll just have to take the first few exams. You may say this sounds daft, but the idea of taking them now was a trial for next Jan, not to pass.

It is a long weekend as Monday is Africa Freedom Day or something and the next Monday is Whit. Everyone is off and shops are closed except of course Lever Bros! Richard was making arrangements for golf and both weekends there are tennis tournaments, which we were going to. Isn't that mean. They also haven't put it on the noticeboard and Richard knows lots of people are going away. There'll be absenteeism I'm sure. Trust Levers to do that. Whoever heard of working a Whit Monday! In the next breath they'll scratch their heads and wonder why they are losing staff and why morale is low and someone will come out from London to investigate!

The dog has just stood and put his paws on Richard's legs to be picked up. Normally he has a sniff at his papers and his adding machine and then satisfied he's not missing anything, gets down. However he's put his head on Richard's shoulder and closed his eyes. Richard wants to know what to do, and he's moved to the armchair. I don't think Pucci's sick, but he can get Richard away from work and into an armchair, which is more than I can. There's more to him than fluff!

Yesterday Richard was playing ball with him and hid the ball, Pucci couldn't find it and went to his basket and fetched another. And Richard shouted – cheat, put it back! And Pucci went and dropped it in his basket and came back and found the other one. You may say it's coincidence! But our dog's not soft.

Chapter 40   Budget Books

Times of Zambia   23 May 1968

Police were called to the Matero market yesterday to investigate reports of illegal evictions from stands as UNIP youths intensified the party's card checking campaign.

Times of Zambia

* A hell run driver's house in Matero has had eight windowpanes shattered and his wife and child injured following accusations that he had killed a child by witchcraft recently.

Letter 128   22/5/68

I had some inconvenient news in a letter, which arrived with yours. The kennels in Liverpool have returned my cheque with a "fully-booked" letter. I am so cross with myself as well as Richard. When we received the letter we didn't have the £10 deposit and for the past month, when asked he said he would do it when he had a minute. In the end I wrote the cheque and just got his signature. My next task is to write to other kennels. The next nearest is Birmingham and the only others that are relatively accessible are Middlesex and Surrey. There is only one in Yorkshire. I just hope we can get in. I hate the thought of leaving Pucci in kennels here, which with his six months quarantine is far too long.

The cashier at Richard's place has been jailed after a police investigation. The other fellow, who owned up too, was put up to it. However all the wages staff are involved in that they knew about it, but didn't say anything, so Richard is working out a new wages system for an accounting machine which he is purchasing and which will save up to 5 clerks. He can then disperse these clerks elsewhere, but they would be wiser to leave, as their promotion chances will have been greatly reduced! As Richard can only put them into vacancies, the eventual saving of wages will be more than the machine rental. These fellows, who are corrupt, are earning the same wage as a European doing an equivalent job and have a lower standard of living, so there shouldn't be money difficulties but they are suckers for H.P. Even Mrs Mhizha in our office is paying £50 a month for a clapped out Rover of about 1960 or earlier and they have to pay £500 + interest. This month there was a mistake in her new tax code, which reduced her wage by half and she was frantic. But even so, she spent £10 on a carpet about 4ft by 6ft, which was the thickness of two winceyette sheets and had a foam back – not rubber backed but foam like on an ironing board or a bath sponge. I could screw it in my hand like a piece of cloth. I would have paid £3 and no more and even so would have used it in a spare room. It will neither wash nor clean and I give it a life of six months. However the pattern was right and would have been fine in a proper carpet.

The way Richard and I work to a budget! We have a book for groceries, which we have used for the past two months and have it set out as follows. (I am also keeping a record of price changes to check on the rise in cost of living since we arrived and in comparison with UK prices)

	Jan			Feb		
Item price	1	2	3	1	2	3
Vim 34	1	2	2	–	3	3
Surf 27	4	2	2	–	6	6

Valerie Lapthorne

Brillo 38   -   2   2   1   1   1

Item price is a list of all possible goods. Column one for each month is the stock held. Column two for each month is the amount required. Column Three for each month is the amount purchased.

Therefore as you see with Surf, at the beginning of Jan we had 4 Surf and required 2 more and bought 2 more (the reason for having columns 2 + 3 and not just one column is that sometimes goods are out of stock and cannot be purchased). At the beginning of Feb therefore we had nil Surf and from the previous months figures the monthly usage had been 6 so 6 more were required (col 2) and 6 were purchased (col 3). At the end of the month the cupboards are almost bare except for stock items, but we only buy what we use in a month. We try to limit the monthly order to £20. This month our estimate was K58 - £29.8.0 so we pruned back and our bill was £20.8.0. We therefore kept to our budget and we don't run out of things unexpectedly and keep a supply of food for visitors and emergency foods like tinned steak and kidney, for when the meat doesn't come. It takes 15 minutes to check stock once a month and about ¾ hr to belt round the supermarket, with one pushing and shouting from the book, and the other diving at the shelves. At home it would be more difficult as there is such changing stock, but here it is always the same and, either in stock or out of stock. We allow 30/- for biscuits and 10/- for cereals depending on what is in. However we deposit a full truck with the cashier and she adds up while we do the second. She then greets us with "Your first trolley is more this month" etc. She says she has never seen anything like it and says "my, but you're organised". She said today how much she enjoyed us coming in. Richard also adds up in his head as we go along and gives her the total, and she shrieks with laughter when he is wrong (he is always within 5/- of the machine total). Then we troop out with three or four boys carrying boxes. This is of course the problem at home. I would have to make about 10 journeys to the shop to load up the car. Here, these chaps troop along the road to where the car is parked and queue up for tips. What a pantomime. I wish you could see us, and the commotion!! Well I seem to have gone on for ages about groceries – P.S. we bought 10 bottles of orange and 10 cokes (family size). Our budget was 14 orange and 12 cokes but was pruned, as the orange is 3/10 a bottle.

P.P.S. And positively the final word – the book list is in the same order as the supermarket shelves, therefore we are not turning pages and not missing items.

In the office we were talking about prices of things and everyone was surprised that Richard only gives me £5 a month for myself, but I think they are selfish, not Richard. For example, Calvin gave Margie £10 this week and she spent the lot on makeup – lovely things admittedly, but extravagant. Everyone said how generous he was. I reckon I must just envious. But she is always immaculately turned out and looks great. But I suppose they earn a lot more than us. This month I have bought a wastepaper basket from a pedlar for 5/6, 10 bob's worth of postcards and greetings cards and will buy Sally Rubner a birthday present for £2 and still have £2.10.0ish over which I will bank for clothes for my holidays. I will get more fun saving for a few months and then buying something than asking Richard for the money, which I'm sure he'll give me. He offered to give me a further £5 a month, with this rise on the way (cost of living) but it might just as well go into our money for our holidays – could you spend £10 on makeup and not feel guilty? Daddy, this is not an excuse for you to reduce mummy's money!! Reading through this it sounds very self-righteous, and I wouldn't say no to a big spend – providing I'd saved it myself, but you do see what I mean don't you? (P.S. Richard buys all my stamps and petrol – 1 gal. a week).

Your Charleston dress sounds a wow. I hope everything goes (went, by now) off OK. Are you glad I'm not around to say disapprovingly, "Oh Mummy" – I think I'd probably join in with you now. Perhaps being out here in the jungle has made me as mad as you!. I don't mind who has my wedding veil. I'm glad it's of use – it's not as though I'll be using it again

Times of Zambia   25th May

Zambia Railways blamed as tin firm closes factory and sacks thirty. Two trucks each containing 40 tons of tinplate have been "mislaid". The railway spokesman declined to comment

on reports that 100 trucks were "lost".

Letter 129   27/5/68

Well it's a Bank Holiday and what a funny Bank Holiday. Richard is the only one in the Court to go to work – everyone else's cars are still here. Andre has the day off, so I'm on my own and it's 9.30. I got up with Richard and he left just after 7.30. After tidying up, I tidied out my dressing table and cupboards and I have just had a bowl of soup. It is too cold to sit out as there is a strong breeze – come to think of it, at home you would have had the windscreen up and the sun oil out. But you know how I sunbathe – in blankets.

On Friday we hired a projector for the weekend, which he let us have for 12/6 even though it was a long weekend, and we have played the films through every night until we are sick of them

On Saturday morning I made up the material I brought with me. I couldn't get the pattern I wanted and settled for one with a centre pleat. It is very effective and although it is tenty, the centre pleat hangs closed and it doesn't look huge like most tent dresses. I really wanted side pleats.

Last night Ron and Elizabeth White came over to see the films at their own request and invited us over to supper as Ron had just been experimenting with Bearnaise sauce and it was good. We had it with steak. On Saturday night we went to the cinema but the film was a Western and not so good.

Pucci is dozing at my feet and his tail has just started to wag. I wonder what he is thinking about. There were tennis tournaments at the club all weekend, but as Richard couldn't play today, he couldn't enter and he was mad at losing the afternoon's tennis on Saturday. We could only have gone to watch. Isn't that maddening. I bet you that Mackie plays golf today. The golf club car park has been packed since 8 o'clock.

I spent today doing the tail end of the salaries, and came in for a lot of ribbing e.g. what would I want to add an O on to a cheque? I said I wanted to have my tea poured every day and the paper for starters, and I would think of something if they behaved themselves.

The David Symonds show is just starting- are you listening? It's very clear tonight – not as though it's being played in a tin bath. I sent a request about two weeks ago, a postcard with a lovely picture of a lion on. It's funny to think that we are all listening at the same time.

Well – well – well ! Fancy that, and there it was, and well, the message was long and the record short, but wasn't that marvellous! I never really expected it to be on, did you!! Wasn't that smashing? I can't wait to tell everyone at work. I wonder who else heard it. Did you tape it? I can't get over it. Yippee!! All that way – it was as good as a phone call, and he put in a message of his own too.

Well that's put anything else out of my mind !

Letter 130   29/5/68

I'm writing this letter a day early to let you know our super news. We arrive home at 8am on April 7th that is, Easter Monday.

I don't know where to start to tell you! We have permission to leave at the end of January instead of February and therefore our stay here is cut by a month. We lose a little money in leave pay and a month's salary but so what. This is just a super dream come true! We also have a far, far better cabin than we expected. It is on the top deck with about 20 odd of the best cabins. It is on the sun deck and has two bunks and private lav. and shower, which we didn't expect. Try and get hold of the accommodation plan of the Northern Star from Shaw Saville agents. Our room is S10. On our deck is the sunbathing area and swimming pool. Above us is the sports deck only.

The agent in Unilever said that below are the lounges, and the cinema and ballroom are well back and we are away from noise. It's like a holiday camp in that it is so self-contained. I won't tell you the price, but we can afford it when our airfare and leave pay are taken into account. We will arrive home as we went – broke, but not in any debt.

There is even a launderette and next door to our room is a bathroom and ironing room, which should be not much used, as there are so few cabins to them. Do try and get a plan. This was obtained without any booking, so I'm sure they issue them as a general leaflet.

Our itinerary is as follows:

Leave Cape Town	noon	Feb 8th
Arrive Durban	8am Feb 10th	
Leave Durban	6am Feb 11th	
Arrive Freemantle	8am Feb 20th	
Leave Freemantle	5pm	Feb 20th
Arrive Melbourne	10am	Feb 24th
Leave Melbourne	6pm Feb 25th	
Arrive Sydney	8am Feb 27th	
Leave Sydney	11am Mar 1st	
Arrive Wellington	9am Mar 4th	
Leave Wellington	7pm Mar 6th	
Arrive Tahiti	7am Mar 11th	
Leave Tahiti	6am Mar 12th	
Arrive Acapulco	7am Mar 20th	
Leave Acapulco	6am Mar 21st	
Arrive Panama (Bilbao)	10am Mar 24th	
Leave Panama	6am Mar 25th	
Arrive Curacao	5am Mar 27th	

Leave Curacao	11am Mar 27th
Arrive Trinidad	1pm Mar 28th
Leave Trinidad	6a Mar 29th
Arrive Southampton	8am Apr 7th

You had better arrange some leave for Easter week. Yippee! Only eight months to go instead of nine!

My African violet is in full bloom and I am going to take some cuttings and start a family of them. Mrs White over the way, looked after my plant at Easter and kept it for about a fortnight and now has about ten rooted cuttings from it. She didn't even give me one – my own offspring.

I'd love a mini-dress or anything for my cruise, like that. Margie is lending me a pattern for a cut away trouser suit – very cruisey!

Richard isn't fatter in the face – I don't think. I think it was just the picture. He's just fatter round the middle. He would also like another shirt. He doesn't like my orange one as he always gets lousy golf rounds and prefers your dark brown one as every time he has worn it, he breaks a hundred. So he is wearing it for the Levers match next Friday, as it's important.

Times of Zambia   June 1968

3rd June   Teachers are urged –resign to frustrate the Government. ANC Chairman made the call

when launching the party's election campaign.

4th June   **Leicester City will never again venture into Zambia, so shocked were they by the barrage of stones and bottles with which the Lusaka crowd greeted their third victory over the Zambian national side.**

While the stubborn stayaways go off to rural taverns, strike is costing Kabwe mine K60,000 a day.

Letter 130a   4/6/68

Well we are well into June, and I am on my holidays- some holiday. I did start looking over my Shakespeare. If I could think of a way to get out of these exams, I would, because I will write all I know in the first half hour of the first paper, and then I could spend my holiday time on sewing and catching up on my correspondence.

Pucci is standing with his nose on the edge of my writing pad with his rubber mouse in his mouth- good he's given up and has gone to sulk under the chair.

I have had six replies to my letters about quarantine. The only one who has not replied is the RSPCA in Birmingham. The one in Halewood is RSPCA and on the whole they seem very lax. The others are all private or Ltd companies. One, the biggest, is run by Spillers and has 178 kennels and forty kennel maids and is £3.00 a week. The others vary from £2.5.0d and £3.5.0d. The one we have decided upon is in Staines in Middlesex, at the back of the airport. It is also a carrying agent. It is in the northwest on the M1 so we won't have to go into London. The one we preferred is in Surrey, run by a vet who said he would drive in and fetch the dog himself. All the letters were very nice and I feel really mean having to choose. I will write and confirm the booking and when they reply, I will write to all the others. The Spillers place sent a hotel like brochure-own heated rooms, comfortable beds changed daily, good diet, and pleasant gardens. I will ask the Middlesex one to confirm that their kennels are heated, as this is my one worry. I hate the thought of him shivering in a kennel in an English January. I must knit him a pullover.

It's mid-winter here and I'm finding it very cold and am wearing my pink woolly jumper over my dress. I've just thought on - I have a white V-necked jersey and a red mohair one; these are still wearable aren't they. You haven't given them to the jumble yet, have you?

On Friday, it was so cold, you could see your breath in the morning, and we had a Tilley lamp on in the office until about 10 o'clock, when the fumes became worse than the cold. I abandoned my office uniform and wore my wool shirt waister, but was roasted at lunchtime as the temperature was 78 -80 by two o'clock. Our house is cold in the lounge as the sun never reaches it at all and it never warms up. At the weekend, Richard and I put the bedroom armchairs in the spare bedroom and we sat in there, as it is beautifully sunny, as is the kitchen below. The blow heater isn't a success as it draws the cold air through the grills along the top of the windows and makes the curtains stand out. We huddle round the heater and get burnt legs and headaches. Tonight is OK and we haven't needed it. We were wondering if our blood was getting thin, as we were moaning about the cold and yet the butter I took out at four o'clock was oil at six o'clock. However, I had a bowl of chicken soup and pretended it was pea whack. *(Liverpudlian ham and pea soup made from ham knucklebones and dried lentils so thick you could stand your spoon in it).*

Chapter 41   Travel Plans

Times of Zambia

27th May   Two men have died in an inter-party riot in Kitwe's Chunwenwe townships. Several others were taken to hospital. Police used tear gas to end the riot.

Assistant minister for State Mr Ntambo has instructed UNIP youth to "check young girls" who roam Lusaka Streets at night but not to "beat the girls, when they find them, but to "chase them away to their homes". He also announced that UNIP was "going to be more strict with pregnant women who go into taverns and bars " There have been shameful instances of women giving birth in such public places and we don't want to see this happen".

* Work has started on a new security road along the banks of the Zambezi on the Zambia/Rhodesia border.

30th May 1968 KK has given the go ahead for youths in Zambia Youth Camps to be schooled in the operation of minor military weapons.

6th June 1968

Mystery hospital raiders executed. The mystery of missing parts on dead bodies in a Lusaka central hospital mortuary was solved this week when hospital authorities trapped three mice. The discovery of missing parts from several dead bodies has baffled city residents for some time. It has aroused superstitious beliefs among many residents. The family whose dead relation was found with missing parts from his body protested and refused to bury him.

7th June Vice-president Simon Kapepwe has told a meeting at Minda that tribalism does not exist in Zambia, only individualism.

Letter 131

Marlene and Peter arrived in Beira on Monday and were expected in Ndola last night, so yesterday morning we went along and examined their larder, and then went out and bought enough to see them over supper and breakfast. I wanted flowers but the florist had sold out! And the garden shop had only a sick looking cactus. The borders in town are full of flowers. We should have pinched a few! Actually, there is never any vandalism of flowers-these people are more interested in food and saleable items, I suppose. Even on the roads by the township the roundabouts and islands are full of shrubs and flowers. The only casualties were rose bushes in Park Avenue, which were dug up after planting, probably by Europeans. How mean. The flowers are such a good display and I am pleased to say that where they have removed the lovely trees which were down the centre of the main shopping road, they have planted shrubs and flowers as promised. However there are too few crossing points and therefore pathways are made through the flowers. When grass and stuff is laid I feel that no paths should be laid until footpaths are worn through the grass and then these should be paved.

Marlene and Peter arrived at twelve, and Richard went round to introduce David (from Port Sunlight) who has been living in their house waiting for them to arrive before moving out. The house was beautifully clean and the garden well kept as David has been chivvying the servants for the last few days and Marlene was very pleased. She asked me to call round, and as I doubted this, thinking Richard had said I would go round as I was on holiday, I rang and, fair enough, the first thing she did was invite me around, so I went about three and sat in the bedroom while she unpacked. I therefore saw all her new dresses and Sally's new mod clothes. However, Marlene says that prices have all very much increased, particularly for children's things, except for Mark's and Spark's stuff. She bought me six pairs of pants, which you wear and throw away- I think they can stand one wash- I don't know as I forgot to bring the packet home with me. I'll have them for my hols; they will be just the job then, won't they. Are they catching on, or are they still a novelty? Marlene bought them as a novelty.

They had a wonderful time aboard ship, and said the ports were a nuisance, as they disturbed their ship routine. The meals were marvellous, (I have seen the menus). However they travelled First Class and probably received special attention. They attended Captain's cocktail parties and a Spanish evening, when they made their own Spanish outfits out of crepe paper and had the use of greasepaint. And lots of themed dances. They never went to bed until the early hours and slept in the cabin or their deckchairs in the afternoon. Sally was deposited in the nursery and screamed when she was dragged away to meals. Marlene said that the waiters used to coax her to eat and she is now eating very well. She was a slow bitty eater, but has put on weight and grown. Richard says that she seemed just the same! I went to collect Richard as Peter was borrowing our car for the evening as theirs were out on loan and due back tomorrow. Peter is looking very tanned and well. Listening to Marlene about the trip, I am certainly looking forward to ours.

What news about Anne! Anyway, they must be both willing and able to have a fourth, as there is no excuse for accidents these days. I don't know that I could cope with seven continuous years of nappies without a break. I think with three that she should have domestic help until the fourth arrives. Boy, I don't envy her one bit. If she is having trouble with varicose veins, she is not in peak condition, is she? Perhaps Jimmy is the domestic help. Out here having a baby is pure pleasure.. One just has to entertain them and cook. If that. *(And then I go on to have four at similar intervals. Serves me right for being prissy.)*

We have had permission from London to leave early. Buchanan has told Richard that Audit would be glad to have him back in no less a capacity than when he left! Richard was that mad. However I said that he could easily find another position with another firm. Anything rather than back in Audit. However, Peter when told of this said it was rubbish, as other people had already started asking for him, particularly financial group. This group is an elite and it would be a plum position, so Richard is up in the air again! Remember Hans Oei, who came here last year from Financial Group? He has just been made the commercial director of Brazil and is only in his early thirties. Don't worry though. We shan't be dashing off again very soon. Not if we can help it!

Richard says he fancies Sweden, Holland or Ireland for overseas postings, as it is as easy to reach home as from Cornwall or Devon. However we both want somewhere where we can garden and potter and make a home. It's just not the same with someone else's furniture in a rented house.

Richard is playing in the Unilever Dash Cup tomorrow. He has a half-day today on an official practice. He is looking forward to it. There is also lunch at the golf club and we are out to dinner tomorrow entertaining a company visitor. Singing for our supper.

Also hoping to go to golf club this evening for steak and chips for fifteen shillings. It will be worth it not to cook and have a few hours out.

Times of Zambia

8th June 1968 The Ministry of Works is to investigate the existence of a number of government caravans in Lusaka's high-density areas. Several of the caravans parked in the yards of some civil servants' homes, have curtains and seem to be used as homes.

10th June Mystery saboteurs blew up the road bridge over the Luangwa River yesterday after murdering the night watchman. , The destroyed bridge spanning about 500 yards is only a few miles from the border with Mozambique. Although only a one-way span, the bridge is a vital link in the fuel route from Beira via Malawi, which brings in most of Zambia's diesel fuel.

Letter 132

Richard was feeling pleased as he came second in the golf tournament with his handicap taken into account. He did a lot better than last year. Afterwards there was lunch in the clubhouse and I was able to linger this year rather than dash back to work. There was a choice of cold meat and salads and curry. It was a nice change.

Richard announced to the assembled golfers that I was late as I was probably throwing up, and I am told he was so excited to be announcing this, that there was no doubt that it wasn't a bug. When I arrived, up went a cheer. Of course every one knew that I had had the miscarriage earlier so everyone was pleased. On coming back from the doctors that morning, I had given him the thumbs up from the terrace and he had bounded back to his tee, waving his club. Of course it was too early to tell parents.

On Friday evening we went to the Savoy with Millers and Dunsmuirs to entertain a marketing visitor. Surprisingly, considering the uninspiring company, we had a jolly good night, and with it being Friday there was a band and we had a bit of a jig. Only the second time since we have been married. Richard says he rather fancies dancing with a married woman.

On Saturday evening, we went to the Copper's Arms to treat Marlene and Peter and we thoroughly enjoyed it. I went in my woolly dress and linen coat as the bar is outside, but each table had a charcoal fire in a saucepan-sized brazier. It was a lovely sight. We were taken into a frequently used bar adjacent to the dining room, which was indoors and there were bar stools and tables around a fireplace which contained about six of these fires. It was very cosy. Instead of my usual stroganoff, I had grilled chicken Yum. We also had crepes Suzettes, which are their speciality. After dinner we went and sat outside and talked and talked and eventually had to go as they switched out all the lights and just left us with the one brazier. We went back to Marlene's for more coffee and started all over again, as David was there babysitting. It was a jolly nice evening, but we always have a good time with Marlene and Peter and we're glad they are back.

They too, funnily enough, are glad to be back. Their stay in England wasn't too good as they were only guests of their friends and parents, which got on Peter's nerves a bit. Marlene says her father is looking old (he is seventy) as he has had two bouts of bronchitis this winter and is very thin. Peter's father, who is seventy-three, has just been retired and is very miserable as he is going to live with his sister, who is a chatterbox. He is also trying to find another job! I suppose, at that age, in two years they will have aged quickly. Both sides of the family gave them the impression that they thought Marlene and Peter should stay at home, now that their parents are getting on. However Marlene's mum is a lot younger than her father and they are exceptional in having such old parents, aren't they, as Peter is thirty and Marlene twenty-eight or nine.

Marlene says that her house here is so nice (which it is) and its nice to sit in the sun, which they also missed. I felt like saying that they are different from us in that they have something worth coming back to.

Richard was informed by Buchanan, that they were having trouble getting a replacement for Richard (they are getting two accountants to do his job when he has gone!) and that they were applying to renew Richard's work permit. Richard politely told him he could stuff his work permit. Isn't that a bit much? If they wanted to keep him on for an extra three or six months, we wouldn't get on a ship, and we would lose our deposits and have trouble re –letting our house at home. Richard said if they had treated us equally with other managers, instead as a young couple, who wouldn't have much anyway at the start of married life, then maybe we would feel we owed them something, but brother we don't, so we are off in February, even if it means Richard falling out with Unilever, which he doubts very much.

Sunday, we breakfasted in bed at nine and read there until twelve. We dozed and lazed until four and then took the dog a walk in Kent Park, a wild area in the middle of town behind the council offices, which we never knew was there. They are gradually creeping in on it with buildings however.

Monday morning, I swotted and in the afternoon, with knocking knees, went to my English Lit. exam. However, I managed it and wrote solidly for three hours and swigged lemonade and sucked sweets. (*I was fighting down morning sickness with these, and the discomfort was distracting. Too soon to reveal this*). The questions were lovely and had I been taking them next January as planned, it would have been a walkover, but I was unable to provide any memorised quotations, which are essential. I am not taking paper two as I haven't covered the work sufficiently, but I will take the third, as this is comprehension and appreciation, Sounds daft to bother without the second paper as I can't help failing however good my other two. But its all practice and I'm curious about the papers. Geography got left behind way back! As you can see from the above, I am not resitting in January as they are in the week of our departure and with packing and clearing up; it's just not sensible.

Richard said before the exam, when it became clear that I hadn't covered all the work, that maybe it would teach me a lesson to try to do two years work in six months, but when I came home delighted by what I was able to answer on the paper, and was determined to have a bash, maybe next year, he started banging his head on the wall. However when I get home I must get down to my piano, as I've two years to catch up on! - more groans from Richard. (*I eventually did redo the English Lit A level exam and got an A. No A*available at this point.*)

Peter says that English TV is now rubbish, and that even supposedly topical programmes like Whicker's World, have been shown before he came out here and that there is very little in the way of new stuff-is that right?

Chapter 42   Exam

Times of Zambia

12th June   Kabwe couple win contest. Miss Veronica Kapapwepwe 20 and Mr. Elias Musanda were chosen as Miss and Mr. Zambia Railways at a beauty and dressing competition held at the weekend.

14th June   Drunkenness, indiscipline, absenteeism and slackness had become "part and parcel" of the civil service these days, the Minister of State for Public Services said yesterday.

Letter 133   14/6/68

Today was my comprehension exam, which I decided not to take out of cowardice. (*Actually morning sickness, which lasted all day, was really debilitating, but couldn't say that!*) I took the dog to the girl for clipping at eight o'clock. My exam would have been at 8.30. and at 8.20, Mrs White came across to wish me luck, and I felt so cowardly saying I wasn't going, that I said, "I'm just off", and I ran upstairs and grabbed some shoes and a pen and some ink and my forms and dashed off. I arrived at 8.29 on their clock, but no one was around. At 8.35, I went into the adjacent office where I was informed that it was probably starting at 9.00a.m, so rather than go home, I sat on the wall outside. At 9.10, this fellow arrives and says he usually started the exams at 9.30, but I could start then, which I did. It was difficult, but I wrote for the two hours. The hall only held me, and it was freezing cold. At one stage I had to rub my hand, as it was so numb. The hall had no windows, only high up on one side to keep it cool in the heat, but with it being winter, the sun couldn't penetrate and it was like sitting in a church. Fortunately my car was like an oven and was lovely, but I couldn't stop my teeth chattering and shivering. I was OK after a while, but now at suppertime my eyes are watering and nose running, so I'm off to bed with some lemon and a hot water bottle. We are going to Tony's wedding tomorrow and I want to be fit enough to enjoy it and eat loads.

Pucci is baldy again and was very nervous and frightened when I picked him up and he howled all the way home in the car. However, he's had a sleep and has forgotten about it, but instead of dozing on the tiles, he does the forbidden thing of curling up in the corner of the settee. He looks like a white velvet scatter cushion with his nose as a black button in the middle. So I've made him a bouncy cushion stuffed with stockings and a tennis ball, and he has cheered up no end, flinging this around and stalking it, and killing it.

Yesterday, I went shopping with almost K4. I bought a block of ice cream and went for some stockings, but they had no 4/11 ones only 8/11 ones, so I bought some 17/6 tights. Richard says he doesn't see the logic of this, but they were the first tights I've seen in Browns, so I lashed out, as the stockings are ridiculously short and with short dresses, its tights or no stockings. I also wanted a bottle of nail varnish, as the bottle I bought for my wedding has dried up. I took the empty bottle, a 3/6 Gala Gem, to match. I had to settle for a size larger and a different colour for 9/6. I also bought a dozen eggs and had about 6ngwe left. I wanted some brown ribbon for a big bow in lieu of a hat for the wedding. They didn't have any brown ribbon, anyway, only blue and pink. How I hate shopping here.

Pucci is flying home and will be in kennels outside London Airport. They seem very nice and assure me the kennels are heated, and they have a special unit for smaller dogs, which have smaller exercise pens, but have more human contact. They have three Maltese terriers in now and they are all settled and happy. He has no changing planes and the kennels will pick him up upon arrival.

David Crawford came for supper last night and we had a good laugh. He is a pleasant enough bloke and is a manager here under Alan Phillips. He is a mechanical engineer and is to train Africans for six to nine months. His Dad is a fireman at Port Sunlight.

Times of Zambia

15th June 1968   **Mr Muzanda said he had killed his uncle because he was a witchdoctor, who had killed three relatives by witchcraft.**

17th June   **Snow has fallen in North West Province. Crops worth hundreds of kwacha have been destroyed by frost in the Luanshya rural areas .**

                          K750,000 earmarked to transform notorious "Valley of the Blind". Bold new plan to fight Luapula sickness. One in very 200 people is affected. Other surveys show that nine out of ten who go blind do so before the age of ten

Letter 134   18/6/68

I have sent all Pucci's documents off for his licenses and all there is to do now is to fix up his flight, which I shall do when we get back from our holiday.

I went back to work yesterday, and back to full time, which I don't mind, although my work has piled up in the two weeks. I am also having a lovely time reading. I got eight books out on Saturday, and I am on my fourth, so I'll have to go back again this Saturday.

It is very cold here at night, and the mornings have been frosty and we have had gas heaters in the office. I nearly put my coat on this morning. As soon as Richard finishes the work he brings home to do in the evening, we are off to bed with our books and a thermos of coffee and it's lovely and warm. I really enjoy being cosy in bed. It's a nice change from sweating under a sheet, but I'm glad this chilly weather only lasts a short time, as in the same way that Britain thinks it never gets cold and snowy and never provides the facilities for living normally in the cold, as they do on the continent, here too, houses are only geared to the heat of summer. Everyone in the office is complaining of draughts at home through the ventilators and grills designed to keep the houses cool in summer. Snow was reported in Choma at the weekend, but I think it must have been the frost and a vivid imagination.

We have just had some tasty lamb chops and I opened a tin of button mushrooms. It was 30ng for the tin and therefore, as there were ten, 3ng each. That's 3 1/2. I had to roll them round in my mouth, savouring each morsel. I could get a 1/3d bag in Marks and Spenser and they lasted nearly all week for breakfasts and grills.

On Sunday night, the odd couple we met at White's invited us for drinks, as Richard gave her one of those cookery books with local cooking in, that he got free, and which she and Mrs White wanted: (He got one for her too).

Pucci won't sleep in his little house. He will go in and out of it and will sniff around it, and lie down in it if we are at the door, but if we move away, he follows us. I think he doesn't like to miss anything. He sleeps now on his blanket, half under the bottom of the bed, and we once sneaked it towards the box. If we put it in the box, he drags it out and under the bed and curls up on it. However at least he will be familiar with his box and his blanket.

Richard has now finished his work and we are going to bed. It is exactly seven o'clock. Rather than go to bed, I would like a glass of fresh milk, a box of chocolates, a bar of M&S chocolate, a big fire and a telly. Just think, what is a pleasant ordinary evening for you, we dream of as a big treat and something to look forward to.

Times of Zambia   18th June 1968

ANC tells members to buy UNIP cards and live safely to keep UNIP youths from their houses.

Letter 135   20/06/1968

I am writing this, whilst sitting at the switchboard at the office doing my stint, as the regular girl is on leave. We received your tape, and we had a good giggle listening to it. I know Hilda was only joking when she said she would come to Southampton to meet us, but as she is staying with you for Easter anyway, she will be on hand. She will also be someone extra to stand up to Mrs L, if she starts bossing you around. Mrs L. won't eat anywhere that doesn't look expensive from the outside or is listed in the Good Food Guide, with the result that you reach your destination, having walked in and out of numerous places at which she has turned up her nose and without having a meal. Hilda wouldn't stand for too much of that, whereas you would go hungry.

You can tell by the disjointed sentences that I am being interrupted. Our stores phones have gone off and upon making enquiries, I find that a forklift truck has ripped down the overhead wires. Makes life interesting. Thank goodness it's nearly lunchtime

I don't think Pucci likes me working full-time again. He makes such a fuss when I come home. We are going to Sally and Stuart's in Misundu tonight. I hope they have some form of heating. I shall put on an extra jersey just in case.

The men didn't come to mend the wires. They were still down when I left. I have just had two syrupy pieces of toast and Pucci has had a crust. I don't know what Sally and Stuart are intending to eat and when, so I am filling in a gap until then. They have got a cooker, which is powered by Calor gas. The cookers though are a terrible price, up to three times the UK price, so I doubt it will be a big one. However they are saving on rent as they get a rent allowance, which, they no longer have to put towards any rent. They only have a few bits of second hand furniture but the floor is carpeted and that will make it cosy anyway. It's still not my idea of fun. I like everything to run smoothly with minimal discomfort.

Do you know, I never walked in the garden at our house in Chester. It was always too muddy, and I was always scrubbing floors. That's the main thing I remember. Scrubbing the floor with Brillo and polishing and having it look no better afterwards. If we stay there, I shall get a polisher. I'll never get the knack like Andres and skate around on a brush and a duster. My floors are Marley here too, but the difference! Admittedly, there is probably a two-inch layer of polish over muck, but so what-it looks clean.

Surprisingly, I shall still be sad to leave, as it has been so different, yet now we are well settled in, it seems so normal. Anyway, things aren't staying the same. All the nicest people are thinking of moving. Cookie has already gone to Lusaka, Susan is getting married in December and contemplating going south. Margie leaves again for Canada next June, Mrs Giles and Mrs Kent are moving to their son and daughters in SA and Rhodesia. Tony has gone. Bob Dunckerley and Naomi move in December and so on. People don't want, or can't, renew their contracts or work permits. So in that respect, I'm not sorry. Ever since we have been here, there has been a downward slide in service and efficiency, although this must improve as the years pass. For example, the man from whom we order our tea and sugar and toilet rolls for the office, has left. For a month or so, we had orders duplicated and messed up generally and then deliveries were stopped completely and we have to collect ourselves, which is a nuisance.

The Airways, too, have changed hands and planes and pilots never seem to come to any set timetable.

Times of Zambia

26ᵗʰ June   ANC men in Mufuilra market melee. UNIP youths stoned in card clash.

Letter 136   24/06/68

On Thursday we went to Sally and Stuart's. The house is fine. The plan is like this

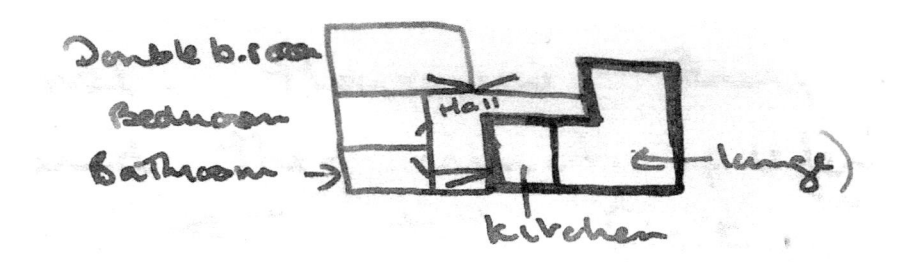

[Floor plan sketch: Double b.room, Bedroom, Bathroom, Hall, kitchen, lounge]

The thick line is the original house and the thin line is the breeze block extension. All the walls are plastered and painted and the floors painted to take polish. They have rugs and some old rocking chairs and a huge fireplace, which is large enough to take the fattest Father Christmas, in which they had a big, log fire. They have no windows, but log shutters, which, in the current weather are very draughty, but we were cosy enough around the fire. Their electricity generator is very powerful and allows fluorescent lighting and lamp sockets. Their stove is gas from a bottle and the fridge is oil. Their water is only cold as yet, but the pump is working and the lav. and taps work and the water is clear and unchlorinated and like stream water. I was most impressed with the plumbing and electricity. The interior is still a little rough, but it all adds to the charm and rusticity. My verdict is that it's fine for a weekend holiday cottage, but a little isolated for permanent use. However they have done marvels, and they much prefer the peace and quiet, as their tiny flat was on the main road above a bus stop, where Africans part-camped, waiting for buses.

On Saturday morning, Pucci only opened one eye on waking up. His other was swollen. He had been whingeing in the night and we had shouted at him. All repentant, I took him to the vet, who said it was a cold infection and gave me some ointment, which cleared it up. He was very miserable and we had a battle to get the ointment in, but today he is fine, and only his ears are sore where he has scratched them. He probably had earache too. I think it's the blow heater, as he has been hogging it, so now the heater is kept on a stool so he is out of the draught.

On Saturday, Marlene invited me round in the afternoon and we sat in the garden eating cake and supping tea. We went back at night for supper and stayed 'til midnight looking at their holiday slides and nattering.

On Sunday, we stayed in bed with our breakfast, a pot of coffee and our library books. We still only got up at ten, but as we had breakfast at seven, it was a long laze. Richard worked at home and I sewed and pottered-very pleasant. I made small plastic bags with plastic and a stapler and Sellotape and put the remaining bits of my clothes into bags. Each jersey and shorts and things has its own bag. My underclothes are kept loose, but the red dust is getting everywhere, even into the cupboards and its best to cover all the items that I am not wearing at least once a week. My shelves in the cupboards are super for this as nothing is more than two or three deep. I much prefer shelves to drawers, as they are easier to keep tidy. One shelf I use as a linen basket- I'm trying to get a cheap basket that the locals make from reeds. My linen and towels are in a big cupboard in the bathroom. I shall miss all this cupboard space when I get home. The spare room has a double floor to ceiling wardrobe and cupboards too.

Yes, women do play golf here, but if you are thinking of me, the entrance fee of £30 odd, plus a set of clubs makes it prohibitive. Richard is certainly getting his money's worth and he really enjoys it, and as he is out from 7 and back at 10.30ish, it doesn't bother me. I can sew in peace. It gives him a good tan too.

Yes, I'm working full time again, but it's OK, as I am up to date and not slogging as I was when doing mornings, and my afternoons weren't all that jolly, studying. It's an easier afternoon at work with company and a cuppa thrown in. I have decided that, having had my week's holiday, that I'd rather work than stay at home. Even with sewing to do and pottering around, there's no radio to listen to, and what's the point of making 11ses, without Mrs Dale and Morning Story, or 3ses without the serial on Woman's Hour. (Are these on Radio 2 now?) I also wait avidly for Richard to come home with news. I can't tell him anything at all, and office gossip is better than nothing. If we were in a normal civilised country, there would be more things to do during the day, even if only "Continental Cooking" at the Tech, or gas showroom demonstrations.

A smart chap in a shabby sports coat has just come to the door asking for work. I feel so sorry for these chaps who are willing to work and can't get any.

Ron and Elizabeth White came for supper last night. Richard had spotted a frozen salmon in Brown's and bought £1 worth, enough for four steaks. We poached it in a white wine and lemon concoction and made potato balls with a little scoop and fried these and had whole tinned tomatoes and mushrooms. It was beautiful and whilst there wasn't much, it went down very nicely and was much appreciated.

Elizabeth is a bit fed up, and homesick. She doesn't work and does nothing but read. And the lazier she is, the less she wants to do. This is unlike her, as she went mad decorating and covering chairs and collecting pot plants. She misses her home and brought some slides taken at Christmas in three feet of snow. Is her house super?! It has a Georgian front and they have altered and extended the back. It stands in two acres of lawn and trees, which in these snowy pictures was beautiful. It looks like this,

The doorway is beautifully Georgian and the façade is genuine. No wonder she misses it. It is not let, just closed up while they are away

Chapter 43   Trade Fair

Times of Zambia

27th June   UNIP to arrange card checks in city centres.

Letter 137   27/6/1068

I have just made a lemon meringue pie and it's in the oven. Someone recommended using soda water instead of ordinary water for the pastry, so I've had a try and I had three egg whites left over from the salmon meal.

We are also getting a new cooker. Richard had a moan some time ago, as he saw the standard list of housing fittings for various size families. Only single people and flat dwellers (that's only us in the company) have three ring cookers and everyone else has four rings. We are OK with our three rings, except for dinner parties and weren't complaining about the size at all, but just grousing because as we live in a flat/terrace instead of a house, we have a smaller size cooker, although one more ring on the same cooker would take up no more room. We also had a smaller fridge for the same reason and are entitled to less furniture even though we have the same area as a house. Richard said he couldn't follow the reasoning. If we were in a house, we would have a larger cooker and stove. I know it sounds petty, but little things like this add up, when people, like the Youngs, have a house and all the extras that go with it and then moan because the kitchen is too big.

We can't open cupboards and Andre and I cannot comfortably stand in the kitchen at the same time. Anyway, the outcome was that a new bachelor is coming and is to have a flat and he is being given our cooker and we are to get a four ring. I wonder if they are trying to soft soap Richard, just as his contract expires, and they want him to stay.

Richard also got a dig in, as the personnel manager said to Richard that Richard's car was so filthy that it didn't look only twelve months old. So Richard said, "What do you expect when I'm not allowed to wash it outside my own house?" He has just paid 10/- to a fellow who comes around with a carpet bag full of rags and brushes, who does the inside and outside very well and also puts a bit of polish on. He did it in the car park outside Richard's office.

Poor Sharmaine was complaining of feeling ill on Monday and yesterday in the early hours, she was rushed to hospital with appendicitis. She had it out yesterday morning and Margie is calling for me at 7.30 to go and visit her, so I must root out some magazines before I go.

Oh my pie! It's OK. The crust is burnt and the meringue very brown, but the meringue has risen and the pastry was pre cooked already.

Flags are up all over the place as it's Heroes and Unity this weekend and we both have Monday and Tuesday off. It is also Trade Fair weekend. The show opens to Trade tomorrow afternoon on invitation only and is opened on Saturday afternoon officially by some minister or other, but we are going first thing Saturday morning to avoid the queues. Everything will be in full swing.

Times of Zambia 28th June

Evidence deficient so court clears two of drunken behaviour. In his judgement Mr Burke said, "The accused said to the arresting constable. "You are a foolish police officer. You are talking bullshit" But the evidence given by the constable was unsatisfactory and his knowledge of English was so bad that I cannot rely on it. Indeed, while I do not agree with the terminology of the accused, I cannot discount the accuracy of his description"

Letter 138   30/06/1968

On Friday, we went out to a company duty dinner at the Copper's. It was a retirement for Enid Case and Richard was host with Marlene and Peter and a Mr and Mrs Lamprey. Mrs Lamprey is now the only white European clerk left in Richard's side now. The meal was O.K. but Peter and I were on one end separated from Richard and Marlene and Enid and Pat by these awful two. He would walk off with the prize for the world's best bore. Only when his mouth was full of food did he pause. Marlene raised her eyes to heaven when I caught her eye. He quite put me off my meal. Some of the things he was saying were so idiotic that I had to keep my mouth from dropping open in astonishment. When Peter or I tried to change the subject, we were interrupted by "when I was in the war" or "when I was a lad I only got a penny a week". He also started discussing the wines Richard had chosen, trying to tell us which was the best, and then asked which was the sweet wine. He would have done better just asking for a sweet wine. His wife wasn't a bit embarrassed. If he had been my husband I would have hidden under the table. However Richard up the other end had a reasonable evening.

On Saturday morning, we were going to for the Trade Fair early. We had members' badges, which entitled us to a special car park, a restaurant and seats in the main stand. We also didn't have to pay and could come and go as we pleased. Richard got them because the chap whose tickets they were is in London. However, Richard got up feeling ill. He took some Andrews, but was violently sick four times and looked awful. He had a normal amount of wine, which wouldn't have caused sickness, and he had a vodka before the meal. I think it was the grilled salmon he had to eat. I therefore went to the library on my own, but he insisted on going to the Fair, as he knew I had been looking forward to it for ages. We called at his office to collect some papers and he was ages. And came out looking awful, but he insisted he felt better and on we went. We went in and I had been looking forward to a real hot dog and bought one for two shillings, but it was just a real disappointment. It was a dry roll with a frankfurter in it -no fried onions or sauces. I had to wolf it down on the way to car so Richard couldn't smell it. We came home and Richard went to bed and slept. As we had had a late night, I gave Andre his pay and came to bed too, with a book. Richard slept until 2.30, and I got up and made some soup and he got up and felt considerably better, and at three suggested going back. I forgot to say that, as we were sitting on a bench in the morning, a crowd appeared at the German stand, so we strolled over, nosey like. I dodged around to the front of the crowd and coming towards me was the President. His Excellency was about ten feet away. I had my camera and started filming and this policeman comes flying at me, so I hastily lowered my camera, thinking I was going to be shooed away. He asked, "Are you the Press?" I said "No" and he said "Oh…Do you know where the press photographers are? We want them to film." By this time the President was passing me, and this aide or whatever he was, told me to wait at the end of the stand, where `I could get a good picture. So I stood at a policeman's shoulder thinking no one would go in front of me. Just as the President was coming to the exit, this chap dashes out and shouts, "Madame, here is your chance," so I raise my camera and His Ex. Gives me a beaming smile from three feet away. I've also got shots of the President of Somalia who was with him. I was so pleased. The presidential party had arrived unannounced for a quick preview and so we were lucky.

We went back in the afternoon and Richard was looking and feeling much better. The official opening by the President of Somalia was at four o'clock so we had time to look at all the stands. Nothing extraordinary. No China or England this year, but Israel, East Germany and Tanzania were new. I wonder why China backed out after last year's success. England didn't appear, as Zambia wouldn't buy unless it was the last possibility on earth, at the moment. We wandered into the main arena in time for a firework display, and sat behind the President, who was on a dais. We sat at a table in the members' enclosure and we had nice coffee and I had <u>two</u> hamburgers for 3/- with raw tomato and onions, but after soup for lunch, was very tasty. I spotted Mrs Giles from the office toasting rolls, so could therefore be reassured that the conditions in the kitchen would be as clean as they could be. We saw a motorbike display where a fellow jumped ten barrels. He turned out to be a foreman in Richard's place. Then there was a high diving display of circus quality, with a burning man jumping into a burning water tank only five feet deep, quite spectacular, which was much appreciated by the locals. I am glad we saw the President in the morning, as we couldn't get much of a glimpse of him in the afternoon. I enjoyed the afternoon as I had the two hamburgers, and whenever we've been to New Brighton, we were always either too mean or more likely too hard-up to buy one. So I had TWO. Rebellious and defiant, I am.

Last night we babysat for Marlene and Peter, and Marlene forgot to tell us that she had a new kitten, which Pucci wasn't keen on. Marlene shut the new kitten in the kitchen, and Pucci and Pinky had a play, but the kitten kept on crying and I didn't like to leave it in the kitchen, so I made Richard take the dogs into the veranda room. It is glass louvered so Richard and I could talk and see each other but the dog couldn't see the kitten to growl at him. We both watched the cat for ages. He is so playful and cute, but swings by his claws on the furniture and chews the legs of the chairs- ouch. I moved to the veranda when the cat fell asleep. We didn't hear a peep from Sally. It was more trouble looking after the menagerie. They also have an African Grey parrot, which shrieks every time you pass the cage, and a fish, which the cat kept eyeing up, and smacking its paws on the glass of the bowl.

We got in at 1am, but Marlene had left us a lovely chicken supper in the oven.

Could you do something for me? Can you contact G plan and order matching stools for our two World's Most Comfortable Chairs, model 6251 in Fabric C128 as G Plan say that the design will be stopped before we get home. (£24/10/-)

The chairs are currently going for £1,000 on eBay. Ours still being used.

4th July 1968

Police yesterday withdrew the case against a young bank clerk who, it is alleged, " intended to insult the National Anthem' at a football match when hundreds of people were running across a football pitch attacking the players.

5th July 1968

The oil link is ready. First fuel may be pumped through

to Zambia later this month.

- **15 firms now under state control. The industrial Development Corporation had completed negotiations for the takeover of 15 companies.**

- **The ANC publicity chief has decided that a a call for his resignation by an ANC regional secretary as "a display of rank insubordination."**

Letter 139   3/07/1968

Wednesday and back to work. On Monday night we went over the way to Ron and Elizabeth's to meet people they had visiting and had roast duck, which was different Tuesday we had a laze, and went to Marlene and Peter's for lunch, which we had outside. It was gorgeous and hot and in the few hours we were there, my arms were red and you could see where my watch had been. We came back to our cold flat and were feeling fed up as we had so enjoyed sitting outside in the sun. It is so disheartening looking out of the window at it. I couldn't stick another year in a flat. Anyway, Ron who had been at Marlene's invited Richard for a round of golf, and Elizabeth invited me for tea while they were out, and we nattered until they came back, and then we had an early night.

At work, we have all agreed there is a change in atmosphere. Easy going Jack Pawson has moved to the offices over the road and is working at a different job and Hitchman has moved from assistant accountant to branch accountant. He is not qualified and is covering his lack of knowledge with bluff and bluster and downright rudeness and we are all heartily sick of him. I am luckier in that he knows little about my job, and therefore interferes little, but the other girls are annoyed at the mistakes he is making, which when pointed out to him, he denies they are his. We are now writing down any instructions he gives us, as proof, if only to satisfy ourselves. Mrs MacDonaugh has written out her notice, ready to hand in at the next row. Jack at first thought it was amusing, but is now concerned as our suppliers and customers are complaining. E.g. we pay all our bills at the end of the month. I process and authorise all the invoices and they then go to Susan, who posts them to customers' cards. The cards are then extracted by Margie and she writes the cheques. This we did on a day each i.e. three days. On the fourth day the cheques went to Hitchman for him to sign-about 100 of them. Today, *three* weeks later, he returns them. Mr Pawson usually returned them the day they were given to him. Of course, this week we have had rude calls and letters reminding us of our credit conditions, and a horrible chap called Lapthorne, rang me to threaten us with suing if we didn't pay up immediately for two measly boxes of soap! This is giving the company a bad name. Every time we reminded Hitchman he was "too busy, far too busy". Yet he finishes at 4.30 and went to the show in work hours for the Trade Preview. And the way Richard works.

At the moment, there is next-door's TV on full blast. We can even sing the ads. It's driving us potty, especially as Richard is working. However, it's the boys next door and they are never much bother. We just loathe their date-less nights, which happily are few and far between.

I don't know why I forgot to mention Tony's wedding. The bride looked lovely in a dress similar to mine but in satin, with train and short veil. Her bridesmaids were in nice styles but lemon, which wouldn't have been my choice. Tony looked chuffed to bits considering it seemed to be a put up job between her and her mother. The reception was peculiar. All small tables with cocktail snacks and champagne. However the barman was one of Richard's staff and the lack of grub was forgotten as champagne was consumed. A band played from four until six and we all danced and staggered in at 6.15.

Andre came in the afternoon instead of the morning, to do his work and we gave him an extra 10/- which was worth it as we left home at one and needed a dogsitter, as five hours is a bit long in the day, particularly as the neighbours would be home. He sleeps when we go out at night (we hope).

However, we thought that the wedding was at 1.30 and it was at 2.30, so rather than sit at home in our wedding togs, we went and had a drink at the golf club and we sat in the sun for an hour. Jim, next door but one was told by Kaffers, his servant, to hurry up and when he asked why, he said that the Bwana and Madame from number Five had already left while he was lunching. He got the fright of his life as he was an usher, and made a few phone calls to check the time. It just shows though how the servants talk. How did he know that we were going to the same wedding? They don't miss a thing!

Are your letters franked from here? Richard now pays monthly and the stamps are put on by machine and he gets a bill.

Times of Zambia   6th July 1968

The national organizing secretary of the United Party has appealed to police to grant meeting permits to his party, "so we can explain to the public our policies and our constitution"

- **Samuel Motowa was sentenced to six months hard labour for stealing 11 pairs of socks.**

Letter 140   8//7/1968

I came to buy a writing pad today and found I only had 8n (9d) which wasn't much good, so I must try and squeeze as much as I can on these bits.

Pucci got better but is now sick again. His paws are red raw as though they had been burnt. We only noticed at lunchtime. I have given him a pill for his rash thinking that might help and am going to make two lint socks for his front feet. If he's not better tomorrow night, back we go to the vets. I'm sure children are no worse trouble.

On Friday we went to a very dull cocktail party to say farewell to Robertson who is doing a stint in London. David from Port Sunlight was there and we invited him back. We invited him on Sunday for supper, and he said we must go and sit in his garden anytime. On Saturday, Richard was working all day, as he has installed an accounting machine and was changing his systems over. I made some oranges in jelly and felt so miserable as the sun was blazing, and I just felt like eating jelly in the sun, and it's not the same sitting on the spare room bed with the windows open. Richard took one look at my long face when he came in and rang David to inform him we were taking up his offer for Sunday. Richard worked on Sunday morning and after lunch we went to David's. I sat in the garden and Richard washed the car. We had cool drinks and a game of French cricket with Pucci joining in, and cheating. We laughed so much that none of us could stand up straight for holding our stomachs. We all came back at five and felt as though we had had a day at the seaside. My face is still red today. We had a lovely roast supper and David left at nine as even he was falling asleep, which we put down to the wine which he had brought for us. All in all, a good day. Even if I were in a flat at home, I could quite safely go for a walk, even if only to Mersey Park and back.

The sad thing is that David's house is Alan Phillips house, which was the Young's old house. This was the house, which was allocated to us, and our flat was allocated to the Youngs, who were satisfied with it, having looked over it. But Chairman Mackie, over the personnel manager's head said, "Oh no, Bill, you have the house" which he did. The thing is that Mrs Young, not being able to drive, was stranded in the house and our flat is handy for the shops. We won't forgive MacKie for his thoughtlessness.

Pucci's toes are a lot less red. Probably the Germolene and pill are doing the trick. I wish I could have identified what bit him.

Elizabeth left us 2lb of sausage as they have gone on a trip, and we already had a 1lb, so I have just put a toad in the hole in the oven as an experiment. It smells OK. But what do I serve with it- peas on their own, or with chips as well.

When David was here last night, I opened four tins of cream, one after the other, and they were all off.

Richard is now home. Its seven o'clock and he's worn out. He brought home all the Times and Sunday Times since the tenth of June, which Peter has had since he took over as Commercial Director in Graeme's absence, so we are making some coffee and are going to bed to read this super store of papers.

I am very cross with Andre. He did no washing on Saturday, which was OK, but tonight the linen basket is full of today's wash – sheets and linen, so he has not done a scrap of work today, but the breakfast dishes and made the bed. As on Thursday, the Whites come home, he must brush and dust there. He has probably been there all day. The annoying thing is that he had the washing bucket downstairs and went out at lunchtime to bring in non-existent washing. How's that for sly. I wonder what he's up to. I shall probably be as sly and drop home earlier in my tea break.

Before Richard came in, I made a lint boot for Pucci, like a mitten but with shirring elastic around the top, but he didn't like it and kept pulling it off. Even the elastic didn't help, as there's nothing to grip, as he hasn't a heel or anything. He sat still while I put it on, but whipped it off very quickly after sniffing it. Cheek. All my good sewing.

I hope Andre isn't starting to turn sloppy, and that he lasts until the end of November until Pucci goes. It's only as a babysitter that we need him all day. I could perhaps manage on my own otherwise for the last few months, (but doing the washing in the bath – ugh!). Only six full months now, and eight weeks to our hols.

I read a lovely book this weekend called The Gypsies by a Hungarian who ran off with the gypsies when he was twelve – a true story.

Chapter 44   Overtime

Times of Zambia   12th July 1968

Paramount Chief Chtimukulu of the Bemba will move his palace near Kalwyu River to an area far from the railway. He said he would completely rebuild his palace and village. He would do away with mud and pole houses as much as possible.

Letter 141

Your bumper bundle letter arrived today. Thank you very much for my lovely surprise present. I can see that I must veto my letters before I send them, to see that there is nothing you can pounce on to send. It's a lovely bow and I wore it last night with my new dress and it's just the job. I can stick in the side or at the back on the top of my lassy band.

Last night, David and Erich, a Swede of about forty who is supervising the installation of a new toothpaste unit at the factory in a room no bigger that your dining room, came. We had a duck, which was killed on Tuesday morning and which Andre plucked in the afternoon. There was loads of meat on it and we left on the wings, so Andre was delighted this morning when he saw the meat left on it. I made a gooseberry pie (tinned goosegogs) and fresh cream and I thought they would never leave. I made three pots of coffee! Eventually they left and I was grateful to get to bed.

Daddy, our house is classed as a flat, I think, because it is in a row of eight or so faced by another two blocks, all of which have a communal yard or square, with washing lines. The front doors open out onto this yard and the back French windows onto a patio, so they are limited like a flat. Words like terraced or semis are unknown and our house differs from a terrace in that it has no private yard nor access, like our Chester terrace. The front doors are all in a row like in downtown terraced houses, but the backs only open on to the equivalent of a balcony. The only other type of dwelling is a detached house in a garden, (actually bungalows, as few are two storied) or in a block of dwellings. Is that clearer?

Do you know that a bachelor, Hutton, just arrived from UK for two years, has been placed in a three bedroomed house with a lovely garden, when Tony's flat is still vacant. Isn't it barmy? Anyway, why should we worry? We're coming home soon!

Thanks for the Birkenhead news cuttings. The girls gasped at Lennon's latest. From the look of Lennon and the "girl", Cynthia looks as though she is best out of his way. I'm surprised it didn't end officially sooner.

We will go and visit Winnie Sword's husband. We have had some funny addresses given to us but this is the oddest. At least all the others are alive. We shall put some flowers on and let her know the damage when we come home.

I have done some calculations and will take no more colour prints. It is cheaper to take slides and have any really good ones enlarged.

Times of Zambia   18th July 1968

President Kaunda having trouble getting missiles from UK....for Zambia's defence.

Letter 142   13/07/1968

Did we have a good laugh at lunchtime? Pucci has received his birthday presents. We opened the parcel for him in case there was a letter or polythene and gave him the slipper, or rather Richard squeaked the slipper at him and it terrified him and he went and hid under a chair, and gradually emerged to examine it carefully. I was sitting on the floor with a "dog chew" and he came to me and grabbed it and ran off with it. He wouldn't let us near. He has chewed it like mad, holding it in his paws like a lollipop. I have just come in from work now and he is still playing with it, although at the end it is like soggy cardboard. It will probably dry when he leaves it alone. If he leaves it alone. He dropped it for a while just to come and sniff the slipper I was holding, but he just saw it as a ruse to get his "chew" and grabbed it again. He is now lying on his back with his feet in the air with it sticking out of his mouth like a cigar. I had seen them advertised on the back of the Times and thought that they were lumps of knotted chamois leather.

We went to Bob and Naomi's with Marlene and Peter on Friday and had a good supper, but it was very cold at their place, and we were huddled round a Calor heater.

The weekend otherwise was miserable. On Saturday, Richard worked until six and on Sunday until four. He is putting all his accounts onto a machine. The transposition was supposed to take place this weekend and the machine operator has been practicing all week and then didn't turn in at the weekend for which she is paid overtime, so Richard instead of supervising the transfer, operated the machine. Then to cap it all, the printers printed the "No Carbon Required forms" back to front so that they wouldn't print. So all Saturday night, Richard chopped forms in half so that they could be used and I typed addresses on the new back copies. I did this all Sunday morning. When Richard came home at four, he was fed up, so I walked with him nine holes on the golf course. We got in at 5.30 ish and then we had to put the remaining trays into alphabetical order. Richard had told a chap to file them in alphabetical order, and he put all the As together and all the Bs together etc. but in any old order, so we had to file each letter more finely. I was whacked, so what must Richard have been? The system wasn't quite ready this morning, but almost. If he hadn't worked over the weekend, it would have meant a complete blockage to the normal flow of work.

The tights I bought for 17/6 lasted a week and a further fortnight until the holes spread beyond the darns. I went for stockings on Friday and bought a pair for 2/11, Italian with no make or colour on the packet, but when I got them home I found them to be as good as those for 4/11 that I normally but which are now out of stock. The next price was 9/11 so Richard made me buy £1 s worth (7 pairs) today, as he is sick of me in darned tights looking like a penniless student.

Richard hasn't been able to use his machine today, as it has been adding in credits with the debits, and therefore throwing out a wrong total. The machine mechanic says it is the programmer's fault and the mechanic is blamed by the programmer. They have been arguing and fiddling with it all day.

Ugh. Pucci has deposited a soggy chew on my knee covered in slobber and hairs and fluff off the carpet. Whose idea was this thing?

Times of Zambia   19th July 1968

Critical KK-Wilson talks. Future relations with UK in the balance.

* "She's my wife, No she's not" wrangle in court. Two men yesterday heatedly disputed ownership of a woman and goods worth K67.50.

Letter 143   17/03/68

Did I tell you where Enid Case is going? She is coming to work for us, and I'm to teach her our office routine! She is going to collect all our old debts via a solicitor. Hitchman is worse than ever. We are having the same trouble with cheques this month, and suppliers are ringing and threatening to cut off our supplies. The cheques are all there waiting.

Richard says he signs 140 salary cheques in twenty minutes, and we only have 100 cheques to go out. Yet he, Hitchman leaves promptly for lunch and at 4.30. Anyway we could moan to our boss, but Richard reckons the most effective thing is to leave it until some suppliers start suing.

I wish I could have gone to George Henry Lees' sale too. I would have gone mad. I am looking for shoes for my hols, but the shoe shop has gone mad on crocodile and skin granny shoes with thick, high heels. I want some beige or mushroom patents.

(Yes, I know, the year before last's colour. I think I'll end up dying my current beige shoes, which are rather shabby. Those dyes they have now are good, aren't they. They even polish properly. I explained to Richard just how successfully one can dye shoes these days, and he said that "one" could, but someone else he knows would end up with red feet, hands and dress, and the shoes in their original colour. He doesn't have much faith in me, does he?

Who on earth is Kelly the kitten? You've not mentioned him before.

David has invited us over on Sunday again this week and he says he has made a better French cricket bat, as I just used a wooden baton thing, which we broke.

Had a sarcastic letter from Mrs. L. saying that she understood why Richard couldn't write, as he couldn't spare the time from the golf course. Then in the next breath, says that if we didn't have dinners to go to, and give, that he would have nothing to write about. She's never satisfied. I asked why he hadn't opened her letter and he said that he knew what it was going to say – haven't heard from you for six months and Mrs W has had 140 letters and ten phone calls. He is also disgusted that she is going on a buying binge, after staying with acquaintances in Sweden, and says she has no ideas of her own and must always copy – I just listen. Anyway, it looks as though, when we get home, that Richard will stick up for me if she gets at me, rather than keep quiet to keep the peace. I suppose being away has established Richard as the head of his family i.e. him and me and Pucci.

Times of Zambia

20th July 1968   Goodwill restored. Kaunda is flying home today. Zambia is in touch with British Aircraft Corporation about missiles.

Letter 144   **22/7/1968**

Thank you for my brown and navy ribbon. I have made the brown into a lovely bow. I found out how to make it when Pucci pulled my other black bow to pieces. It wasn't badly damaged; just a few stitches had come undone. The navy I have made into a headband.

On Saturday morning, I went back to Bernina and was one of only two for a lesson. It was a jolly good lesson about applique and I came out all enthused to have a bash at some sewing, but I only had 10ng (1/-) with me, which was just as well.

Pucci doesn't half recognise sounds quickly. I only have to pick up the biscuit barrel and he's at my feet from three rooms away. The same with a bar of chocolate wrapper rustling and Richard accidentally gave him a peanut, which was a mistake as Richard only picks up the plastic peanut box and his head appears at his knee, begrudging every mouthful. However, he doesn't pester us at mealtimes, because he has his supper at the same time as us.

Mrs L should have had three letters now, as Richard has written regularly for the past few weeks. I will chivvy Richard to write, but do not feel inclined to write myself as she is only interested in hearing from Richard. Remember last time I wrote for Richard, she said she had had no letters from Richard, but we have had one from Valerie. She doesn't see that the letter is signed, from Valerie and Richard, and it shouldn't matter who wrote. No I'll just natter at Richard and see that he doesn't leave it too long.

Andre is OK again, touch wood. Must have been an off day. We have got £6 towards his bike, and will have £8 at the end of this month. His bike is £16, and a bit more than we thought, so as the Whites are going at the end of the month we will have to add £6 towards it. I still lose out on cleaning things – four packets of Surf extra a month, and I found Andre had used my Brillo when she asked him to do her oven while she was away.

We went over to water her flowers yesterday, as they are away this week and the house was a midden. Lunch dishes in the sink just rinsed, and she had been dressmaking in the lounge and the material was all over the floor and material and patterns all over the chairs. When she is away, Andre does the floors in lieu of washing. Fancy expecting him to clear that mess. Believe it or not, I make sure everywhere is tidy before I go out to work in the morning. With such ample cupboard space and a home for everything, a linen basket on the landing, wastebaskets everywhere and few possessions, being tidy isn't difficult. Let's hope, without the incentive of a servant to keep tidy for, that I can manage it at home. We will have to have fitted wardrobes in the spare room. I must admit, I prefer shelves in a wardrobe to a chest of drawers, as everything is much more accessible on a shelf. I do wish you could see my tidy cupboards. I've developed quite a fetish about them. Just wait until I have kids! Then you'll get your own back.

We got six little grapefruit today, our monthly shopping day, for 9d. They were very nice although there was only a spoonful in them. Tonight we had, -guess what? Birds Eye Fish Fingers. Phil Dwyer has just tried importing them by refrigerated ship to Dar Es Salaam and by airfreight to Ndola. We have also bought lemon sole and plaice. Richard left instructions for fish, chips and peas, bread and butter and a pot of tea for two. The fish was lovely but we didn't touch the bread and butter as the bread was Ugh and the butter was slightly rancid, but the tea was great. Richard said we were playing at "being at home"! Mrs Mac in the office first said these fish fingers were in and rang all her English friends. One of them wanted to know if there were chicken and turkey pies too. Phil Dwyer said that these were under consideration too. Yippee! Such luxury. However ten fish fingers were 4/6d. Anyway, we certainly had our 4/6 worth of pleasure out of them. Yum, yum.

Pucci is on his second chew stick as we lost his first in David's garden where we spent Sunday afternoon. I took my relaxy chair and had a lovely laze. It was super. David came back for supper and we had a casserole which I had left in the oven in the afternoon and I did pancakes and had them dashing in and out of the kitchen with their plates. I make lovely filling fattening pancakes. We then played "Risk".

Richard went all round town looking for Jaktari or Joktari, a game with two bats and a ball anchored by elastic to a block, to play at David's. No one knew it, although we have seen people with them. One girl on being asked for Jaktari, a game with two bats and a ball on elastic, said Oh yes! And produced table tennis. Another girl said that yes she knew of it. " Its just the thing for the garden. We've got none in though." However another couple of chaps came and we just sat and chatted. Pucci never stopped belting around the lawn all afternoon. You'll be pleased to know that he doesn't dig or run on the flowerbeds, and that the shrubs we watered last week are flourishing this week.

Times of Zambia   23rd July 1968

It's away. A flick of a switch sends first oil through pipeline.

- **UNIP names traders in "protection racket"**
  The Lusaka UNIP regional office has issued a stern warning to Indian shop owners in the capital who were allegedly contributing money to the ANC so that their businesses can be protected.

Letter 145   24/07/1968

I wish I could cine Pucci at the moment. I brought the supper in and put the oven gloves on the shelf under the stairs. He loves this cloth and grabs it whenever it is in reach and fights it. He couldn't reach it and walked round the shelf on his hind legs sniffing. He then went up the stairs and poked his head through the bars of the stairs looking down at it. He was so persistent that I gave it to him. Isn't he ruined? He doesn't damage it, but as the ends are padded and weighty, he can throw it into the air and it swings out. He runs round with it over his head like ears, or on his back like a saddle with bags, or with his head or feet in a glove.

I know Sharmaine was dense, but she brought a scrapbook of her modelling photos, very nicely set out, but on the front in neat lettering was "My Pearsonal Modeling Fill" or translated, "My Personal Modelling File" She is 17. Do you wonder why parents are keen to send their kids to boarding school! The only correct word was "My", but the lettering was good.

Weren't we lucky going to Rhodesia at Easter now that communications have been cut off? We have been forbidden by the company on instructions from London to have any dealings with, or visits to Rhodesia. This will create complications going to Salisbury on the way to South Africa. And more expense travelling via Malawi or by plane to Jo'burg. No restrictions have been issued by the Zambian Government and nothing official has been confirmed, just the company instruction and rumours. Its probably just Unilever keeping its nose clean.

I have just rescued Pucci from the bathroom. He goes into the bathroom and tries to pull the towels off the rail as he can reach them if they are hung untidily, and in the process knocks the door to; and then whines to get out. He always does this when we ignore him or are busy and I think it's a trick, like the baby throwing its boots out of the pram.

Richard's system is on its feet but going slowly, and he is sick of calling in the machine man, to right basic programming errors, but it's now an established part of the company and the editor of the Lever News wants to do an article on it.

Chapter 45   Explosion

Times of Zambia

29th July 1968 — Police step up hunt for cattle rustlers, after reports that 48 head of cattle were stolen from a ranch on the old Mumbwa Road.

31st July 1968 — "Shoot on Sight" order after dog attacks. Police in Kalulushi are under orders to gun down all stray dogs on sight after one child was savaged to death and another boy mauled by a pack of rabid dogs prowling the area.

Letter 146

We had a commotion on Friday as you can see from the newspaper cutting. About nine o'clock, there was this almighty explosion and we all ducked as the roof and walls shook. Mr King from the plant, was coming into the office and he turned and ran like mad through the plant door, and then the alarm started, which we are used to at works' practices. The girls said, "What do we do?" And I said, "Get out fast, because I had seen Mr King act so concernedly. I shouted to shut the windows and turn off the electricity, as this was the only fire precaution I could think of, and helped fling cash and valuables in the safe. We then all picked up all our bags and went out into the street. Africans were coming from miles around to see what had happened. All I could remember was Jack Pawson telling us that if anything started at the plant, the whole of Ndola would go up. We persuaded Mrs Bailey to come out, but she is 72 and was sitting at her typewriter saying, "If my time's come, my time has come."

The fire brigade and ambulance arrived as Mr Cole ran in and shouted to the terrified Mrs Mhizha at the switchboard-'Stay at your post! And then he ran off.

Apparently two cylinders of hydrogen blew up and a fellow with them. Mr King was first on the scene and they controlled the blaze before they could reach the man who was badly burnt. The blast had blown off the roof of the H2 plant and damaged the equipment and the main concern was to stop the blaze spreading to other cylinders. They put the man on the back of a truck and drove him to the hospital, but his arms were off and he was badly shattered. He died yesterday. He had only been with us for two months. The cause of the explosion is still unknown.

People came from all over the place, just from nosiness. A private car even drove into the works and around the fire-with that danger too. Aren't people fools! Apparently even the glassware shelves rattled at Brown's in the centre of town.

Fight for life after factory explosion

By Times Reporter

AN NDOLA plant attendant, Mr. Robon Chansa, of Twapia township, was last night in a critical condition after an explosion at the hydrogen plant of the Zambia Oxygen Company in Chisokone Avenue.

Mr. Chansa, 22, was apparently testing a hydrogen cylinder when it exploded. He was rushed to hospital, where he underwent an operation. Last night doctors were fighting to save his life.

The plant was extensively damaged, said the general manager, Mr. David G. Woodworth.

A fire caused by the explosion was put out by company employees. The Ndola Fire Brigade were called in but found the situation under control.

There were about 60 people at the plant at the time of the explosion, which was heard all over the city.

Senior Assistant Commissioner of Police Louis Wapamesa said that police investigations so far ruled out sabotage.

The works managers were very shaken by this. They sat at the bedside of the injured man in shifts until he died. He was talking to the end. They must have so dosed him up so that he felt nothing. It was this that upset them more than everything, as the man had lost both arms and legs. They think that it was caused by an employee filling a gas tank, whilst smoking a cigarette. And there were No Smoking signs on huge panels all over the place.

On Saturday, Richard had to work again to ensure his programme went to schedule as the faults with the machine have set it back. He took the dog back with him at lunchtime, so that I could go to a sale of work and then join him. The sale of work was dreadful and I fought to buy a 5/- cake, (which was very nice) and left five minutes later and arrived at the factory just after three. We stayed until six. I tore off payslips and filed cards to facilitate Richard's progress. He couldn't ask the girl to work the weekend as she is on overtime all week. A month's invoices have to be entered to the accounts in less than a week.

We arrived home with colossal headaches and had supper out of tins and fell into bed at seven. We woke at 1am as there was a noisy dance at the golf club, so I made coffee and then we slept until 7.30a.m, and Richard was up and out for work for eight. After lunch at two, we went to David's, sat in the garden with Richard doing his regular weekend work on his files. David arrived back from Kariba and as seems to be the habit on Sundays now, we came back home to the roast lamb I had left in the oven.

I'll be heartily glad when we go on leave and have a good two weeks rest. Richard certainly deserves it. This firm has certainly had their pound of flesh. The thing is, that if his system works as it did at Mitcham Cardboard, then it will be forgotten, but if it fails, Richard will certainly be remembered.

Times of Zambia   2nd August 1968

President Kaunda said yesterday that he had no doubt that Zambia would be one of the few countries where post independence elections would not bring "some confusion".

*   **Retiring staff putting off local recruits. The acute staff shortage which threatens to disrupt many local authority services has been blamed on the bad image being projected abroad of retiring officers on contract and the cost of living.**

Letter 147   1st August 68

I am glad Nanny is so well. I suppose it makes a difference to your mind when your physical comforts are looked after. She now no longer has to buy and cook and wash her clothes. I don't suppose I'd be very clean and tidy if I had a cold house and had to wash clothes in a dolly tub. Look how horrid it is to bath on a cold day.

Peter says confidentially, that Financial Group and the Overseas Committee and a large UK company (he wouldn't or couldn't say) have asked for Richard already, so we are assured of something nice. The first two are London based but are bound to be plum jobs, but the last is anyone's guess. At least London is only a train ride away, and very close after being this far away.

Richard hasn't yet ordered a car. There is an eight-week delivery for Volvo so we will order in November to be sure. Don't worry about the journey up. I'd hate to travel by train with all the bits we will accumulate on the voyage and with two months luggage. It will be a lot easier to dump the whole lot in a car. You can also bring a couple of blankets in case I feel the cold.

Doodle says he feels common, having just read in The Times, that one million Doodles have been sold. I cheered him up by telling him that he was the only Doodle in Zambia, and none are as well travelled as he.

We had a board meeting today and Margie and I bought 16/- worth of biscuits, knowing they would probably only eat 5/- worth. We now have enough biscuits for one each with every cup of tea for a week. I was disappointed however that we weren't told to buy flowers. Must be economy month.

We laughed in the office today. We were moaning about the junk accumulating in one corner of the room, e.g. an old typewriter, files, ledgers and a clumsy out of date machine, so we stuck up a notice, "Zamox Museum of Antiquities" and labelled everything. Broken wire waste paper basket, "Basket used to catch Anne Boleyn's head", the typewriter "Caxton's first printing press", ledger, "Domesday Book", files

"Dead Sea Scrolls", calculator, "Abacus used by Archimedes", chair with stuffing protruding "King Canute's throne used when repelling waves" and so on, all corny but fun. However instead of stimulating management to throw it all out, we have had a steady stream of visitors. I think we should charge.

Margie didn't know Caxton or an abacus, but her cousin topped the lot. She looked vaguely at it all and Susan asked if she knew the Dead Sea Scrolls. She just shrugged and carried on talking to Margie. I then said. "Do you know Anne Boleyn, Sharmaine?" and she said, "Does she live in Luanshya?" However we didn't tease her further and fortunately she didn't realise she was being teased. As I've said before she is lovely and she'll make a great model.

I made tinned tuna fish cakes tonight, as we had no meat, but with fresh cabbage. An unusual combination but a good economic meal.

Its getting warmer now and I'm going to work now without a cardigan, although I still need a bit of choke to get the car started. Probably as there is such a difference between day and night temperatures at the moment. Batteries go flat very quickly too.

My pen is running out and as I am in bed, I am too comfy to go downstairs and fill it. It's 9.15pm and Richard is already snoring.

Times of Zambia   6th August 1968

The Government has made it clear to companies involved in state takeovers, that book value only will be paid for controlling interest.

* A shortage of fish has caused a mad scramble by housewives whenever traders reach Kitwe and other Copperbelt centres.

Letter 148　　　5/8/68

On Friday we went to David's for supper, so we had chicken in front of a TV! Haven't gone out to see someone's TV since the Coronation.

On Saturday, we went out to find Ndola Hill, but couldn't find it. My map must be out of date. We shall try again next week, maybe. We ended up in Kent Park and sat there while the dog had a good run round.

On Saturday night, we went to a party at Sally and Stuart's, which was great. On Sunday, Mrs Lindique next door said that the dog had howled a lot. Goodness knows why he did, but the flats are so noisy. We apologised and envisaged not going out again until the dog goes! Anyway, David said he would look after the dog when we want to go out and this will solve the current problem as both David and the dog leave in November. But it doesn't solve the long-term problem. Perhaps six months in quarantine kennels will accustom him to his own company. Whoever heard of a dog sitter?

Today is Monday, a Bank Holiday, and David came for lunch as he was working and Richard and I came and sat in the garden. We have just finished a cheese, egg and onion pie and a lemon meringue that I made this morning and we are watching, of all things, an ancient "Maverick". Pucci has belted around and sunbathed all day and is now sleeping. It was lovely in the garden and we also had a week's supply of Telegraphs to read. Super!

We have been reading animal books on Kenya and are very keen now on our holiday. I can even tell the difference between a Masai giraffe and a reticulated giraffe. Also, did you know that it is a cheetah that has spots and the leopard that has rosettes?

My second cardigan has also 'washed tight". The sleeves are to my elbows and I washed it myself!

Yesterday, we sold Richard's rat eaten jacket, an old dress and a pair of my shoes which had gone sloppy to a rag man and got 25/- Not much, but we wouldn't wear them again and I'll put the 25/- towards some material for a holiday dress.

The earliest we can book Pucci's flight is October, but we have all his licences and permits.

Do send him some chews for Christmas, as he loves his chews. The second has been thrown out and I am saving the third for November.

Times of Zambia   12th August

K17 million power plant for Kariba Dam.

Letter 149   7/08/1968

I am writing this in the office, as I have no post to work on yet, Enid Case started work for us today. She has got rid of one Lapthorne to get tangled with another.

Richard is ringing his mother on Saturday for her birthday. The call is booked for 7 o'clock Zambian time, 6 o'clock U.K time.

Four weeks to our holiday. David will take us to the airport. He wants to stay in our place while we are away, as he isn't so keen on the Irish electrician he must share with. At least the house won't be over run with insects and he can keep an eye on the car.

I have taken some cuttings from the office red and white geraniums to go with my pink ones. The weather is hotting up here. I no longer wear my jersey in the mornings as it's not cold enough and the afternoons are beautifully warm.

I like New Brighton in the off season best –its twice as seedy and the Victorian element stands out more strongly when the hot dog stands aren't there. Do you know what disappointed me, pop music over loudspeakers instead of the hurdy gurdy music. However, I think the Tower Grounds roundabout still has its own organ. *Odd that fifty years later in 2008 I did my dissertation on "New Brighton Out of Season"*

One thing about water ski-ing on the Mersey – no bilharzia.

Times of Zambia   14th August 1968

Gun patrol hunts panga killers. A man dies and a Minister hurt in funeral attack.

A gang armed with axes, pangas and spears hacked a UNIP official to death and left an Assistant Minister of State lying on the ground with head wounds in Chililabombwe yesterday

Letter 150   12/8/68

We are attempting to fix up our long trek to Cape Town. We have made up our mind to travel to Salisbury by bus on 31st January at 4p.m. from Ndola with Richard finishing work at 3.30! The bus is suited to the heat – sunroof, bar and lav. on board. The latter suiting me no end. However it is a long journey, arriving at Salisbury at about eight in the morning, a sixteen-hour journey, and a dull run, being hundreds of miles through the same bush country. However we stop for dinner in Lusaka, and can sleep before reaching the Zambian border in the early hours. We fly from Salisbury to Jo'burg by Skycoach on the Sunday, which is just a little dearer than the bus as luggage is limited to 15k instead of 20k. but we can send a box on ahead a few weeks beforehand to the ship. We then plan to continue to Cape Town by train via Kimberley, heart of the diamond country, to meet the boat on Friday. It's all very exciting and makes me feel weary to think of the travelling but as we have two months sailing to recover, it doesn't bother me very much. We have made provisional booking for the transport subject to seats being available. I am now looking at a hotel brochure to book hotels.

What did your friend mean? There are no White Nuns in Ndola, only White Fathers, who do similar work. As it happens, we gave a donation to an organisation this week: A woman came to the door. I'll keep my ears open for an actual White Nun. Ordinary nuns are often seen shopping in town (in their Mercedes!)

Let's hope you don't have to strike Daddy. Fancy being lumbered with all that decorating. You'd be better off at work.

On Saturday, after a morning at work, we went to try and find Ndola Hill again- we had been on the right road but had approached it from the wrong side. The hill is an outcrop, which sticks right out of the trees and gives a splendid view through 360 degrees. It is quite a climb and almost hands and knees in places, as it is very dry and sandy. Pucci managed OK, running on ahead and looking back at us, toiling and sweating. I took a Tupperware of water for Pucci and we all shared it at the top.

Do you remember when Gran went to a Tupperware party and was horrified at the prices, so ordered the cheapest on the list and when her order arrived, she had bought three lids?

David is moving house today with the electrician as the Phillips are back, and he rang Richard to say that he had inspected the fence and it was dog proof. The only thing is now to find somewhere to put the other chap. A third bloke is moving in, in October.

The Phillips' family came home this morning, so we had to stay at home. However, I had bought some dress material and some shoe dye in the same shade of orange. I realised all my new dresses had high collars and therefore weren't much good for hot sun. I started sewing at 11 and with a quick break for lunch had finished at 3.30 – all pressed and ready to wear. I set up the iron in the spare room so I can press as I go along. I then started on the top of another, a repeat of the dress with the unusual back with the covered buttons. But I was tackling too much, so I gave up for the day. I've just to finish that and then I'll have two new dresses from the material from home and four new ones made in the last few weeks. We have spent so much on our holiday that it leaves little for clothes and Richard is going in much Bosticked sandals, but we might as well skimp for this holiday while we have the opportunity. Only 16 working days to go.

The phone call. Richard went on talking after the pips as the operator didn't butt in and he got charged another £2. Was I mad? I said that he had rung his mother for 5 minutes this time and 5 minutes last time, making 10 minutes, whereas I only had two times 3 minutes, and that he owed me another four minutes. However he didn't follow my reasoning.

Letter 151   14th August 1968

I went into the travel agents today and booked all bus/plane/train journeys and have written to the hotels in Salisbury, Jo'burg and Cape Town.

We have also sent off deposits to all our Kenyan holiday hotels to avoid carrying too much cash with us and so we can budget our spends a little better. We have decided to hire a car for the whole time, so that we can sightsee as Nyali is ten miles outside Mombasa and there is a small game park outside Nairobi. At 12/6 plus mileage and with so much to see, we do not consider this an extravagance.

I am eating the lemon cheese I made, and it's lovely, with just the right lemon tang and with just butter, lemon, eggs and sugar must be better that shop-preserved stuff and here it is cheaper than shop bought. David gave me some under-ripe paw paws for chutney, but they have ripened and unless I make large quantities it will work out expensive as the added ingredients are expensive – tomatoes and raisins – and will outweigh the saving on paw paws. Richard doesn't like paw paws anyway!

Making jam is expensive too as fruit is imported all year round, except for oranges and lemons, and there are no cheap seasons as for blackcurrants and strawberries at home. Kenya grows strawberries so we shall gorge while we are there.

Richard says that Bob Dunkerley didn't come to work today, as there were two leopards at Misundu. One was shot, but the other is female and believed to have cubs. Bob is bothered about his chickens attracting them. I hope Sally and Stuart are not bothered, as they are so isolated and have no glass in their windows only wooden shutters.

Today's photo is of me up a tree. Isn't that a lovely climbing tree? However I found that I was too nervous to climb very high – frightened of damaging my dress or myself. Dear me, such is growing old.

☐

Chapter 46   Sharing Gardens

Times of Zambia   15th August 1968

President Kaunda yesterday banned the United Party. Mundia sent into restriction.

End of petrol rationing not far off.

19th August 1968

The period from now until the general elections early next year would be a most difficult one during which, if the leaders were not careful, Zambia's enemies would attempt to destroy her, President Kaunda warned yesterday.

Letter 152

On Friday, we went to Phillips' for supper and to hear about their trip and took Pucci with us. He had a play in the garden and then we put him in the car where he slept until 11.30 and then started yapping so we came home. We couldn't have him in the house as the Phillips have a dachshund, who has already taken the ear off one of their friend's dogs. Pucci had enough room in the estate, and his blanket and toys, but what a performance!

On Sunday, we went to David's new house at Borrowdale at ten and stayed until 5 having soup for lunch. The house had been repainted and furnished. The other lodger went out for the day with friends, so there were just the three of us. We sat on the terrace lazing and reading, and although Richard had taken his briefcase, I'm glad to say that he ended up reading the papers too. Marlene and Peter popped in with the post for us all, so on went the coffee.

Pucci has a girlfriend. He spotted two little Maltese, just like himself, watching him through the fence. He approached cautiously, and then all we could see was a white woolly ball and three tails wagging in the air. They made friends and raced up and down either side of the fence.

The neighbour said that her two were father and daughter, and the little female dog kept sniffing Pucci and dashing to and from the fence and when he ignored her and came and sat with us, she would sit and gaze at him. We did laugh at them. Pucci fell asleep on the way home and then woke up to have three helpings of supper, one plate of liver, one of chuck steak as he finished the liver in two gulps. And then a plate of scraps from the leg of pork. No wonder he didn't budge until seven this morning.

Richard and David were under our car most of the morning, cleaning and pottering. We can't do this in the flats, understandably, as I suppose some people would take their tinkering to extremes. It was just like being in our own garden and the day went too quickly.

There were lots of fruits in the back garden, lemons, limes, paw paws and grapefruit. We shook the trees and they fell down. (the fruit, not the trees). We had lime in our coca cola and sucked grapefruit. One grapefruit had a maggot in it, which David dropped onto the path. We then watched it being set upon by tiny ants, which pulled chunks off it until it was dead. Quite hideous. They just ate it without any bother. At least spiders paralyse their prey before noshing it. I suppose this is a hygienic way to dispose of dead matter, but not living things!

This morning we left the house at seven o'clock to wait to register for a National Registration card, as the rush had died down a bit. We were first, except for a woman in a shawl sitting with her cooking pot. Only six had joined by 7.30 when it opened and they were very friendly, being people from the "outskirts" who were not familiar with town attitudes. We all nodded and good-morning-ed, like old friends. But these people were so nervous when being questioned for their forms. I felt sorry for them as we were able to take or leave any official bullying, but these people were obviously terrified by officialdom. We then had to queue for our photos and had our cards fitted in plastic. We were out by 8.30, which was no worse than our Ministry of Pensions and National Insurance offices, and no one was unduly unpleasant. We had decided to get these cards on hearing that entry to and departure from the country would be facilitated, being concerned about our holidays and particularly our final departure as the cards have to be surrendered, and not having one to surrender might be difficult.

Times of Zambia   20th August 1968

The first toothpaste to be made in Zambia. Cleanliness is King at Levers…(who are) giving the final impetus to yet another "Buy Zambia" enterprise by this forward looking group.

Letter 153

Well sometimes things do happen worth recording between Mondays and Wednesdays. Firstly I have had a huge bunch of flowers and Margie has announced she is pregnant, and believe it or not, there is a connection between the two. Margie has been wanting an addition to the family since Christmas, and as the months have passed, she has been getting more and more miserable and the gap between Michelle and a new baby was widening. Anyway, I rooted out my family planning booklet and going by her previous dates and things, arrived at a new date on the calendar and ringed it on her calendar and told her that that was THE night. She took the information home to her husband (poor fellow, I don't know what he must have thought) and duly carried out the book's instructions. Monday she went to the doctor's and announces the news yesterday, when the results of the test were known and today, I get a flipping bouquet of flowers, half a dozen roses and half a dozen carnations, delivered to the office in cellophane, and even her mother rang and spoke to me. Everyone is highly delighted, and we all had sausage rolls with our tea.

The second bit of news is that we have bought a new camera for our travels. Here they have little duty and are cheaper than the UK and of course RDL negotiated discount on it. It's a beautiful camera; a Canon with a light meter and rangefinder built in and as extras an ultraviolet filter, a lens hood and a telephoto lens with 8 times magnification. Richard saw his bank manager and he Okayed us going into the red with our holiday as he had the security of Richard's terminal pay. We bought it this afternoon and Richard has taken it and the brochures to work with him. I wonder if he brings it home still wrapped up or if he is as impatient as I am to have a fiddle with it.

I arranged my flowers in two separate containers, a bowl for the carnations and the roses in the vase Sally bought me for Christmas. They make such a display and it's nice having flowers around, just like at home.

Andre for the past week has been doing extra washing for two of the White's male visitors, and boy, has he had a lot, daily clean shirts for three of them and Richard, plus all the extra linen. Mrs W. said she would give him extra and good enough she gave him £2 for the extra washing, which was from Friday until today, and he couldn't tell me fast enough when I came in. Lets hope he doesn't booze it all. One thing is for sure, he won't have it left tomorrow.

I have studied the camera. Apparently you either set the shutter speed or aperture and then adjust your other setting depending on which you set first. I find it easier to choose the f setting, thus giving a certain depth of field and then adjusting the shutter speed until the automatic in the viewfinder is correct. A hairline moves across the O. It is quite unobtrusive. There is also automatic focusing, very useful. We have a time switch too and can take photos of us together on our own if you see what I mean. I have bought a black and white film and we will use it at the weekend.

☐

Times of Zambia   22nd August 1968

Zambia accuses Russians of acting like imperialists. Naked

aggression condemned by President Kaunda. The President assured Czechoslovakia that although Zambia "could not help, we really and spiritually support Czechoslovakia".

26th August 1968

21,000 houses are needed to solve our squatter problems …in Lusaka and Copperbelt areas.

Letter 154   26/8/68

It's 6 o'clock and I've just flopped into a chair with some coffee. Sally, Stuart, Sally's sister, Valerie and David are coming tonight and everything is well on the way and I'm having a breather before Richard comes home. Menu- roast pork, roasties, spinach, cauli, stuffing and applesauce, then paw paw, pears, ice cream and chocolate sauce. All nice and easy.

We spent Saturday afternoon at David's with his two lodgers, Roy, and Ken Norris, who worked at Price's when Richard worked there in his summer holidays. Ken arrived on Thursday and is very green. We only realise how acclimatised we are when someone new comes. Unfortunately there was a huge spider behind him, which I have since confirmed was poisonous. We sprayed it and it lay dying in its web and Pucci walked past Ken and licked his elbow and poor Ken nearly leapt over the verandah wall. We had a lovely afternoon and Pucci had a chat with his girlfriend next door. David came back with us to dog sit. I made him a shepherd's pie and fruit and cream and didn't feel like going out, as it smelled so good. However out we went and had a reasonable evening. The couple had gone to a lot of trouble with their braai and the food was good. The host asked Richard, who was drinking beer, if he hadn't seen the vodka. Apparently he had seen Richard drink vodka when we last went out. But it was on the company, hence the vodka. The fellow had bought a bottle of vodka especially, so you can see they had taken the trouble to please. We brought Marlene and Peter back and we sat and drank coffee until 12.30. It was actually nice going out and not worrying about fanny next door and whether the dog was being a pest. David said he lay at his feet snoozing all night.

When we came back from David's in the afternoon, fanny was standing on her doorstep. We pulled up outside White's to unload our car of chairs and stuff and she put her hands on her hips then pointed round the corner, indicating we should move it, as our big car was outside our place already. As we got out of the car, Elizabeth shouted that she had coffee on the go and to come in. This was what Richard wanted. If the woman had ignored us, we would have unloaded the car and driven away as we normally do, but her standing there like the Gestapo, made us mad. Richard was cross-mad and I was fed-up mad, having had a lovely afternoon and coming back to that. We stayed at Elizabeth's for half an hour. Ron was away for the weekend and Elizabeth said we could say we were having his space on loan. When we came out, she was sitting in her lounge, with the light on in the hall and the door open to watch us come back, so we sneaked in from the other side, and reluctantly Richard moved the car,

Which, incidentally, we had to hike to, when we went out an hour later. She habitually drives up and honks her horn, and her poor servant has to scurry out to take her bag out of the car. I'm going to paint "Big Brother is watching you" on her door when we go.

Yesterday Richard entered a golf competition and came second. He was so pleased and came home with a huge hors d'oeuvres dish with five glass dishes set in stainless steel. I'm going to christen it tonight. When Richard arrived, the other three people had agreed to bet a ball on the first nine, the second nine and the match. He concurred, but not enthusiastically, at the possibility of losing three balls at 6/6d each. He ended up winning three from each, nine balls in all £2.10.0d worth. So was he pleased with himself!

Good news too. All travel and hotels booked for home trip. We panicked on hearing the Kafue Bridge was closed from 6pm to 6am, due to the number of lorries bashing it in the dark. Richard rang the travel agent and asked if the times would be altered as we are on an overnight trip. She said it was O.K. as the northbound and southbound coaches met at this point and we would swap coaches. Richard then said, "So we'll walk across the bridge", and she said, "Oh no, we'll have to row you across". Fancy at two o'clock in the morning, with our suitcases, being rowed across the Kafue, in and out of the hippos and crocodiles. In fact, I rather hope we do, as it'll certainly be a yarn to tell, won't it?

Your letter arrived via Marlene, who put a note on it asking for the stamp. Have you one of the church? I think its 1/6. And any of the others will be snapped up by folks here, if you can get hold of any used ones.

Times of Zambia   27th August 1968

Bandits shoot three in raids on Copperbelt Houses.

Chapter 47   Margie and Marlene to rest.

Times of Zambia   **30th August 1968**

Dragnet out for "fun" poachers. Organised expatriate gang hunted by game rangers.

Letter 155   **29/8/68**

I've been doing your share of sick-visiting today. Margie wasn't so good and from all the symptoms, I ran her to the doctors at two o'clock and sure enough, he has given her injections to prevent a miscarriage and ordered her to bed until her innards settle. I ran her home and saw her into bed and left the nanny making tea for her and then went to tell Calvin and met him on the way home. After I had been back in the office for an hour, Richard rang to say that Marlene had been sent to bed with a pending miscarriage and would I go round. As it was 4.20 pm, I nipped up for some flowers and went on to her house. Peter was home minding Sally, and Marlene had all she needed, so I just tidied Sally's toys and stuff and got Marlene's shopping list. Whereas poor Margie was miserable, Marlene was more annoyed at missing three nights out in a row. However the doctor is calling to see both on Monday, so all that can be done now is to cross our fingers and hope for the best. It must be something in the air today.

David is coming tonight to put some extra wire on the radio aerial to make it fit along the window ledge instead of straight across, thus making it less obtrusive. I am at the moment making a steak and kidney pie with horrible ox kidney, and we have got, guess what, celery! I've added this and carrots. Yum. I've still to take Margie's shopping up tonight.

Supper here with Stuart, Sally, Sally's sister and David was a success, except for the fact that at 9o'clock all the lights went out. We had no candles or matches, just a torch. We drank our coffee and played guessing games until 10, when we decided to give up. Just as everyone was getting into their cars, the lights came on again and they all dashed back inside for more coffee for half an hour, when the lights went off again.

On Tuesday morning, we asked Andre what had happened to all the half used candles from the previous power failure and he said they were used ones so he had "tidied them". He's had strict instructions not to tidy the new ones.

The electricity was off for an hour on Tuesday and two hours last night. Tonight I have a pie in the oven, and so far the electricity has not gone off. I have been to Margie's and she is a lot more cheerful and is on a bed settee watching TV.

Richard and David are playing Scalextric on the table. David has done some soldering of Richard's lousy wiring and they have spent far more time improving the cars' performance and setting out the track, than racing.

Did I say that I have dyed my beige shoes orange? They don't look like new, but look almost new. It's quite good stuff. The shoes don't look dyed. In their beige state they were so shabby, they were fit only for the bin, so they have a new lease of life. I'm not wearing them until my hols. I've also bought a new swimsuit. The one Mrs L bought me for Christmas still doesn't fit even with the alterations, and is too short in the body.

Mrs L was always buying me things that were too small. She was obsessed with her own weight, whereas as long as my clothes fitted me, I didn't think about my weight. When the children were small she bought me a beautiful suede long skirt and waistcoat from her smart dress shop. She bought me a size eight. I was a twelve. When it didn't fit she exchanged it for a bigger one, a size ten. When I reported that this was too small too and that I really was a twelve, she refused to take it back as she didn't want the women in the shop to know she had such a fat daughter-in-law. It was a lovely outfit, but being suede there was no give in it. Years later it ended up in the Oxfam shop. I had never been able to wear it.

Times of Zambia

3rd September 1968

Oil together. It's no longer a pipe dream. President Kaunda of Zambia and President Nyerere of Tanzania turned a valve at the Ndola terminal of the K32 million TanZam pipeline yesterday and, to the cheers of thousands, ended Zambia's 32 month oil famine

Letter 156   2/9/68

On Friday we went to David's for supper and he and Ken had made a roast chicken with sausage and veg but no spuds, as they didn't know how to roast them. It was very tasty. We watched TV in the evening and Pucci played in the garden until late.

On Saturday afternoon Richard played in a golf competition and was second again, winning a serving spoon and fork in stainless steel. However he played to four below his handicap, therefore his handicap will be reduced and he won't win so easily anymore although he played his best round ever on Saturday. Richard wants to get his handicap to 18 so that he can join a UK golf club more easily on coming home.

(Never did join a golf club. There was never any spare cash and the experience would never compare with hopping next door at 7.30am and playing 18 holes before it got too hot.)

Well we have the suitcases down, but won't pack until Wednesday morning. We are due at the airport at 3.30. We are taking one car to Marlene's and one to David's for safekeeping and David is taking us to the airport. Richard is taking Pucci to kennels. I couldn't bear to, as he will be so excited going out in the car and then will cry so when we leave him. It seems such a dirty trick and we can't explain that we are coming back and not just deserting him. We are spoiling him. He has had minced meat and tomatoes tonight. He'll be on hippo meat next week! I'm more bothered about this spell in kennels than the long one, as here the employees work just for a living, whereas in the UK, kennel maids must be dog mad and will therefore treat them better as he is such a cute looking little chap. David is going to pick him up before the kennel closes at 12.30 on Saturday, as we get home late afternoon and he can therefore have Sunday to be ruined and settle back in. We have bought him a brand new flea collar, as we're taking no chances with insect life and we will bath him when he comes home (he'll be sorry he came home, when he sees the bath!).

Both Margie and Marlene are improved and things look as though they will be OK. I went to see Margie on Saturday. Her little girl is so cute. She is just 2 ½ and was still in her pyjamas when I arrived. She said she wanted a ride in 'auntie's' car. Margie said she was too grubby and had to put a clean dress on. Anyway Michelle went and picked a dress and underclothes and wiped her face with a flannel, and when dressed spent ages combing her hair, patting it down after combing. She had obviously watched Margie. She then went and fetched her best patent leather shoes and a huge patent bag of Margie's. I then had to take her on a ride to the PO to post a letter. We never thought she would complete getting ready and if she did, she would forget the purpose of it. She looked so quaint trooping along with her huge bag over her arm, and her letter to post. She wasn't happy on the way home, and said she wanted to go to Granny's. I said that Margie would wonder where she was, and she shook her head saying, "Mam sleeping. Mam got sore tummy. Michelle noisy and Sophie (the nanny) smack Michelle. Michelle go Granny's." She's not daft is she!

I want Richard to polish the cases. However he says that getting them down is a Daddy job and polishing is a Mummy job and I disagree. Polishing is a Daddy job and packing a Mummy job. The cases are either staying dusty or it's going to be an Andre job!

Letter 157   4/9/68

The Kilimanjaro Hotel.   Dar Es Salaam, Tanzania

Arrived safely on our 1st leg of journey. Just posting this to record a Tanzanian stamp, before moving to Kenya at 9.00 am tomorrow.

Letter 158

Nyali Beach Hotel, Mombasa, Kenya   Tuesday 10.9.68

I'm writing this on the beach after breakfast. The sun is strong but so is the wind, so we are going out for a couple of hours in a glass bottomed boat at 10.30 where the tide is at its lowest and we can go and look at the coral reef.

Yesterday we drove 80 miles up the coast to Malindi, where there are a few hotels and little else. It was a very pleasant drive including a trip on a ferry over a river where we got out of the car and sat with the locals, a thing we wouldn't do in Zambia. The locals here still wear beads and just skirts and silver arm bangles and things. I didn't take any photos of them, as it would have seemed rather rude, especially as they were taking no particular notice of us. Malindi is a fishing place and stank of fish but had a lovely beach and the hotel at which we had a drink was right on the beach and with every self-entertainment you could think of.

I didn't tell you that we flew over Zanzibar and its surrounding islands. It looked beautiful and they were all set on a coral reef and you could see all the various colours of the water for miles around the islands

Ten miles south of Malindi is the ruined Arab city of Gedi, set in the bush and overgrown. They are just starting to excavate it and it's rather weird. They have done a lot of work on a small corner but have just hacked paths through the undergrowth to various other buildings they have started uncovering. We took one of these paths to a mosque and saw the most gorgeous plants and butterflies, the latter of which Richard tried to photograph, unsuccessfully as you would no sooner focus than they would be off. We also heard a rustling near our feet which we knew to be a snake we had disturbed, but as neither of us knew whether it was going or coming we ran – aren't we cowards!

Gedi was magical. No one knows why it was abandoned. I checked on the Internet, but it appears very little work has taken place since we saw it. Of course, no sooner would it have been left untouched for a year, the jungle would have taken over.

Anywhere else it would have been declared a world heritage site and been covered with a glass and stainless steel dome.)

Later, we went out in this glass bottom boat and stopped on the edge of the coral reef where we drifted along watching the fish and coral and things. He anchored us to a section of reef, which was now above the water and said we could walk on it. It was a bit prickly underfoot but the coral had a generous spread of sand and weed. We spent about 20 minutes (5 of us) wandering along with the sheltered water on one side and the huge thundering Indian Ocean waves on the other. Mombasa is safe for bathing as there are no sharks inside the reef. Richard picked up a starfish in his hanky, as big as a dinner plate but when it put one of its arms around his hand, he decided to leave it where it was. We settled for two smaller ones, which seemed to be dead, and which are now very dead. The boatman said they would all be dead before the tide came in again anyway. There were lots of small pools in the reef with tiny fish and pretty plant life and in all we were out for 2 ½ hours, and for 10/- each we reckoned this to be worth the money.

We went back to the beach this afternoon with me in a dress, having caught too much sun on Sunday. However at three a squall blew up and it started to rain, so we came back and had some tea, and went into town for some paperbacks. Richard is sorry he did, as I did my souvenir shopping i.e. two Arab necklaces. I am very pleased with them. One is a sort of beaten silver links, and the other is a medallion with a tiger-eye stone in the middle (not a very good quality one). They both look as though they have just been dug up, and one style's similar to those in the museum at Gedi. I think it is just that they are traditional designs. Richard says I should get the Brasso on them. I wore one for dinner tonight and it looked most unusual. Richard retaliated by buying four wooden, what he calls "peanut bowls". I don't mind as he serves peanuts with his beer, in my fruit dishes and as I now only have four of these and can't get more to match (although I bought them here) it'll save breakages. *(Peanut bowls still being used fifty years later, which is more than the fruit bowls are. (Subsequently, in the UK, both necklaces were stolen by a man who came with a team to treat the wordworm, downstairs in Surrey. I caught him coming out of my room. He said he was just checking the upstairs floorboards and that he had put the carpet back so carefully, I wouldn't know he had been there. Nothing appeared* to have been disturbed and it was only when I went to put on my best watch some months later, that I found all my jewellery had gone. Nothing of any great monetary value, just sentimental stuff and I kept adding to the list for a number of years after. The woodworm company was nowhere to be found. This is where the Internet is so useful in tracking people down, both burglars and burgled.))

Remember Margaret buying me a tiny bean with elephants in it in ivory, which I lost on taking it to school? Well I found them in the junk shop I got the necklaces at, and bought one for me and two for the twins, which I shall put in their next letter, that is if I don't lose these!

I have just been in the bathroom to find that a few of my 'empty' shells, which I collected, have crawled up the wall, so they'll have to go back in the sea tomorrow!

We have a mixture of people in the hotel, but mainly the majority are Germans, who are as bad as South Africans. But unfortunately the English here are either weedy squirts or paddling with their trousers rolled up types and the Germans certainly adapt better to the heat. They are all on tours, the first tried by the hotel, and we seem to be one of the few coming on our own, although once, this hotel was for regulars and faithfuls, coming year after year. I think they have been hit by not being allowed to take South Africans and Rhodesians, as these were the people who used to frequent it. Mrs Cleveley in the office used to spend two months a year here!

The hotel is in a beautiful setting and for the price we are paying, good value. We were spoilt by that one night at The Kilimanjaro, as that is known as the best hotel in Africa, and that's why we went mad for the night.

Letter 159   13.9.68

Nyali Beach Hotel

Mombasa, Kenya

The manager here is a German so I don't know how he is McCrindle.

We call him Von Grundle.

We move on to Nairobi tomorrow, stopping tomorrow night at Kilaguni Lodge in Tsavo Game Park. It says in the brochure – 'in the heart of elephant country' and I'm petrified of meeting all those elephants. This is just a short note, just to let you know we are on the move.

I had a lovely tan yesterday but it is peeling today, although my arms and legs and face, which have been reasonably weathered over the last year or so, have got a good colour. Richard has also evened up his tan. His legs, arms and face had an excellent colour as you can probably see by the snaps but he was still white where his shirt and shorts were. He has now lost his 'white shirt' and looks very well.

Chapter 48   Nairobi

Letter 160   16.9.68

Panafric Hotel Nairobi, Kenya

Well we are on the last leg of our trip now. We thoroughly enjoyed the change over from Mombasa to Nairobi. We set off early Saturday from Mombasa and arrived at the game park entrance about 11. We drove straight to the lodge for lunch, which took us an hour, as it is a 20-mile per hour speed limit. The main road (a dirt road) in the park was smoother than the lousy pot holed main Mombasa/Nairobi road. We intended to dawdle in the park on our way to the lodge but we were detoured around 30 miles to another entrance as rain had made our first choice of road impassable. We had a super lunch and the lodge is marvellous. It is a main lodge with groups of thatched chalets forming an enclosure, which is walled in between and contains a pool and a lovely garden. The chalets have terraces overlooking the waterhole, which was presumably responsible for the siting of the lodge. We sat outside on the terrace until about two watching zebra and deer come and go. It was very relaxing. We then decided to do a little safari and off we went. The scenery was fantastic, beautiful rolling plains and hills, and a variety of foliage from grassy plain to thorn scrub. We saw mainly deer, zebra and some giraffe. It's great fun spotting them and keeping our eyes skinned. However we were disappointed not to see any lion, but had we stayed all week we still might not have seen any (rather like Chester Zoo). We stopped at a waterhole with a viewing platform where you can see hippo below, which we did and crocs too. I wasn't fussy on being out of the car even though there was a ranger at this point. When we pulled up, I spotted a tiny monkey on a rock and rolled down the window to photograph him. Richard shouts 'look out' and apparently a monkey had jumped onto the roof and over the side and I had to push him off with the camera with one hand and roll the window with the other. He then sat on the bonnet with his nose against the window looking in at us. Didn't he realise we had come to look at him! As Richard says, perhaps some giraffe runs a trip to Kilaguni waterhole advertising it as the perfect place to spend your evening, eating and drinking in comfort, watching humans only 100 yards away feeding and drinking in their natural surroundings.

In the evening we had another super meal with strawberries and cream (in which Kenya specialises). Yummy. We then sat with coffee watching the waterhole with the aid of our binocs, although this only helped us see detail. The pool is lit by an 'artificial moon', a very pale glow, and we saw allsorts, deer mainly, a civet cat and jackals. Then came the elephant, first two huge monstrous bulls and gradually out of the shadows from all sides loomed sixteen elephants in all. We watched them quarrel, fight and play for over two hours, when they drifted away. These fellows are so huge; they are terrifying and with tusks so long!

Letter 161   19/9/68

Ndola again

After spending a fantastic evening watching the waterhole we went to bed in our little chalet. However the lights went off at 11.30 (generator closed down) and after sleeping restlessly, at 4.00 I awoke to hear growls and snufflings and various other unsettling noises outside and there were small animals running between the thatch and the ceiling boards. I was petrified and I woke Richard and he grovelled around for a candle and I could only doze off again with the light flickering. I was glad when the dawn broke. At 8.30ish we did a roundabout tour out of the park and saw deer and giraffe and other small game and then the thing I had been dreading. To our right was a huge bull elephant. Richard stopped and was photographing like mad, while all I could do was watch it, watching us with its ears starting to wave. Anyway it started to sway towards us and Richard started the engine and we eased away, and its ears subsided. They are monstrous things not like the moth eaten tiddling things in zoos. They are really prehistoric. Anyway we saw lots more and up to ten at a time, but they were all from 50 to 100' from the road, which was a much happier distance. One feels so vulnerable in a teeny weeny car.

We then had 150 miles to go on leaving Tsavo and we arrived in Nairobi for lunch. The hotel was very good but unfortunately their new pool wasn't finished, which was a disappointment although their tariff was lower because of this. We window-shopped. The shops in Nairobi are just splendid (comparatively) and we oohed and aahed all afternoon. Richard wasn't daft taking me around on a Sunday afternoon, when they were all closed. On Monday we did a snake and bird park and the museums and public buildings and sat in a park eating ice cream, but late Monday, we couldn't see what we could do for another 5 days especially as the temperature was only in the 60s and as we had seen most things already (we intended half days for this, that and the other, but with having the car and leaving the hotel at 9 and arrived back for supper at night we did most of the things in the two days). So we dashed to BOAC and they altered our flight from Sat to Wednesday. We should have spent 2 weeks in Mombasa and the odd 3 / 4 days in Nairobi. On Tuesday we actually went in the shops and I bought a small clay African head and some raffia coasters. Most things although beautiful, catered for Americans and were from £10 upwards. Even the clay model I fancied was £4/10/-. The one I chose was 25/- and the mats were 15/- and a banana palm picture (like fretwork) was 10/-. The mats and picture were Richard's choice.

We took a sandwich lunch, and I bought some beautiful flowers for Winnie Sword. *(A relative of ours, whose husband had been a policeman seconded to the Kenyan Police and had been murdered by the Mau Mau)* The shop made up a gorgeous bouquet with 1 dozen red carnations, 2 dozen daffodils (which I've not seen in Africa before) and some iris, for £1.0.0, all in cellophane with a card.

We went to the cemetery and his grave is in a pleasant spot, shaded by trees, and a little man came with a watering can and a pottery urn, and I spent a pleasant half hour arranging the flowers. It was worth the trouble to do that, as the flowers here are so expensive, and it's not often I can do it. You can tell Win that the grave is well looked after, and with being gravelled, it looks neater than the gardened ones. The flowers made a lovely show and we have taken some snaps to show Win how it looked when we arrived and of the flowers.

We then went on to Nairobi Game Park (which being only 44 sq. miles has no elephants). We cruised around for over three hours and saw allsorts of game (mainly deer, zebra, wart hogs, giraffe and ostrich). Then as we were coming out we saw a ranger car off the road (or track) and in the middle of the plain. It was just still. Anyway, it looked from the position through the binocs, that it was lion, so we found the track the car had made through the grass, and followed and sure enough there was this lion just sitting there with ½ dozen lionesses and cubs all curled up asleep. The ranger motioned that we take photos which we did and when we had finished another car came and we turned and went back, thoroughly satisfied at having seen our lions. A very fitting end to our hols. In the evening we blew out on a night out at the best eating place in Nairobi, which was super and the food was smashing, so all in all we had a cram full three days instead of a drawn out six days and saved a little (or rather didn't spend so much).

We arrived home at 5.30 and got a taxi to Marlene's to pick up the car, but she insisted we stay for drinks and then for dinner. We had also unfortunately spoiled a surprise welcome home dinner which she had planned for Sat, and invited David and his lodgers. We picked up Pucci this morning and he is so pleased to be home and keeps putting his head on my knees and giving long contented sighs.

Well before you turn the page and hear my next news, which I have been saving, take a big swig of brandy. I'm six months pregnant – perhaps you ought to have another swig. I've been keeping it secret until now, although we have been bursting to tell you, as you would no doubt worry, especially with me going on safari, and flying. However there it is, and your grandchild is due on Jan 4th giving us four clear weeks before we come home. The doctor is pleased with my progress, and also said we could happily plan our journey home, as it would in no way harm junior and the cruise could only be beneficial to me.

However, we are officially telling you in our next letter, after my 6 monthly check-up and Richard is writing to his mother too. However I couldn't bear the thought of his letter arriving first and you hearing the news from Mrs L instead of me, so just you tell anyone you like except Mrs L until the next letter arrives. I won't say anymore now except that I hope you will be as thrilled as we are and that I and baby (who is kicking away like mad) are both well (touch wood!)

Letter 162   22/9/68

By the way, you'll have to ask Auntie Kit to get down the cot from her loft, as we shall need it if we stay with you when we come home, as your grandchild will then be over three months old. You will now understand why all my new dresses for my hols were all high waists and tents! And also why I've not yet answered your question as to why I'm not playing any tennis at the moment, and also why you have commented that I perhaps look fatter in the face, as I was 4 months pregnant in that photo of me up the tree.

I have sent to "Mothercare" for £30 worth of basic items i.e. nappies, pram sheets and blankets, a few nighties and stretch suits but nothing exciting. I'm relying on Mrs L for cardigans and things, although I've made two incomplete jerseys, both incomplete because when I went for more wool it was sold out. Even with postage and duty (sea mail – keep your fingers crossed!) it will cost no more, and also things are available which they aren't here. I have also ordered a bottle warmer and flask mainly for the boat home. There is no sense in you sending anything here as our luggage home is restricted, so he/she can live in a stretch suit until we get home and then you can go mad and buy quilted coats and things for the cold as we can't get or even need anything like that here.

We spent most of our holiday spends on a second-hand pram/carrycot on wheels. The previous owner was the wife of the Israeli Ambassador. It was £17/10/- and cost £5 to send back to Zambia, but new would have cost 30 odd pounds. I reckon it would have cost £14 at home. However, he (I'll call him 'he' for convenience) will have to practically live in it until we get home, so we wanted a reasonable one. It is also weather proof and I can use it until he needs a pushchair. I would have liked a crib, but by the time he arrives home he will be cot size. Never mind.

(The hassle we had at the airport with the pram. Freight cost was worked out by volume not weight, so the first chap measured it from handle to floor. So we then took the cot off and collapsed that down and then folded the chassis down. To reduce the price even further we took the wheels off and put them in our suitcase. Seems a

performance, but prams were not available in Zambia, not even second-hand. The wheels never fitted on again properly. I remember having Andrew as a new baby in the pram, Nigel in a harness sitting on a tea tray on the top, when three of the wheels came off at once and rolled down the hill. The tea tray slipped off and Nigel landed on Andrew. I had to unstrap Nigel and carry him under my arm and leave Andrew in a pram at forty-five degrees while I fetched the wheels. Is it any surprise that I bought myself a Silver Cross for my grandchildren?)

The doctor reckons a cruise is ideal and says not everyone is so lucky. We will both be on hand to attend to him and I will not be concerned with anything like cooking, and he will be on the ship long enough to establish a routine.

I am working half days again during October and am then finishing. I shall then be seven months, which leaves me only two months to wait, one of which unfortunately will be without the company of Pucci.

On Friday I went to see Margie. Unfortunately the baby had started growing in the fallopian tube and she has had it and the tube removed. She can still have children as she still has the remaining one, but the doctor said her blood count was far too low and that she was undernourished and must either take a holiday or finish work, so she is not coming back to work. However her little girl is a tonic and is keeping her very cheerful. I also went into work, as when I rang Sue to see how Margie was she said there had been changes and I must come in. I was rather cross as my desk has been moved and all my personal things put in a tray and some new local staff taken on to take Margie's place. Mrs Giles who is in her late 60s has also been taken ill and has gone to hospital in Salisbury leaving the wages job vacant. My own work is up to the ceiling and I am expected to clear this and train an African which is OK, but the snag is that there is a rumour that I am to do Mrs Giles' job too until new staff arrives. This would be too much. If I were taken off my own job and the African left to train himself, I would not work the month out, as the only point in me stopping the extra month mornings was to train someone else, as they hadn't found a replacement. This is all Hitchman's doing, not Jack Pawson's, as he is now Head Office. Mrs King, Kent and Sue are most unhappy, as they feel that they will be pressurised to leave. This will happen, not by management but by circumstances. We have already noticed the ladies' lavatories becoming unpleasantly dirty (we have a new receptionist too) and it is these sorts of discomforts that will make our super office disintegrate. It's a pity the changes can't have come more evenly, as we worked so well as a team as you know. We could absorb new staff easily one at a time, but not in such volume.

Anyway, I look forward to hearing your reactions to our news.

Letter 164   27/9/68

Thursday. Well by today you will no doubt have our news. I wonder what your reaction is!

On Monday I went to the doctors for my six monthly check-up and everything, touch wood, is fine. The doctor can now hear his heart beating loud and clear. He also told me to start relaxation classes given by a private person at her own home, so I went today at 2 o'clock. The girl is only about 26 and a trained physiotherapist and there were four other fatties there. One due next week, another in two weeks, one the same as me, and the other in between. The exercises were not strenuous, mainly muscle control and consciousness of various muscles – a bit like yoga I suppose. The relaxation was super. I was nearly asleep. We were relaxed and had to screw up all our facial muscles and relax them. I don't know how the girl instructing us kept her face straight. We must have looked awful. I'm sorry Daddy, that for the next 3 months you are going to get blow-by-blow details.

I have given Pucci the leg of lamb bone as it's only a little one (too small for Andre) and he doesn't know what to do with it. He is chewing it but not managing very well, not gnawing it or anything but he's enjoying it. I've tried to take it from him but he picks it up and hides under the table. He is taking advantage of my current hugeness and reluctance to chase him.

My parcel arrived safely from Mothercare and included the following. Tell me if there is anything that you think I still need.

2 pairs pram sheets

1-doz nappies (I hope to use disposable on the trip)

1 waterproof pram sheet

2 pram blankets

4 woollen vests, 2 cotton vests

6 nappy liners (to stop moisture seeping back onto his behind)

2 pop-on waterproofs, 3 waterproof ordinary (Richard thinks this child is going to be permanently wet with all these things)

2 woolly nighties, 2 cotton nighties

4 growy suits

2 bath towels, 1 bottle heater, 1 bottle warm-keeper

1 Bri-nylon sleeping bag, 1 brush & comb, 1 nail scissors

This seems to cover essentials. He can live in the nighties and the suits until we arrive home. In fact vests and nappies are the order of the day here, fancy dresses etc. being rather hot.

Chapter 49   Hot

Letter 165   29/9/68

I received your letter posted 24.9.68 on Sat. morning after Richard had been to work, and I told him I had cheated and written to you early but he didn't mind and said that knowing his mother it, was probably the best idea.

I'm very glad you are pleased. I knew you would be, but thought you might either be cross at us for not waiting until we got home (when I should be 26 before I had one) or at not telling you before, but as you see we had excellent reasons for both.

I'll now answer all your questions, which I've probably touched on in my last few letters but still – I'm having him at Ndola Hospital which is shabby, but which has competent staff and a good atmosphere. The doctor is Dr Hayes and the best in the area and there is also a surgeon gynaecologist resident in Ndola. In fact I'm probably as well off here as I would be in a production line like Clatterbridge. Here babies are only born every few days and there are usually less than half a dozen in at a time. Also, I will have met these girls previously at relaxation classes.

The whole procedure is expensive but we have a medical insurance, which pays for most and the company will pay the rest, as medical bills are covered by contract. I'm not getting any baby furniture. A cot would only involve cot bedding and is not in any case necessary for the month we shall be here with him. I'll borrow a bath and he can use his carrycot to sleep in. He can sleep in our room possibly, as the spare room will be taken up with packing cases at that time! If Mrs L knits, it better be for three months or older, as it won't need any cardis here and only the odd one on the way home.

How can he be South African if born in Zambia? If anything he'll be

Zambian! However we will register him at the British High Commission. I'm going to write so as to avoid any pitfalls re passport etc. He'll be christened at home, if anywhere, but I don't even know that I'll have him christened. I don't know any suitable godparents, and no one that I would entrust with the upbringing, religious or otherwise of my child. There's only Tony and Joan and they are Catholics. I'm sorry if it means being done out of a do. I'll speak to our vicar, but he'll probably say go ahead because he hasn't done a christening for ages and he likes using his christening robes.

I shall repeat (again touching wood!) that I am fit, except for being more tired in the afternoons at work, but these will be OK with me working mornings from Tuesday. Junior is very active – in fact I think there's half a dozen fighting around in there. I'm not fat. I've not put on any noticeable weight anywhere but around my potbelly! I was 118 lbs. or so before and am now 131 lbs. – and the doctor is happy with this. And Hilda should just see my cleavage! It quite makes up for having a fat middle.

Daddy, aren't you glad I told you now instead of before, because instead of 8 months of this you'll only get three! Perhaps I should tag on a supplementary page labelled 'Gory Details' because you'll suffer every twinge of this one more than you did the last one (me!) otherwise.

It is 5.30pm now and we have been sitting in David's garden since lunch. They have left us the key and Richard has cleaned the engine and body of the Minx as he did the Imp last week. He is just on the final polish now and then we will go. David and Ken have gone to Vic Falls on an all in day trip by plane and are due back at 8, and are coming to us for some supper. It's been like a Sunday afternoon should be. Pucci has run around for the past three hours and is now flat out with his tongue hanging out.

David came to us most apologetically yesterday, as he had been invited out to dinner and forgot until the fellow said 'see you tonight'! This meant no dog sitter. Anyway Enid has no dog so we took Pucci along and left him in the car with his rug and a plate of supper and biscuits. He was fine, but after dinner Enid looked out of the window and she could see his little face looking out of the car, and he looked so pathetic –

419

although he has loads of room in the car and plenty of air etc. especially with the back seat down – remember we got my wardrobe into the back of the Minx! Anyway she brought him in and until 10 when she went to bed, Anne their 11-year-old daughter played ball and things in the hall with him. We played darts on the terrace until 1.00! And Pucci sat and watched us in between sniffing around the garden.

Monday. Had a hectic day today. I have been shopping last week for patterns and material for this year's office uniforms. What an exasperating job. I chose 6 patterns in one shop and they had only <u>1</u> size of <u>1</u> pattern! It was the same in the two other pattern shops. I had to buy 4 sizes of 4 similar patterns to get the design in 10-16 sizes! Then material. We wanted 25 yards of each colour material and similar patterns on 4 dresses, but no shop had any suitable rolls with more than 25 yards on (25-30 yards is a full roll, and once one person buys a length then it is useless to us). However this morning I went to a wholesaler and after a little reluctance on their part and hearing I wanted at least 100 yards they took me to the store. The materials were mainly plain and check but in a variety of colours and qualities so I instantly spotted a shelf of these and they had four colours so I took a roll of each at 9/11 yard (2 x 28 yds, 1 x 30 yds and 1 x 35 yds). However I saw our last year's uniform material which we bought wholesale at 17/11 yd (linen) and asked the price and was told 11/6 a yard. What we could have saved! The stuff is drip-dry terylene/cotton. I was then dashing around with buying orders and cheques and bought 32 zips in various sizes and colours, and 32 reels of cotton. Mrs Kent and Mrs King have asked me to make theirs (at 25/- per dress – so that's £10) but I am not rushing so don't worry and will just do as much as I feel like. The back room can be the sewing room! Unfortunately both girls' are unusual size 16s. However as there is extra material I needn't be too afraid of making mistakes. I now have to cut off the lengths and make up parcels for everyone with appropriate zips. I even have allowed for one hook and eye per dress.

I go on mornings tomorrow. Unfortunately my replacement, unknown to him, is suspected of a large fraud at his previous place of employment (guess where!) so I await the outcome of investigations. This puts me in a spot, knowing this and unable to say anything as yet. At least I can keep an eye on him. *(I have obviously not said anything in case my letter was opened. This fellow worked for Richard. He had A levels and was very confident and well turned out and charming, but they began to suspect he was running fiddles with the wages and were gathering evidence to prosecute him when he took up my job. Richard had to get in touch with my boss and tell him what was happening and advise him not to let him handle any cash until it was sorted. The following morning the police went to pick him up and he had done a midnight flit into the Congo, having been tipped off. With A levels and the Zambianisation programme he could have been running the company in a few years. Pity I don't recall his name. Maybe he is running computer scams in Nigeria.)*

Times of Zambia   2nd October 1968

Thousands flee homes in riots. As thousands of refugees from riot torn Old Kanyuma township streamed back to their houses yesterday, ANC leader Harry Nkumbula claimed that moves were afoot to ban his party.

3rd October 1968

K70,000 buys Munda Wonga Botanical gardens for the nation. The ten and a half acre gardens, a popular tourist resort and pleasure destination was bought from its owner Mr. Ralph Sader, who has devoted all of his spare time and money over the past eighteen years to developing the gardens.

I am delighted to read that Munda Wonga is now a fully-fledged member of BGCI, (Botanical Gardens Conservation International) which supports plant conservation and education worldwide and whose illustrious members support each other.

Letter 166   4/10/68

A very quicky letter as we went out last night and I forgot to get cracking on your letter as we had visitors.

Valerie Lapthorne

Yesterday afternoon I went to relaxation classes and one girl rang to say she didn't think she was going to make it, so we should see her announcement in the paper shortly. It's funny to think that in just three months I shall probably be ringing up to say that too!

I started some sewing at 3.30 and David came at 6 to dog-sit and then Ron White (just back from UK again) came to say he was back, and when Richard arrived I was doing David's supper and we had two visitors supping. At seven we went to Sally and Stuart's for a braai and had a good evening.

I received your letter after the official announcement, on Wednesday but still haven't heard from Mrs L. Wasn't it a jolly good job I wrote beforehand!

I love my daisy slide. It's ever so pretty. I wore it out last night. I need something frivolous to make me feel nice, now that I'm getting huge (hugeish!)

The weather here is stinking hot. "Stinky, sticky, sweaty 'ot". Everyone is irritable and lethargic, hence why they call it 'suicide' month. The only breeze is a hot one, like opening an oven door.

I am well on the way with my first four dresses and have cut out the prototype of my next four in case I finish the first lot over the weekend. My second lady is a lot less fussy than the first and if I suggest altering this, that or the other, she readily agrees with me. Even so I let the pattern out 2 inches in the centre as a guess and I needed it!

Times of Zambia 4th October 1968

President Kaunda has sent a circular to all electoral offices and returning officers warning that incompetence or dishonesty will not be tolerated in the course of the forthcoming general election and instructing all officers concerned to keep themselves free from any political interference or pressures.

6th October 1968

Gang holds mother at gunpoint. Miner's wife and three children locked up as armed men walk out with goods worth K700.

Letter 167   8/10/68

Your letter no. 167 received on Saturday morning when I went to Richard's office to see his new desk and chair (very posh).

Daddy, please rescue my wooden train out of the shed. I think it needs just new wheels and a coat of paint. Let me know, as I shall repair it, as in the toy catalogue from Galts, these trains are from £7-£8. *(still in the loft)*

I daresay, Mummy, that I'll let you send something, as an oz or two won't make so much difference, and I know that I was longing to buy up all the gorgeous baby clothes in Nairobi, and your choice must be even wider. What would be lovely is one of those angel tops (that is if you've not already spotted something you like). As babies here just wear vests in the day, these are posh to put on for visiting and showing off, and I've nothing in the pretty line. Everything is calculatedly practical, as you can see by my list. Won't we have a super spend on baby stuff when I get home! That's one consolation for all the abominable clothes available here.

Still no sign of our second roll of slides. It's a 24hr service in Nairobi and Mrs King's were all waiting for her when she returned to work. They have been away three weeks now. I hope your snaps all turn out OK. If your camera has had it daddy, you can have my Sportsman, now that we have our new one, it's the one that took our colour prints so you can see it's in good working order.

I was mad when I came in at lunchtime. Remember me saying that my plants had been pulled up while on holiday? Well my huge creeper is thick on the terrace latticework about 10ft high and 6ft wide. It separates us nicely from next door and from the road, and is privacy making. Well it grows on a single stem, which is very woody and about 1" thick at the base. It was all limp and dying so I went to tell Andre it needed watering when I realised it had been cut at the base about 6" from the soil. The whole stem had been cut through. Andre said he didn't notice anyone except the normal gardener who does the lawn. Andre wouldn't have done it, as he takes time to train all the new shoots into any gaps and it's just as much his creeper as mine. I felt like taking a chopper to someone. I can't think who is doing it. If the caretaker had thought it against regulations surely she would have told us, although it's been there for two years at least! I was so blazing mad.

On Sunday, we spent the afternoon at David's and he came back for supper and last night, Ron White, Ken Norris, Roy, Rodger and David came for supper (what a bachelor night). Elizabeth is coming back on Sunday. Fortunately Richard takes my car and she won't know I'm home in the afternoons. I won't mind in November, but this month I'm up to my eyes in dressmaking. I'm at it from 2 until 6 with a break to start supper. Yesterday Margie and her friend called at 2.15 and left at 5 (hence my letter being a date late) and I didn't do a thing. Today I have given Mrs Kent's four a final press (I had to redo the hems as she thought perhaps they were in fact too short by half an inch – she tells me after I've sewn them, not when they are pinned! The trouble is that she can't sew and doesn't know what's involved). I then cut out Mrs King's four and tacked two to try on tomorrow. I'm thinking of asking the other couple in the queue, to find a dressmaker on the pretext that I'm too slow.

It's still roasting hot here and we are having a lot of trouble with mosquitoes. We spray the bedroom an hour before bedtime and the ventilators and go in and out shutting the door after us, but they still wake us up. One night I counted twenty-nine bites on my arms and legs and even on my behind where my nightie rides up. Fortunately we have cream, which we slosh on and they are gone by morning. I'm still covered in scabs where I've scratched at them in my sleep. We have tried tucking the sheet up to our chins but in this heat it's impossible. As we only wake at 2ish I think they must come in through the ventilators.

Tell Auntie Vera that we also now let people in and out through two-inch gaps in the door, as there are hoards of moths about. There is one above me now around the lamp. They are huge, with brown furry bodies. Fortunately I only dislike them when they fly around my face.

Things are hectic at work as my replacement has not returned and I'm doing my own job plus weekly wages to be accumulated and paid at the end of the month, as the wages clerk (Mrs Giles) is sick. Most of my calculations are guesswork and I bet there will be a queue of complaints at the end of the month. Well, I've only 17 more working mornings. Margie goes to the pool (9d swimmers, 6d non-swimmers!!) which is fairly empty in the mornings, so I shall go every morning with her until the rains, as the air will be good for me and Mrs Chapman (the physiotherapist at my class) said swimming is excellent for all the right muscles.

I've tried Richard on names, but all he can suggest is Bert and Fred and as you can imagine the names I fancy, we never get very far

Times of Zambia   7th October 1968

Foreign Traders under fire. Zambians will triumph over "selfish" barriers to speed the economic handover. Southern province Minister of State said that Zambians were waging an economic war against foreign traders and businessmen.

10th October 1968

Public theft rate soaring claims MP. The incidence of theft by public servants has increased "manifold" over the past few years…At one time it was comparatively rare and severely dealt with, but this was no longer the case There also in some cases seems to be a certain reluctance to prosecute.

Letter 168   10/10/68

Were all your timetables accepted at the Union meeting? Is there any improvement in the turns for a 5-day week or are they worse consequently. I hope your cold is now gone, Daddy. This year I am so used to our seasons here. I have to think twice to realise you are now approaching winter. The sweat is rolling down my nose and I have a pint jug of lime at my side and it's ten past eight. Brother, it's hot!! I haven't had a cold for over a year (touch wood!)

Coming home we will only have two suitcases, a holdall and a carrycot so you see we are limited and we are sending a cabin trunk on, three or four weeks beforehand, with our stuff required on voyage, so you see all the baby stuff must come with us. I had set my heart on a crib with frills and things, but have had to scrap this idea. Never mind. I think, Daddy, that you must never let Mummy out with more than her train fare, the way she is browsing around the shops!

You are paying 1/- for a lemon!? When I think that they are falling off David's trees for lack of use. And we give aid to Zambia! Zambia needs to give UK lemon aid. (What a horrible pun).

If you win on Ernie you can come out in January and travel back with us.

Today I went to my class, and it was so nice after belting around the office in this heat. I nearly fell asleep. One of the girls has gone off pop. Anneke (a Dutch girl) is end of November, then Diane (the little fat girl) is 19th Dec, then me 2wks after and then Rosemary 4wks after that, so there are 2 before me. I won't think of it. It gives me the jitters! I'll never remember all my breathing. The idea of this psychoprophylaxis – or what have you, is to strengthen the muscles beforehand, and the breathing is to alleviate pain at various stages mainly by giving you something to do and concentrate on, rather than being overwhelmed by pain. The relaxation bit is to help you relax properly in between times ready for the next onslaught.

I'm glad I've got my pram and parcels, as the other girls are having such trouble and are relying on people in the UK or South Africa to send things on request, so you see I'm very well organised.

You should see my factory. All the dresses in various stages on the clothes airer. Everything is tidy and Andre sweeps and empties the basket during the morning so I start tidy everyday. I have finished Mrs Kent's four, and finished one of Mrs King's, the other three being in various stages of tacking. I'm pleased with my progress.

Poor Richard came home at 6.45, had supper, and it's now nine and he is still working. It's not his own work. A group of clerks got in a mess with a ledger while Richard was on holiday and didn't balance and they didn't do anything about it, and went from bad to worse. Richard has just found out that they were thousands of kwacha out and has brought two cabinet trays of debtors' cards home. They are not even filed properly and some of the terrible mistakes a child of ten wouldn't have made. Just when he thinks he's getting somewhere, he's back in the bag of detail again. He is just sitting there shaking his head and tearing his hair. I'd better make some coffee.

Photo of me and one of Rich. The one of me is my favourite. I'm in an old fort looking out of a spyhole to the Indian Ocean. Who says I'm fat. Look at my gorgeous hollow cheekbones. See how long my hair is? I'm getting a couple of inches off it soon.

Chapter 50   Inventory

Times of Zambia   11th October 1968

In one of the most amazing documents ever to be tabled before parliament, Zambia's Auditor general, yesterday flayed Ministries and Government Departments for "confusion, lack of planning, unconstitutional spending, inexcusable lack of control and making a monkey of the law." He revealed that millions of kwacha are unaccounted for.

Letter 169   14/10/68

As we seem to have to take on a new tenant – I suppose Mrs L has told you, would you please buy for us <u>6</u> new <u>cheap</u> chairs in as near as possible teak finish. I reckoned on not more than £6 each but am behind on prices in the UK now. We would rather spend £36 than ruin our leather chairs especially as we have the other four to match. Sad, but one of the penalties of an abroad post. The rest we will have to take a chance on. Mrs L seems to think we would not want to re-let and said to someone that we would only let to February anyway! I'm afraid we would let until at least the end of March, as if we have no rent, then we can't pay our mortgage and insurance standing orders. I don't fancy the house left empty through the winter anyway.

I'm getting one of those little baby chairs. They are popular here and even have little sunshades. It will be useful to prop junior close by while we have our meals if he isn't sleeping. They can only be used after 1 month old, and as a high chair and swing or car seat if you have all the attachments.

We are paying more now for letters, as the little post clerk who does

Richard's mail is very keen and weighs all the letters. However she is also keen on catching the relevant post so it is worth paying any extra.

I have finished my second lot of 4 dresses today, and nice they look too. I finished them at the weekend and tried them on my lady this morning and as none needed any alterations I trimmed, tidied and pressed them this afternoon and then cut out my next four, which are a size 14 and need no alteration to the pattern. It has no sleeves, a front tab and collar and looks pretty even being a size smaller than the size 16s. I have tacked one to try tomorrow, to use on a guide for the others. It is taking me roughly a week for each set of four as I have done eight in 2 weeks. It's nice to have a slight change of design.

On Saturday we took some snaps around Ndola, and went to Kent Park to walk the dog and then to Marlene's to see her new suite (Gimson & Slater and a terrible price – but such an improvement on the other cardboard effort). On Sunday, such a hectic day! I was up at 7 and did some washing after breakfast. I then made a cheese/onion/egg flan for lunch, two dozen cheese scones (a success) and one dozen jammy scones. Sally, Stewart and David arrived for lunch and then the chaps went to play golf. This arose after Stewart and David teased Richard about his keenness for golf. So Rich offered to give them a game. They arrived back at five and wolfed all the scones! Helped by Rubners, who called with some newspapers. We had a lovely full house and made such a noise laughing and talking (probably get an eviction order tomorrow!) Good job I did all that baking! The lads thoroughly enjoyed their game. After going over every detail of each hole and every stroke, we had our supper, a huge leg of lamb and things. After supper we showed our cine and slides (I hired a projector for cine and Sally borrowed one for slides). Our holiday snaps are lovely, although our second reel of game shots is still missing.

Don't we have trouble! My creeper is now completely dead and my chameleon after straining himself going brown for a few days has disappeared.

My replacement has done a midnight flit to Dar-es-Salaam, so perhaps I'll get someone else – probably at the beginning of next month after I've left! Ah well, it won't be my worry, although I would have liked to do a proper handover as no-one else knows the details of my job! It's not detailed in codebooks like the Civil Service.

How about Nigel Jonathan and Clare Louise? Richard just grunts and is no help. He definitely won't have Cressida or Gemma or Kate. Mean thing!

Times of Zambia   17th October 1968

President Kaunda yesterday dubbed Britain's new proposals for a settlement in Rhodesia as a despicable surrender to racism.

Letter 170   16/10/68

Don't overdo the knitting and strain your eyes. You've not long to finish it though and post it. (11 weeks to countdown).

I'd like one of those bags. I think I said in my last letter I was going to get a sponge bag for the bits, and this sounds just the job for travelling. Wet nappies! Ugh! What on earth have we let ourselves in for! Pucci won't be put out. He knows all about his new brother (sister). But one always has to be prepared for jealousy between the 1st and 2nd child. Poor old Pucci won't see the new addition until he's 6 months old. Two years is a good gap between one's youngsters isn't it?

Pucci's trip is in the process of being booked on a flight for the 12th or 5th December, depending on availability. That leaves me only three weeks on my own.

I've been dressmaking again this afternoon and received my first cheque for £5 for Mrs King's 4 dresses. However I'm not doing anymore – 25/- each or not! Mrs Mc's that I'm doing now are the nicest. Probably Mrs Kent, who, when she saw Mrs King's collarless ones, decided she should have had no collars, will decide that she should have had no sleeves on seeing Mrs Mc's.

Went to my class today. I enjoy it. I'm very good at relaxing. We are really briefed on what to expect and at what stage to do what, like fire drill. She has a baby of about 12 months and carried out her own drill and said she was completely in control except for the last ten minutes when she was a bit overwhelmed. Ah well, enough gory details.

Things are hectic at work. I've a new clerk to train as from tomorrow. I hope he does OK. I'm also doing the wages still! It doesn't look as though Mrs Giles, the wages clerk is going to be in before payday. I couldn't keep up this pace and am definitely leaving on 31st. I shall be seven months then anyway, and it's stinking hot. I'm not looking forward to November. It's so noisy in the flats with nattering mothers and screaming kids and houseboys throwing coffee parties with all their cronies on the grass. I am going to the pool for an hour in the morning anyway so can just potter in the afternoon starting to clear out for packing. We should know in the next month or so what is going to happen next. However to me, a house with a 6ft fence and soundproof walls and no neighbours is high on the list of requirements. Never, never again a flat except as an 'in transit' home.

I'm having trouble with my knitting and have given up until I feel the urge again. I'm a lousy knitter. I have managed a cardi, and bonnet and boots to match for coming home. I have just received my latest Mothercare catalogue, and want to order loads of 'unnecessary' stuff. By the way what do you fancy being called? Have I asked you before? If not, have a think, as you'll get first choice. Granny? Too old? Nanny – oh no! Nana? Grandma? Grandpa? (not you mummy) Gramps (sounds about 90!) Granddad? Or just Chul (not respectful enough!) Probably whatever Jnr calls you first will stick, however derivative. So you may end up being Chullychully! Dreadful thought. Enough rambling!

Times of Zambia 18th October 1968

Rodney Malcolmson, blunt speaking Independent member of

Zambia's National Assembly was yesterday suspended from his duties as an MP for the rest of the life of the present parliament…It brought to a climax the furore which followed Mr. Malcolmson's gaff in the House earlier this month, when he made his remark about certain people "who not long ago were jumping from tree to tree."

* Hitler pleads Not Guilty. Hitler Salombo pleaded not guilty to doing grievous harm to Chuma Chanda on October 13th.

Letter 171

I must try and write smaller if they are still charging 30n a letter. It would be pointless to write on both sides with the paper so thin as you would never be able to read it.

The key to P.O. Box 1609 is lost and Peter has the duplicate and only opens it at weekends and will not release it during the week. Unfortunately it takes three wks for a replacement key and it looks as though we will only get mail at the weekend. I'm sure however Peter will have to open it midweek as if the box is left for a day, the mail piles up on the floor behind the box out of reach. Good news – Richard says they have found the key making what I've written a waste of space, when I'm trying to conserve it.

Richard has heard nothing of any job in London. Do not bank on us being around for very long, as our leave finishes on 31st April. If we are away however, Richard can go on ahead and reconnoitre housing, and you will be lumbered with me if we sell the house more or less right away. You will probably be glad to see the back of us, with nappies and yelling and untidiness and maybe even our bouncy dog. Pucci, by the way, is very well and great company for me. He's someone to talk to, and when I think of him in kennels I give him a big hug and a tickle, which he quite likes even when I wake him from a doze in the cool. He sometimes is asleep, but if I go out of the room, however much on tiptoe, he is there behind me and if I change direction I'm always bumping into him.

Gory details – be warned, Daddy

I went for my monthly check-up today and the doctor said everything was 'grand'. My weight is only a lb or so up on last time and blood pressure OK. I asked him which bump was what and whether the little bumps jabbing me in the ribs were feet, and he said the head was down and it was sideways with is feet and arms to my right hence all the bumping on that side. If he sticks a foot or hand out and I poke him, he pulls it back in again. I wonder what terrible psychological effect that has on him! At least he's obedient. I met a girl in the surgery who had her baby last Monday (the second to go off pop). She was out of hospital on Wednesday after an easy birth, although is worn out coming home so soon and with a 4-year-old daughter. She says the breathing exercises helped a lot particularly as the birth was quick and she had less time to be tired.

We went to David's on Friday to Muirheads" house, which he was minding while they were on leave, and I had a lovely play on their grand piano. They also have a large Labrador and I thought Pucci would be eaten, but after a few growls they completely ignored each other except for a sniff. David also let their cat in and I half closed my eyes for the ensuing scrap, but while the cat arched her back and waved her tail, Pucci went up slowly and sniffed and then licked its face and the cat clobbered Pucci with her paw for being cheeky. Instead of charging teeth barred, Pucci just retired and the cat stretched out on a chair. When we introduced Phillips' dachshund to Pucci they went for each other like tigers. I think if the other animal isn't bothered then Pucci is fine but if any attack is shown then he's in, regardless. Another thing I think is Pinky, whom Pucci has known since he could crawl, and a Labrador is much the same colour and build. At the vets it was the little snappy dogs and Alsatians Pucci growled at and ignored the Labrador, bulldog and boxer types.

On Saturday, Richard played golf in a competition and drew a good partner, and as the game was played between them (e.g. best score of either taken on each hole) he came in a drawn 1st with another couple. As it was a friendly competition they tossed for 1st and Richard lost. He still got two glass butter dish things on a wooden stand. One is unfortunately chipped, and Richard doesn't like to ask where it was bought. This prize was won too on his new 18 handicap. He seems to have given up tennis, a) because I only go to watch and b) because the standard of the club has gone down and he can go all afternoon without a proper game. He didn't mind playing a few games with poor players as long as he got a good men's doubles, but all the men have joined other clubs and Peter is going more often to the boat club with Marlene for the same reason. I have finished my 12th dress and have cut out my last two. Enid wants me to make two of hers but as she wants a roll collar instead of ordinary, I think I'll not take her up. It's such a heck of a lot of work departing from the pattern. On the size 16s with collars, I had to cut one out of paper as the pattern didn't have collars. I wouldn't have minded keeping my last four as these were very pretty.

I have just paid 1.50 (15/-) for a pest strip, a piece of insect repellent plastic as we have had such disturbed nights and as there is a lot of malaria about. Let's hope it was worth the investment. Richard says if he gets one night's sleep it's worth 15/- and I'm inclined to agree.

Sunday we spent at David's new place and he came back for supper. It was sizzling hot and Pucci had a few bursts around the garden before flopping with his tongue out on the stone porch. However he still exhausted himself enough to drop asleep after his supper and not wake properly until morning. He's dreadful on Mondays. Normally on hearing Andre he bounces around full of life, but on Mondays after dashing down to say hello to Andre, he comes back up and under the bed and only comes down very reluctantly with us to crawl under the settee and continue with his sleep, ignoring us when we go to work.

Well all for now or we'll be charged 45n.

Times of Zambia 24th October 1968

Another train crash. Railway officials would not disclose the cause of the collision but said police were investigating.

24th October 1968

Eviction notices have been served on spongers living at Mitanda Old People's Home in Ndola. Some of the residents are said to be "teenage youths and mini-skirted girls"

Letter 172   25/10/68

Boy it's hot. I've never known it so hot. My ink is just drying up on the pen nib – I've just filled my pen but as you can see I am having trouble getting it to write. The nib is perfectly clean too!

Your letter 172 received. Oh dear. I'm sorry you don't like our choice of names. They were the only ones we agree on. I thought Clare Lapthorne was quite acceptable alliteration. Surely you don't find it so awful! We will no doubt think of other names, but be forewarned. Junior is at present kicking the writing pad, which I had balanced on his behind. His present position so Dr Hayes says is upside down with his feet and arms to the same side. My book says this is the most common position, and also the best position for him to be in, so let's hope he stays that way until he 'engages'. See all my knowledgeable terms!

As you will now know, we had a useless conversation by phone with my in-laws. We had a letter from Beresford Adams saying that we had said the chairs were to be changed but Richard's father had said 'No', and would we make up our minds. So we rang up, to say put new chairs in. We want new chairs in as, because we don't want further damage to our expensive ones, we were willing to buy 6 cheap ones to sell when we get home, and to prevent any damage to our set of ten. We reckoned it was worth the expense, to save our set. The same with the cutlery. As we were so broke when we left, we had to leave a pair of knives and forks of a set of 6 we had, as we couldn't afford to put even Woollies ones in. Now one of the knives is lost, so you can see our ½ dozen set is spoiled. We were afraid of our chairs being damaged and spoiling the set of 10. However all Richard's father would say was that there was nothing wrong with our chairs and that they were fit to leave in. He seemed to think we were putting in new ones for the benefit of our tenant and not for us. All we could say was OK, let them stay, as to argue over the phone was costing as much as the chair replacement. So despite what we think best, we have decided it is simpler to let the things stay. I'm so sorry for causing you bother, but it is so difficult trying to control things satisfactorily at this distance, especially as the main thing is to get a tenant in quickly, to save us money. At three minutes, Richard said 'cheerio' but his mother wanted to speak; at four minutes she wanted to speak to me and said what she was knitting etc. In the end at 5 minutes, I was in a cold sweat thinking of the cost and said 'that's lovely – cheerio times up' and Richard grabbed the phone back and we shouted cheerio and rang off – but what else could we do. The line was excellent, as though we were ringing locally, hence probably why Mrs L wanted to stay chatting. Anyway we spent £5 getting nowhere and we both felt so helpless this end. Neither of them either said Congratulations or anything. Mrs L just said I was a naughty girl – presumably for not telling them sooner – or more probably as Richard said, she was horrified at the thought of me seducing her little boy – brazen hussy that I am!!!

Yesterday was Independence Day and unusually quiet as all the rallies were held in other towns this year, so the town was quite empty. We went to Borrowdale (as David was away for the weekend and not in his new house in Ambleside). Ken Norris is still at Borrowdale with a new chap called Tony Thwaite, who used to go to St. Anselms and who used to be one of the heartthrobs of Park High. He still is gorgeous. 6ft 4", so he says, and he has blonde hair and is very good looking. He arrived two weeks ago and is with Norris until his wife arrives. She had a baby four weeks ago and is staying with her parents until he moves into a house. He has just given her the OK to book her ticket. She is 25, and it seems a pity she didn't arrive early, as she is the nearest in age to me, and Tony gets on well with Richard. Tony is here to design a projected extension to one of the plants.

Ken, Tony and Len Allen, the new technical director, replacing Miller, all came for supper. We had a jolly good evening. All Pommies together and all wifeless except Richard. And to think when we arrived Peter, Mackie and Richard were the only English. We are almost outnumbering the South Africans and Rhodesians. It's good being in a majority! Believe me, the English despite their faults are still a race apart, even if only in sense of humour. It is a help too, that all these people have interesting jobs to work on, and are not here solely for the money, as most of the southerners are, and there is more enthusiasm to see the company do well.

Mrs Mc. was very pleased with her dresses and when I looked at the cheque she had given me £10 too much and I took it back. She said it was OK, as I had made them so nicely and she was delighted with them, and she wouldn't alter the amount. Wasn't that nice. I have finished Mrs Mhizha's two today; that makes fourteen and is my lot. Enid wants me to do hers if she gets stuck on her first two, but I have parcelled up her material to give to her on Monday. She can then give me them back later, if she likes but I don't think she will bother if she has the material rather than me. I couldn't face even another two! I've got stripes in front of my eyes.

My next job is a complete household inventory for packing and customs purposes, which I must do before 15th November.

I can then write more as I have time, but I'll have nothing much to write about. Just think, it's not so long now is it!

Chapter 51   Andre's bike

Times of Zambia

8th October 1968

Kitwe City Council is waging war against bilharzia and malaria-the two killers which appear with the rains every year. Armed with deadly DDT and molluscacide, teams are about to move into all of Kitwe's townships to spray the scattered pools of water, dambos, ponds and creeks where the malarial mosquitos and bilharzia infected snails lived.

Times of Zambia   29th October 1968

Mr Chimba told the House that under a new law passed in Parliament last year, there will be 800 businesses vacant to be taken over by Zambians. "Then it will be practically impossible for a non-Zambian to obtain a trading license, thereby surrendering their businesses to Zambians", he said.

Letter 173   28/10/68

I'm sorry you were put to so much bother over the chairs. The ones you chose sounded just the job and Richard still would like to have gone ahead, but we have had no choice. We could have sold the chairs on coming home at half price and would only have lost the cost of one of our dining chairs. Still, let's hope the next tenants have no children or animals. Those chairs have to last us the next 40 years. *(Still going strong in their third household)*

Thank you also for offering to clean the house, but apparently Mrs L is seeing to this.

We had a lovely day yesterday. We went to Borrowdale at Tony's and Ken's invitation after lunch and we stayed outside until six and then Len Allen joined us for supper and boy, what a lively evening we had. We talked and talked. At one stage Ken who is a mad TV addict, said 'shall we watch ….' And was drowned in boos. Len is thinking of putting on a review at Christmas. Led by this clique of Pommies that is forming, aided and abetted by Tony. You know how Richard imitates people. He does a superb one of the managing director and when relating a conversation he uses all the appropriate voices. They pounced on him in the middle of his tale and told him about the review, and Richard says he is doing no imitation of the MD until his next job is fixed and the papers signed! We made up some super limericks and new words to old songs and if the thing gets past this initial enthusiasm, then it should be jolly good! However that remains to be seen.

On Saturday we went to Hutton's cocktail party and it appears Pucci was good as our dear neighbour hasn't been in touch with us yet. Ken invited all three of us out to watch the Saturday film (an old thriller I have already seen on TV at home) so Pucci got an evening out anyway. He is no bother at all at Borrowdale. He belts around the garden for a while and when we came indoors, he had his supper and flaked out under the settee, and hardly woke when we took him home. He is definitely booked on the December 12th plane to London, I would like you to ring on 13th to the kennels and then telegram us to say he is OK. I will find out first if the kennels do this or not and then let you know definitely. I will pay for any costs incurred. It's worth it, so that I can sleep. I'll miss him so much and am dreading his departure.

Work is awful at the moment. I have no one proper to train and having finished wages on Friday, I am trying to catch up on some backlog of my own work let alone tie up all the loose ends and leave memos on this and that. It is also unbearably hot. It was 95 yesterday according to the newspaper and has gone up to the 100 mark in the last week and even at night it hasn't dropped below 83. And there isn't a breath of breeze. It's like walking with your head in a plastic bag. Everyone's hair is stuck to their necks and faces. When the rain comes I shall dance in it and sit in the storm drain and float in it.

This afternoon I cut out my white dress for the wedding – have I told you we have been invited to Joan Williamson's wedding on the 9th Nov. Well, we have. I didn't have the strength to do more and sat in the bath sloshing myself with a sponge.

Richard brought home Andre's bike today at lunchtime. It is a Hercules, New Yorker in maroon with white wall tyres and white seat and saddle bay and a stand. Very smart. His friends' bikes are all the cheaper ones in black. He spent all lunchtime adjusting the seat and polishing it. He kept a deadpan face when we gave it to him and just said "sank you", and we didn't know whether he was pleased or disappointed. However he was standing amidst an admiring crowd with it while he polished, and Elizabeth when I saw her this evening said she wondered why he bounced into her home with the laundry and went skipping back across the court singing to himself and then bounded in two leaps over our drain and up our steps. So it seems he was pleased. He has had strict instructions to leave it on the terrace instead of outside the kitchen until I buy a lock for it tomorrow.

I was as excited as he should have been.

I'm having my tea party this week, so that should keep me busy all Thursday afternoon.

David went to Salisbury this weekend with Mr and Mrs Van der Westhuizen and stopped overnight with Cookie and George, not knowing we knew them. Cookie asked if he knew us, and he said 'know them, I'm their lodger'. David said to Richard that he had bought a new record in Salisbury and wanted to try it out, but Richard told him to bring it Friday, when all the fellows were coming to supper. But no doubt we shall see him around before then!

Times of Zambia   30th October 1968

The European dominated Commercial Farmers' Bureau was yesterday attacked by the Agricultural Minister for " being very intemperate" and "attacking the Government".

31st October 1968

The Government is to form a company with the country's two major copper producers within the next four months, to supervise the marketing of Zambia's copper exports.

Letter 174   31/10/68

Well my last day at work today and I'm fagged out!

I worked like mad this morning trying to clear up a number of loose ends. We had ice cream and Chelsea buns instead of sausage rolls at tea-time. Yesterday, Sue said that there had been a collection and what did I fancy and I said a stainless steel gravy boat, which were about 8.25 (4.2.6d) and she said that I could have four because £20 had been collected. Well, have you ever tried spending £20 in half an hour? We wandered around the shops – all half dozen of them and eventually after a lot of going back and forth and two stops for coca-colas I decided on the following – a carving set in a fancy box, and with bone handles £7.10.0. A gravy boat and stand and divided vegetable dish in stainless steel (K21.00 - £11.10.0), a morning tea set and tray (K 7.50 - £3.15.0) and I had 60n (6/-) left over so I bought a pusher and spoon for 10/6 putting in the extra. What a display! It was like getting married all over again.

Anyway today while I was still filing at 12.30, everyone drifts in and I had an official presentation, which made me feel quite spare. But a lot of nice things were said and it was quite lump-in-throat making, as until then it hadn't dawned on me I was leaving. I got full pay plus full leave pay on leaving and on the whole they have been jolly good to me. I don't think I could ever hope to get a nicer job. Ah well, let's hope my retirement is worth giving it up.

When I got home I made two dozen cheese scones – very successful, and a dozen fruit muffins (scones with grated apple instead of milk to mix – very fruity) and loads of fancy sandwiches and snacks. I had a bowl of pears and oranges and ice cream and lots of cool drinks, orange milkshakes and coffee. I had just washed my sweaty face at 4.30 and was pouring out the hot milk when they arrived.

The idea was to keep Sue in the living room and everyone would sneak their presents in the kitchen into the basket I had made. But I asked Sue to hold the dog while everyone came in, and she said OK, just let me rinse my hands and she bounced into the kitchen where by now there were loads of presents. Her face dropped when she came out but she didn't say anything. We then all started eating, and I brought out all the gifts and made Sue sit in the centre. Then the light dawned. She said she had spent a horrible ten minutes as she had thought everyone had brought me a present for the baby and that she was the only one who hadn't. Anyway the idea is to guess the present by feeling it and to guess the sender by a clue on the gift. All the gifts must be for the kitchen (hence kitchen-tea and everything was yellow which we had ascertained beforehand). I put on my present, which was a washing up bowl – "from someone the same shape" which the cheeky thing guessed straight away.

Everyone left at six on Richard's arrival, and David arrived five minsutes afterwards and they proceeded to wolf the debris. I then went up to see Mrs King who has been ill since Monday – she went to the doctor with swollen ankles and was told she had a weak heart and must rest and lose weight. Apparently all she could say when she arrived back at the office was – 'but I'll miss the tea party!' So I took my leaving presents round to show her and to give her a full report of all the happenings.

Her daughter had made a dress thing for the baby in winceyette. It's miles too small, but she was dying to give it to me, and had made it at school. Wasn't that a nice thought?

Anyway I'm writing this on the bed with my aching legs on a pillow. What a day!

We had our best night's sleep last night for ages, with our fan on and chairs holding the curtains away from the windows to keep the sun out and yet leave space for a draught, and I was coated with insect repellent! The rains are late this year. They had started in earnest this time last year. It was this time last year we were nearly flooded out. Talk about long hot summer – phew. However, I like it better than the miserable cold. What on earth will I be like in April? I have forgotten what it is like to wear a coat, and gloves! What peculiar things are they?

Times of Zambia   1st November 1968

After a slight holdup caused by the recent concrete crisis, building has resumed at Ndola Central Hospital.

2nd November   Water goes on ration in Luanshya.

4th Teenagers, both boys and girls have developed a really queer way of dressing themselves. Boys have fantastically designed clothes, for instance, Lone Stars, tight shirts and jackets with no collars. They have high-heeled shoes like those of ladies. Some have chains around their wrists. Even girls have a similar way of dressing.

Letter 175   4/11/68

Well here I am, a lady of leisure. It seems most odd, and I feel that I am off sick, or on leave or something!

On Friday, I went shopping and to the library and on to the pool for 10 o'clock. Just after 10, Diane a girl from relaxation class arrived and us two fatties sat together. I had already been in for a swim. It is a beautiful Olympic size pool and there were only half a dozen people there and even when it increased to about 30-40 (including children) it was still empty as only a dozen or so would be in the water at one time – if that. I was going to leave at 11.30 but Diane was stopping to 12.30, so I did too. I then went to collect Richard, as my car is still out of order. In the afternoon, I put my feet up and had a read, before getting the supper for

David, Ken Norris and Tony Thwaite. They had a racing evening with the Scalextric, which Richard had set up on sheets of hardboard borrowed from work. They didn't finish until midnight! Talk about second childhood!

On Saturday, David put the new ball bearings in my water pump and the car now runs beautifully. It was in running order before but was making a horrible noise – just two ball bearings had rusted together as the oil had dried out of something or other. We all had lunch and then decided to visit a lake we had heard about and had traced on the O.S. map. We turned off the main road and after travelling a few miles up the dirt road; it was like being miles out in the bush. The road was lined with clusters of villages, not shantytowns but proper thatched huts and grain bins and things just like on the photo of the village I sent. Not only were the villages different, but so were their inhabitants. As we passed they would wave and the children would run to the road. We had our cameras but again I felt it rude to use them. We saw people drawing water from wells and a woman pounding grain and chickens being put into baskets made of grass and strapped to bicycle carriers and what delighted me most was a beautiful bonny baby who toddled to the road after his older brothers, wearing just a piece of string around his tummy, unlike the older ones who had khaki shorts on. All this just about five or six miles from the centre of town. After a few wrong turns, all of which proved interesting, we arrived at the lake which is at the bottom of a crater made, it is believed, by a meteor. It was very green and there were fish in it although it wasn't approached in any way by streams. It was too far down and the sides too steep to be accessible and you would have hated the sheer drop Mummy. We had a much needed drink of orange sitting at the top and Pucci had his drink and was so thirsty he nearly choked with it. He finds it very hot in the car and usually shelters under the passenger seat where it must be cooler.

When we got back the car was covered in red dust and so were we. When Richard and I washed our hair, the water was like red mud.

Yesterday afternoon Richard played in a competition. He wasn't keen, but he had agreed to partner a chap who couldn't find a partner. He was even less keen when he saw the weather. On Saturday the wind came, and it was cool instead of hot, and we suspected the rains were about to start. Anyway at about 12.00 after a cloudy morning, down it came. And did it smell good. All grassy and fresh. Anyway it's continued until the evening and Richard played in his mac and umbrella, and when I saw him coming back I turned on a hot bath for him. At six we went to David's at Ambleside again to watch TV. Len Allen and Tony Thwaite joined us, but Ken had gone to Kariba for the weekend. We watched TV from 6.00 until 11.00! It was a good show. We had the Girl from Uncle, Millicent Martin Shaw, The Avengers, Mogul and a documentary, all of which were new series (to us at least). Unfortunately Saturday night's film was Ice Cold in Alex, which we had all seen more than once, but it was still a very watchable film.

This morning at 8.00 I went to the cobblers and for bread and some bits. Normally the office messenger would do all my shopping but now I have to make special trips into town whenever I need bread etc. I then went to Customs for an export form for Pucci, and on to the Library, arriving back at 10.30 (the pool is closed on Mondays). After writing a few letters and having some toast, it was 12.00 and I must think of lunch. I shall start on some sewing this afternoon or I'll become terribly lazy.

Times of Zambia

5th December 1968

Despite the "tremendous surge in prosperity" hailed by President Kaunda, four out of every ten Zambia children die before they are five years old. They die because they are malnourished and lack resistance to disease. What is more, two of the remaining six children who survive their struggle against malnutrition are seriously affected physically and mentally by their experience. The feeding pattern of father, then adults first and children given what is left, must be broken.

Valerie Lapthorne

6th December A Western consortium led by Lonrho, now seems certain to give Zambia its first rail link with the coast to be outside the control of colonialist governments.

7th December Just arrived. Gladioli bulbs.

8th Wanted. Large travelling cage for Alsatian.

Letter 176   9/11/68

We have had a Christmas parcel from Mrs L. She has knitted two nice jerseys for junior, which I am very pleased with. I looked at the names on the other two parcels but didn't even have a feel, but put them into the cupboard. I know what mine is anyway, and if I opened it I'd only regret being fat.

More names coming up. Richard has suggested Ben and Melissa. Can't say I'm struck on Melissa but I think Ben is a good little boy's name and a tough sort of man's name. Richard not sure about Nigel, although he likes it with Jonathan. I shall certainly not discard a name because you don't like it, but junior is your grandchild too, so I must reconsider if you loathe a name. I'd also like to tag Charles in too, but Richard says that I'd also have to add on Eric! So that ends that!

I think you had better enquire your end of Shaw Saville re letters, if they have a Liverpool office. Otherwise I will write to London. The Zambia Airways chap was most discouraging about Pucci, implying that he would have a dreadful trip, so I wrote to B.U.A. London and got a nice encouraging letter back, even saying that I should put his name clearly on the box so he could be talked to, and attach his lead so he could be exercised when they stop down, or when there is any delay anywhere, so that's a bit better.

This morning I went into the office when I had finished my shopping and couldn't get away. Sue had a dress for me to put some Bernina stitching along and I went to collect it and was inundated with gossip and queries about work and didn't get away until 9.30. I won't go to the pool until 10.30 as I'm keeping Pucci company (the cheeky thing is snoring at my feet and he prefers Andre's company anyway). However Andre will soon want to clean down here and will hover with his broom until I shift myself – what a life. At least Pucci can crawl under the settee or stretch out under the bed out of the way. I'm best at the boat club. You will be pleased to hear that everyone in the office commented on how well I looked. Mrs Mc said – "You don't look half as tired!" I don't know whether to take that as a compliment or not. I must have looked as I felt. I am getting a nice tan however, although my shoulders are peeling and I am cross about that.

Andre has said no more about his bike, but he is keeping it spotless and when it rained on Tuesday, he dried it off before going home. He doesn't know we are going yet – we are rather afraid things will start to disappear. We will tell him when the dog goes, which will be the first indication. Also when I go into hospital he can work until lunchtime only so that he will be too busy to get into any mischief. We are hoping the next tenant will take him on, but are afraid that the flat may be vacant and just held for people over here for short spells. Did I tell you that the new accountant replacing Richard is going into Borrowdale, the house with the nice garden and all those fruit trees in the back? Huh! Not that I begrudge him it......

We still see Marlene and Co at least once a week. I don't mention it so much as it's a normal occurrence like buying bread. And they often pop around with post arriving at the weekend.

Chapter 52   Checking the Hospital

Times of Zambia

7th November   An 80-year-old woman who set out on a long journey by rail has been missing since July. Her daughter, who was waiting for her in Mufulira, seems to have lost every hope of finding her mother.

9th November   British and Rhodesian negotiators were reported today to have made some progress towards agreement on the Rhodesian Independence deadlock.

10th November   A man who set fire to a house belonging to an old man, whom he believed had bewitched his niece, was sentenced to nine month's hard labour. He said he had only burnt the house down after warning the man to move his property. The man's seventy-year-old wife happened to be in the house and she later died.

11th. November   President Kaunda warned yesterday that he would act firmly against any UNIP supporter who attempted to stand as an independent candidate at the forthcoming elections. He would regard such a member as an enemy of the nation.

Letter 177   11/11/68

Re Andre's bike. The rain came down suddenly this afternoon and he dashes out and stands it in the hall. So he cares!

On Saturday, we dropped Pucci off with David, and Pucci sat by the gate and cried when we left but David said as soon as the car was out of sight – all of 20 seconds, he forgot us and went romping around the garden, so perhaps he will adapt quite well to kennels. We then went on to Joan Williamson's wedding. She looked lovely and her dress and the attendants' outfits were super. When I went and dropped off her present in the morning, she said that there wouldn't be seats for everyone as she had been inviting people since the invitations went out and there were now 250ish! Well the guests were mainly the rugby club and the hard drinking core from the golf club, so after the photos we decided rather than fight with that lot for a sausage on a stick, we would prefer to sit at David's, so we came home and changed and were back at David's for four o'clock. We had supper and watched TV with David. Yesterday we again spent the afternoon with David and took our own supper and cooked it there and again watched TV until midnight by which time I was asleep. David's settee is old and shabby but large and very comfortable and I just can't sit comfortably in ours anymore as I fidget because junior, if he's not got his feet in my ribs, goes to sleep right under my lungs and makes me sit bolt upright so I can breathe properly. I also can't fasten my shoes in comfort. I'm not fat anywhere else – in fact I still have a waist. I'm just all stomach and it looks even funnier in the mirror now that I am sunburnt.

Pucci has just made a tooth hole in my slipper and is proceeding to enlarge it, so I'm afraid I shall have to take it from him if it gets so that he can pull plastic off. Would you send a small parcel of toys to the kennels for me if I give you the address, including some chew sticks and preferably without any whistles as I have just rescued the metal piece out of the slipper, before he swallowed it. He might settle better with toys. A small yellow Spratt's ball with or without bell would be the job (the one I have is numbered 249 design!) I will send his own with him if you can't get a similar one, but the less he is cluttered up with moveable, rattley objects in his travelling box the better.

We are tonight writing an inventory, or rather bringing our previous one up to date so that shipping and insurance forms can be made out. We intend to pack up on 28th Dec. Richard wanted to pack before Christmas, but this means being without a Christmas tree or any ornaments or rugs or anything and the house will be a bit bleak, so we have extended it to 28th Dec. That gives us the Christmas holiday and weekend to pack up. We pack roughly in tea chests, which are transported to Salisbury and repacked for sea and sent on from there. They should arrive at the same time as us.

Elizabeth and Ron White are going away again next week, and they have a visitor who arrives this afternoon and may stay after they have gone, so Elizabeth asked me if Andre would do his bed and dishes, and I bravely said I thought the visitor wouldn't object to washing his own dishes if Andre did his laundry. The situation today was that she brought loads and loads of washing over (Andre did a week's holiday washing and changed the bed on Friday) including sheets and towels and all her underclothes (as Richard says – Ron wears funny shirts and underclothes (which was the original arrangement). I am using 4-5 packets of soap extra per month, which is over 10/- worth. It's partly my own fault; I suppose I could ask for soap, but she might stop sending washing and at least Andre is benefiting. But I today did some baking, but as Andre was up to his ears in her ironing I washed up myself. You may say that this was no hardship, which it wasn't, but the thing is that I am paying him to do *my* work. Ron is just as much a nuisance; they are loaded with money as they are paid salary in UK and live here on expenses, and so save all their salary, yet Ron never has change on the golf course for green fees and Richard is always paying 5/- here and there for him. And here's us living to a strict budget so that we can have our super trip home.

We advertised our car but have had no replies – the ads were in on the wrong days from the ones we said and also instead of putting "extras include front seat safety belts, burglar alarm…." The ad read -extras include front seat, safety belts, burglar alarm… However Stuart Parker rang up and said that he is going to approach his boss to buy it for him (his job includes a car) as their car has had it, and they need a larger one with Sally having a baby and also Stuart has made a long trip (Kariba) with us and knows the car's performance.

Still no news of where we are to go. The ten days is up at the weekend (Mackie said we should hear within 5-10 days). It's quite nerve-racking. We have already waited 6 weeks from the first hint he dropped!

Slept well last night – it rained in the night and was cool and kept the mosquitoes away. By 10 a.m. this morning however my clothes were sticking to me. I wish you could hear outside tonight (above next door's TV that is). The crickets and locusts have stopped and we are getting a froggy chorus from the dambo.

Our phone no is Ndola 4987. Book your call to me, and then if only Richard or the houseboy is home they needn't connect you. The normal time is three minutes at £1.0.0 a minute. So if you ring and I'm in hospital you can ring again without a loss to yourselves.

I went to the library today and got seven new books. Should last me a day or so! One I will only read in the mornings, as it is an omnibus collection of ghost stories – lovely.

Well the pool is open again tomorrow. It's closed Monday for cleaning, I must admit it's a very well cared for pool and less chlorinated than our tap water. Let's hope the rain sticks to the afternoon.

I planted some seeds in the bare patches of my box – morning glory – they grow fast and are creepers, so I'm training it to grow all over the front and on to next door so that it will grab our next door neighbour when she comes out – lovely science fiction stuff.

Times of Zambia

12th November 1968 The Government has drawn up a master plan to end colonial inspired segregated housing by creating cosmopolitan communities in all towns. In future residential blocks will be built comprising 200 families of varying

educational, income, and social levels.

13th November   The Minister of Commerce says that non-Zambians should avoid wasting time and money of both the applicants and the licensing authorities with applications that could not be successful.

13th November   A plane, which had taken off for Ndola, returned to Lusaka 40 minutes later. No announcements had been made about the bad weather in Ndola. "We all thought we had landed in Ndola. Imagine our shock when we found we were back in Lusaka"

13th November   A cheap protein packed food is being sold in the shops all over Zambia having been tried in hospitals, prisons and clinics as part of the war against kwashiorkor. The food is a powder to be mixed with water to make a soup or relish. It comes in four flavours, curry, oxtail, chicken and stew.

14th November   Zambia's first full-scale sugar crop has been a bumper success.

Letter 178   14/11/68

It's 9.30 and I'm having my elevenses – well I'm thirsty. The weather has been dull and miserable this week with almost continuous rain, so I haven't been to the pool once.

Tuesday however, Diane came around for coffee and we arranged to go to the new hospital to find out where the maternity ward was. So yesterday, Wednesday we went along. We had difficulty parking as all around the new hospital is as yet unpaved and the rain had turned everywhere into a red quagmire. We went to the desk and were directed to the 1st floor and hence along a warren of corridors to the ward, where the sister on duty was. She was African, but very efficient and a sister as opposed to ordinary nurses (here nurses are ward maids and sisters the nurses). We asked where to report and she showed us and as we hesitated to go (purposefully) she asked if we wanted to look around. She then took us along past the post natal wards (two-bedded rooms) to the ante-natal ward – 12 beds and past the 2 nurseries, one ordinary and one premature baby one. She even took us to the delivery room, which is like an operating theatre but with a bed and cot instead of an operating table. She explained procedure as she went and was most helpful and pointed out the more cheerful aspects – the babies in the cots, rather than dwelling on the horrifying instruments in the delivery room. Visitors are normal (not just husband) although the husband is the only one to be able to go through to the nursery section. The babies are kept in cots at the foot of the bed, and removed for the night before visitors arrive. That seems fine, as we won't be complete strangers when we come away from hospital and at least I'll know how he breathes, and his sleeping patterns. So, all in all, it was a worthwhile visit. There will be less risk of infection in a new hospital and the sister and staff seemed cheerful and as you can see, helpful. We came away with our list of things to bring in. Nothing very expensive, just Dettol and Vaseline and things like that (no N.H. Service!). However our insurance will cover hospital and doctors' bills and any actual prescriptions.

Andre came and went this morning. He says his wife's throat is swollen and she can't eat and he wanted to take her to the hospital. He will probably have to sit there all day. He did breakfast and then went. So I'll have to make the bed and do the dishes! I may even flick a duster around. I'll draw the line at the washing though. I don't fancy kneeling over the bath.

I have just thought on. I've six people to dinner tonight. On Tuesday Ron and Elizabeth invited us over to meet their commercial director. He is staying in the house while they are away as from today and arrives back from a trip to Lusaka this afternoon, so of course benevolent Richard invites him here tonight, and again, of course, we must have someone for him to meet so as Peter and Marlene are already going out we have invited Bob and Naomi and Douglas Hutton (whose cocktail party we went to). The very thought of it makes me feel tired, but Richard is a help and does a lot of the cooking. I have insisted that this is the last dinner, our only other entertainment being the little party we are throwing for David before he goes. But Richard's replacement arrives on 9th Dec so I can see us being lumbered with showing them around. At least after 30th Dec we have a good enough excuse, as all our stuff will have gone and we will be on an emergency kit. We also run into trouble in that we are the first people on contract, i.e. with our own cars and effects (unlike Youngs who only supplied their own clothes) to leave. We have asked for a subsistence kit – bedding and pots and a dinner service etc. for the last month and have also asked for a car for use as from when we sell the Imp. It's a pity we have to be first, as the firm will act as though they are doing us a big favour, yet having set a precedent all those following will have better treatment (as in housing – here I go again). Mackie is moving into a larger house and everyone is moving up one, including Marlene and Peter. Peter says perhaps the 2nd accountant will go into their house (one of the two replacing Richard). Richard said that would be just the last straw (Marlene's house has two bathrooms, dressing room, 3 bedrooms as well as the huge ordinary rooms and garden). It doesn't look as though any of the other moves will take place before January, but Richard says if they offer us Marlene's house two days before we leave we will take it otherwise, when Richard complains in London, they could reply 'well we offered them a house!'). Even for a fortnight it would be OK as the pram is only out of the way in the spare room or on the terrace. It's even too cramped under the stairs. Moan over. But it is galling when people like Hutton, a bachelor, is in Graeme's huge three bedroomed house and we are here. And he is only a manager like Richard.

Thursday late. Good news – I think. Richard has had his next appointment confirmed as being at Unilever House – it is a 2/3-year special hush, hush assignment. Will let you know more when we know more. It is also a promotion.

Times of Zambia

14th November 1968, Opening the new Luangwa river bridge built over the remains of the sabotaged structure, President Kaunda said those responsible belonged to the racist clique. "I am aware that they are very angry at the fact that in six months we are in a position to open a new one. I am sure they now wish they had waited a little longer in order to blow up the new one."

Letter 179   18/11/68

I could clobber Richard's mother. Isn't she a panic monger? Richard wrote and said he had been offered a job in South America, but this was overruled by the UK one. It's partly Richard's fault even mentioning it, because I'm sure she never reads his letters properly when she does get them, as we can see by her replies that she's got things wrong. Richard is at this moment perusing catalogues and looking at the London maps to see the best place to live. Tony and Joan are trying Tunbridge Wells but we are quite keen on northwest London near the M1 and M4 so we can be easily accessible to and from the north. In fact, if we move in before we collect Pucci, we shan't have far to go for him after all.

If we can't get a tenant by Christmas we must consider selling our house, as we will be unable to support our mortgage repayments as well as rent here without jeopardising our cruise. This means however that it may be necessary for me to stay with you until we get a London house, but this shouldn't be too long so don't worry that you will be lumbered with me for months. We shall (horrible thought) maybe take temporary accommodation in London whilst looking around.

Our dinner went extremely well on Thursday, and Bob, Derek and Douglas Hutton all got in touch with Richard to say how they had enjoyed it. We argued and told yarns until all hours, and the meal was one of the best yet, possibly because I am home and can start about 3 o'clock with preparations.

On Saturday we went to David's and sat in the garden and had chicken and chips (David's cooking) and watched TV. On Sunday David, Stuart,

Derek and Richard played golf and in the afternoon we three went to David's, repeating Saturday's performance but it was our turn for grub and we take it up all prepared. However there was a storm and we were forced indoors. However Marlene and Peter and Sally Anne called with the mail and that occupied us until time to do supper.

David has suggested coming down to Southampton too with his fiancée, and wanted to know where you are staying, and if you would mind. This will actually be useful as he can take our luggage and leave plenty of room for Hilda and our carrycot and trunk. Have you booked a hotel? Remember that it is Easter weekend. David goes home on 27th i.e. a week on Wednesday but is holidaying in East Africa for three weeks arriving home for Christmas, and will call on you about then with his slides and stories.

I went for my 4 weekly check-up today and horror! I have put on 10lb instead of my usual three or four. I have put on 22lb altogether, which is OK, but I was doing so well! I therefore have to cut down on bread and spuds etc. I have steak, peas, 2 mushrooms and <u>no chips</u> for supper. It was awful watching Richard eat his. I've got a recipe book from the library, which uses all fresh fruit and veg and gives well-balanced calorie low recipes. They are all expensive here though. I don't want to lose weight – just not put on anymore. I think it must be finishing work and not dashing around but loafing instead. I must go for a swim tomorrow even if there's snow in the air. It was too miserable last week and it was closed today.

I have bought a load of things to take into hospital as per my list. £3's worth! I also bought Sally Anne a box of plastic farm animals for 1.69 (16/11). Tomorrow I do my month's shopping for the last time. After Christmas we shall be using up all our accumulated stock and just be buying things, as we need them. The shop has Christmas food in; all tinned. Even puds, mincemeat, and I shall get some. I will also need to get extra things for David's party.

I had a nice letter from the kennels, who assured me that they would fetch Pucci with the minimum of delay and would telegram us immediately, so that saves you a job, thank you anyway. I also asked when to pay the balance, having just paid one month and they said it is month by month in advance but if we had exchange or bank difficulties it would be OK to pay when we got home. That too is nice, although I don't suppose that anyone who is willing to pay a dog's airfare will leave it stranded with them willingly.

Thank you for my parcel – I got sidetracked. The angel top is gorgeous. I am buying some stretchy pants tomorrow and he/she will really be kitted out. Last week I made a dress complete with smocking, which I did with the aid of transfers and diagram. I can cut it into a shirt if she is a he. I did pants to match.

I also made a matinee coat with matching pants and boots to match both outfits. The jacket had loads of my Bernina embroidery on it. These have been made out of the leftovers from the office dresses. I still have enough to do a blue and pink outfit (the other is yellow and the dress outfit beige).

I bought also 3-8oz bottles and one 4oz bottle. Do you think this will be enough? I will have a bash at feeding it myself but at the first sign of any discomfort from me, or baby, I shall go on to bottles. Dr Hayes is very keen on 'feed it yourself' and you stay in hospital seven days if you feed it, to establish a satisfactory routine

Chapter 53   Sewing

Times of Zambia

19th November 1968   The ANC hit back at UNIP officials who suggested that foreign powers had backed the ANC leader.

19th November   Waiters in Kitwe's two city hotels are defying the bans against tipping. Notices placed on tables throughout the lounge and bar at the Edinburgh advising against tipping have now disappeared. The managers have been told that waiters accepting tips are liable to instant dismissal.

19th November   At the squatter settlement in Monkey Fountain, the rains are a constant threat to traditional thatched roof and grass houses. Although clothing and bedding are stored in trunks or suitcases they still become damp. Children have coughs and stand in forlorn groups as rains churn up the ground outside their houses into small lakes of mud. In between showers frantic patching is carried out and the children are sent to scour refuse dumps to find anything, which could be used.

Letter 180   20/11/68

This is posh paper called 'onion skin'. I've a good mind to write on both sides as they were out of my normal 2/6d pad. Mean aren't I.

Had a busy morning yesterday. I first altered a dress for a girl in the office (not one I made) and then at 8.00am I went for my monthly shopping and finished that at 9, having kept within my budget. I then had a long list of things to get, and which I was determined not to come home without. I got some things on my hospital list, and barbeque sets (long-handled utensils) for Marlene and Sally Parker and things like hinges for our trunk and a new flea collar for Pucci for his journey. I even ended up at a crummy Indian shop for ribbon for the two outfits Browns didn't have ribbon in white and blue – of all colours to be out of. I still couldn't get any dog dishes, or anything nice for Christmas for you at home. I have bought you a small present, and have left the price on just for you to see how scandalous it is. David is taking the presents for us. We have exactly the same problem as last year – all the things have been imported and have the duty and freight charges slapped on, and it seems silly to buy them and send them back! We can't do the same as last year as we have had a warning from our Eastham bank manager. We have paid our cruise deposit and will not reimburse the account until we leave when Levers give us our fare. We are also unable to transfer our Jersey money until after the end of the tax year or we lose half in UK tax and to crown it all, we still have standing orders for our mortgage, without having any rent cheques coming in. Doesn't the position sound awful – and it isn't really, because in Jan we get our gratuity which pays for our cruise and also we can transfer our Jersey money when we get home, which looks as though it will have to go towards a house deposit in London, prices there being what they are!

Anyway, having visited an out of the way bookshop for nice paper and a card for you, I called at the office. Last year this awful shopping made me quite miserable it was so un Christmassy, but this year it doesn't matter so much. Even the Christmas pudding I bought for 7/6 (smaller than those M&S puds) has the label almost illegible because of rust from the tin!!

However I bought an advent calendar for me, and one for Sally Anne. Peter was very pleased with it as they had them in Austria when he was small, and the first he saw here was the German one I had last year.

At the office I had some forms filled in to reclaim my pension fund, had a cup of tea, a quick natter, answered a few queries and then went to the customs office to have Pucci's forms stamped; however they needed his licence and I had to come away. I came home, had a drink (unsweetened) unloaded my shopping and then went to the pool for 11.30. I spent a lovely hour at the pool. Diane was there, and I was the only one in the big pool, the others being with their children in the small pool. It was lovely. In the afternoon I sewed.

Today, I carried on my sewing and then went to a canvas place for some deckchair canvas. I bought 5 yards for 1.90 (19/-). This is to make a huge duffle bag. Our luggage to go down south is

1/ a trunk to be despatched four weeks before our departure,

2/ a small suitcase for baby's clothes (don't nappies take up space!),

3/ an expanding case for Richard's and my stuff,

4/ a holdall for bottles and nappies etc.,

5/ a holdall for cameras and odds and ends,

6/ the pram.

Richard and I took the two suitcases and one holdall to East Africa and had trouble staying underweight, so as we are only allowed 30lbs each on the plane excluding baby and the pram, it's going to be a tight squeeze. I therefore decided to make this mammoth bag and take it in the trunk and we can then fill it with all the excess things we accumulate en route e.g. clothes for us and baby and presents and souvenirs. You can see therefore that it will be a good thing if David comes down as at Southampton there will be a trunk (only the size of a suitcase), 2 suitcases, one very gay duffle bag, 2 holdalls, one pram, and somewhere amongst that lot, three of us!

Ron White has just phoned to say his plane has been delayed and would we collect him at the airport at 7.30, as he can't get hold of the lodger. (Derek has gone on a trip and is due back this evening and has their car).

The cheeky thing reversed the charges. I couldn't refuse either could I! Remember me saying that he keeps borrowing 5/-s. He probably thinks our phone is on the company, like his.

There now appears to be twelve coming to our little party. I am doing nothing elaborate. I shall do salads and 2 chickens and some ham. Drink is the only problem, but we have dregs in all bottles and when that is gone, the short drinkers will have to stay on beer. We don't want to be lumbered with half touched bottles on leaving.

Back to the canvas factory – the building on the outside was smart but the back and roofs (or rooves?) were corrugated iron. There was canvas and machines and operators everywhere. What with the heat and the smell – talk about sweatshop. They seemed to be making army camouflage clothing and tents. I waded across the building with all these big eyes on me and my middle, bought my 5 yards and fled. Then back to customs where my forms were stamped. There is so much shopping and paperwork a) for Pucci, b) for baby, c) for our packing up and disposal of household, d) sale of our cars, e) transfer of money and f) final trip. I send Richard off to work each day with lists I have made during the previous day of things to be done and enquiries to be made. This afternoon I finished my two final baby outfits and started this letter and am now waiting for Richard to come home.

Times of Zambia

22nd November 1968 Members of the Lumpa sect living at the refugee camp in the Congo, are in a bad way. Food, medicine and clothing are scarce and water can only be obtained after walking many miles. They are determined to never return to Zambia until Lenshina is released

22nd. November A spokesman for the four star Ridgeway Hotel yesterday denied that regulations had been introduced forbidding African girls to sit with European men, unless they were married. He described as a mistake, an incident on Friday when a Zambian woman journalist sitting with two

Valerie Lapthorne

European friends was insulted by a security guard who demanded to know which of the men she was married to.

Letter 181   25/11/68

Well we have had quite a full weekend. On Friday morning I went to Kitwe with Marlene in a chauffeur driven car, to buy curtain material for the new house they are to move into, as the selection in Ndola is very poor at the moment. It wasn't much better in Kitwe, but we had been over every inch of shop space in about an hour and a half and eventually had to compromise on material that was OK but very ordinary and very curtainy. I also bought 2lb of plasticine from a hobby shop where Richard had sent me to get a new car for his set. When I got the parcel back here, the woman had put the wrong car in the bag, after me picking the correct part. Was I mad! They don't stock these parts in Ndola either. We had coffee and then James brought us home again in time for lunch.

On Saturday, Richard worked until two-ish and we went to David's for a few hours. In the evening, we deposited Pucci at David's, where even if he howled no one could hear him, and we went with Marlene and Peter at David's expense to the Tudor Inn and had a good supper and a bit of a dance i.e. a few quicksteps before the shaking and twisting took over (aren't we doddery). Actually I'm the wrong shape for twisting. We had a good night and got back to David's about two, and Pucci was fast asleep when we peeped in the window and didn't hear the car draw up. The only thing that marred the evening was that Richard knocked his chair over and his jacket was on it and he smashed his glasses, not just the lens, but also the frame. He went for new ones today as they were beyond repair. They will cost about £15 to replace! We could have done without that expense, but he's got to have glasses.

On Sunday we went to David's at 11, Richard going into work for an hour first. We sunned ourselves until two and had our lunch outside but then it began to rain and they set up the Scalectrix in the lounge and no sooner had they done this than Eva and Allan Phillips and the children arrived with a box of chocolates for babysitting for the past 2 Fridays (I forgot to mention that – we babysat last Friday and watched a lousy American thing which only revealed at the end that it was in 2 parts). We also watched an incomprehensible "Ratcatchers". This Friday we thought we would see Part II but it hadn't arrived at the TV studio! We then saw the second part of the previous week's Ratcatchers, which showed why the previous week's ended in the air. On Wednesday last, when we went to Ken Norris's, they announced that they would not be showing Part II of a series, as they had shown it the week before part I by mistake, but they would give instead the end of the plot – which the announcer then proceeded to read!

On Sunday after we had provided coffee for the Phillips', Marlene and Peter and Sally arrived with the post and we didn't get rid of all our visitors until six. We then had fish (Birds Eye – just in and all sold out the same day) and chips and an assortment of veg that David was using up. We then had jelly and cream and raspberries (also Bird's Eye which David had bought and kept as a surprise).

Today I went for coffee to Eva's and David arrived for lunch, with the trunk all fixed up with new locks.

Diane called while I was out and left a note to say she had met the swimming pool attendant who had said the pool was closed until further notice because he couldn't get any chlorine. He expected it to be open in a month! What a blow. How long do you give me before I go barmy! This week I am going to Enid Case's for tea tomorrow, and to Marlene's on Thursday and Eva's on Friday, however.

Tony Thwaite's wife arrived yesterday and today I thought of going to say hello, but they are staying at Borrowdale, where we used to sit in the garden, and I had the thought that it might be thought I was getting in quick so that we could visit them when David went, so I didn't bother. They are both coming to David's party tomorrow anyway and Eva, who has met her, is having her to tea on Friday. Richard asked Buchanan if we could have the key to Ambleside at the weekends as it will be empty for about a month and we would like to sit in the garden, but he said he "didn't think so". It would be setting a precedent. Don't you think they could let us use it? We only need access to a lav. if that. We could I suppose just go and sit there and go away again – the houseboy knows us, and he is being retained for the next tenant (also a bachelor or man without his wife, who is a process worker foreman and is coming to train process workers for a few months). But it will look less odd to the neighbours if we are able to go in and out with our own key. I can go to Marlene's anytime or Eva's, but I feel reluctant to do so as I can't invite them back (although I'm sure they won't mind). But it's so much nicer to be able to say 'come and see me next time'.

Richard has just picked up your parcel. We paid 25/- duty, which was OK. I have put the Chrissy ones away without peeping. It's no temptation to peep as otherwise our Christmas wouldn't even seem like Christmas if we had no presents to open. But Junior's things I looked at (I think you intended that). They are just _gorgeous_. I bet you enjoyed buying the tops. Aren't they beautiful? And the jacket is by far the nicest I have – I haven't one jacket that is anything the same yet. I have seven all different and two that I haven't completed because the wool is finished. I don't see how Mrs L says it's too thick. This child is going to be so spoiled! Perhaps it's as well we are moving to London before it takes over!

Well, I'm just going to get cracking on an apple pie, mince tart and a fruit jelly. I can serve them cold tomorrow with ice cream and cream. Then tomorrow all I have to do is prepare all the salady things and cook the chickens and do some shopping. Everything must be ready by four as I'm going to Enid's for 4.30. I rang to say did she mind if I came Wednesday, as I had forgotten I was having visitors. She put her hand over the phone and said, "It's Val, and she can't come tomorrow!" So I'm wondering if the other girls are going and it's a surprise tea or something. So I said – well I'm mainly doing a cold buffet so I'll just not have to stop long, and she said – oh that's good because I've made a cake! Well we shall see!

Times of Zambia   28th November 1968

Eight of the 14 ANC candidates flown to their constituencies by Air Force planes on the order of President Kaunda failed to lodge their nomination papers. ANC leader Harry Nkumbula said they never left the aircraft. "They were too frightened. They were to be met at the various airstrips by police escorts, but there were no police to meet them"

Letter 182   27/11/68

It's a hectic life I'm leading! Yesterday I was grocery shopping for the party and I also bought some Christmas presents for David to take home, but unfortunately he is now overweight and my parcel is 3lb. By removing Dad's presents it is reduced to 2lb so David is thinking of sending some unaccompanied luggage.

Anyway after leaving home at eight, I arrived back at ten and started cooking. I did three chickens, an apple pie with orange rind and an open top which I let go cold and covered in whipped cream, a mincemeat tart which I served hot and a jelly cream. Richard carved the chickens at lunchtime and I prepared eight large platters with salads, chicken, ham, tongue and salami, and also had vegetable salad, potato salad, red cabbage, pickles, capers and olives. It looked a super spread. We moved the furniture around to leave our tiled space for dancing. At 3.30, I had a bath and got changed and went to Enid's for tea and sure enough it was a baby shower. There was a gorgeous spread of cakes and sandwiches and a big basket full of presents, which were as follows: sheet and pillowcase from Sue, thick flannelette blanket/sheet from Enid, overall bibs from Mrs King, 3 bibs from Mrs Bailey, pillowcase from Mrs Mhizha, boots from Mrs Kent, bonnet from Mrs Giles, brush and comb from Mrs Mc, and pair of frilly plastic pants from Mrs Cleveley, the boss' secretary. Didn't I do well! I must quote the rhyme on Kay Cleveley's present:

This tiny pair of pants size one

Will cover up a little bum

The last few weeks will quickly go

A boy or girl you soon will know

If on the day you find there's two

I'll buy another pair for you!

Lesley King had made a matinee jacket complete with embroidery (she is 10) and Ann Case who is 11 or 12 made me the sweetest felt bear about 5" high. He is green and yellow and one of those animals that you can't really tell what it's supposed to be, but she has made and stuffed it very well and it has an expression all its own.

We all talked ten to the dozen and I came home at 6.30. Richard had come home early and carried on where I left off. Everyone arrived before eight when David arrived. He was careful not to come before we told him to, as he had twigged it was a party. Apparently Mrs Van had said "See you Tuesday at the party", and David said 'Oh no, I'm going to Val and Richard's' and Mrs Van, realising she had boobed, tried to cover up, but the secret was out! It was a jolly good night, food and ale in plenty and didn't flag, but it broke up at twelve, mainly because people had to get back to babysitters. We had Phillips' children in our bed and they were thrilled as we put Thwaite's baby on the dressing table in its carrycot. It slept until woken at twelve, and although only ten weeks old, just chuckled at us and fell asleep again before they had got her to the front door. She is a very pretty and placid baby with big eyes and black hair. I hope ours is as good. She sleeps from 6 until 5.30a.m., which I think is very good.

Unfortunately at midnight my feet had swollen for the first time, so I had instructions from Richard to sit with my feet up today. However this morning at eight I went into the office to thank the girls, and Mrs Bailey who sent a present but who couldn't come to the tea. I stayed for tea and had a weigh on the scales and am now 139 instead of 140 despite yesterday's grub! Although I've not really lost any, the thing is that I'm not putting on more. As I arrived home, David called to dump his suitcases while he went around saying cheerio. We had coffee and some mince pie and just as he left, Margie and Michelle and a friend arrived and I started again. It is now 11.30 and I've got my feet up. We are going to see David off at 3.30. The lucky thing!!

Thursday 8.30. We went at 3.15 and had a drink with David before he was called through at 3.30. Richard hung on until 4.00 and we waved David all the way to the plane. Richard then went back to work and I took the borrowed glasses back to Ken's. On passing the airport again at 4.30 when the plane was due to go, it still hadn't gone so I sat in the car alongside the runway. It started up its engines but it was ten to five before it actually moved down the runway. David should have seen me as the plane moves down then turns round and comes back, so he will know someone stayed until the bitter end. Marlene and Sally gave up and went home and no sooner had they left then the plane started to move. Buchanan has now said he will do a check inventory of David's house and if everything is satisfactory then we can have the key for this Sunday. Someone else is arriving on Wednesday and is stopping at The Savoy, so depending on whether this chap wants to move in straight away, will decide whether we have the key for next weekend.

What made David overweight was the hideous copper lamp the firm bought him which weighed 14lbs. They tried all morning to get an extra allowance, but no luck and he had to send a suitcase on its own direct to London. Then Buchanan comes to the airport about ten to four with a chit for 7 kilos extra. Just too late!! Typical Levers.

Andre's wife is now out of hospital. He doesn't have to pay. There are the paying and non-paying wards. Non-paying wards are more packed and as you can imagine, a bit rough. They are given clothing and bedding and free medical treatment. The paying ward is less crowded but of course the fees are high unless you are insured. I couldn't make out what was eventually wrong with her. A dose of penicillin probably did the trick.

Oh dear! If you are going to buy a 4ft bed, I hope there won't be any friction or hurt feelings when we stay with one or the other. At first though I shall stay with you as I shall be home during the day and at least

Daddy will be home during the day. I couldn't bear to sit in Lapthornes' all day without even a magazine to look at.

This morning I made up my holdall for hospital. A bit early I know (5wks) but if Junior is early like I was, the more I can do now the better. I am also starting to fill a suitcase with clothing that I will not need in the next eight weeks nor on the cruise, so that if baby is early, Richard will know what things to send by sea and what to leave. Activity will start 2wks today when Pucci goes. We can then start piling up stuff in this back room having recovered our tea chests from Marlene. We still haven't had confirmation from the firm that we can have an emergency kit so I can see us living on cold meat off paper plates, or else we shall eat out and charge it to the company.

Chapter 54   Layette

Times of Zambia

29th November 1968 A gang, 23 strong, swept into Zambia from Angola killing one woman and burning fourteen villages. One thousand have been made homeless. President Kaunda blames ANC for the raids. Police have amassed spent cartridges, two ancient muzzle-loading muskets and an assortment of bows, arrows, axes and spears.

29th November President Kaunda accuses ANC men who failed to register. He accused the candidates, in spite of being given an Air Force plane, of spending their deposits on food and drink at Mokambo. This claim brought an angry outburst from the Opposition leader, who said that his candidates had returned with their deposits intact.

29th November The body of a European, a recent arrival, was found behind the Lusaka Hotel. Police say there was a wound to the back of his head.

Letter 183   29/11/68

I went to Marlene's yesterday morning to a tea party. Marlene asked if I would bring Elizabeth. However Elizabeth rang to say she was busy and would be a bit late and would I mind waiting for her. I said OK but thought she could have been on time. Anyway instead of 10.30, we arrived at Marlene's at 11. Only when I had walked in did I realise that being late was a put up job. Blow me if I wasn't the cause of another baby shower. Sally Anne's bath on a stand was full of parcels and I had to sit in the middle and open them. And were there some nice things – here goes:

Marlene	- sheet and pillowcase
Naomi	-Swiss embroidered pillowcases and three tiny woolly teddies on ribbons to tie to a pram
Moira Dunsmuir	- one of these receiving blankets thicker than a sheet but thinner than a blanket
Eva	- a big thick white nylon blanket
Elizabeth	- three small towels
Mrs Mackie	- a bowl and cup set
Sue Thwaite	- a bib with arms in
Chessy Muirhead	- a receiving blanket & pillowcase
Janet Sadler	- a receiving blanket *(I've still got all those blankets)*

And from Mrs Mackie's mother, who is paralysed down one side after a stroke – two baby hangers that she had covered in crochet work.

I now am in the marvellous position of having <u>too much</u> stuff to travel with!!! Yesterday afternoon I cleared a shelf in my cupboard and put on this the entire things junior will need in the first weeks. Then in the tin trunk for Cape Town due to go after Christmas, all the extra blankets and larger items, mainly the dresses and cardigans I have made, and in the third pile I have put the small things he won't need until we get home. There were only about four items in this pile! So what a surprise. I have also put aside the nappies and sheets to be washed. Everything else can be worn straight away.

From eight this morning, I have been backing my books with all the lovely paper from my presents. David gave us a sturdy box about

24"x12"x12" which has a lid. This will be ideal for our books. I have lined it with a cut up plastic bag and have packed most of my books all backed. Richard is getting some silica gel from the lab for me to sew into bags and pack with the books. When we came all our books were in a cardboard box and were very damp. The pages on our Robert Carrier are still wavy. Our clothes were all damp and covered in mould, so everything is going into plastic bags with a sachet of silica gel. I have also painted our name and the wineglass this way up sign on our boxes. *(This trunk is still in the barn with all the sports kit in.)*

My next job is sorting out my clothes into three lots.

A) to go home by sea direct – i.e. sweaters and sports clothes.

B) to go in trunk to Cape Town i.e. things I don't need from now until going on the ship i.e. mostly beach clothes and my heavy coat for Southampton and

C) clothes I will be wearing continuously and which must travel with us – the cabin trunk needs to be twice the size.

I am doing all this so that if I am in hospital when the removal people come, Richard will know where he is. The household stuff is easy – everything must go! It's just clothing and baby stuff that is the problem. From Jan 3rd to April 7th we will be living out of one suitcase of clothes between us, the other being for the baby, and will be supplemented from Feb 8th by the cabin trunk. Boy, are things speeding up!

Saturday 10.30am. Well another busy morning. I started off at 7.30 by sorting out my wardrobes, into the three piles already mentioned. The things I shan't need I have already packed. I have lined the airfreight chest with plastic and all the clothing is in plastic bags that I have been hoarding. I've not packed dresses into the Cape Town trunk, but have hung them altogether on one side of my wardrobe. An extra pile has grown of out of date stuff to be passed on to Andre. Richard is starting on a sort out as well, with a lot of pushing e.g. "Surely you don't want to take all those ties" "These shoes are a bit past it". After I had had my fill, I washed all the nappies, sheets and towels for junior – in the bath!

Phew! These no doubt will be the first of many – no turning back now. Elizabeth shouted from her window, outside of which are the washing lines – "Just you wait until they're dirty ones – it's OK washing clean ones!" Ugh! I am now supping my coffee after which I shall do a bit more, then we are going to David's – alas with no David but there is the garden and TV and we shall take our supper, and we won't suffer the weekend radios and squawking children in the court and we will be getting fresh air. I have also heard that there is enough chlorine to open the pool again on Tuesday for a week (they clean the bath out on Mondays).

Monday 3.15. We spent a nice afternoon and evening at Ambleside on Saturday and left all our grub and chairs for Sunday and we went back there after going to Bob Dunkleys for a braai at mid-day. Sue Thwaite was there with her baby, which I fed (getting my hand in). A three year old little boy – I don't know to whom he belonged, came with me as I put the baby in her carrycot in the bedroom. He had a chungalorlor about eight inches long on the end of a stick (they are horrid black centipede things as thick as sausages. Ugh! I'm afraid I'll never be a good mother as the conversation went like this:

"Here's a chungy for the baby"

I don't think the baby likes chungies.

Why not?

Because she doesn't know what it is.

I'll just put it in the pram then.

No don't do that, the baby might eat it.

Why?

Because babies do things like that.

Why?

Because she's small and doesn't know any better. You had better put it back in the garden.

Why?

Because I said so!

Oh! – and he went out. So I can see I should have said, "Because I said so" at the beginning, although I don't know whether Spock would approve.

We entertained Marlene and Peter for a few hours at our "weekend cottage" on Sunday and then we had supper and watched TV. It certainly keeps Richard from working. Buchanan however recovered the key first thing this morning and will hand it over to the new bloke on Wednesday for him to move in when he feels like it. Richard's replacement arrives Saturday, but we are going to Sue's wedding and can only entertain him on Sunday and we are to entertain him all day i.e. from before lunch until after supper. How on earth am I going to keep a six year old happy, I don't know. We shall have to take them for a run in the car. Unfortunately, Whites took their visitor to the Dag Hammerskoeld crash site but couldn't reach it for water. They then went to Ndola Hill but couldn't get near, as there was a Forestry Notice up saying No Entry! We forgot our cameras the first time when we went with David and intended to go again later!

Marlene says we will have trouble leaving a baby so young with a babysitter and this will botch up our farewell dos. We intended taking out Bob and Naomi, Peter and Marlene, Sally and Stuart and Enid and Pat, all on one night. I don't know how we'll do this. I'm afraid I am not having them at home as it will be too much. It's a pity we haven't a garden (here we go again) as we could have a braai and this is just a case of supplying meats and salads, which Richard could do. The only other alternative is a midday cocktail party using up the dregs of our liquor and ordering snacks from a hotel. We shall have to see how it goes.

Let's hope we get invited out as we can lug baby along too.

I've reached rather a stalemate now. Everything packable is packed and all my repairs are done and I went to the library this morning and got eight more books. What can I do now? Baking is restricted as I don't want to buy new packets of currants and flavourings etc., and I must just use what I have. No point starting any oil painting. Have wrapped Christmas presents – all three of them and sent off my cards. I think I'll go and make a cheese pie and a milk jelly.

Monday 7.00. Well I made my cheese pie and milk jelly and also a coconut sponge to use up some coconut. We have had supper and are just off to bed, having listened to the BBC World News. We have also just cut the bits off Pucci that would be too difficult to untangle. We have just to brush out his head and face – the most difficult part as he wriggles so much, and I'm frightened of poking his eyes. Then Wednesday he will have a bath ready to be given the once over by the vet on Thursday. On Saturday we must take him to the government vet for a health certificate and on Monday I shall take his completed docs to the airport offices and on Wednesday we and Pucci will have a chicken supper and on Thursday! – I don't like to think about it.

Times of Zambia   December 1968

2nd December   Portuguese bombs were dropped by aircraft on a village near Chipata. Dr Kaunda said he was becoming convinced that Portugal was waging an undeclared war against Zambia.

*   "The eradication of English would mean that Zambians would enjoy the fruits of independence in every category. It is absolutely possible that one of our vernaculars could replace English." Says Winter Mashimi, Chingola

3rd December   The Zambian Government is to lodge a strong protest to the UN against recent Portuguese bombing attacks.

3rd December   Police have been alerted to be on the lookout for trucks believed to be involved in an extensive copper smuggling racket.

Letter 184   4/12/68

Wednesday 3.30. Sitting on the bed with a cup of coffee. Well we look as though we have a customer for the car. We asked £750 for it, wanted £700 but were prepared to accept £650. Stuart's boss has offered £650 from 1st Jan. so this timing will suit us as the tax runs out then. He is reluctant to pay more because they are in no desperate need of a car and have not sold their other one. Their financial year starts in Jan, hence the date they will take it. So in view of the fact that we need to dispose of it in order to pay for our new one, and that Stuart's was the only enquiry after the advert then we feel we must let it go. We still haven't lost on the deal. Richard has circulated an ad through the firm now for mine. I wanted to hang on to it as long as possible, but we had the balance of the cruise to pay for and again, the fact that we may have difficulty selling it, has decided Richard not to hang on. We are also going to advertise our tape recorder – Richard wants a new one to match the hi-fi and we could sell it here for what we paid for it, the electric fan heater which we were forced to buy but have no use for – we will have to take a loss on this. We offered it to the company, as the next people will need it. They retail at £30, but Richard got a discount. – (People in houses have grates and don't have to buy electric fires!)

Another blow. Remember that I said our insurance pays a good portion – approx. ¾, of medical expenses and the company pays the balance; well Mackie has decided that in view of the number of confinements (Marlene, Chessie Muirhead and me) all of which were premeditated, then no shortfall will be paid and we will have to foot the bill. This will be at the minimum about £50. Richard was cross as we had not budgeted for this, and prepared a memo of all the UK benefits we are foregoing e.g. 18wks at £4.6.0 a week (I was working and would have been entitled to this) – that's £72 – my maternity grant of £22, plus free National Health including any medicine, free equipment in hospital, and cheap milk throughout. So even with the shortfall paid by the company I'm still losing out cashwise. I never thought £4.0.0 a week was much, but when you drop to one income, it certainly would help to gradually get used to it.

I went for a swim and met Dianne yesterday, but today has been very rainy. I took Elizabeth shopping at eight and then had coffee with her, and have just been pottering since. Richard wants a bathrobe, so I will draw out the remains of my dress money and make him one, and one for me. He reckons it will save taking his dressing gown and save on taking bath towels and will double for drying after a dip on the boat. I think he's just too lazy to dry himself.

We have had a postcard from David saying 'It's all you said it was – wow!' I'm glad about this as we enthused so much about East Africa that I hoped he would not be disappointed. The lucky thing! Anyway you shall hear about it before us. You will probably see loads of photos of us that we haven't seen as David put his home address on them. Did I tell you that on the cruise I shall put your address on the films and address them to V.A. Lapthorne, V.B. Lapthorne, V.C. Lapthorne and so on and then you can see if any are missing at once and also you can tell me when they arrive, easily and I know where they are. In fact I will start with the film I have in the camera now, as we can't guarantee getting it back on time. I'll use this film up on Sue's wedding, local views and Christmas.

Recapping on the medical expense business, Peter told Buchanan that it was so petty and he was so fed up with the miserable co-operation he was getting that he was handing in his notice. Buchanan told him not to be hasty and to wait until Mackie returns. Mackie is at present in Lusaka with wife and mother-in-law viewing an art exhibition. They are stopping at a £7 each bed and breakfast hotel all on the company. Richard will get the expense claim and reckons it will be more than the medical claims of all three of us!

I have just sprayed a matabela ant. They let off a terrible stink when trodden on and the room now stinks of this. I must find it and shift it!

Thursday evening. I didn't find it. I just had to have the doors all open. Pooh!

Richard is hoping his job may have something to do with their takeover, especially as they won't let him know the nature of it. On things like this they usually put people in to Unileverise a company and Richard rather fancies the idea. If it is anything like this, it really is a plummy one, but again this is only daydreaming based on a few facts. Richard was home just after five. Brother, is he cheesed off. There is a farewell party on Friday for Ken Norris —you know how friendly we have been with him — and we haven't been invited, again! It's not Ken's fault, as the guest list is made up by Buchanan and Ken is the guest of honour, not the host. I bet he'll be mad when he finds us not there! So coming home at five is Richard's retaliation. He reckons it's all work and no play for him and vice versa for most of the others. We have been out to dinner as guests of the company only twice. Peter goes out once or twice a week (not that we begrudge Peter that!). We shall just wait and see who is invited out with the Prices, one of Richard's replacements, to his introductory parties with Mackie etc. Richard says that if we don't get invited with him, then he will claim expenses for Sunday when we are under company instructions to entertain them. Richard asked Buchanan three weeks ago to contact London re some queries raised re our transfer and he has been "too busy" to write although he plays golf on Wednesday afternoons. That's all the moaning for now.

Never mind – soon be home – Y I P P E E !!!

Chapter 55   Replacements arrive

Times of Zambia

4th December   1968   Another village raided. Fifteen men believed to be a part of an ANC gang trained in Angola, have raided another village. The government newspaper in Tanzania said that the Portuguese bombing was a "grand plan by Western Imperialists to establish a white hegemony in southern Africa.

5th December   Lusaka Police were investigating the death of a UNIP supporter, whose body was found near where ANC leader Harry Nkumbula held his first election meeting.

5th December   Portuguese authorities have accepted responsibility for as many as six separate incidents of shelling or bombing of Zambian villages. They have undertaken not to continue to provoke Zambia in cold blood.

5th December   Townships were bewildered at the sight of hundreds of miniature parachutes ballooning out and making for earth. The packages they carried were cigarettes. British American Tobacco Zambia Ltd had used this method to introduce its new Players No.6 cigarettes. Townships in Lusaka were "invaded" on Wednesday and Lusaka itself on Thursday.

Letter 185   9/12/68

Well I have just heard infant's heart beating. I went for my check-up and Dr Hayes handed me the stethoscope and there it was di-dum, di-dum, loud and clear. It was quite exciting, and he timed it very well as it still doesn't, or didn't, seem real. It does now however and I felt like shouting "Hi there!" back down the stethoscope. I've only put on 2lb in the last three weeks as opposed to 10lbs in the previous four and I now have to go every week.

We babysat for Alan and Eva on Friday again, and on Saturday, Andre dogsat while we went to Sue's wedding. It was only a small church and so rather full. Sue looked lovely and the dress she drew and which I made up in stiff paper about eight months ago looked super, and just like the model, which she gave to the dressmaker, to copy. Our office crowd, Enid and Pat, Mr and Mrs Mc, Mrs Giles, Mrs Kent and Mr and Mrs King all were at one table. There were cocktaily snacks and champagne, and dancing, and as our table acquired more champagne than any other, we were the noisiest table in the room. We had a really good time and arrived back here at seven. I gave Andre 10/, which was for shampooing my bedroom rugs. However when I went upstairs, all he had done was brush them. He hadn't even opened the dog's food or switched any lights on except the kitchen ones. I give up, it's too late to argue with him now, and it's not worth him being all grumpy.

Prices arrived on Saturday and were entertained by Peter and Marlene. We picked them up at 10.30 a.m. James is Ann's second husband and they have only been married since October. Her first husband was killed in an accident, which must have been dreadful for them. Maybe this is why the child is so precocious. James is very good with her and perhaps she will settle down. We had coffee on their arrival and nattered and then I did steak and jacket potatoes and salad for lunch. We then toured Ndola (petrol is now off ration) and went to the Bull and Bush for a drink. (Pucci stayed in the car for 20mins). They were pleased with their house and they move in at the weekend. We had roast lamb for supper etc. and boy was I whacked, although Richard did a great deal. The little girl kept saying 'I'm hungry' and then wouldn't eat her lunch. Then she spotted a choc-ice in the fridge (one of two Richard bought for us) and asked for that. Just before supper she started again, and when I said supper would be just ten minutes and offered her a biscuit she said she wanted another choc-ice. What could I do! She just turned down her mouth and said 'but I'm hungry now, I want my dinner now!' You can expect this from a 2/3 year old but surely not a 6yr old. After leaving her empty ice cream wrapper on the sideboard, she said she wanted to draw, whereupon I provided paper and crayons. She then wanted to cut out and wanted scissors. I told her to hang on as I was doing cauliflower cheese, and the scissors were upstairs. Whereupon she sulked. After being provided with scissors she wanted glue, so after dinner I put newspaper and glue on the table and this kept her quiet for an hour. She also kept asking for drinks and would drink two mouthfuls and then complain that it wasn't fizzy anymore. She turned up her nose at some coconut cakes I made especially for her, and I felt like stuffing them down her throat. Fortunately at about eight she started whingeing through tiredness and they removed her. Richard and I dropped exhausted into bed. I should have Ann and child around during the week, but I just haven't got the courage.

I met Dianne this morning and have invited her for coffee on Friday so maybe I shall ask them too. Elizabeth and I went shopping for baby presents as Mrs Mackie invited us to a baby shower for Chessy. I bought a pair of frilly waterproofs like I was given. We went around about ten and most of the Lever wives were there. Chessy also got some lovely things, and Mrs Mackie had put on a lovely spread. She also has loads of garden furniture – more than allowable, and which has been allocated to under furnished houses like ours for the sake of the account books! So I picked one of the six garden umbrellas, which I fancied! Their garden however is beautiful and is a riot of colour and she obviously takes a keen interest in it – I'll give her that!

Today I've had a letter and card from John and Sue Gibbon. Do you remember them? They went to London, but she says John's father died and they were recalled out of duty. He has now been transferred to Jo'burg and she says that if we were passing through on our way home, then to call and stay. So, as we have no contacts or hired car in Jo'burg I must reply immediately and take her up on that.

Monday evening. Peter has told Richard this evening, when Richard presented his 'introduction programme' for Price, that Price is only going to do one quarter of Richard's job. Richard asked why and was told – well you couldn't expect anyone to take on all you have been doing! They are getting a secondment for 12 months to tide them over with the rest. Ah well!

Also, that fellow who was supposed to move into "our" house, doesn't want to and is staying in the Savoy for the month that he is allowed, but he still has the key – humph!

I have just one page left of this pad. I seem to be going through them quickly unless the weeks are passing more quickly. I think it's the latter.

I hope the weather is reasonable at home, as although Pucci has a heated house, when it rains here it takes him all his time to go for his regular walk around the terrace. Well we are both going to bed now, as Richard has brought no overtime home. We will have a read. I have brought Richard four books from the library – three Dennis Wheatleys and a 'Plan your Garden' book – his own request. He says that he is getting leave happy. On Friday, I wrote to eight more estate agents in northwest London. Richard says he is looking forward to living as he chooses to live and not as someone else chooses. It does annoy us when Len Allen who is in charge of housing says that we were very lucky to have our own house getting married, as he didn't when he got married – the fact that not many people did 20 years ago compared with couples today, doesn't enter into it, neither apparently does the fact that we saved and budgeted hard and planned everything ages in advance. Ah well. Seven weeks on Friday – the freedom bus out!

Pucci's address is

Willowslea Farm Kennels

Spont Lane Stanwell, Staines, Middlesex

Times of Zambia

10th December Details of the Portuguese offer of compensation for border raids is being worked out between Lusaka and Lisbon.

Letter 186   11/12/68

I'm feeling miserable today. I have just dusted Pucci's travelling box and stuck on all his labels and a plastic bag onto the side of his kennel to hold his lead. Pucci sat and watched me for a while, had a fight with the roll of sellotape, killed it and is now asleep in the doorway of the box in his blanket. In the middle of doing that, Richard rang me to say he has sold my car. We asked £550 but have been offered £500. The fellow is one of Richard's staff and he has arranged a bank loan and will let Richard have the cheque tomorrow, so it looks as though I will have lost the car by the weekend. My best friend and my second best friend going on the same day! I will therefore have to taxi Richard to work in the mornings so that I can have the car. No more popping out when I feel like it! January will be the worst however as Richard will have a company car which I won't be allowed to drive. However I expect I shall be too busy anyway to bother much and I can always push the pram into town. However, once Pucci is gone, I will start collecting packing cases from Marlene's garage. Richard is browsing through the travel brochures, but I'm not interested yet as there seems to be so much to do beforehand.

I wrote to Mrs L to thank her for the jerseys and Mr L wrote back and said what a delightful surprise to hear from me. Cheek.

It's rather like school holidays at the moment. I went out at 8a.m. for bread and a chicken and then did a few jobs. It's pouring down with rain. The only thing is that, Daddy, you aren't due in, in the middle of the morning and I can't make a cup of tea and listen to Morning Story with you.

Goodness knows how my letter got to Senanga. This is a place right up the far reaches of the Zambezi, and it doesn't have any telephones – just a radiotelephone, as it's so far into the bush. It probably travelled by canoe for the last part of the journey. I should keep that postmark!

Richard hasn't got his glasses yet. He is wearing a terrible old pair with clip on sun pieces, which are too heavy and pull the glasses off his nose. He gets into such a temper with them, but really he looks so odd that I have to try very hard not to laugh.

Friday. Well this letter is being posted a day late I'm afraid. I was too miserable to write yesterday. We took Pucci to the vet at 8am and he didn't even squeak when the vet gave him his injection although his little heart was going ten to the dozen. Richard then went into work and when he came in at nine Pucci was very subdued and he had been curled up on my knee dozing. We took him to the airport and there were a cat and a dog already in their boxes. I didn't want to leave Pucci then as the plane wasn't due out until 10.30, so the official said we could pass him through customs, but we could leave him out until they were ready to load him aboard. The injection had made him lose all his excess bounce although he was still lively. We walked him about, but for most of the time I just nursed him and he dozed. He didn't make things easier by licking my face every now and then. At 10.30 however the plane hadn't even arrived but we had to part with him. I handed him to Richard who gave me time to run to the car, so I wouldn't see him in his kennel or hear him crying. He did cry however when Richard left him, but I hope the drug would make him doze off, or at least stop him from getting too worked up. Anyway it should have been me who should have had the injection as I howled all the way home. The plane took off at 11.30 and it was awful seeing it disappear into the clouds. I took a photo of it taking off.

In the afternoon I went to relaxation class and then to Marlene's with carnations for giving my baby shower, but she was out. It was horrible coming back to such a quiet house. I sat downstairs with a cup of coffee, rather than upstairs where Pucci and I have our three'sies and half a ginger biscuit each.

I shall be happier this time next week because then both he and I will be settled in our new routines. In the evening Richard and I went again to Marlene's and then to the pictures. We saw the Honey Pot, which was

OK but I kept looking at my watch wondering where Pucci was, and also junior makes me wriggle when he wriggles, as there's not much room for him now.

This morning Dianne (due next Weds.) and Anneke (due yesterday) from relaxation class came for coffee, so I was busy making scones this morning and a cheese pie for tea. They were successful and after turfing out all my baby things to look at, they left at 12.30. A right fatty trio we made.

Andre doesn't know we are leaving, but with the dog going and me fetching two tea chests from Marlene's, he is probably guessing – we shall tell him at the end of the month, by which time we will be packed and there will be less likelihood of him stocking up on our things to tide him over. We may then know if anyone is coming into the flat, who will be willing to continue with him. Failing that we shall advertise in the paper for a new job for him. We will give him an extra month's salary if we can't find a continuing job, but I think we shall be able to, as people are happy to take a recommended servant, especially one with his own house and transport.

<u>Friday</u>. Well talk about Friday 13th. We have just had a telegram from London to say that the boat is not leaving Cape Town until 16th Feb i.e. 8 days later and is arriving in Southampton on the 14th i.e. a week later. We now must try and alter our bus, plane, train, hotels and car hire all to fit in with the new date. Either that or stay a week longer in Cape Town.

Times of Zambia

12th December 1968   **Ndola to Kabwe road travellers face yet another hazard apart from oncoming tankers in the middle of the road. With mushrooms popping up now that the rainy season has arrived, young children have been throwing them at motorists.**

Letter 187   **14.12.68**

Well we have spent an expensive morning on the phone to Rhodesia and South Africa. We thought it was better to ring and enquire if the dates were still vacant the following week, rather than write and have some perhaps say 'yes' and others 'no'. We rang the bus and plane people and have booked on trips the following week. These were the most urgent as the trips are only once weekly and the most likely to have no vacancies. We decided to stay here the extra week instead of letting the original travel arrangements stand and staying in Cape Town an extra 8 days a) because if junior is late there will be no panic and b) staying a week in Cape Town would be too expensive in view of the holiday we were having and c) an extra week's pay here which would go towards our holiday. We have also changed two hotel dates and on Monday, Richard has booked calls re the Jo'burg/Cape Town railway trip and the other hotel. So although getting home a week later, we gain a day in Cape Town. I'm afraid it messes up your Easter weekend though, and your leave arrangements, so you too will have to start making fresh plans! The telegramme said "letter following" so we wait for details of the postponement.

Yesterday afternoon I took Ann and Rose to Monkey Fountain Zoo. We stayed until 4, as the child was quite happy on the swings. We came away then as it was raining and we all went to the factory at five – me to collect Richard and to dump them on James. I was wise taking them out as the child was OK playing, but was a pest from 4 to 5. However I had brought a cut out book in case it rained and didn't need to produce it, so that can wait until she comes again! In the evening, James and Richard went to this marketing conference, so I went and had dinner with Ann at the Savoy, and nattered until they returned at 10, when we carried on until nearly 12.

This morning Saturday, we spent telephoning all over the place! With good results. This weekend is the first we haven't been out for months and months. Our evenings are full though. Tonight we are going to Phillips' as guests not babysitters and tomorrow we are going to see Walt Disney's 'Jungle Book'.

This afternoon we have been 'gardening'. We have two bushes the same in the front and loads of geraniums in the back so we have swapped half over to change the colour a bit, and done some pruning and tidying. The boxes now look more varied. Let's hope sour face next door approves of our colour scheme. At least I'm home and can watch out! I hope we soon have a telegram about Pucci. I've dreamt of him for the past two nights, but funnily not about parting with him or his being in kennels.

Yesterday, I was very pleased to get a card from David's mum and dad, thanking us for looking after him and making his stay so enjoyable. Wasn't that sweet of them!

Chapter 56   Now We are Three

Times of Zambia

13th December 1968 Susman Bros and Wolfson Ltd have handed over their chain stores to Zambians after 67 years of trading in this country. Expatriate staff will continue to act as secretaries and advisors for the next five years.

13th December More than 3,000 ANC members have handed in their party cards in disgust at the recent Mwinitunga murder raids.

14th December In a pre-dawn swoop, police surrounded opposition leader, Harry Nkumbula's house and began to search for firearms. They left with a single barrelled shotgun found in a bedroom cupboard. There was no ammunition.

Letter 188   17/12/68

Yesterday Monday, Elizabeth came over in the morning to sew on my machine, so that filled that in nicely. In the afternoon I went to see Dr Hayes and he said 'the head was well down', which means that my pelvis can cope with the baby and that everything is OK. He also said I was having a contraction, which I didn't notice. Apparently this is common now as it gets itself ready. We had an incomprehensible letter from Richard's father congratulating us on the birth of our child, as it should have arrived by now. Have they got the date right? It's due on 4th January not December. Most peculiar.

Yesterday afternoon after the doctor's, I went out to Misundu to see Sally and Stuart, having collected Richard after work and we stopped for supper. I am taking Elizabeth out there on Friday to see the house and will take some photos. They have just had a dining room table and benches made fitting into an alcove, out of ordinary 'tongue and groove" wood polished and clear varnished which Pat Case made (Enid's husband). It's just like something out of Heals or Habitat. Sally has covered the benches with long corduroy cushions and it is very effective. Elizabeth is interested as they have a Georgian house, which they are enlarging without spoiling the front, and a Welsh cottage, which they are renovating. Sally and Stuart wanted to convert a cottage but have had their fill with this house. It's really marvellous what they have done, and now they have overcome water and lighting and waste problems, they are adding refinements like fitting cupboards and Marley floors (all offcuts) and carpets and rugs etc. I never thought they could make it so cosy. They had a tarantula inside however, a huge hairy thing that Sally didn't believe was real. Stuart knocked it into a bucket of meths with a broom handle (before knowing they can jump 6 feet). They had it photographed and identified by their friend who keeps snakes for a hobby!

I have just taken Richard to work and Elizabeth and I are going to the hairdressers. I want my hair done for tonight as we are going to see Kismet.

<u>Wednesday</u>. I had my hair done and it was super and only 25/-. She did three pony tails down the back and turned each one into curls and the bottom one into ringlets as well. As you can imagine it was very elaborate and I felt it was quite wasted just going to the theatre. The remainder of the morning I spent supping coffee with Elizabeth. In the afternoon I ran Richard to work then called to see Dianne to see if there was news about Anneke, but she was still the same! Dianne's baby is due tomorrow. She is coming for coffee in the morning if she can make it! I can see all three of us being in hospital together. At three, after tea and cake, I came back to lock up and send Andre off and then at five, I went for Richard. Richard nipped down to the golf club for a farewell drink with Derek Sadler and arrived back for us to be at the theatre for 6.30.

The show was quite reasonable, the lead being played by a girl who sang in Birkenhead Operatic.

This morning I took Richard to work and then went to Ann's to take her shopping and to choose plants for her garden. As she is living in Borrowdale, Richard and I had already planned with David what to do with the garden, and I knew what shrubs were already there and what were needed. As for the child, I find myself telling her to stop showing off, or being silly and surprisingly enough she takes notice. I think she just tries it on to see how much she can get away with. She is getting a Labrador pup this evening. Poor little animal! We stayed for lunch with them, and I am now sitting on the bed with the intention of writing and then snoozing, but it's so odd without Pucci snuggled alongside that I'm going down to make a cake for Dianne coming tomorrow. I shall take the remains with me to Sally's as Richard made a pig of himself on Monday and had chunk after chunk of Sally's cake, and yet he hardly ever eats cake at home!

After a lot of fuss, Buchanan is handing us an emergency kit. He agreed this eight weeks ago and told us to go ahead shipping our stuff. Then yesterday he says it's too early. There's not so much difference in letting us have a kit for one week or three weeks. We can have a kit on the understanding we spend no more than one night in a hotel. That suits me fine. We are getting a half tea and dinner set, some pans, cutlery and bedding. Just enough to survive on. We have a good excuse for not entertaining. I shall have to leave behind my brushes and mops and cleaning things though, but that is all. I still would rather pack before baby arrives, as I will have enough to cope with then. I have today bought five tinned meats for Richard e.g. steak & kidney pie, beef & veg curry, roast lamb slices in gravy – for when I go into hospital. I have also ordered my turkey. The only invite we have over Christmas is to Enid's on Christmas morning for drinks. Ron and Elizabeth are away and Marlene and Peter have asked James and Ann for Christmas dinner and Sally and Stuart have been invited out, so we shall have a very quiet Christmas, although I can think of no better place to go than Enid's. We have a bottle of gin over from David's party unopened and so we can take this up. We will go for ten and stay until they throw us out! *I don't seem to be bothered that Marlene and Peter are asking our replacements for Christmas lunch and we appear to have been abandoned. Twas ever thus. We are now part of the past, not the future.*

Thursday. Went to the pictures last night to see La Ronde. This morning Anneke arrived instead of Dianne to say that Dianne had flown round to her in a panic as the baby was on the way, so she had taken her to hospital and then felt odd herself so went to the doctor's who said that she was to go into hospital too, to have the baby, not induced, but "encouraged", as it has already shown signs of coming. So Anneke came straight around here to tell me about Dianne and she phoned around from here to try and find her husband, who is a sales rep. So we had coffee and then she went to get her things and to go up to hospital, so they are both in together. I feel quite out of the excitement. Although Dianne was petrified and Anneke could hardly hold her coffee cup! If my infant is as early as I was, then we could all be in together! Dr Hayes is away for Christmas, and that is why he wants Anneke in hospital, so I hope really that I'm not early.

Friday. Must close in haste. Rang hospital. No news of the other two. They should produce this afternoon.

Times of Zambia

16th December 1968   ANC President claimed that UNIP supporters had already filled a number of ballot boxes with forged ballot papers for the general election on Thursday.

16th December   ANC workers are said to be posing as UNIP officials and telling people to put a cross on the lion to vote for UNIP thus spoiling their ballot papers.

16th December   A UNIP candidate said that December 19th

would see the end of political opposition in Zambia. "You can't have two bulls in one kraal. Dr Kaunda is the only bull in Zambia"

19th December Zambia goes to the ballot box. Prime Minister Harold Wilson told Parliament that Britain would help to strengthen Zambia's defences if President Kaunda wanted her to.

20th December Zambia records nationwide peak voting.

Letter 189   **23/12/68**

Ndola Hospital

Zambia

I dare say there is no need for me to say that my son is the most wonderful, most beautiful child in the whole of the world, but having said that I had better start from the beginning.

At about 4.30 on Saturday afternoon I developed the most awful backache. We were at the tennis club and I thought it was with sitting on an uncomfortable chair. Anyway I asked if we could go home and Richard and I came back to the flat, by which time I had my suspicions. At five the contractions were coming at regular 5-10 minutes so I rang the hospital, who said to ring my doctor. Dr Hayes wasn't due back until 7.30 so I hung on until 5.30 and then rang the hospital again and they said to come in, which I did. By 5.45 I was in hospital and didn't have a bath or an enema or anything as I was coming along so quickly. At 8, Richard was sent away and I was transferred to the delivery ward, when the sister on duty told me she had contacted Hayes and I was to try pushing so I did but got nowhere and made myself very tired. Hayes arrived and was ever so sweet but said I was not fully dilated and should not push but try to revert to controlled breathing and he gave me an injection as he said it would take a further hour and a half and he would be back. Well the next two hours are best forgotten as the injection knocked me into a stupor between contractions, which was good and slowed them down, but the contractions then came in uncontrollable waves. I was in the delivery room with the lights out to help me rest. In the end I pressed the bell, and the sister contacted Hayes, but she said to hold on until Hayes arrived, as I was going to tear. Those next minutes seemed an eternity. Hayes came and we started work. That was the best bit as with an awful effort, my son emerged. First, on one push came his head, which turned around of its own accord then on the next push out came the rest of him accompanied by the bellowing of a healthy pair of lungs. The doctor held him up for me to see and said 'it's a boy' and all I could see was a thrashing pair of arms and legs, and a wide-open mouth. He was put into a cot in a towel while Dr Hayes saw to me. It only then occurred to me to ask if he had all his toes and fingers and things, but he appeared so perfect (and is) that I never doubted it. I checked my watch and it was ten to eleven.

They then gave him to me but I was worn out. Dr Hayes then chatted but I can't remember the conversation, as I was too tired and excited. The sister then made me comfortable and I was given a hot cup of Milo, which tasted like nectar. I was then put into a two-bedded room and dozed for an hour. As I passed the nursery, sister held Nigel Jonathan up, all clean and in a nightie. Richard had been ringing from Alan and Eva's every hour and at 11pm, sister said he could pop in quickly at 11.30 to see us. He bounced in on the dot with a face glowing like a big sun. He only had time to say hello and to peer at Nigel through the nursery glass, as he officially wasn't allowed in until visiting. After about 12 o'clock I didn't sleep at all. I was too excited and restless and I am alongside a picture window, which is level with my bed on the 2nd floor. I watched the traffic come and go and watched the sky grow light. At 4.30am!! Nigel was brought to me, and the sister gave me a tray with allsorts on and said to change him and feed him. Fortunately the other girl in the room who was going home, knew what to do and showed me. Then I went and had a bath which took me hours. However as breakfast still isn't until 8 o'clock, this is just as well. I was absolutely starving particularly after missing my supper. Anyway I had a lovely plate of porridge and Nigel was brought in again and the new sister on duty showed me how to give him his boiled water and to change him.

Visiting wasn't until 3.30. Apparently all Richard had done all day was booze. First at Ron and Elizabeth's, then champagne at Marlene and Peter's, provided by Peter. Then a round of golf with Ron and in to see me, after which he was going to tea at the Phillips'. He came in again at 7.30-8.00 with loads of things I requested and at 8.30 Nigel came in again for his last change and feed. The sister gave me a sleeping pill, which I didn't want but she said it would be good for me, and I did get an excellent night's sleep from 10.00 to 4.30. I had a bash feeding him myself supplemented with his bottle until we get the hang of it. We have made good progress so far. I had a shower this morning under one jet of cold water, but I reckon this is better than a bath as I have no need to sit in the water and no trouble scrubbing the bath out with Dettol before using it, and I reckon it's healthier using the running water. An African girl was moved in with me this morning. She had her baby on the floor, while her husband was filling in the admission forms.

By the way, the nurse, who made my bed, said I was a good girl, as I was very quiet and didn't scream the place down like some. Little did she know I had half the pillow stuffed in my mouth when I rang the bell for help, and the contractions had subsided when the sister arrived. (*However the "nurse" last night, who was telling me to push and then to wait for the doctor, was not a nurse, but a ward maid, only there to feed the babies during the night if required. Glad I didn't know then. And she checked to see if she could see the head!*)

Nigel stays by my bed until meals and visiting and I am now used to him and am quite eager to go and fetch him from the nursery. I knew he was his father's son after his first boiled water as he gave a big burp. Perhaps I'd better say how he looks. He has a good shaped head and Richard insists he has his nose and ears, but I think they are more my eyes and nose! He has a soft layer of hair, which is dark but inclined to be blonde and the front looks as though it has some of Richard's kink in it, so I'm hoping he will be blonde like Richard was when he was small. Well goody here's breakfast!

Times of Zambia

21st December   President Kaunda said that he was very humbled by the overwhelming vote of confidence that the country had given him.

*   An ANC member was shot after UNIP candidates were named as the winners. ANC blamed UNIP for the disturbance and the slaying of their member.

23rd December   As President Kaunda is preparing to announce his new cabinet, the threat of a secession movement loomed in Barotsi Province. One of the leading figures of the Lozi Royal Family, Princess Nakatindi warned that if it gained strength it could spell disaster for the province and its 300,000 inhabitants.

24th December   Zambia Flying Doctor is negotiating for funds to start eleven more airstrips throughout the country. They hope to bring every rural dweller within ten hours reach of a doctor.

Letter 190   Christmas Day 1968   Ndola Hospital

No doubt you are celebrating today. Lever Bros and Zambia Oxygen have sent bouquets and I have had cards and presents for Nigel from Marlene, and 30/- from ZamOx for his first savings account but I shall ask if I can buy a baby record book and have them all sign it.

<u>Boxing Day</u>. I gave up with the pen and my biro has disappeared. To continue. On Christmas Eve, Enid came around with her church choir

and nipped in to my room. All the lights were switched out in the corridor and the choir had candles, and it was very choke-making as they sang Silent Night, Once in Royal and Away in a Manger and they all seemed so relevant, especially as they came right on feeding time and there was Nigel clutched to my bosom. Enid says he's just beautiful too.

(This was really special. The choir didn't normally do the maternity ward as the hospital usually sent everyone home who could walk. Just as I had started to feed Nigel, the lights went out and I thought, "Not another power cut" but wasn't unduly bothered as there was still light from the street. Then I was aware of a flickering light in the corridor, but only thought it was the staff organising candles. Then came the singing and I slipped off the bed and carried Nigel to the doorway and looked out. At the far end of the corridor there was a procession of choristers with lanterns. I clambered back on to the bed and with Nigel still clamped on, tried to make myself respectable with the sheets. They sang "Once in Royal David's City" as they gathered around inside the doorway and then started on "Away in A Manger". The funny thing was that as they came to the end of the carol, the singing was faltering as everyone was choked, me included. They, presumably, because the words made sense with me sitting inside a candle lit room with a new baby, and me because I was happy with my new baby, but it was Christmas and I was thousands of miles from home and my own Mum.)

I'm going home at ten this morning instead of tomorrow which is a Christmas concession although I'll have to return tomorrow to have my stitches out. I'll be very glad to get home, as at the moment Nigel needs feeding irregularly. Yesterday morning he was so hungry at the 4.30 feed that he guzzled for an hour and even after me bathing him (for the 1st time – what a way for him to celebrate his 1st Christmas!) he slept right through his 8.30 feed and nothing would induce him to wake. He slept until 11, when Dr Motala (Hayes' locum) woke him and then he remembered he was hungry, so I whipped him out of his cot. This is OK in the morning but the babies have to be surrendered to the nursery before visiting and this means he screams before I can get to him and by the time I can collect him he is too cross to get started. On Tuesday it was worse as he was still on a bottle and now that I am feeding him I can give him a sly sup. He cried so much and got so windy that he held his breath and went blue much to my horror (Spock says this is OK and normally happens with contented babies!)

Richard is crackers about him. He visits early to see him before he goes to nursery and yesterday the baby was allowed to stay during visiting and he couldn't take his eyes off him and commented on every movement of his face or fingers 'look at that – watch him, quick!' As if I hadn't done anything else for the last four days.

The hospital made quite an effort yesterday. Nigel had a present in his crib in the morning – a bib and a vest. We had a mince pie with morning tea, turkey lunch with Christmas pudding and trifle and Christmas cake in the afternoon complete with cracker and trifle bowl of nuts and sweets. Richard brought in his presents to me and mine to him. He bought me a petit-point brush, comb and mirror set, a guidebook to England with restaurant recommendations and recipes, and after delving into my bag while I was away he took pity on its tatty state and brought me a lovely handbag in brown leather.

<u>Later</u>. 9.20am (feels like afternoon) Both Nigel and I are bathed and fed and I am dressed ready for the off. I can't dress Nigel as Richard brought everything on the list I gave him except a nappy! He brought Nigel's bath towel! He must have thought he has the bottom the size of a baby elephant.

Yesterday we also had a visit from the Mayor and Mayoress of Ndola, who made suitable seasonal and congratulatory remarks.

Saturday. I missed the post with this I'm afraid, but we are home again and it is rather chaotic. We slept OK last night but Nigel cried for about 3 hours with wind on Thursday night. However we have invested in a bottle of gripe water and he has been as good as gold since.

Thursday afternoon Marlene and Peter called. Yesterday morning Mrs Mackie called with a bouquet of roses from her garden. In the afternoon Nigel and I slept from 2 until 5 when Richard came home. Today Richard collected our emergency kit and we have started packing although slowly. I seemed to have done nothing except wash and iron, and feed Nigel! I put out washing at 6.00am this morning after feeding him and made up feeds and then lay in the bed. Nigel then decided to have a windy spell and that took up an hour by which time it was changing and feeding time again! Phew!

Richard, as a surprise, has hired a TV for six weeks. He knows the man as he has recently ordered £6,000 worth of new office furniture from him and he waived the six-month minimum hire rule. Richard reckoned we would be housebound and as I would be doing nothing but get used to Nigel all day, I would be glad of a diversion in the evening. Hang on, his Lordship is coming to (dead on grub time) and chewing his fists. Here we go again.

Sunday. Whew what a night! We got about 2hrs sleep. However at seven he went to sleep and I have just fed him again and he is sleeping again. I've to go to the doctors tomorrow as the hospital have left a stitch in which is rather uncomfortable, and I shall ask him what's giving him all this belly ache. I reckon that it's this mixed feeding – one feed me, and one feed bottle, that's not doing his digestion any good. We are packing crockery this morning. Richard has nipped to Rubners' for all their old newspapers. With the packers coming on Thursday, please excuse me if letters are late or scrappy.

Times of Zambia

30th December Zambia economic and defence problems will be discussed when visiting Labour Party MPs meet President Kaunda this week.

- Harry Nkumbula denied that he said Zambian society was too primitive to require election posters. He had said that they were not sophisticated and election posters would mean nothing to them. In any case, he added, there was no printing firm in Lusaka, which was willing to print election posters and election manifestos.

31st December British Civil Service System scrapped.

Letter 191   2/1/69

Ndola, Zambia

Well our effects got off safely today, after a week of climbing over packing cases and cardboard boxes. You can imagine the chaos particularly as it has rained for the past three days and there are wet nappies everywhere. I'm a bit weary of these four-hourly feeds. In the book they don't mention that it takes almost that long to change him, get the food down him and deburp him so that when you finish it's time to start again. Every time he sleeps I try to get an hour's kip too to get up my strength for the early hours of the morning.

We went to Alan and Eva's on New Year's Eve to see in the New Year and to Mackie's on New Year's Day where Richard played tennis and where Nigel snored all afternoon to get up his strength for the early hours.

However we watch TV in the evening until his late feed and it's a good anaesthetic if he cries. Marlene took me to the clinic and Nigel has jumped from 6lb 9oz on leaving hospital on Thursday to 7lb on Monday. So the mixed feeding and all this wind, isn't doing him any harm.

Well he's awake again, or rather he's cried himself hungry again so here we go!! I feel like an automatic milk machine!

Chapter 57   Sleeplessness.

Letter 192   5/1/69

Two minutes breather. Phew what a night. I was up until 2 and then he was awake again at 5.30. And he slept solidly all day. He just doesn't know the difference between night and day! If he has slept beyond feeds, we have left him but again good old Spock says to not let him sleep too much beyond or we will never establish any regular routine, so as from today, we are taking our courage in both hands and are going to wake him when he oversleeps.

We went shopping yesterday, or rather I stood outside with the pram and Richard dashed around the supermarket. I met Dianne whose baby is now 8lbs and sleeping well. Anneke's baby however is also on the windy side.

The house isn't looking as bare as I thought it would, as the sideboard is full of baby cards and we have the TV, and library books and magazines about.

It seems ever so odd you talking about snow and fog etc. I do hope we settle down well and don't hanker too much after the sun. We will be bound to miss it a little, as one would after a holiday. But I'm so used to wearing cotton shifts and no shoes and stockings. Then again I like woollen dresses and my suits, and will probably be able to afford to get some smart clothes. Richard hasn't had anything new except for presents, but it's only shoes and heavy stuff like suits and trousers that are looking the worse for wear. His sandals are awful, one had no strap at all; they are far worse than anything you wear in the garden Daddy! Won't it be nice to have a spend. We have allowed £100, all being well, for clothes which sounds super, but after Richard's and my suits and a couple of pairs of shoes I dare say we will get little change. Just think, there's you lot celebrating like mad, while we pace the bedroom floor! I think you are celebrating the fact that it's not you that has to do it!

Monday 9am. Washing and feeds done. Nigel asleep. Me with feet up. Well we tried out our new routine. At 6pm Nigel was asleep and we woke him and by the time he was clean and changed he was hungry. He ate and was then windy, but after what seemed a reasonable amount of patting, we put him back in his pram where he howled on and off for an hour and then slept. At 10pm we woke him again and this time he went straight back to sleep after feeding. At 2am he awoke and was fed but we put him in the spare room when he wasn't asleep by three. He screamed his head off but we all fell asleep simultaneously. 6am awake again and put back after feeding and he is now again sound asleep. This is a great improvement. The result is that we are far less tired in the morning, and that Nigel instead of screaming until his next feed, now dozes off. We think that continuous nursing and trying to deburp him just makes him more irritable and he is happier left alone in the quiet. Also, for about an hour before he wakes he makes 'coming to' whimpers and grunts and I awake at the first and lie waiting for him to fully awake. In the spare room we can't hear these small noises but can hear him cough, sneeze or cry out. I do so hope this isn't a flash in the pan as it's very depressing being so tired, and I feel full of beans this morning.

It was smashing hearing you on the phone and I'm glad you heard Nigel. I handed Nigel to Richard; hence the reason Richard couldn't hear you as Nigel was bellowing down his other ear. It was nice to hear you Daddy, but on hearing you it seemed like only yesterday that we were talking. The first time we rang, it was exciting. The second time also, but I felt miserable because we were smack in the middle of our tour and it was horrid having to put down the phone, but this time it was super as we were able to say, "See you soon!"

Hurray too! I put on the dress you sent for my birthday and it's a lovely fit so I retried on my Christmas dresses. The silk one is now a super fit too and the blue one only needs a bit more off my hips. However all my straighter dresses are the same, so I must do a bit of rolling. Your letter No 193 arrived yesterday via Marlene and Peter, who now seem to be making a habit of calling to see Sunday children's TV for Sally.

How I miss my motorcar. We are at present using allsorts of odd cars from the firm. We had an old huge Wolseley for the weekend and have also been using a Peugeot. This means we can only shop on Saturdays, or nip in to the deli in the evening for a loaf. No more browsing around the shops to fill in an hour or so. Sally and Stuart are very pleased with the Minx – it rides their dirt road very well – with their 1100 you felt every bump. Sally is having her baby in March in the UK and is staying until May, so we shall see them in London, and they have offered to take us house hunting as they live in, and know, North London very well.

10 o'clock feed over. He cried for about 10mins and when he stopped I popped in and he was restless but asleep. Keep your fingers crossed.

Times of Zambia

11th Jan 1969   **President Kaunda has condemned as an idiot, a fool and nincompoop anyone who behaves like a tribalist or copies a tribalist.**

Letter 193   **10/1/69**

Nigel is very fit. I'm now organised to bath him at 5.30pm for his 6.00 feed, instead of a bath every other day when I could fit it in. Yesterday too was the first time he didn't think I was trying to drown him, and instead of screaming blue murder he sat there and I splashed him for a bit just making the most of his reception. I also had the water a bit hotter instead of tepid. He still is very windy and has some good sleeps and then a screaming fit. I feed him myself for the 10pm, 2am and first morning feed which is very convenient, but I am very unpredictable as sometimes when I think there is too little and I bottle feed him, half way through the feed my bosom gets jealous and drowns us both. It would be more satisfactory one way or the other, but although breast-feeding at home is fine, I will have to revert to bottle for the trip, as I can't be continually changing and washing my clothes.

We are taking Nigel to Enid's tonight. Richard has warned her it might be the end of our friendship! Peter is taking us out to dinner on the company, with Bob and Naomi, who are leaving on 31st Jan – after being both born and bred in Zambia! They are going to South Africa and are selling up their farm.

Pause while Berit Dwyer called. She is the one with the twins. I thought I am tired but she has been telling me how she coped at first trying to feed two. She practically never slept because as soon as one finished feeding, the other had to be fed. Phew! She has brought Nigel a plush blue and pink clown with a cute face. (*Still have it.*)

Our revised itinerary is as follows:

	Arrive	Depart
Cape Town	Feb 15th	Feb 16th
Durban	Feb 18th	Feb 19th
Fremantle	Feb 26th	Feb 28th
Melbourne	Mar 4th	Mar 5th
Sydney	Mar 7th	Mar 9th
Wellington	Mar 12th	Mar 14th
Tahiti	Mar 19th	Mar 20th
Acapulco	Mar 28th	Mar 29th
Panama	Apr 1st	Apr 1st
Curacao	Apr 3rd	Apr 3rd
Trinidad	Apr 4th	Apr 5th
Southampton	10.00am	April 14th !!!!!!!!!!!!!!!!

I am not sorry we came away though. I have a lot more confidence in my own abilities (did I hear you say blowing a trumpet appears to be one of them!) but I adjusted to a new way of life and tackled and did well at a job I had no previous knowledge of, and made a lot of friends on my own e.g. people who are friendly with us because of <u>me,</u> and not Richard or you two. In other words I suppose I've learned to stand quite steadily on my own two feet – although Richard must take a big chunk of the credit. Just hope Nigel isn't as revolting a teenager as I was.

(?? I was a perfect teenager. I was a wimp and never did anything vaguely rebellious. Even took the most boring, horriblest job in the National Insurance Office at Mum's recommendation: a nice secure pensionable office job. Used to cry in bed every Sunday evening as I had a whole week of work before seeing Richard at the weekend again. At least my frugality as a teenager paid for the deposit on our house. Thank heaven for Richard, for marriage and Africa.

Pause for change, feed and a scream. I have discarded his growysuits for a while as he was wringing wet and his hair was sticking to his head and his head was beaded with sweat. So at the moment Nigel has a nylon nightie, vest and nappy on and no covers. I'll put a winceyette sheet on if his feet get cool. It's very humid at the moment and it's difficult to judge the temperature, as everywhere is so damp.

Gosh he's howling again. Just a mo! ….. Peace again – a couple of pats on the back and a jiggle of the pram. Spock says (how many times are you going to hear this!!) that if picking him up makes him feel better, go ahead, but if not leave him alone, before he gets too used to being nursed every time he cries.

Richard took some champagne into the Zamox office today together with Nigel's baby book which they had bought and which I want everyone to sign.

You will probably be pleased to know that I am reconsidering a christening.

Times of Zambia

12th January   **UNIP men living in fear after Barotsi swing to UP**

Letter 194   **12/1/6**

I have two jerseys but nothing to wear with them as my trousers have had it, so I went to the four clothes shops to buy a mini-skirt. In all the shops there were about 12 skirts to choose from, mainly plain grey permanent pleats! I was quite surprised. Must be an after Christmas lull. I am buying some material in the week and will have to hand sew one and borrow Marlene's scissors.

We did get a telegram from the kennels. He was diverted to Manchester, because of fog and then re-flown to London. The kennels also have just written to say they had received Pucci's parcel and say how 'very thoughtful it was of Mrs Waring'. I'm a bit apprehensive about him though, as they say that although he is very happy (!!) he has lost weight because of the long journey and change of environment and that he is on a special diet to remedy this. I do hope he is not pining. Poor little sausage. He probably missed his lunchtime lumps of cheese and savoury tangs and his 3'sy ginger biscuit and the odd liquorice allsort.

I think you had better bring my Dutch blanket in the car, as my green coat was too bulky for the trunk and I only have my linen coat to land at Southampton in. The big coat took up too much room especially as it was only to be worn on the Southampton-Birkenhead journey in a heated car.

On Friday night we went to The Coppers with Marlene and Peter and Bob and Naomi. It wasn't a company do. It was Peter's treat. We took Nigel to Enid's at 7.30 and we had sherry with them. He started to cry as we were leaving but Enid bustled us off and told us not to worry. We laughed in the car as both Enid and Anne were longing for him to wake and we knew that as soon as we were gone he would be picked up. Anyway when we went to collect him she said that he had gone to sleep and then woken up at 10pm. She had fed him and at 11pm when we arrived he was sleeping. She insisted we had coffee, which we did and stayed half an hour and then went back to Marlene and Peter's where they and Dunckleys were having liqueurs. We arrived home at 1.30 and I was in no hurry as he was due for another feed at 2am. I fed him at 1.45 and we went to bed.

On Friday, Dianne took me to the clinic and then we met Anneke, and also the other two girls who were in our class at the beginning. All five of us were madly comparing notes. The two other babies are 12 weeks and look so huge compared with our tinies. However they look ever so bonny and laugh and chuckle and are really interesting, not just food demanding machines. Nigel is advancing splendidly. In 10 days he has gained 1lb, 1oz a day, and is now 8lb 1oz. Anneke's little girl who was 6lbs 13oz at birth is only 7lbs 13oz and Dianne's boy who was 7lb 11oz at birth is 8lb 6oz. So Nigel is doing comparatively well even with his unfortunate mixed feeding. The other two are completely breast-fed.

Monday. Today I went with Dianne to Anneke's. They have a lovely house in Northrise and a complete nursery of white furniture even to playpen and highchair. They have certainly planned in advance! At one stage all three babies were awake at once, and I wished I had taken my camera. As you can imagine, every burp and sneeze of our respective infants was compared and discussed!

We've had some estate agent gen. and are pleased as it looks as though we will be able to manage a detached house even if it's not new, but at least one not much more than ten years old.

This letter is very scrappy, and I do sound very cabbagey, but perhaps in a few weeks when we start on our travels I hope I will be able to send more interesting letters.

Today Richard ran me in to town in his lunchtime (2.30-3.00, the only time he could get a car) and I bought some material for a skirt. Again the materials are awful and all cotton. A month ago they had loads of Courtelle and woollens. It must be a change of season. Anyway it's pale blue with a navy line and will match my navy jerseys. How it will hold together with hand stitching, I don't know!

Times of Zambia

13th Jan 1969 Kaunda warns Watchtower against foreign leadership. He has ordered the Watchtower sect in Zambia to Zambianise their clergy.

Letter 195 15/1/69

It's 7.30pm and we are watching TV with Nigel supplying a chorus. From 6 'til 10 he cries but we don't mind this as we have TV and the more he stays awake in the evening the more likely we are to have a quiet night. Dianne's baby is on cereal already. *(3 weeks!)* When did you start feeding me solid food?

Do you know that I still have 13lbs to lose before getting back to normal. I'm still 127lbs instead of 115ish. I went up to 144ish! The thing I regret about my cruise is not being able to have accumulated cruise clothes. I was too fat to make anything and now I have neither machine nor time. I have about 5 dresses that fit me. Richard says I can get some bits in South Africa.

Another blow. We have come across sanctions in reverse. Our Salisbury/Jo'burg flight we picked as it was an economy flight. We have just been informed that we are to pay double the listed price, as we are booking in Zambia and the special price is only available to Rhodesians and South Africans. Also Mackie has changed his mind again about our baggage allowance despite appeals from Graeme Muirhead. This, in all, sets us back about £70 we hadn't budgeted for. Isn't that a blow! We will probably end up working our passage on this cruise!

We are throwing a farewell party a week on Sunday. We have asked Sally and Stuart for a loan of their garden and braai and we are having a barbeque. We are having everything disposable, with knives and forks and trays on loan from Richard's canteen, and paper plates etc. There will be beer and cool drinks, and our invitations state "bring your own tankard"! We have invited Marlene, Peter and Sally, Bob and Naomi and their children Robyn and Linda, Eva and Alan and their children John and Kirsten, Sally and Stuart of course, Sue and George, Enid, Pat and

Anne, Ron and Elizabeth and their lodger Derek. We have not invited Prices, as their child would ruin it and it's only for old friends anyway. Ann now has her own car, and has had it for about 2 weeks. She has not asked if I want shopping or anything. And the way I waited on her and ran her shopping every other day. The Prices are full of moans about their accommodation, and as you can imagine we have very little sympathy with them.

Sally is taking me to Misundu tomorrow to sit in their garden (a ride in our own car!). Stuart is in Lusaka and she is collecting him from the airport at teatime and coming back to us for supper.

Today Nigel followed Richard's finger from left to right moving his eyes and his head. No doubt about it this time. He does it every time so it's not coincidence. Richard is convinced he is the brightest child out. Nigel is definitely watching our faces and will move his head in the direction of the speaker, but this is not as definite. He also enjoys his bath better each day and clutches at things including my hair – great fistfuls he grabs and swings on it when I put him back in his cot.

Today I put him out in his pram in the shade in just a vest, nappy and nightie and after half an hour he was crying and I brought him in and boy was he hot. His rash had exploded and he was whingeing. He was in the shade too! I changed him and left him in his vest and nappy in his pram in the bedroom, and his rash has subsided a good deal, but not disappeared. And Mrs L said to be sure to keep a jersey on him!

We are now watching "Whiskey Galore" a 1943 film. There has been a series of Ealing Studios films and they are crammed full of today's TV actors. And corny! Wow! Thrillers don't seem to date so much but general films – oh dear. They're OK to watch during the 10pm feed otherwise it means the 10, 2am and 6am are all done in bed and it makes the night so long.

Chapter 58   Partying

Letter 196   17/1/69

Monday 9.30am. Jobs all done. Nigel grizzling in his cot. Saturday, we went to the swimming pool just to get me out of the flat. Ron and Elizabeth came too. It's more crowded at the weekend but still very welcome. Poor Richard didn't go in as he can't swim and feels daft as everyone here can swim like fish. I enjoyed my dip and Nigel slept. Yesterday we went to Marlene's in the morning where I spent half an hour on her Bernina making my skirt. It's not a success as although my waist is fine my hips are huge. I am almost a stone heavier and it's all around my behind. In the afternoon Richard played golf with Ron, with Elizabeth's clubs and in Graeme's shoes, and I went for the walk pushing Nigel who slept all the way although he had been an absolute horror all day and all evening. It must have been the onions I had for my supper. Elizabeth says I should have a tot of whiskey on the Friday we leave and he will sleep all night! It'll probably knock me out too! We had drinks with Whites after golf and came back here in time to see the last episode of the Count of Monte Cristo.

I'm writing this with Nigel on my knee. Andre just shouted downstairs 'Scuse Madame' – which means that Nigel has just yawned or hiccupped. It was the latter so rather than let him get on with it, I have to pick him up. I think that Africans think it wrong to leave babies, as Sue Thwaite's servant is forever rocking the pram when her baby stirs.

It's cooler today and there is no sign of any heat rash. On the golf course I tucked a sheet in his mosquito net around the hood to keep out any sun. I keep his net on all the time, and keep my eye open for mozzies, when he is out of the pram, as malaria would be awful at his age and he's only protected from the pills I take. I have made an appointment for his smallpox vaccination on Thursday, and I am dreading it as the vaccine here is strong and although good, knocks toddlers out for a few days and Nigel will only be 4 ½ weeks. I do hope Dr Hayes can give him just a tiny dose. We can't leave it longer, or nearer to when we go, as the worst is at 8/9 days after the jab and Spock (again) says that those days should be quiet and it's wise not to be busy or to do any travelling. So think of us at the end of the month coping with wind and a fever.

I don't know how we are going to arrange things when we come home. We are hoping to sell our house when these tenants move out, probably at the beginning of March, and if it is sold before we arrive home then our furniture can go into store with Hardings who are holding our other things, and to whom we have sent the sea things.

Richard has written to Mr L about all these things, but I am repeating them to you so that you are also in the picture and can see if Mr and Mrs L do something daft. Mrs L is also taking it for granted that we are staying with them the weeks after we arrive home and she has taken the week off so that she can look after Nigel while we sort out our Chester house. This is unnecessary as there will be little sorting out to do, and Nigel can come with us anyway. I can't just dump him with a stranger. She would also be better saving her leave to visit us when we are straight in London. Also Richard is going to London on the Wednesday after we return to find out about his new job, and I shall stay with you, when he is away at least. The rest of the time we shall unfortunately have to divide between you. Richard thinks we would be better staying at the Central!

2pm. Do you recall how many times we have not been invited to company dos? Well our farewell party is on Friday and Alan and Eva Phillips have not been invited and Richard went to see Buchanan who for once agreed it was ridiculous as Alan is the only manager who has not been invited – correction, Jim Sergeant also. Buchanan went to see Mackie who issued the invites and was told that they couldn't come. Our reaction was that they could stuff their flipping party. We are only friendly with a few couples and Alan and Eva are one of them. There are people invited that I've never even heard of, let alone met. Isn't it barmy? Apparently the way they work it, is that all the departmental heads are invited regardless of grade, together with the lower grades in the department concerned. Our party is an accounts department do, so all the accounts supervisors are invited together with the representative heads of departments not directly concerned. Richard is assistant chief accountant, and Bob Dunckeley is an assistant, and Alan is the assistant engineer and Jim Sergeant is assistant sales manager, so these four are consistently left out of parties. In Richard and Bob's case, Peter is the department head. So out of almost 40 managers, depending on the type of party, one to three managers are omitted. Alan invited us to dinner afterwards before he knew he hadn't been invited. However we are still going out to dinner and will leave the cocktail party early rather than not go at all. We weighed up whether to not go at all, to make up for all the parties we've not been to, but it's Bob's party too and we don't want to embarrass him by not turning up, but we are very much tempted! Tell David when you see him. I bet he'll explode!

Eva says she doesn't want to go anyway now. It all sounds so petty, but I know how she feels. It's miserable being the only ones left out. I wonder if I've the nerve to say when someone is introduced that I don't know "how ridiculous to be introduced just to say farewell" but I haven't the nerve. Perhaps a couple of whiskies would do it. Never mind, our party on Sunday has all our friends going and that should be good.

A high chair for Nigel sounds super, but do wait until I come home as I am so looking forward to going around the shops! We can have a good old browse when Richard is in London.

Daddy, will you feel any financial benefit from your 5-day week or will it disappear in tax. Will you still get your rise and back pay, or is this a way around it.

On Saturday, we picked up all our tickets for the journey. Yippee! 2wks on Friday!

Don't blame Win for not having her baby adopted. I couldn't part with Nigel however strong the pressure. I think to do that you must be a real hardknock and very callous, or very far sighted and very courageous.

We have loads of gen. from house agents and there appears to be lots of suitable houses available. The main thing is the siting in relation to a station and unfortunately all the big houses with lovely gardens in our price range are cheaper comparatively because they are miles from a station and even then about an hour from London. Ideally we want a post 1960 house, 3 / 4 bedrooms, detached with a private fenced in garden, and we have seen some that meet most of these conditions. Let's hope similar ones are available in April.

Richard starts work on 5th May 1969 and will have to stay in digs if we have no house. Depending on the digs and Nigel's behaviour, I shall either go with him or stay with you.

Letter 197   22/1/69

Last night we went to Ron and Elizabeth's for dinner with Marlene and Peter and Derek Williams. Richard came home green at lunchtime having been sick at work and went and lay down. He went back to work half an hour late, but feeling better. Peter and Marlene were up all night with upset stomachs. We can't think what they had eaten last night, but I had everything they had and (touch wood) feel fine. Poor Elizabeth. Wouldn't she feel awful if she knew? I saw her this morning and she didn't mention that they had been ill at all.

We have had quite a lot of invitations to dinner, Enid, Prices, Alan Phillips and Mackies (paid for by the company!). Well it saves us cooking in the last weeks. The junk we are eating at the moment, all the odd tins and packets e.g. orange jelly and blackberries, and lemon meringue filling with no pie! The braai on Sunday will use up all our sauces and pickles and chutneys – if not we can leave them at Sally's. My other stuff – baking powder, spices, icing sugar and the like can go to Eva. Basic things like flour, tea and sugar and coffee and salt can go to Andre. This can be done after lunch on the Friday and we can go straight to Eva's or Marlene's for a cuppa before either Peter or Alan takes us to the bus at 3.30.

I can't say I will enjoy having no news of you between here and Freemantle, but if anything urgent crops up about the dog or house or anything you could always telegram the ship or what have you. I'm living in limbo at the moment. Now I have taken down the baby cards, the place looks barren. Being without a car and our household effects gives me absolutely nothing to do apart from walking to Dianne's. I suppose that at least Nigel keeps me busy. It's rather like waiting for a taxi to go on your hols. Once the cases are packed and the water and electricity is switched off, you just want to be off.

Although we won't see the place again, there is the consolation that most of our friends will probably crop up in the UK in the next few years. Even Dianne is leaving for the Cheshire area in March. *My cousin made friends with a new mother in Cheshire and found out it was Dianne, so we did meet again.*

I took Nigel to Dr Hayes and he says that Nigel is too small for smallpox injection and that it was not worth having him very poorly at this stge. He has given me a letter to that effect, and I am to produce it if it is queried. I hope there's no trouble at any ports. I'm rather glad really as I couldn't bear him to be poorly on the eve of our trip. Sorry this is a scrappy letter, but the highlights in the last two days have been coffee at Dianne's and a visit to the doctors!

Letter 198   24/01/69

I have lost my sunglasses! I went to the opticians and he can get new ones for me before I go. I'm very pleased about this as the sun is so glaring out and I've never been outdoors without them on; fortunately I don't need to drive, but when I walk to Dianne's the glare from the road is awful. Anyway, the optician suggested all-purpose lenses, which are tinted to take away the glare but can be worn indoors too which my others couldn't. The optician also had in some new frames, that he was just unpacking, and I picked a very smart pair. He also informed us that, as they were tinted and on a prescription we can claim on our medical insurance and therefore only have to foot half the bill. So what was a great inconvenience and a financial disaster turned out to be an advantage – a better pair of glasses for a reasonable price.

On Friday we went to Mackie's for our farewell do. It went off very well – about eight people were sick, Mackies themselves and Marlene and Peter and Richard and a few others. Richard was ill all night and I went and slept on the sofa for some peace. What a night. We were presented with two copper tankards with Lever Bros 1969 engraved on them. They are rather nice. *Must have cost Levers all of a pound. I wonder what happened to them? It tasted awful to drink out of them. Mainly used them for flowers.*

Yesterday, Sunday, we had our braai. It went off very well, but all Saturday night there was a tremendous storm and it was still raining when we arrived at Sally's at 10.30a.m. We had prepared all the food at home and even cooked the baked potatoes for an hour in the oven before putting them in tin foil. We then loaded the car to the brim and drove five miles up the Mufulira road to seek out a charcoal burner. We bought a sack of charcoal for 12/6 and we had to re-organise the car, putting the crates of ale on the front seat, and me in the back by the carrycot with my feet amongst cakes and meat etc. I did no baking, but bought apple pies, egg custards and a lemon meringue. We had 12lb of steak, 30 lamb chops, 3lbs of sausage and 1lb of burrewoeurs, and loads of salad and bread rolls. I also bought ice cream and choc-ices for the babies (5 of them) which kept them quiet as it drizzled until 12.00 and then the sun came out and we sat on Sally's new lawn. Everyone went home at about 3 o'clock and I fed Nigel and we had a cup of tea. Clearing up was easy, with all the paper things. It was a jolly good afternoon and everyone thoroughly enjoyed it. It was miserable coming back to the empty flat!

This morning Richard arrived home to say that there had been a whopping collection at work and he was to go and choose something, so we went and chose a slide projector and an electronic flash gun. Isn't that super. I'm longing to see them, and have a play but we have to wait until after his presentation.

Here is an independent unbiased opinion. One of the secretaries said to Richard "How is the baby, I believe he's gorgeous" – One of the other secretaries had seen him and told her. So there you are. It's not just us who think he's a smasher. Richard calls him 'Superman'. Another way Nigel is growing is his paddy. If you take away his bottle when he is in mid-suck, he will go bright red, screw up his face and scream and thump me with his fists until I ram it back again. He knows what he wants!

Letter 199   30/1/69

On Tuesday, we went to Jack and Marge Pawson's, and had a smashing supper. We left Nigel with Enid, and I was relieved, as he had been crying off and on since two o'clock. However the monkey fell asleep when we arrived and still hadn't woken up when we came home.

We are going to Alan and Eva's tonight and they are taking us out tomorrow. We are going to Enid's Saturday and are keeping Sunday completely free to do our packing. We will never get everything into our cases I'm sure!!I bought 3 packets of disposable nappies – 30 for 15/-! They will last me for the last two days here and a day travelling, so that I will buy more in Salisbury. I shall only use them for the week travelling unless they are very much cheaper on board ship. They are little thicker than paper hankies!

We are sending some stuff off by airfreight – all the bits and pieces that are left. Tea cloths, iron, projector, etc. A group of girls in Richard's office from one of his departments have sent Nigel a present – a mug, eggcup, napkin ring and spoon all in a set. Wasn't that nice.

Chapter 59   Leaving

Letter 200   2/2/69

Mrs. L redeemed herself and rang us yesterday. She didn't say how gorgeous Nigel was, just that he was just like Richard at the same age, which I suppose in her eyes is the same thing!

Yesterday we spent a very pleasant day packing. It's a tight squeeze into just two suitcases. We are sending a further small box home by airfreight, with the odds and ends we haven't room for. This includes Nigel's clown – I will have to buy him toys on the way if he needs them.

I can't get into the spirit of coming home yet. It still seems such a long way off and we have such a long way to travel.

It's Andre's last day today and he is polishing all the furniture. He washed out the kitchen cupboards and paintwork yesterday. The cupboards are now practically empty. Our suitcases are packed but for Nigel's things and our things for this week. We are going to the Price's tonight. Enid, Pat and Ann are coming to us tomorrow to eat our duck with us. One of Richard's staff, Mr Njamba, presented him with a duck. He kindly chopped off its head for us and Richard brought it home in a cardboard box. Andre's last job will be to pluck it and clean it. It's rather sad that he is going after being with us for so long, but Richard has found him a good job in the factory, which is about £6 more a month. There is also a medical and pension scheme and of course the job is secure. His punctuality and attendance record with us is good, so he should have no trouble in holding down the job.

I'm going for my post-natal check-up this afternoon – I just timed that well.

A lot of people seem to be coming to see us off (the radio is playing 'Yesterday' – making me quite nostalgic – for what I don't know – but it's a sad tune) so we shall keep our cine out. I hope it doesn't rain, as people might not want to come to get soaked!

We leave here on Friday morning and go to the Phillips for lunch and then to the bus for 3.30pm. We arrive in Lusaka at 9.00pm and in Salisbury at 6am. It's a long journey isn't it? Let's hope we get some sleep. If we don't sleep because Nigel is crying – neither will anyone else and won't we be popular! I have bought a dummy and he doesn't cry when this is in his mouth – but it keeps falling out so I shall have to stay awake and keep ramming it back in again. Someone has said that the movement of the coach will help him sleep – I hope so.

As you can see I'm waffling. My next letter will probably be an airmail letter posted before we go, and then probably another from the boat. I'll try to write on the way down, but expect at every free moment to be fixing up a new load of bottles. I have made three insulators out of newspaper. I wound thick paper around a bottle, stuck on a bottom and made a lid and covered the lot with some Contact I found when clearing out. They won't keep the bottles warm, but I hope will prevent the milk from going off too soon.

Just spotted a house in the estate agent pamphlet - £8,750 – Mill Cottage. 4 bedrooms, 17th century cottage with ¼ acre with frontage on the R. Wye. Sounds lovely – probably full of dry rot and gets flooded from the Wye twice a year!

Letter 201   7/2/69

A very short note indeed. Everything apparently under control but seems chaotic. Richard's coming home at 3, and I've just had a super lunch with Ron and Elizabeth. The electricity was switched off a day too soon at 8am and it was only at 12 that I rang the Electricity Board and found out it wasn't a power failure. Hence I couldn't iron and have lost 4 hours drying time with the electric fire. Have been into the office to say Cheerio, which was rather sad, and Dianne is taking me to Mrs Chapman's (the physio) with Anneke to show her and the rest of our class our results.

We arrived at The Savoy Hotel in good time for the coach to Salisbury, with all Nigel's bottles prepared for the journey. However there was a problem with the coach and they reckoned it would take a couple of hours to fix and we should come back at 5.30pm. Dianne invited us back where happily I could feed Nigel and make up another bottle. All the folk who had come to wave us off said Goodbye and drifted away. Dianne brought us back at 5.30 but had to leave because of the baby, so there we were without a bus or flag waving farewell party. The coach company announced that they would be replacing the coach, by which time it was dark. The replacement bus arrived. It was a regular local township bus with metal-framed seats, no air conditioning, no loo, no catering. When everyone complained, we were told it was that or wait days for the other to be repaired. We set off. Every time we stopped for a loo stop in the bush, I had to wrap Nigel up in his pram mozzie net until we moved off again after the driver had sprayed the interior of the bus .I have never seen such a variety of flying creatures. It was a long, long fifteen hours. Can't think why I didn't mention it.

All for now and all from Ndola.

Letter 202   11/2/69

The Rand International Hotel

Johannesburg

South Africa

Well I'm writing this on the Karoo Express from Jo'burg to Cape Town. I don't know so much about express, as we are chugging along. Where did I get to last?

In Salisbury in the afternoon we went out of town to a lake. We saw some giraffe and deer and a monkey! We had a picnic lunch by the lakeside, which was very pleasant. Our only problem was keeping Nigel cool in the car. He was OK when we stopped, but driving we draped nappies across the back windows. We went out to Salisbury airport at

7.00pm and left for Jo'burg at 7.40.pm. Nigel slept from arrival at the airport until we arrived at the hotel in Jo'burg at midnight. Our suite at the hotel, on whose paper I'm writing, was super. We had a huge bedroom with a full size business desk and office area, and a lounge with fitted-in armchairs and coffee table and a cocktail cabinet thing containing a fridge and glasses. This was ideal for Nigel's bottles.

It's the first and last time we'll probably be staying in such a smart hotel. We didn't hire a car in Jo'burg, so couldn't get out of the city centre, so we spent the whole day shopping. Lovely. I was rather disappointed however with the shops as they were in the middle of "end of summer" sales and the stock was a mixture of sale goods and winter clothing most of which was from the UK – particularly "Harella" stuff. I'm blowed if I'm buying stuff made in Beaufort Road when I'm out here!! *Harella was a clothes factory, which had a low-paid workforce, which gave me a lot of problems while I was in The Ministry.* However we found a boutique, where I bought five dresses. They were most interested in us and we had a cup of tea in the back of the shop and I fed Nigel there! Wasn't that nice – although Richard says that he more than paid for the tea. I also bought a pair of sandals, a pair of shoes and a velvet bow, which was as dear as the shoes! I'm glad I bought it – we even went back to the shop to get it, as I knew I would only hanker after it and it's rather frivolous. I wore my new navy and white spotty dress with my old green shoes and bag to match last night at dinner.

Later, Tuesday, on the Karoo Express– 7.30pm

We are very lucky to have a four-seater compartment. The train journey is 10am this morning to 4pm tomorrow, that's 30 hours! Nigel is already filthy. Our hands have been grubby and his new cotton rompers are covered in grimy prints and he has smuts on his face. We have had lunch and dinner and the man is now coming in to do the beds and I am going to have a sleep.

Wednesday – 9.30am And still we're on the move. We saw the dawn rise over the desert this morning. The countryside is fantastic in its bleakness – not the attractive bleakness of the Yorkshire Moors but a dry, dusty waste. Nigel was fretful all of yesterday but is at present catching up on his sleep. It's not the making of feeds that's difficult –just the fact that I can only rinse and not sterilise his used bottles. I must boil them all when we get to the hotel. We are in the hotel until Sunday so we will be more settled. You can see by the first page how dusty it was last night.

Hotel Metropole, Cape Town.

Having a splendid and very busy time in Cape Town. It's a tremendous place. Sorry letter is scrappy but we have been out all day and arrived back at six. The hotel has sent all his dirty bottles back, all sparkling clean on a silver tray covered in a linen cloth. They offered to do this without any request from us. How about that for service?

It's magnificent here.

Letter 203   16/2/69

Northern Star   8 miles from Cape Town

Well we are now truly on our way home. We finished off our sightseeing yesterday and also managed a few hours on the beach. In the morning we called on your friend May Blackmore. She was in, but just dashing out to the hairdressers and had to catch a bus. She was so flustered when she heard who we were and went flying round combing her hair and tidying. She really is a fusspot. However we took her photograph with John who is a very nice, polite and chatty little boy. She said she would phone the hotel and I never thought she would as she didn't know our name but she found us and we had a good old natter for about 15 minutes. They are in a small but pleasant flat and are quite settled. We invited them to the hotel for a drink but her husband had just come in from work. I got the impression she would have been delighted to have come, but that her husband wouldn't make the effort. She looks years older than you (I've got to say that haven't I!) Her hair is grey and she is very dumpy although quite smart. You wouldn't think that she was the pretty girl in your old Ministry photographs.

Nigel is being super. Friday and Thursday I let him sleep through and he slept from after his 6pm bath and feed until 4am! And last night he slept until 5am. Isn't that smashing? This means we can quite happily leave him for the evening and just pop back every half hour or so to check on him. *This makes me wince, but we were only in the hotel dining room. But post McCann, I would have had room service.*

We left Cape Town at 12 noon today, with streamers flying and "A life on the Ocean Wave" being played on the loudspeakers. It's rather like a modified Butlins afloat, but it should be fun. We are sitting on the aft deck – the only place to sit as it's blowing a gale everywhere else as we are just rounding the Cape – the roughest part of the whole voyage apparently. Nigel isn't allowed in the dining room, and we take him to the nursery and put him in a cot. The nurse said he fell asleep as soon as we left and he was sleeping when we collected him. Dinner is at 6 – too early unfortunately as he has a bath and feed then. I shall have to give him a few ounces beforehand as he must wait until 7 – or I may take him to the children's tea at 5.45 and give him a spoonful of Heinz bone and vegetable which may make him last the extra hour. He will then be bathed and in bed for us to join in the evening's activities. All the lounges and writing rooms are very comfortable but the boat is very full – mostly Australia bound people.

Monday 3pm. Well this is more like it. I spent this morning queuing at the launderette! But we have now found a space, which is very sheltered just outside the nearest door to our cabin and we are relaxing.

The food is ok, but the meal times are very rigid – only an hour for 1st sitting but at least the service is quick – it's a wonder we haven't got indigestion!

We are at present cruising along the South African coast. We have passed Port Elizabeth and should be passing East London at 3.30. I shall feed Nigel on deck so that I don't miss anything. Nigel is wearing his first cardigan, as it's rather cool in the wind – but he's well wrapped up – it's just his arms and neck that need covering. We have joined the library but I must write some letters first.

I must close this letter this afternoon as 6am is the last collection for post to be put ashore at Durban.

We have a newsletter each morning, which I shall save to show you. There have been keep fit lessons and art classes and yoga today, but I was in the launderette!! There are films this afternoon and evening and also a dance and singing in the tavern, so there's plenty to do. There are always card games in the various lounges and discussion groups in the library. However at the moment we prefer to be very anti-social and just laze up here on deck.

At no point have I described the cabin. We had booked an indoor cabin for two: the outside cabins were extra, but on the Sun Deck, the best deck. As we had booked twelve months in advance, we had to let Shaw Saville know there was an extra to include in the cabin. They said that it wasn't a problem; they would just put up a cot. When we arrived at the cabin, the steward, whose name was Elsie, was flapping, as there was no way a cot would fit in this tiny window less room. And boy was it tiny. It had bunk beds. We said that we could keep the carrycot on the floor, and put the wheels in the shower. It was grim trying to feed Nigel, as the top bunk was too low to allow me to sit upright. I had to half lie down on the bed propped up with pillows. Elsie took pity on us and pitched up with a small, upholstered chair, which we jammed between the bunk and the sink. We had to put a pillow on the sink so I wouldn't crack Nigel's head on it. It wasn't good, but it was much better.

Letter 204   Saturday 22/2/69

Durban to Fremantle

Nigel was two months old yesterday. And only 7 weeks to go now! It's rather a pity because instead of just enjoying the cruise, I can't wish it to go fast enough. Seven weeks seems the longest time of all!

We spent most of our time just sitting in our sheltered spot. I'm glad I didn't have time to lash out on beachwear as I'm sitting here in my jersey, but it feels very healthy. We saw a feature film on Thursday and last night went to a race meeting with wooden frogs. It was just like horse racing even to the music and the Honest Joes taking bets. There was quite a good atmosphere.

In Durban we went on a bus tour with all the old dears. However it was probably the best way to see Durban, but after Zambia, the state of the black Africans here seems quite ludicrous. The South Africans seem to treat them like monkeys in a circus, encouraging them to perform begging dances for the coach loads of tourists. Unless it was just the ones we saw.

We also visited Durban's Indian market, which was fascinating. Unfortunately Richard is very cunning and only cashes enough money for a couple of Cokes, so I don't go as mad as I did in Jo'burg. We are not doing so badly on board ship, we just buy a drink at meals and maybe in the evening, and the odd bar of chocolate and packet of crisps. It's the ports that are more expensive as we pay for the bus tours, lunch out and camera films – but on the whole we are doing better than expected.

So far we are going through a library book a day. I particularly like mine for Nigel's early morning feed between 4am and 5am. We were disappointed at first as the books looked so tatty, but on closer examination we find that the books are current ones. As every other person has a book, and if they change them as often as we do, it's no wonder they are well thumbed.

Nigel stays on deck all day with his blanket up to his chin and is quite cosy, and all this fresh air should do him good. For the last three days he has had a teaspoon of Farex mixed with four teaspoons of his milk. This makes about four teaspoons of cereal, which he eats well. We laughed the first day at the faces he pulled and more went down his bib and sleeves than down his throat, but we now have the knack and he doesn't lose any at all and swallows the lot. I give him his milk after, not before, as he can then wash it down, otherwise he can't swallow what's left in his mouth and chews and sucks for ages.

I shall just be posting one letter at each port. We should be home before our last letters! We are looking forward to getting mail in Fremantle.

Tuesday 25th? I am sitting on deck soaking up the fresh air. Poor little Nigel's got a runny nose and a cough. I sat up with him almost all night and we stayed in bed until 11 to recuperate. He has got some cough mixture from the doctor. All the children on board have it and a lot of the adults – a good number of whom are in bed. He sleeps OK during the day, all snug in his cot but in the air-conditioned cabin his nose runs and he can't breathe and hence coughs. He's such a brave little boy. He'll cough himself awake and then open his eyes and gives a big smile. It should only last another day or so. He is still eating heartily and is otherwise fine, but Richard and I are looking the worse for wear! Just when we were starting to get some sleep!

Last night was a fancy dress party, which was ever so good. We wrapped Nigel in a blanket and went and sat to see the parade. We then collected our buffet supper and came up to our cabin for a feast to give us strength. The costumes were super. The best were the improvised ones with towels and things, and the witty ones. The funniest were the boys dressed as silly things e.g. a great beefy man in a crepe paper tutu as Queen of the Fairies complete with hairy chest. One winner was 'A bust' which was a cardboard ring around the neck draped with a sheet to make a column, a complete white face and Grecian wig made of cotton wool. It was very simple and most effective. The evening meal was a special one and the dining room was decorated with balloons and hanging streamers and things and there was piped music, which we don't normally have and the atmosphere was very festive.

Yesterday, we played deck quoits in the morning, which was good fun.

The sea is an absolutely gorgeous shade of blue and from the top deck you can see a complete circle of horizon. It's like sitting in the middle of a huge blue saucer. My favourite pastime, when I get the opportunity, is sitting looking for flying fish. There were two whales on the starboard quarter on Sunday, but I was in the launderette and Richard on the port side with Nigel and he couldn't get there quickly enough.

We get bulletins of the land we are passing and the weather forecast and bits of sea gossip over the loudspeaker e.g. the names and history of the ships we are passing and where they are going.

I wash on one day and iron the next, and it takes me an hour a day. I am completely in favour of these tumble driers in the launderette. I wash and spin in one room and dump the whole lot in the drier in another room, and after thirty mins or less in the drier it's ready to put away. I'm trying to convince Richard that we need one. It's just the job with nappies. Even at Dolphin Court in that heat, I had always a clothes airer full of nappies.

We have bought <u>SIX</u>!! more slide films and 3 more cines and that should easily last us. Golly, aren't you going to be bored silly!! The ship's shop is closed until we leave Australia in 10 days so we have stocked up.

We arrive in Fremantle tomorrow. We had a 'landfall' dinner and dance last night as we approached Australia, with paper hats and decorations. For the last eight days we have put the clock on 45mins each night and boy do you feel it. We shall lose another 6 hours before arriving home. Ah well – we shall be home sooner!

Nigel's cold has almost gone and he is a lot better, but I now have an awful streaming cold and cough and we have not even reached the northern hemisphere yet!

We have a funny Cockney waiter at our table and when we told him we were from Zambia and not South Africa, as he thought, he says "Cor! You ruddy missionaries or somat?" Can you imagine Richard a missionary?

We always have the waiter's choice. He says 'What'll you have?' and then replies – 'Nah, I wouldn't have that – it's as tough as old boots' – or 'don't have those beans, they'll ruin your teeth'. We wanted braised beef instead of ham but he said it was stringy, and we told him that he said it was stringy because he had to walk further for the beef. So he brought the beef and with misgivings put it in front of us and sure enough it was stringy!! So now we listen to him. *His ambition was to have a fish and chip restaurant, where you would eat in as well as take out. He was only the same age as us. I hope he managed it.*

I am now sitting in the lounge while Richard is writing. Nigel was sleeping soundly before supper so we didn't take him to the nursery. It is now 9 o'clock and I popped up (we take it in turns every 15mins) and he is still asleep.

We are writing to Mr L as he has been asking about the selling of the house. We must take a chance and leave it to his judgement, but we will make a list of what he can sell at the same time e.g. cooker. I'm not sure about things like curtains and venetian blinds. I'm all for selling them if the house buyer will take them, but I must talk it over with Richard. Two things are definite – no loose furniture or lamps or light fittings (except the globe ones) or the Hygena base units (2 of them) must be sold. It's so difficult to remember what was in the house and must accept whatever Richard's father thinks is for the best. It must be just as difficult for him as for us. He has reminded Richard that he promised to buy him a record cabinet to replace ours. I think we will have to leave ours, although Richard is reluctant as I bought it for his 21st. He also asked what records Richard was leaving for him! We will have to put something towards their new suite, particularly as theirs was ruined by the tenant's cat.

Chapter 60   Between Fremantle & Melbourne

Letter 205   2.3.69

Northern Star

Super – four of your letters received today on arrival in Fremantle. We went and looked at the "L"s but there weren't any, so Richard said. After breakfast I nipped back and had a root about and found four from you and one from mother-in-law. He needs glasses – No. 206 was posted to Melbourne but arrived here – wasn't that clever, either of Shaw-Saville or the G.P.O.

We had a super day today. Ten customs or immigration men came aboard on the pilot boat at six a.m., as the ship wasn't allowed to berth before a check. By 7.30 we were all through; only a matter of stamping the passport – and at eight we docked. The car hire girl was waiting (in a red mini skirt-white blouse and red cap, bag & shoes like an air hostess). She handed the car over and we piled in (except the mini-girl – Richard said he wished he'd had chauffeur drive instead of self-drive!). We went through Fremantle to Perth and up the coast and spent the morning along some beautiful beaches. The waves are surfers and I put Nigel in the Indian Ocean (just his toes) when the wave was on the ebb, but he screamed like mad and drew up his knees. However he liked squiggling his toes in the sand. We didn't sit in the sun, as it was too hot (98° recorded on the ship) and when Nigel is out of his pram I have to carry his pram umbrella or drape a pram sheet over his head so that just his nose shows and he looks like a sheik.

We then had Cokes and milkshakes and drove back to Perth to a beautiful park. Here we had a lunch in the open air and Nigel woke as we finished, therefore just timing it nicely.

While I was feeding him we got talking to some real Australians. There was an old dear whom they called Auntie and whom they were visiting, who had been born in Australia, and her nieces and the niece's daughter of about twenty-five. We talked for about half an hour and they were so friendly and stood waving when we drove off. One said she was born in Salisbury and Richard said "Salisbury, Dorset or Salisbury, Rhodesia" and she said no – Salisbury, Parrawirra.

We then drove to a memorial fountain, in which was a white swan, which all these Australians were photographing. I took a photo and then one lady said she had never seen a white swan before. Apparently the indigenous Australian swan is completely black! And this one had been specially imported, hence the interest.

We then drove back to Fremantle. We posted a still film and a letter at the main G.P.O. where I asked for Mrs. King's sister (in our office at Zamox). However the man said no women were employed there. I must have got the wrong G.P.O. or Mrs. King must have made a mistake.

I'm sending a letter from every port, so that's Melbourne (this one), Sydney and Wellington. I expect I shall be home before any from Tahiti onwards. We are a Royal Mail ship and perhaps the letters will arrive home on this same boat depending on the regularity of the air services.

Tuesday 4th For Southampton we are going to get a balloon to wave so you can spot us on board. If you won't feel daft, see if you can get one too, or a flag or something. It's impossible otherwise to pick anyone out.

Also – the ship is able to take radio telephone calls when it's a day out of port, so you can ring the ship on the Sunday if you like.

Letter 206   Thursday 6/3/69

Between Melbourne and Sidney

3pm mid-way between Melbourne and Sydney, and this will be a quickie as I've been mad busy today washing clothes and my hair and writing my postcards and this is the first time I've sat in the deck chair all day and

527

Nigel will be waking about 3.30!

Richard says that I will have to have a rinse as my hair is going grey at the sides – no wonder! We had a super time in Melbourne. Yesterday we visited an Australian animal sanctuary and saw koalas, platypus, echidna (what!!), emus and kangaroos, which I tickled! I said I'd like to take a cuddly koala home, but I was already taking home something cute and cuddly, and Richard said 'Yes that's right – me!'

I am also still putting on weight despite cutting out bread and potatoes, so I'll now have to cut out the fish course and the puddings. All I can wear are my new dresses and two of my maternity tents, and I can't pluck up courage to wear my new swimsuit and I can't get into my shorts, so now my wish to lose weight is greater than my wish to not waste the meals we've paid for! So I must be very strict or I'll be waddling down the gangplank. I'm only 10lb lighter than when I was 9 months pregnant!

We were cross (again) with the letter from Richard's father. First of all he asks us what we mean by ringing Beresford Adams Estate Agents when he is supposed to be dealing with things. However we received a letter from B. Adams wanting clarification on some points and we could only do this by phone, as we obviously couldn't exchange letters. Richard wrote on the same day confirmation of the phone call to Beresford Adams and details of the phone call to his father. Secondly he was mad about us not telling him the projector was in our parcel of effects, and that we had better be careful about trying to get away without paying duty in future, as we could have been fined etc. etc. We had absolutely no intention of not declaring the projector. The airway bill said household (or personal) effects and Richard spent a long time at the airport listing every single item in the boxes for customs declaration purposes before we were allowed to dispatch the boxes and we were in no way underhand at all, and had no intention of putting Richard's father on the spot. In any case where was the Zambian inventory we filled in? Eric also said that because he was nice to the customs people they were prepared to overlook "the other little things" – what "other little things"? Nigel's clown and his EPNS spoons? – I repeat – we were certainly not trying to smuggle anything in. In any case the company will pay for any duty paid on unsolicited gifts at the end of tour anyway so we would be unlikely to try anything. It makes me cross to have him think we were being dishonest. Surely he can give us the benefit of any doubt without jumping the gun like that. Ah well, I can only see our point of view! The sooner we can attend to our own affairs and make our own mistakes, the better.

The Australian coastline here is incredible, all long, beautiful beaches. I took out a book from the library about Captain Cook – the one that was featured in one of the Sunday colour supplements and he travelled the same routes as we are, so it is super seeing the same things and reading about the same places. I keep thinking someone will shout "Land ahoy!" from the rigging. Richard says that, when they see me, the sailors shout "Avast behind".

Hope to met Roy and Brenda tomorrow. Next stop Wellington, then we feel we are nearer home as the distance between us starts to decrease, as up to now it has increased.

Letter 207   Monday 10/3/69

Sidney to Wellington

Well we had a super time in Sydney. We arrived in port at 7am and we were allowed ashore at 8am and shortly afterwards Roy, *(a relative)*, came. Visitors were not allowed on board until customs had done their stuff but we were allowed off and fortunately, I recognised him straight away. He is just a younger edition of Uncle Bob. I have only ever seen him fleetingly more than ten years ago. Brenda couldn't come on Friday as she was working, so Roy took us all around Sydney and to Botany Bay and Bondi Beach and to some super views and to many places he had never been himself, even living so close.

We had lunch at a place specialising in fish. It was gorgeous eating fresh fish again. It was guaranteed swimming the day before. We arrived home at six and then Roy had to drive 1 ½ hours home. He said they both would set off early tomorrow to avoid the Sydney rush hour traffic between 7 and 8am. At 7.10am on Saturday there was a knock on our cabin door and there they were. They said we must have breakfast, but we said we wouldn't wait, as that would have been an hour before we set off. So by 7.30 we were on the road. We stopped at a roadhouse for coffee and doughnuts from which, at that hour of the morning, we had a choice of forty do-nuts, with the cook bringing more trays out while we sat there. The smell was mouthwatering. We had chocolate do-nuts, being very conservative, but there were melon do-nuts and peanut do-nuts and apple and honey do-nuts – you name it and they had it. Yum-yum.

We went to a viewpoint above Wollongong, where they live, but didn't go the ten miles down as it was out of our way. We continued to the Blue Mountains, a lovely area, which is the boundary of the outback. We had a ride in a train that went down a cliff at an angle of 52º! The seats were positioned at an angle so that you sit upright going down. When you are hauled up again backwards you are forwards. One trip forces you backwards and the upward trip is like being hauled up by your braces. It was super. Brenda can't stand heights so she minded Nigel at the top. We went for lunch and then went to see a Rotolactor, which is a very swish milking machine. The cows are reared in paddocks and then by habit walk into the machine where the milking things are fitted on. The machine rotates – this sounds odd, but I will explain when I get home, as I need my hands to show you. By the time the machine has rotated, the cows have been milked and walk off leaving room for the next cow.

When we parked in the pub car park, we took up a table about thirty feet from the car, which was parked in the shade. Nigel was asleep in the carrycot on the back seat. Roy said to leave him there with the windows open as we would hear him if he cried. Which we did, but when I did hear him cry and went to fetch him, he was purple in the face, and he had beads of sweat all over his head and his growy suit was soaked with perspiration. We stripped off his suit and gave him a bottle of milk, which revived him, but we were badly shaken. I didn't want to leave him in the car, and I should have stuck to my guns.

We had lunch again and we managed to pay for this only by snatching up the bill. They wouldn't let us pay for a thing. We got home at 8.30ish and they came aboard and Roy was funny because of course he hadn't had a pint of English beer for ten years. Here in Australia, they don't have pints, only glasses of beer, like America, so he was delighted to have it in a big pint tankard.

They do not intend coming home at all, unless they win the pools. It's no easy matter to raise the £1,000 odd to come home as you can imagine, especially as they are building a house, and Brenda is stopping work when their baby boy arrives (adoption – did you know?) and Roy has given up his polo and is trying, most regretfully to sell his horse. They are most anxious for Bob and Mary to come out to stay. They say that now that they have no one in the UK to keep them there (e.g. Mary's mother.) they must come and that they have thrashed it out no end of times with them. I said that I thought the heat wouldn't do Uncle Bob's chest any good, but Roy said the doctor here said that he sends asthmatics to the Blue Mountains but the doctor there sends them to the coast and Roy reckons that, as Uncle Bob was so very well in Majorca, it would be better for him to try Australia and he couldn't possibly be worse than in the UK winter in a coal heated terraced house Unknown to Uncle Bob, Roy even had a job lined up for him. It's a pity Bob and Mary couldn't manage a holiday here just to see the place. Anyway we have taken loads of snaps and they can see for themselves. We have had instructions from Roy and Brenda to tell them what it is like, but they say we would be flogging a dead horse to persuade them to come out.

The big surprise was that when the adopted son arrived to great excitement, Brenda did not know that she was pregnant, so two sons in the same year. Surfeit of happiness all round. Mary did end up in Australia but only when Bob was dead and she was showing signs of Alzheimer's. If they had gone earlier, their final years would have been so different.

Tuesday afternoon. Just spent my hour in the launderette to get my washing up to date before we arrive in Wellington tomorrow.

Again rather than buy souvenirs, we are hiring a car and seeing as much as we can. All the noisy children are off the boat now and there are only about 10 little ones in the nursery.

We went to a dance last night at 10 o'clock after Nigel was fast asleep. It was very gay and all the decorations were Maori type things. We didn't stay too long as we like our sleep too much!

We are going to wave either balloons or the baby's sunshade, which is blue and white, so you can see us straight away – but try and telephone the ship the night before if it's not too expensive.

Well 4 wks 4 days – so see you soon.

P.S. Wellington

Have just had your letter about Pucci. I knew what it was before even opening the vet's letter. I won't say any more as you know how I will feel and how we shall miss him. Don't you feel too badly about it either.

We had chosen a kennels near to London Heath Row airport to reduce the time in the travelling box, but after that awful long journey, the plane was diverted to Manchester, because of bad weather. The dog was sent back to London the following day. Although he had a travelling bag with food and water and a lead, I don't know if he had been taken out or fed or whatever. I hope so, but he was very stressed when he arrived at the kennels. He then didn't want to eat and deteriorated and they diagnosed a heart problem, and after speaking to Mum, recommended having him euthanized. I reckon he died of a broken heart. The thought distresses me even now.

Letter 208   15/3/69

Enroute to Raratonga

Today is Saturday 15th – and so is tomorrow! I thought we would lose a day but we don't, we gain a day, isn't that a pest. We had a good time in Wellington – we called on Trish only to find that she had moved out ten days previously, but her flatmate rang her at her in-laws and Trish and fiancé Errol came and took us to their new house, where Trish is staying. The house is old and wooden and shabby on the inside, but Errol has started to convert it. On first impressions he seemed a bit gormless, but our opinion changed somewhat on seeing the inside of the house. In retrospect, he was just awkward and shy. He has practically knocked down the inside of the house and made the living rooms and kitchen open plan. He is a carpenter and as you can imagine, his kitchen fitments are works of art made in the natural wood and beautifully finished. He imported his favourite woods from South Africa. They have little furniture but have a fitted carpet, so it doesn't matter. Trish is very capable and made a lovely supper with cheese and things and cake and we nattered away at ten to the dozen, Errol losing his shyness, when going into detail about his conversion. He has also put a large picture window in the lounge. The original kitchen is a laundry room. One bedroom is as yet untouched and is awful – layers of peeling wallpaper, mouldy lino, etc. They reckon they will leave this to emphasize the difference. How he could have envisaged such a conversion when the whole house looked like this I don't know. Trish is very happy and Errol is the sort of chap who will thrive on her 'mothering'. The house itself is right on the beach but for a narrow road, and the sunset from there is beautiful. While we were drinking coffee, Errol's mother rang to ask where we were. Trish apologised to us and asked if we minded going over to see them. We didn't mind a bit, and when we arrived we were treated like V.I.P.s and mum-in-law had put on a huge spread and an aunt and uncle and cousin were there. We eventually left about 12.30 and still stood in the driveway for about half an hour. Both mum-in-law and her sister are fussy little bodies who are as fond of Trish as she appears to be of them and showed me the wedding cake and dresses and all the preparations with great excitement. The wedding is 12th April. I will add the address on the end of this letter. So I am sure she will be very happy and well looked after – it's about time isn't it! *Trish had emigrated to escape a bad family life*.

We also visited a zoo, botanical gardens and a beautiful begonia house. I have fallen for begonias and we have taken loads of slides of them! This place was lit up at night and we took Win and Graeme, a nice couple from Sydney on our dining table.

As the gangplanks were removed yesterday, a girl fell into the dock from the quayside. A deckhand from the ship dived in off the bows of the ship – a heck of a drop and grabbed her, by which time she was unconscious. It was about 15mins before they got them out, as the dockside was so steep and the poor chap was holding her up all this time. Eventually they managed to tie a rope to a ladder and get them up that way. Three police cars and the ambulance had arrived by the time they were out. The girl was wrapped up and stuck in the ambulance and the chap walked away and only went about 10 feet and collapsed. No one noticed, as there were hundreds of people waving as the ship started to move. All this happened at the bow end where we were, as we were more interested in watching the tugs manoeuvring. The crew shouted 'get him aboard' and a couple of men helped him up the crew gangplank and that's the last we have heard. About half a dozen of us who were the only ones apart from the crew, watching from the ship, clapped him as he came aboard. She would have drowned if he hadn't jumped in as only a few on the quayside and ship saw her fall in!

Innocents that we are! The waiter gave us the real story. Apparently, the girl was the rescuer's girlfriend and it was all prearranged that she should "fall" in and he would rescue her, and that they would both go to hospital in the ambulance. He wanted to stay in Wellington with her. If he jumped ship, he would never be able to work on a ship again. He would also not have the relevant papers to stay. This solution was their way out. The crew however knew what he intended to do, and when he collapsed-the ruse to be taken away in her ambulance- they hauled him back on ship to save him from himself. I think he might have been punished. I wonder if they ever got together again.

I'm annoyed about the extra day as I thought we would be home quicker. The tours in Tahiti are a terrible price – between £3 and £6 each for a morning or afternoon. The one with Tahitian dancing is £4.15.0 each and a bit beyond us, so we are going on a morning 9.30-12.00 general tour – not as exciting, but we will at least see the place, as car hire here is prohibitive and it is not advisable to eat out as last time in Tahiti a lot of people were very ill with food poisoning.

Monday – Just arriving at Raratonga – looks beautiful – real South Pacific stuff.   Love from the crew of the Endeavour.

Chapter 61   Raratonga

Letter   209   17/3/69

We had a super afternoon yesterday. We anchored off Raratonga, in the Cook Islands at 2pm but the island itself appeared on the horizon about twelve. It was marvellous watching it approach with the mountains gradually making themselves distinct and then the colours appearing, purple to green and finally the waves on the shore and the trees. It really is a lush tropical island and I wish we could have gone ashore, but perhaps this would have spoilt the illusion. Dancers came ashore in boats and we had a show on the sports deck in the blazing sun. I couldn't see to film as the crowd was about 4 or 5 deep around the edge and I told one of the crew (who has 6 girls and one boy and makes a fuss of Nigel) that I was too small, and he went and found me a wooden box and I was about 2 feet higher than anyone else and filmed like mad! Although we resolved not to buy souvenirs I bought a wooden hanging house for Nigel for 10/- with bone hanging pegs that jingle in the wind. Isn't he spoilt! An old man bought me or rather Nigel, a lei, the garland of franjipani flowers, which smell so gorgeous. We have loads of film and pictures and will leave them to show you how colourful it all was. We are now en route to Tahiti, which seems from all reports to be very expensive, dirty and unfriendly! Anyway we are only there for a day!

Nigel is sampling beef dinners and banana dessert but it's making him a bit windy and so I think I'll not push him at all, but try in earnest when we get home. Unfortunately the heat has increased immensely and he is only comfortable inside, so when he is sleeping we leave him in the cabin and pop in and out until he wakes, unless it is coolish.

I don't know how many more letters will reach you. Maybe this will be the last one that arrives before we do, so have a safe journey to Southampton and try to get in touch by phone before we dock.

Letter 210   25/03/1969   En route to Acapulco

I will save this letter until Panama, as it is the American and not the Mexican GPO and it's more reliable.

I had a mad dream about us arriving home last night. We landed by ferryboat at Woodside Ferry and couldn't get ashore as the gangways kept falling off. Such frustration. Time is crawling somewhat on this eight-day stretch as we are in the equatorial zone and the humidity is 97% and it's raining off and on and too wet to sit out. We could sit out under shelter, but the damp and heat make Nigel unhappy so we prefer to keep him in as constant a temperature as possible to prevent the return of his cough.

He is being a good baby, touch wood, and has now started to chuckle when he smiles, and kicks his legs and makes noises like conversation when you talk to him. He is small though. The baby who is two weeks older is a lot bigger and not fat. Nigel isn't skinny at all-we think he is just right, just don't expect a bouncing baby. Richard is hoping that he will not be small as he was always teased at primary school as he was always the top of the class and the smallest as well, not a popular combination.

Saturday was Tahitian night and you should have seen the outfits, or rather the lack of them. Bikinis with a few flowers pinned on, and swimming trunks with facecloths sewn on back and front! I was definitely overdressed. It was all rather colourful. The walls had been covered with palms and flowers taken on board at Tahiti.

Monday was the "Crossing the Line " ceremony, which was a bit silly, just a lot of slapstick mess, and we got bored and came away.

The man in the library has had to open a new page for us. The practice is to note the number of the book as you take it out.

Last night we made the second performance of the film. The films are all good. We had "Thoroughly Modern Milly" on Friday, so you can see they are reasonably up to date.

Unfortunately, our day in Trinidad is on Good Friday and everything is closed. Isn't that a shame? I wonder if we will have Easter eggs and an Easter Parade.

Later. Just up from the launderette to catch a school of dolphins leaping around, presumably disturbed by the ship. People do make work for themselves. I have two days washing and ironing down to fiftyfive minutes. I first wash the ironables and put them in the dryer. I then do Nigel's one and a half dozen nappies and the underwear, adding them to the air dryer as I take them from the spin drier. By the time the washing is in the spinner, the first lot is dry and I iron while the remainder is drying. I then fold the nappies. This means I am only idle if something is taking longer to dry. *(What a performance)* Some dears do their washing and collect it in a basket and then move into the dryer room and sit for 30 to 40 minutes watching it dry. The most efficient are the under thirties, probably because they are easily adaptable to the machinery. The worst are the old men. One old bloke filled his machine and then proceeded to wash by hand with a bar of soap. He was quite adept at the spin dryer though. Young bachelors are surprisingly efficient until a blonde starts using the machine next door, then they lose their memories and have to ask which switch is for what.

We have just been watching flying fish and saw some rain ahead and hoped the bridge had seen it too, as the ship changes course to avoid "scattered showers". Sometimes we are dodging around all day and you can see the patterns in the wake. Sure enough we veered to port (dig the lingo) and the rain has passed. You can see it actually raining only yards from the ship and all we get is a few spots. We asked about this and apparently it is company policy to avoid rain as it is a cruise ship and apart from all the outdoor things coming to a standstill, the interior of the ship becomes damp and dirty with footprints and everyone is miserable. You should have seen all the miserable faces yesterday when the rain was unavoidable.

Saturday, 29th March   Had a super time in Acapulco yesterday. We went for a tour in the morning ending with the divers of Qubrada. However we went back to the ship between twelve and four, as it was too hot for Nigel. We were anchored off shore and were ferried ashore in the ship's launches, which was a novelty. The atmosphere is very like Spain, lazy and happy, but with an unfortunate American influence, flashy cars and drawling accents and trashy souvenirs.

30th March 1969. Happy Birthday to me. Richard bought me a book, (a big one, all glossy) and a bow, (hair not violin).

Must close to catch the Panama post

PS Monday 31st March Richard wouldn't let me seal this letter but rushed me to lunch, and then I realized why. He had received your telegram and had put it on my plate in the dining room. Many Thanks. That was a good surprise. In the evening, we invited an old couple to have a drink with us at 5.30 and the soft pair brought me a box of chocolates. When we went downstairs, the table was all covered in decorations and balloons, and there was a big birthday cake in the middle. Win, who shares the table with us, had put a present on my plate, a pair of stretch tights. *(a novelty at this point)*. So we had a bottle of wine and dished out cake to all and sundry and a great crowd came and stood round the table to sing "Happy Birthday" quite spontaneously.

We are now cruising along the coast of Costa Rica and reach the Panama Canal entrance at the unearthly hour of 4am.

No more letters now…..home soon

Arrival

We had a brief telephone call in the evening from the parents to the ship. They said that they would be dockside first thing in the morning. It was cold on deck on the morrow, so we had taken the baby to the nursery. We then dashed up onto our sundeck to get the best view of the dock. And there they were. Dad in his overcoat and trilby, Mum in a new coat and hat. They were looking up at the ship, scanning the rails. They hadn't spotted us yet.

They seem so small.

Mrs Routledge, Mrs Kent, Joan, Cookie. Mrs Giles Margie Mrs Mhizia

Valerie Lapthorne

Me and Pucci

Zambia Letters Home